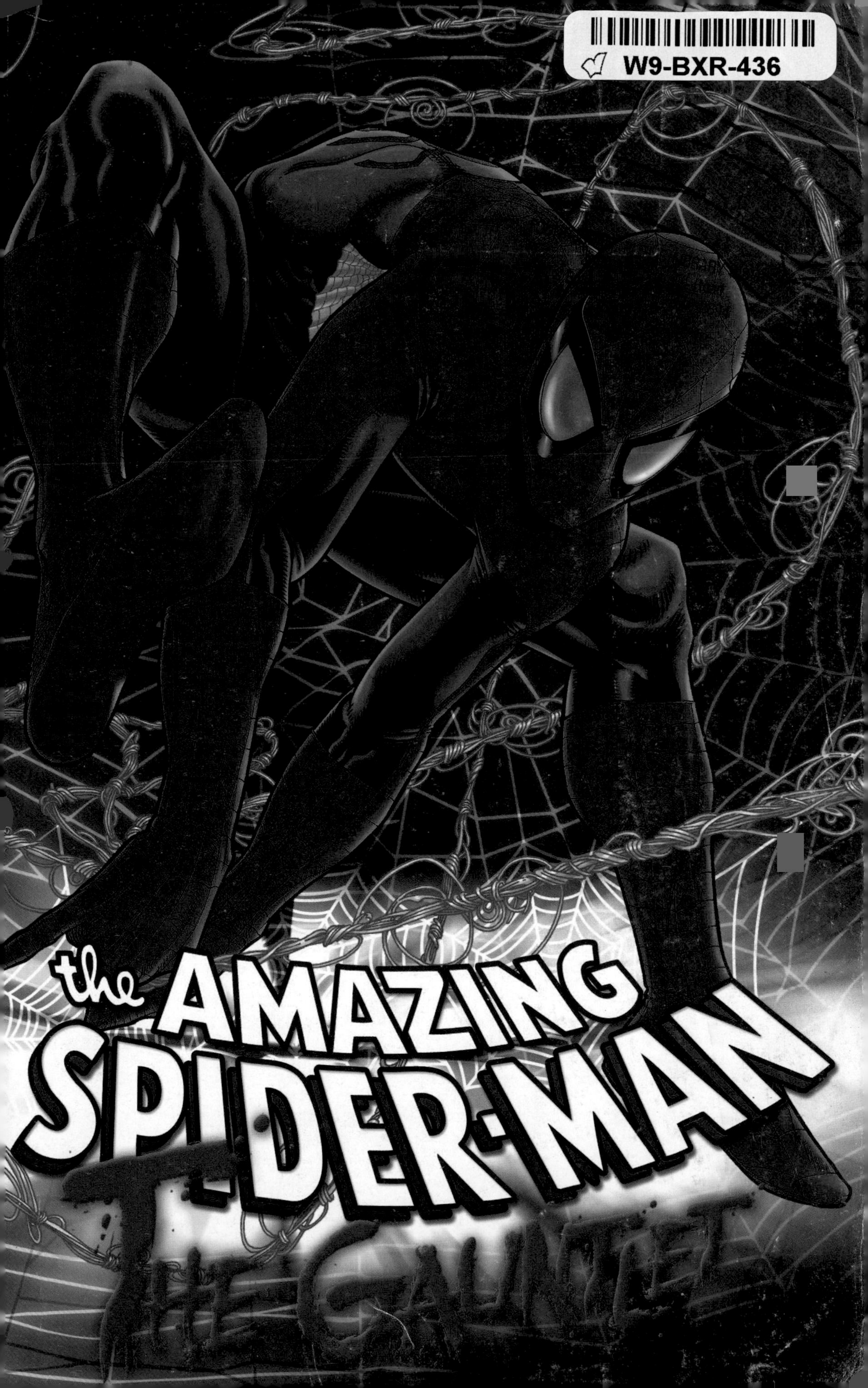
the AMAZING
SPIDER-MAN
THE GAUNTLET

the AMAZING SPIDER-MAN

THE GAUNTLET

JUGGERNAUT

ISSUE #626
Writer: **FRED VAN LENTE**
Artist: **MICHAEL GAYDOS**
Letterer: **VC'S JOE CARAMAGNA**

ISSUES #627-629
Writer: **ROGER STERN**
Artist: **LEE WEEKS**
Colorist: **DEAN WHITE**
WITH **MATT HOLLINGSWORTH (ISSUE #629)**
Letterer: **VC'S JOE CARAMAGNA**

"BROTHER, CAN YOU SPARE A CRIME?"
Writers: **MARK WAID** & **TOM PEYER**
Artist: **TODD NAUCK**
Colorist: **ANDRES MOSSA**
Letterer: **VC'S JOE CARAMAGNA**

ISSUES #229-230 (JUNE-JULY 1982)
Writer: **ROGER STERN**
Penciler: **JOHN ROMITA JR.**
Inker: **JIM MOONEY**
Colorist: **GLYNIS WEIN**
Letterer: **JOE ROSEN**
Editor: **TOM DEFALCO**

Web-Heads: **BOB GALE, JOE KELLY, DAN SLOTT, FRED VAN LENTE, MARK WAID** & **ZEB WELLS**
Assistant Editor: **THOMAS BRENNAN** • Editor: **STEPHEN WACKER** • Executive Editor: **TOM BREVOORT**

Collection Editor: **JENNIFER GRÜNWALD** • Assistant Editor: **ALEX STARBUCK**
Associate Editor: **JOHN DENNING** • Editor, Special Projects: **MARK D. BEAZLEY**
Senior Editor, Special Projects: **JEFF YOUNGQUIST** • Senior Vice President of Sales: **DAVID GABRIEL**

Editor in Chief: **JOE QUESADA** • Publisher: **DAN BUCKLEY** • Executive Producer: **ALAN FINE**

SPIDER-MAN: THE GAUNTLET VOL. 4 — JUGGERNAUT. Contains material originally published in magazine form as AMAZING SPIDER-MAN #626-629 and #229-230. First printing 2010. Hardcover ISBN# 978 0-7851-4613-1. Softcover ISBN# 978-0-7851-4614-8. Published by MARVEL WORLDWIDE, INC., a subsidiary of MARVEL ENTERTAINMENT, LLC. OFFICE OF PUBLICATION: 417 5th Avenue, New York, NY 10016. Copyright © 1982 and 2010 Marvel Characters, Inc. All rights reserved. Hardcover: $19.99 per copy in the U.S. and $22.50 in Canada (GST #R127032852). Softcover: $14.99 per copy in the U.S. and $16.99 in Canada (GST #R127032852). Canadian Agreement #40668537. All characters featured in this issue and the distinctive names and likenesses thereof, and all related indicia are trademarks of Marvel Characters, Inc. No similarity between any of the names, characters, persons, and/or institutions in this magazine with those of any living or dead person or institution is intended, and any such similarity which may exist is purely coincidental. **Printed in the U.S.A.** ALAN FINE, EVP - Office of the President, Marvel Worldwide, Inc. and EVP & CMO Marvel Characters B.V.; DAN BUCKLEY, Chief Executive Officer and Publisher - Print, Animation & Digital Media; JIM SOKOLOWSKI, Chief Operating Officer; DAVID GABRIEL, SVP of Publishing Sales & Circulation; DAVID BOGART, SVP of Business Affairs & Talent Management; MICHAEL PASCIULLO, VP Merchandising & Communications; JIM O'KEEFE, VP of Operations & Logistics; DAN CARR, Executive Director of Publishing Technology; JUSTIN F. GABRIE, Director of Publishing & Editorial Operations; SUSAN CRESPI, Editorial Operations Manager; ALEX MORALES, Publishing Operations Manager; STAN LEE, Chairman Emeritus. For information regarding advertising in Marvel Comics or on Marvel.com, please contact Ron Stern, VP of Business Development, at rstern@marvel.com. For Marvel subscription inquiries, please call 800-217-9158. **Manufactured between 6/21/10 and 7/21/10 (hardcover), and 6/21/10 and 12/22/10 (softcover), by R.R. DONNELLEY, INC., SALEM, VA, USA.**

10 9 8 7 6 5 4 3 2 1

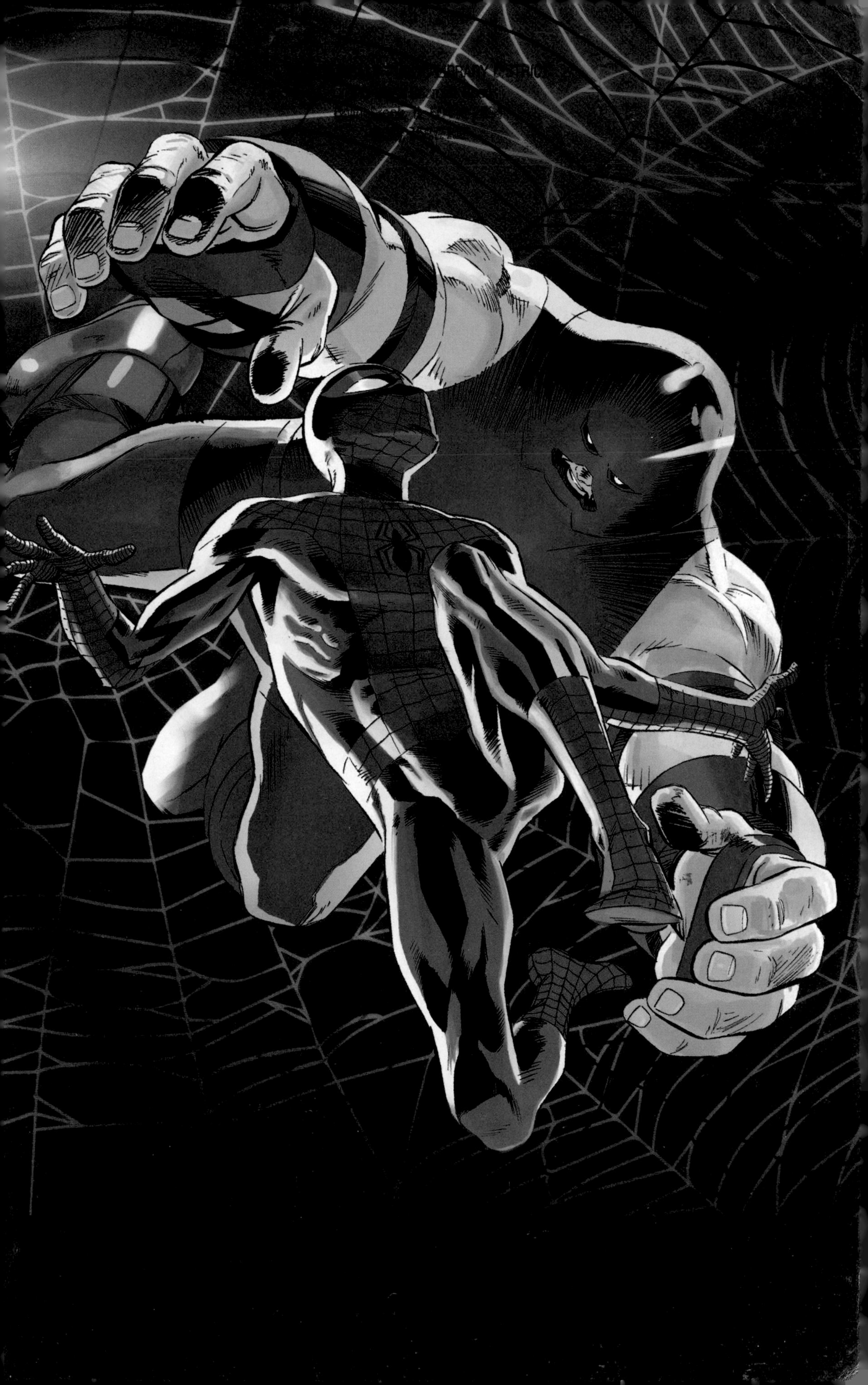

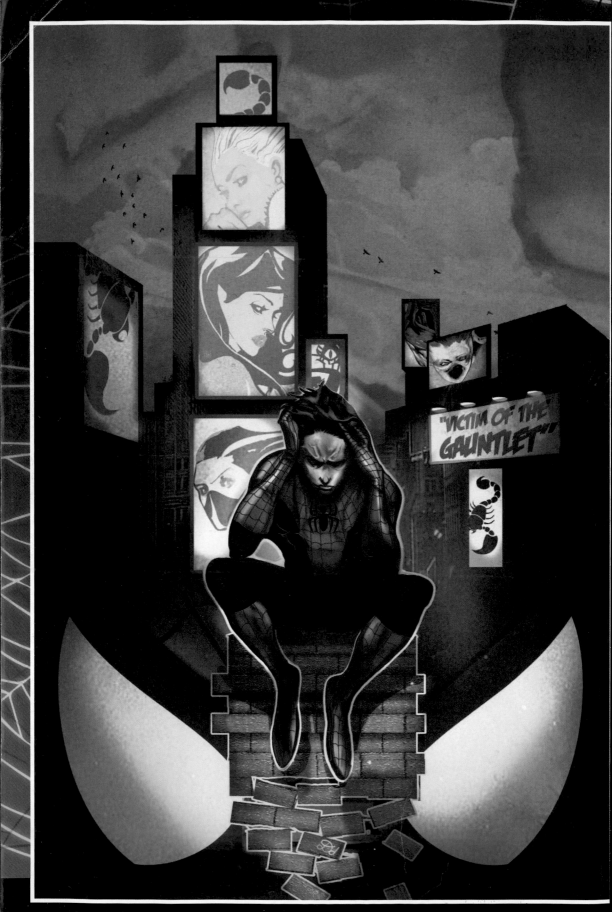

AMAZING SPIDER-MAN #626
COVER BY MICHAEL DEL MUNDO

RSS | ARCHIVE | ABOUT | CONTACT | ADVERTISE

NEW USER? CREATE AN ACCOUNT!

GALE, KELLY, SLOTT, VAN LENTE, WAID & WELLS – WEB-HEADS

SEARCH GO

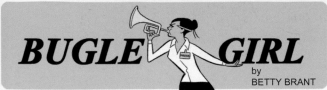

BUGLE GIRL

by BETTY BRANT

Fred Van Lente – Writer
Michael Gaydos – Artist
VC's Joe Caramagna – Letterer
Michael del Mundo – Cover
Tom Brennan – Asst. Editor
Stephen Wacker – Editor
Tom Brevoort – Executive Editor
Joe Quesada – Editor in Chief
Dan Buckley – Publisher
Alan Fine – Executive Producer

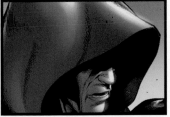

BOYS WITH THE HOOD! Who is Parker Robbins? Our investigative report into the small-time crook who became Kingpin to the city's super villains, organizing them... more...

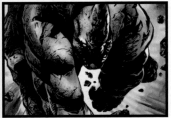

RUMBLE IN THE BRONX! Aleksei Sytsevich, the man known as Rhino, disappeared late last night after rampaging through the Bronx and then up to his old neighborhood of... more...

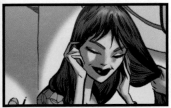

CUTIE CALL? Who's fashion model and reality TV host MARY JANE WATSON talking to? Paparazzi couldn't confirm, but sources say the TV star recently invited Harry "Son of an" Osborn to live with her in her Brooklyn... more...

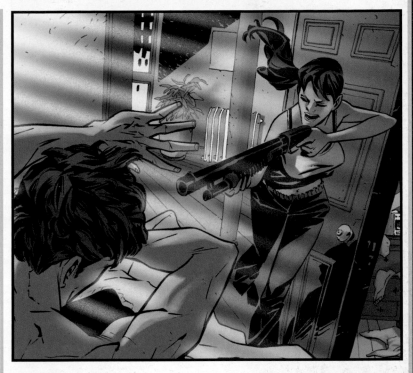

Peter Parker has faced some incredible odds in his life as Spider-Man, but his roommate, no-nonsense lawyer Michele Gonzales, may prove to be his toughest challenge yet. Michele took over the apartment when her brother, Pete's former roommate Officer Vin Gonzales, entered protective custody for testifying against police corruption.

Initially considering Pete a freeloader, she began to warm to him and even accompanied him as a date to his aunt's wedding – only for a night of ill-advised romance to throw any progress out the window. The two have rarely shared any words, let alone kind ones, and their relationship has gone ice-cold.

If his home life wasn't tough enough, Pete's faced a veritable gauntlet of his greatest foes lately, with each step costing him more than the last. Between Electro's destruction of his prime source of income, The DB, to the tragic downfall of the Rhino, who returned to a life of crime after his wife was murdered, Pete's had his mettle thoroughly tested.

But perhaps the most damaging blow came when he lost his job as official photographer to the mayor's office. Forging a photo to exonerate an innocent Mayor Jameson from a crime he didn't commit, Pete found himself on the wrong side of Jonah's journalistic ethics...and lost his job, ruining his reputation in the process. Battered, exhausted and unemployable, Peter Parker's luck may yet take a turn for the worse, as the gauntlet of evil doesn't seem inclined to stop...

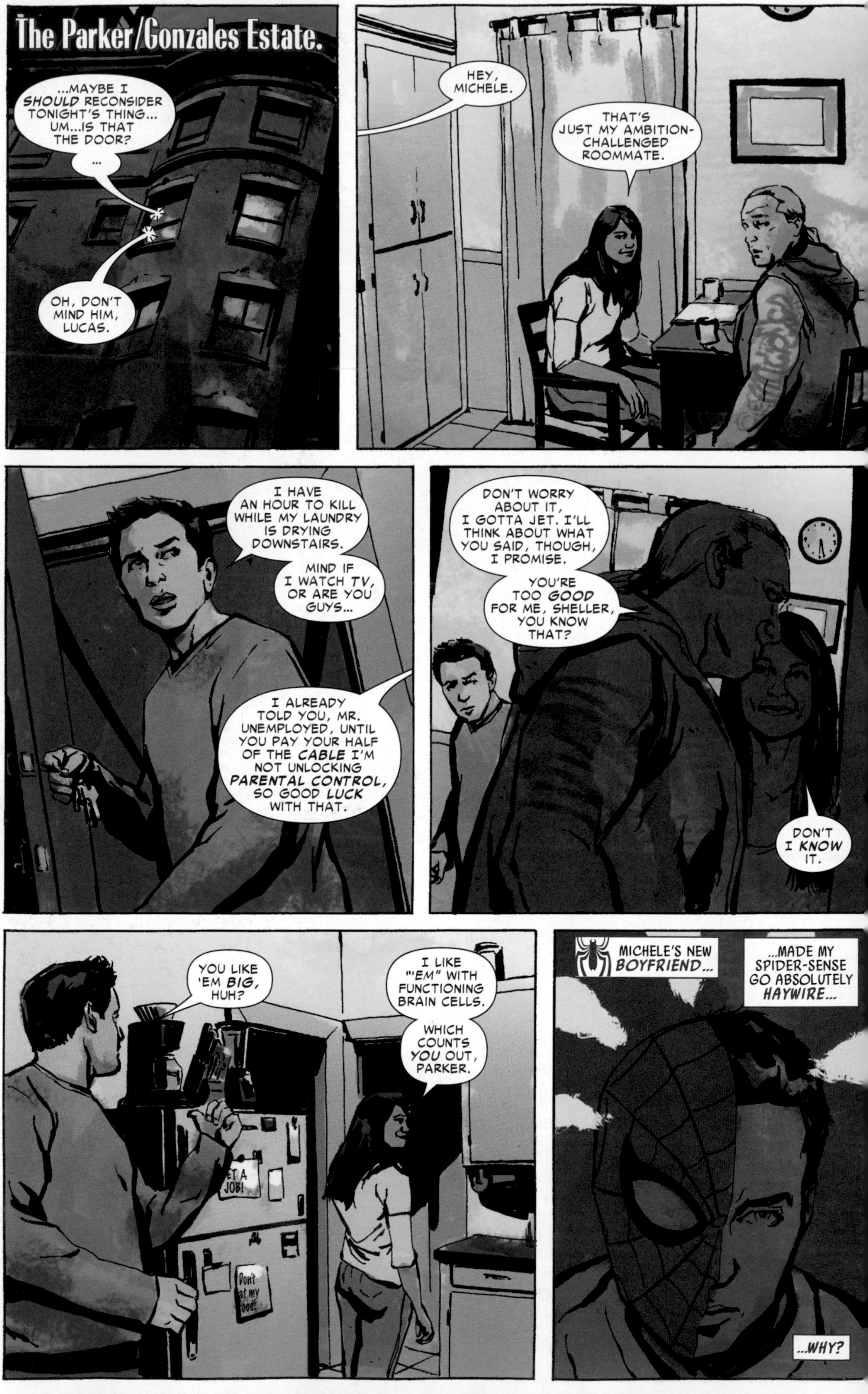
The Parker/Gonzales Estate.
...MAYBE I SHOULD RECONSIDER TONIGHT'S THING... UM...IS THAT THE DOOR?
...
OH, DON'T MIND HIM, LUCAS.
HEY, MICHELE.
THAT'S JUST MY AMBITION-CHALLENGED ROOMMATE.
I HAVE AN HOUR TO KILL WHILE MY LAUNDRY IS DRYING DOWNSTAIRS.
MIND IF I WATCH TV, OR ARE YOU GUYS...
I ALREADY TOLD YOU, MR. UNEMPLOYED, UNTIL YOU PAY YOUR HALF OF THE CABLE I'M NOT UNLOCKING PARENTAL CONTROL, SO GOOD LUCK WITH THAT.
DON'T WORRY ABOUT IT, I GOTTA JET. I'LL THINK ABOUT WHAT YOU SAID, THOUGH, I PROMISE.
YOU'RE TOO GOOD FOR ME, SHELLER, YOU KNOW THAT?
DON'T I KNOW IT.
YOU LIKE 'EM BIG, HUH?
I LIKE "'EM" WITH FUNCTIONING BRAIN CELLS.
WHICH COUNTS YOU OUT, PARKER.
Don't eat my food!
MICHELE'S NEW BOYFRIEND...
...MADE MY SPIDER-SENSE GO ABSOLUTELY HAYWIRE...
...WHY?

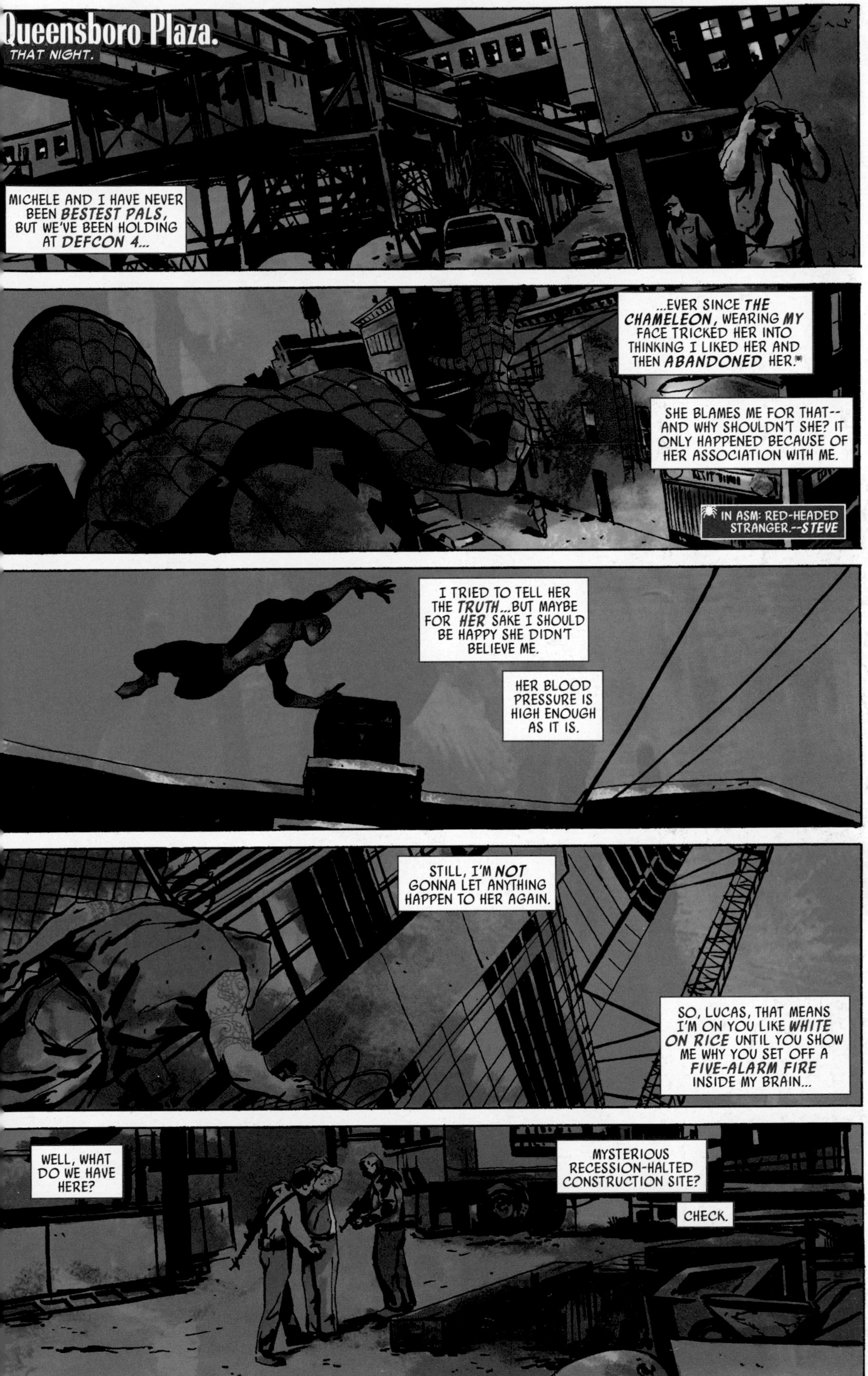
Queensboro Plaza.
THAT NIGHT.
MICHELE AND I HAVE NEVER BEEN BESTEST PALS, BUT WE'VE BEEN HOLDING AT DEFCON 4...
...EVER SINCE THE CHAMELEON, WEARING MY FACE TRICKED HER INTO THINKING I LIKED HER AND THEN ABANDONED HER.*
SHE BLAMES ME FOR THAT--AND WHY SHOULDN'T SHE? IT ONLY HAPPENED BECAUSE OF HER ASSOCIATION WITH ME.
*IN ASM: RED-HEADED STRANGER.--STEVE
I TRIED TO TELL HER THE TRUTH...BUT MAYBE FOR HER SAKE I SHOULD BE HAPPY SHE DIDN'T BELIEVE ME.
HER BLOOD PRESSURE IS HIGH ENOUGH AS IT IS.
STILL, I'M NOT GONNA LET ANYTHING HAPPEN TO HER AGAIN.
SO, LUCAS, THAT MEANS I'M ON YOU LIKE WHITE ON RICE UNTIL YOU SHOW ME WHY YOU SET OFF A FIVE-ALARM FIRE INSIDE MY BRAIN...
WELL, WHAT DO WE HAVE HERE?
MYSTERIOUS RECESSION-HALTED CONSTRUCTION SITE?
CHECK.

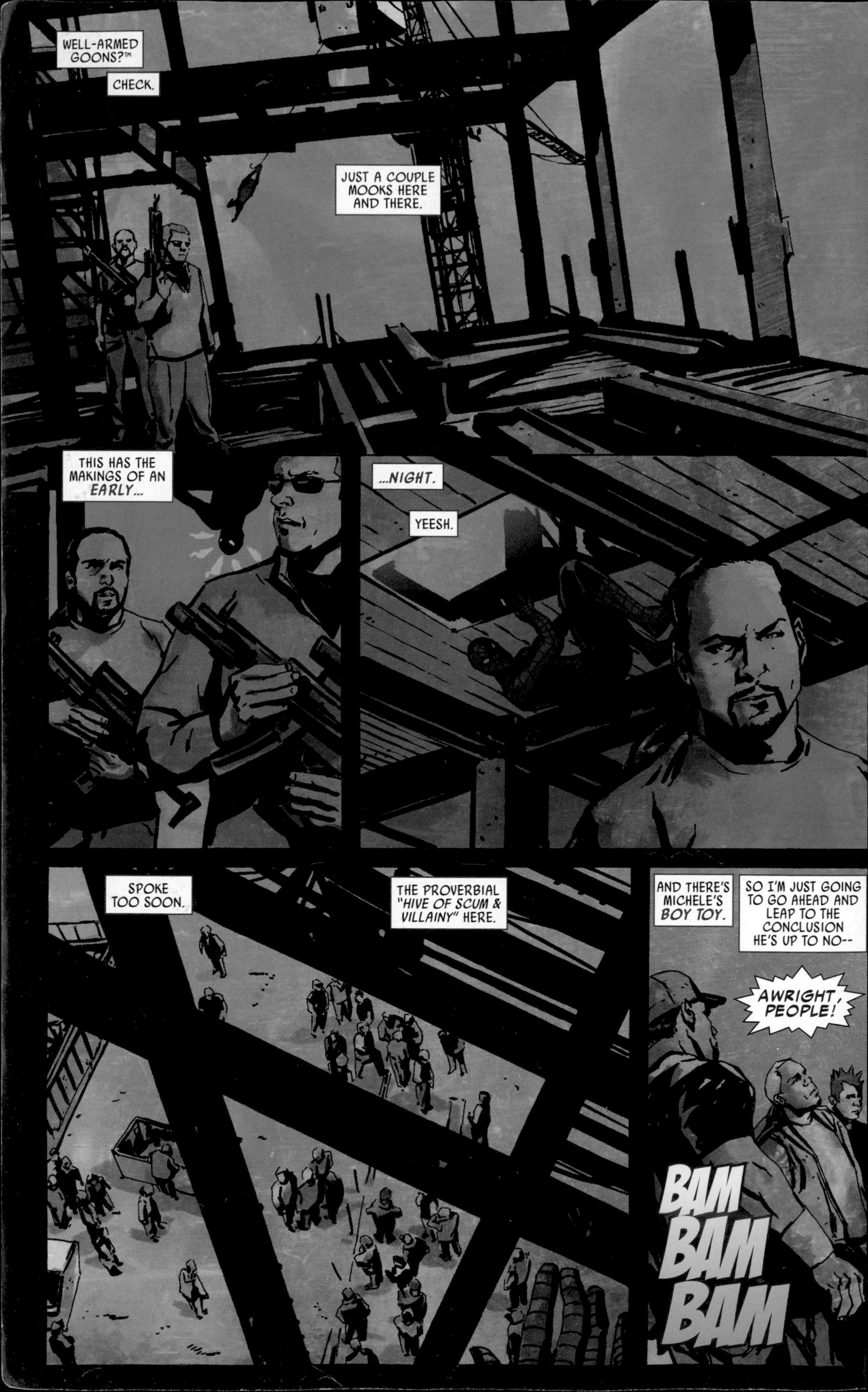
WELL-ARMED GOONS?™
CHECK.
JUST A COUPLE MOOKS HERE AND THERE.
THIS HAS THE MAKINGS OF AN *EARLY*...
...*NIGHT*.
YEESH.
SPOKE TOO SOON.
THE PROVERBIAL "*HIVE OF SCUM & VILLAINY*" HERE.
AND THERE'S MICHELE'S *BOY TOY*.
SO I'M JUST GOING TO GO AHEAD AND LEAP TO THE CONCLUSION HE'S UP TO NO--
AWRIGHT, PEOPLE!
BAM BAM BAM

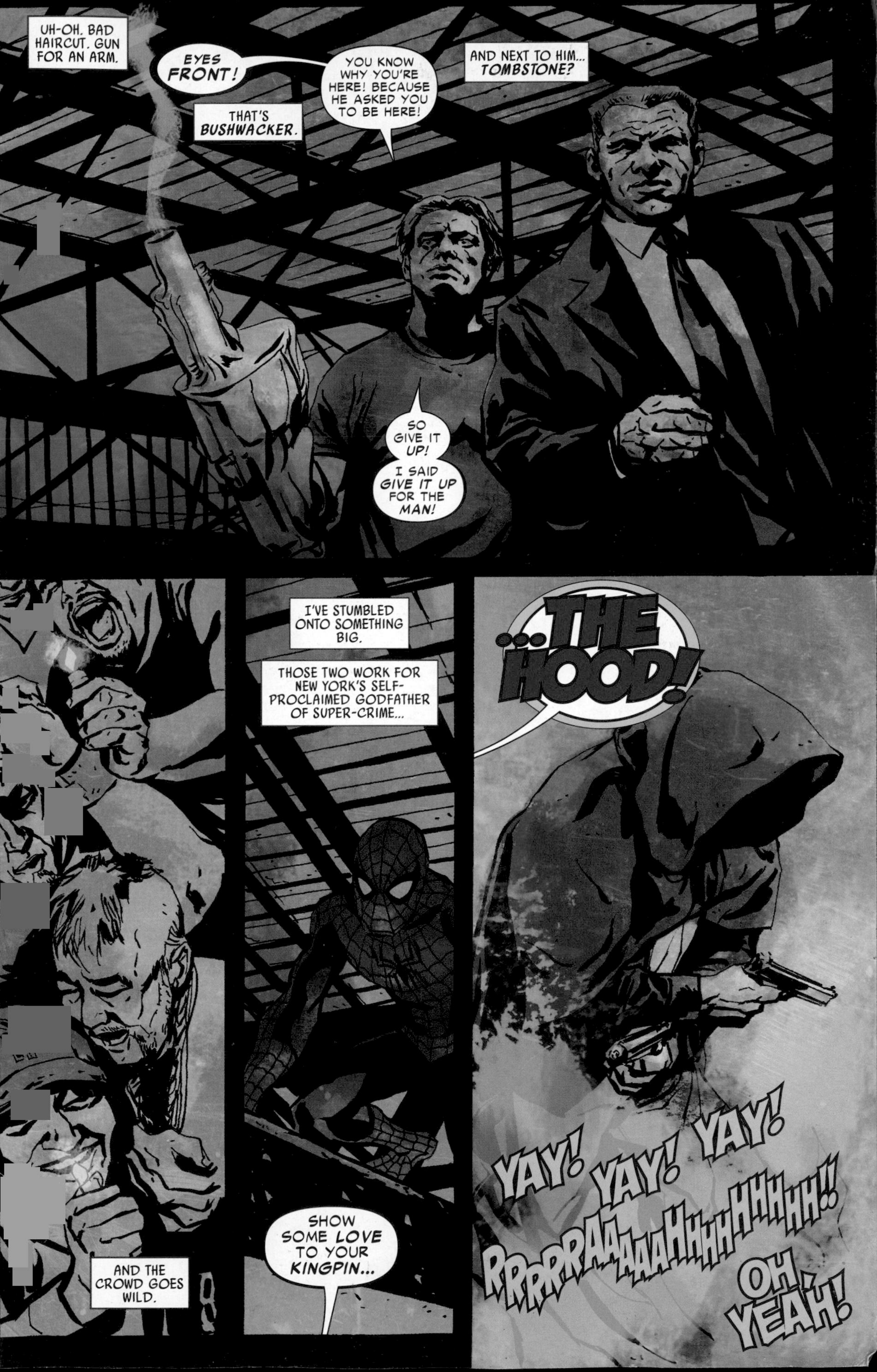
UH-OH. BAD HAIRCUT. GUN FOR AN ARM.
EYES FRONT!
THAT'S BUSHWACKER.
YOU KNOW WHY YOU'RE HERE! BECAUSE HE ASKED YOU TO BE HERE!
AND NEXT TO HIM... TOMBSTONE?
SO GIVE IT UP!
I SAID GIVE IT UP FOR THE MAN!
AND THE CROWD GOES WILD.
I'VE STUMBLED ONTO SOMETHING BIG.
THOSE TWO WORK FOR NEW YORK'S SELF-PROCLAIMED GODFATHER OF SUPER-CRIME...
SHOW SOME LOVE TO YOUR KINGPIN...
...THE HOOD!
YAY! YAY! YAY!
RRRRRAAAAAAHHHHHHHHH!!
OH, YEAH!

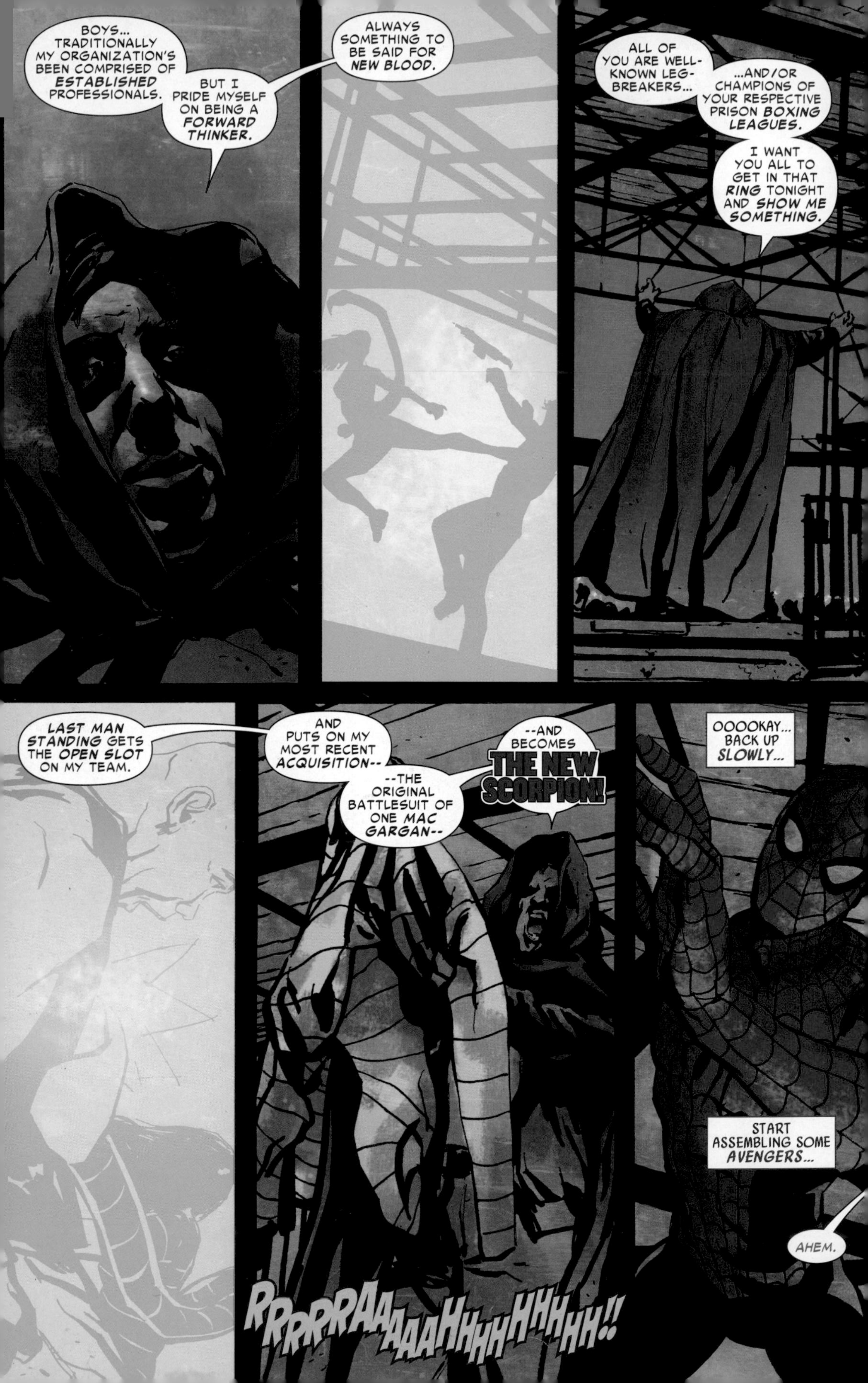
BOYS... TRADITIONALLY MY ORGANIZATION'S BEEN COMPRISED OF ESTABLISHED PROFESSIONALS.
BUT I PRIDE MYSELF ON BEING A FORWARD THINKER.
ALWAYS SOMETHING TO BE SAID FOR NEW BLOOD.
ALL OF YOU ARE WELL-KNOWN LEG-BREAKERS...
...AND/OR CHAMPIONS OF YOUR RESPECTIVE PRISON BOXING LEAGUES.
I WANT YOU ALL TO GET IN THAT RING TONIGHT AND SHOW ME SOMETHING.
LAST MAN STANDING GETS THE OPEN SLOT ON MY TEAM.
AND PUTS ON MY MOST RECENT ACQUISITION--
--THE ORIGINAL BATTLESUIT OF ONE MAC GARGAN--
--AND BECOMES THE NEW SCORPION!
OOOOKAY... BACK UP SLOWLY...
START ASSEMBLING SOME AVENGERS...
AHEM.
RRRRRAAAAAAHHHHHHHHHH!!

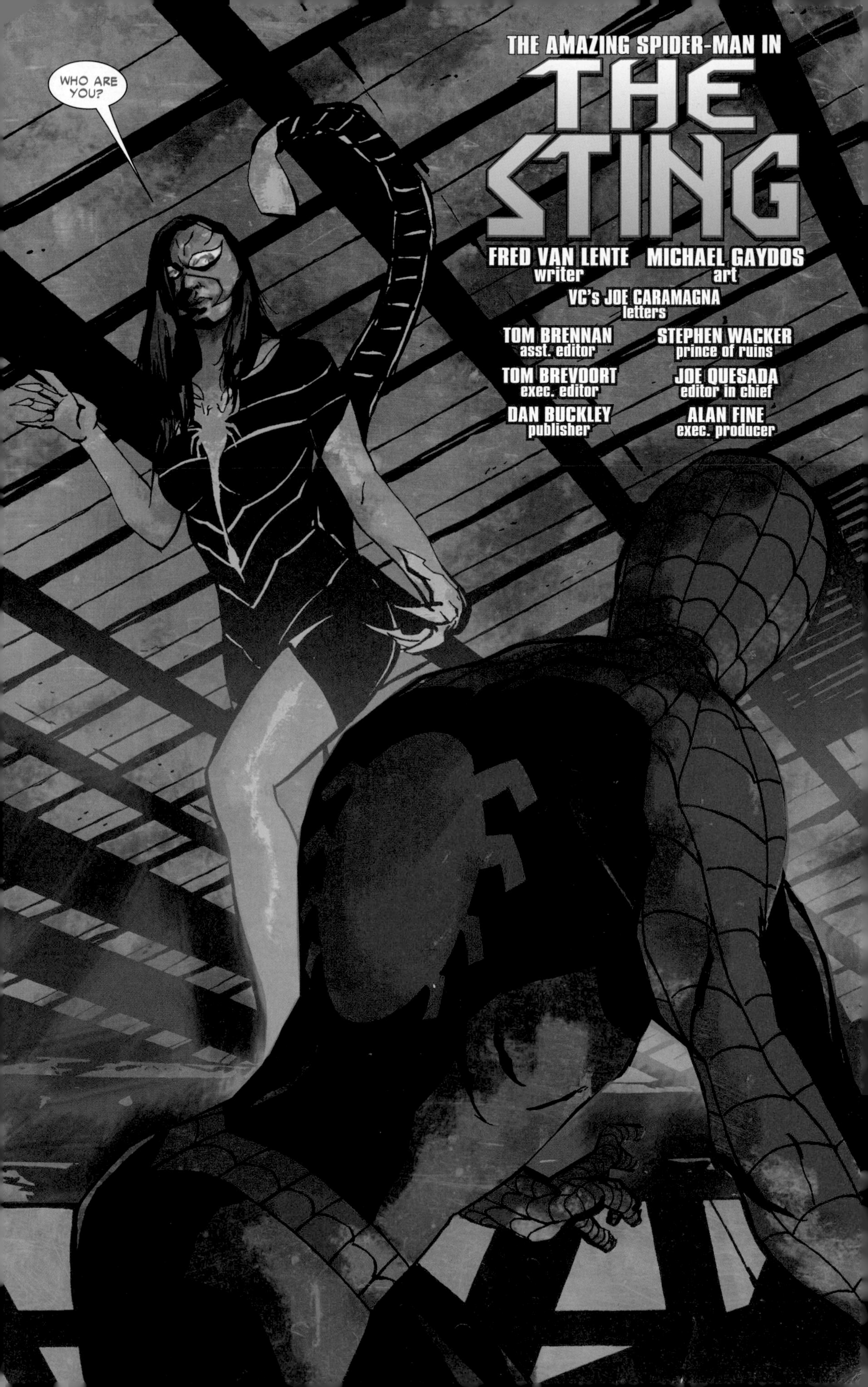
WHO ARE YOU?
THE AMAZING SPIDER-MAN IN
THE STING
FRED VAN LENTE writer
MICHAEL GAYDOS art
VC's JOE CARAMAGNA letters
TOM BRENNAN asst. editor
STEPHEN WACKER prince of ruins
TOM BREVOORT exec. editor
JOE QUESADA editor in chief
DAN BUCKLEY publisher
ALAN FINE exec. producer

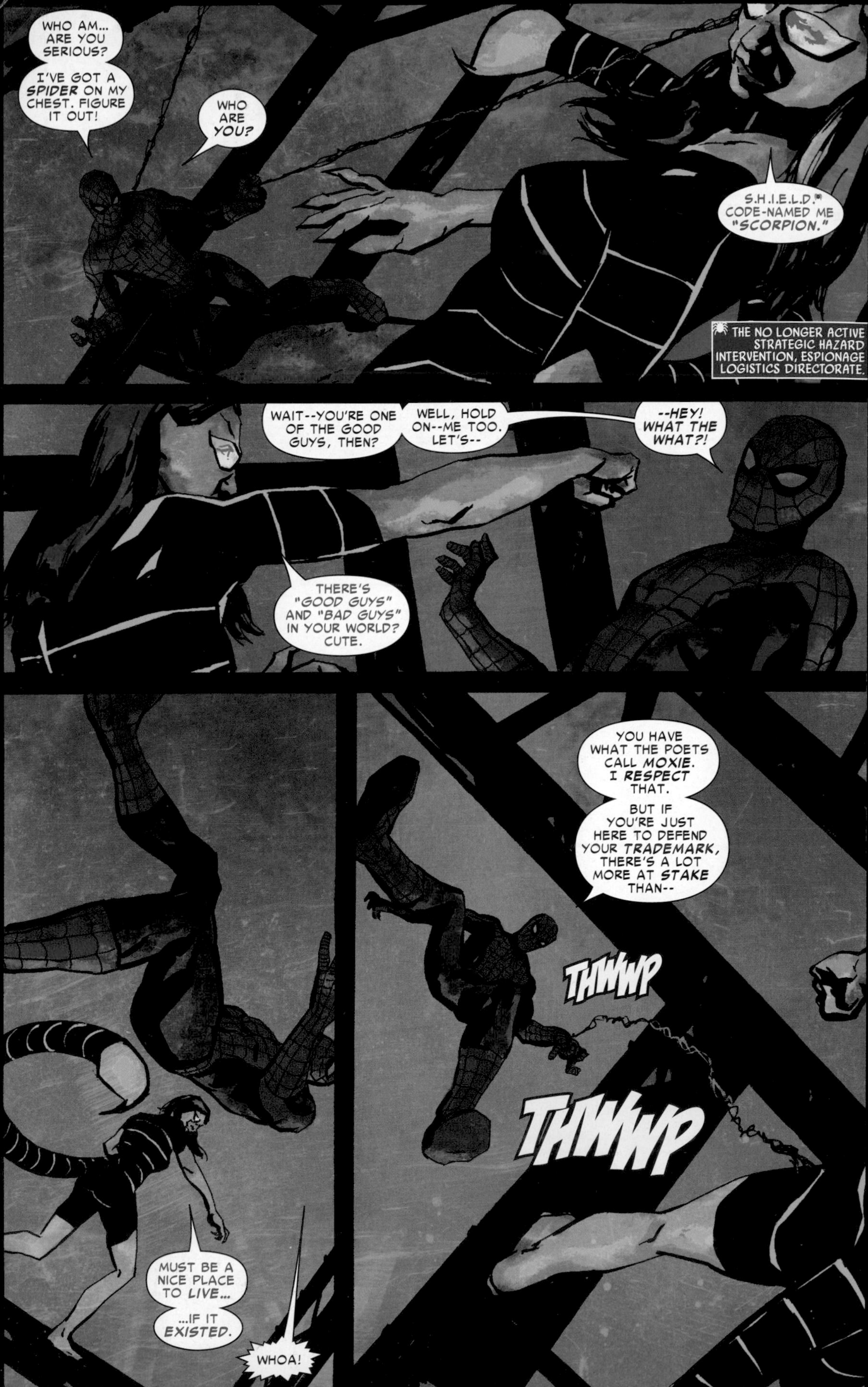
WHO AM... ARE YOU SERIOUS?
I'VE GOT A SPIDER ON MY CHEST. FIGURE IT OUT!
WHO ARE YOU?
S.H.I.E.L.D.* CODE-NAMED ME "SCORPION."
*THE NO LONGER ACTIVE STRATEGIC HAZARD INTERVENTION, ESPIONAGE LOGISTICS DIRECTORATE.
WAIT--YOU'RE ONE OF THE GOOD GUYS, THEN?
WELL, HOLD ON--ME TOO. LET'S--
--HEY! WHAT THE WHAT?!
THERE'S "GOOD GUYS" AND "BAD GUYS" IN YOUR WORLD? CUTE.
MUST BE A NICE PLACE TO LIVE...
...IF IT EXISTED.
WHOA!
YOU HAVE WHAT THE POETS CALL MOXIE. I RESPECT THAT.
BUT IF YOU'RE JUST HERE TO DEFEND YOUR TRADEMARK, THERE'S A LOT MORE AT STAKE THAN--
THWWP
THWWP

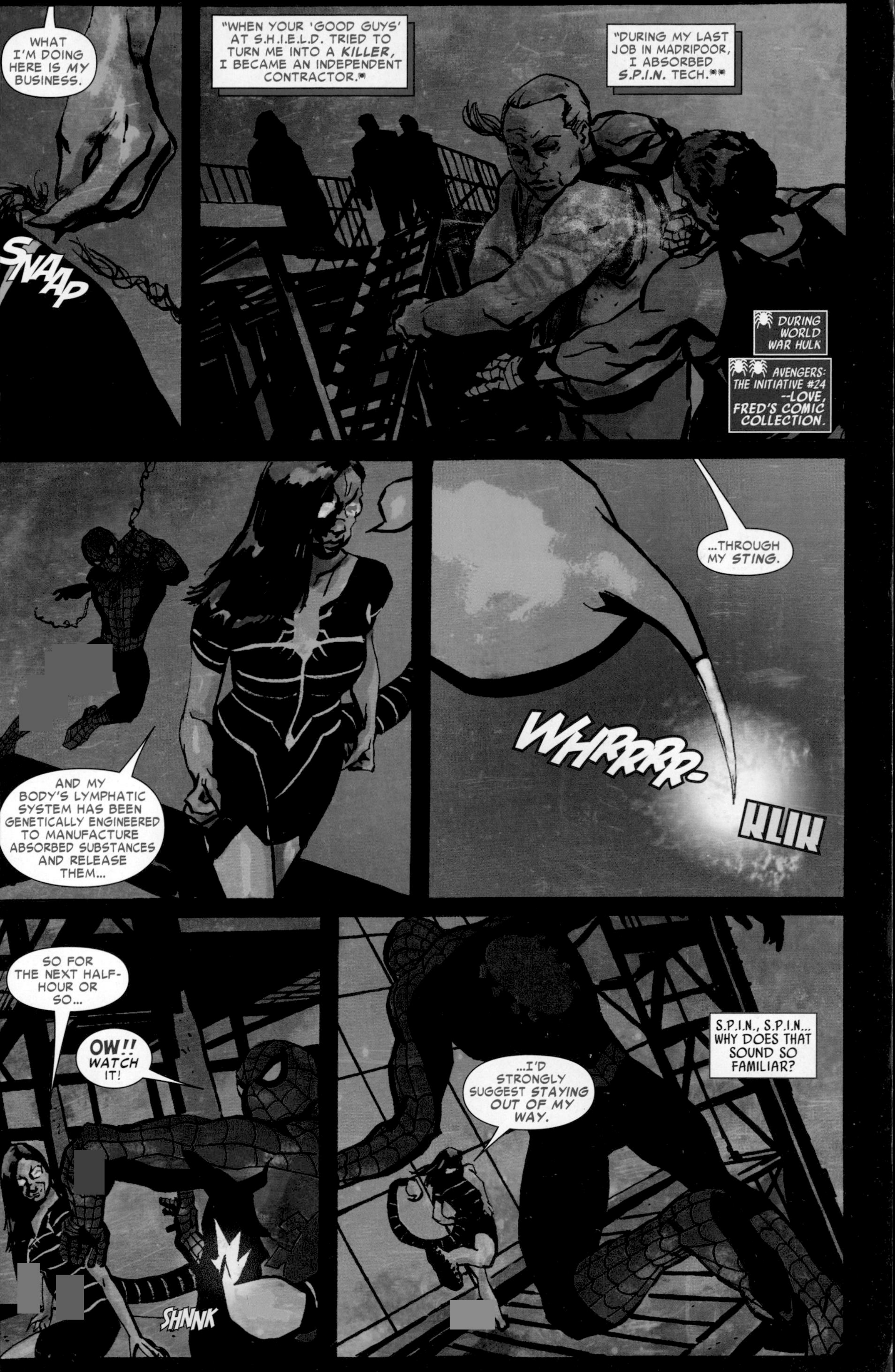
WHAT I'M DOING HERE IS MY BUSINESS.
SNAAP
"WHEN YOUR 'GOOD GUYS' AT S.H.I.E.L.D. TRIED TO TURN ME INTO A KILLER, I BECAME AN INDEPENDENT CONTRACTOR.*
"DURING MY LAST JOB IN MADRIPOOR, I ABSORBED S.P.I.N. TECH.**
* DURING WORLD WAR HULK
** AVENGERS: THE INITIATIVE #24 --LOVE, FRED'S COMIC COLLECTION.
AND MY BODY'S LYMPHATIC SYSTEM HAS BEEN GENETICALLY ENGINEERED TO MANUFACTURE ABSORBED SUBSTANCES AND RELEASE THEM...
...THROUGH MY STING.
WHRRRR-
KLIK
SO FOR THE NEXT HALF-HOUR OR SO...
OW!! WATCH IT!
SHNNK
...I'D STRONGLY SUGGEST STAYING OUT OF MY WAY.
S.P.I.N., S.P.I.N... WHY DOES THAT SOUND SO FAMILIAR?

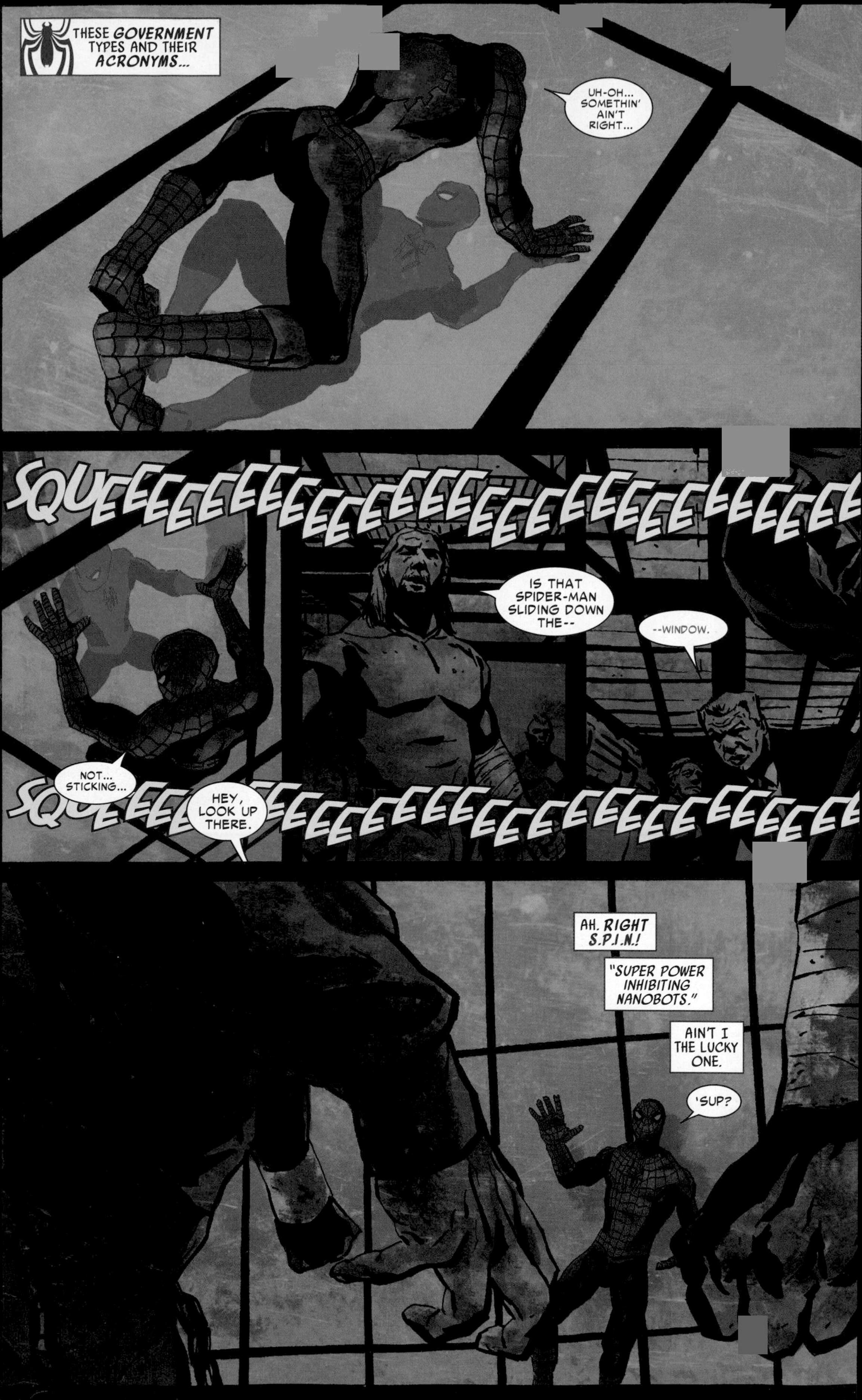
THESE GOVERNMENT TYPES AND THEIR ACRONYMS...
UH-OH... SOMETHIN' AIN'T RIGHT...
SQUEEEEEEEEEEEEEEEEEEEEEEEEEEEEEE
IS THAT SPIDER-MAN SLIDING DOWN THE--
--WINDOW.
NOT... STICKING...
HEY, LOOK UP THERE.
SQUEEEEEEEEEEEEEEEEEEEEEEEEEEEEEE
AH. RIGHT S.P.I.N.!
"SUPER POWER INHIBITING NANOBOTS."
AIN'T I THE LUCKY ONE.
'SUP?

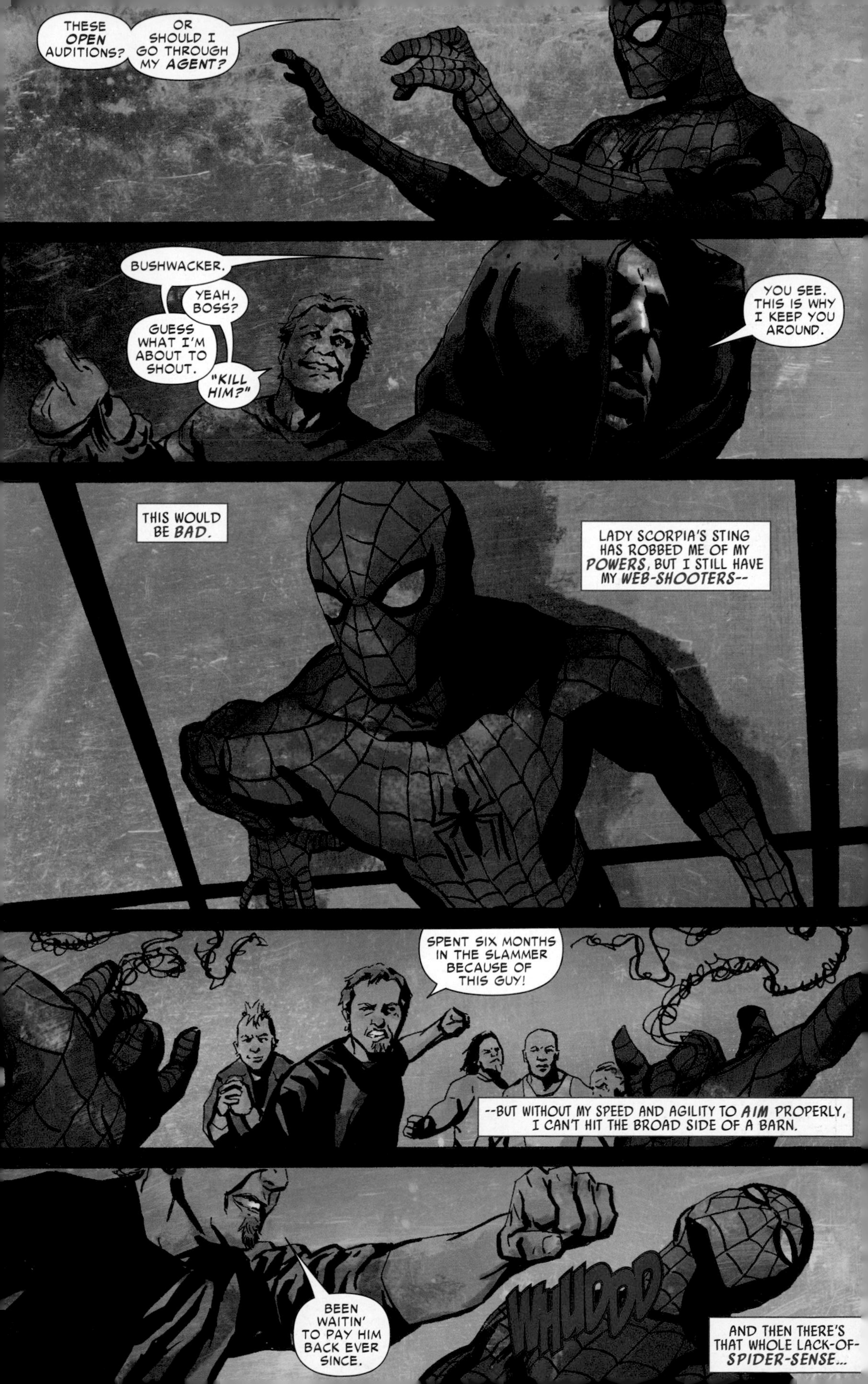
THESE OPEN AUDITIONS?
OR SHOULD I GO THROUGH MY AGENT?
BUSHWACKER.
YEAH, BOSS?
GUESS WHAT I'M ABOUT TO SHOUT.
"KILL HIM?"
YOU SEE. THIS IS WHY I KEEP YOU AROUND.
THIS WOULD BE BAD.
LADY SCORPIA'S STING HAS ROBBED ME OF MY POWERS, BUT I STILL HAVE MY WEB-SHOOTERS--
SPENT SIX MONTHS IN THE SLAMMER BECAUSE OF THIS GUY!
--BUT WITHOUT MY SPEED AND AGILITY TO AIM PROPERLY, I CAN'T HIT THE BROAD SIDE OF A BARN.
BEEN WAITIN' TO PAY HIM BACK EVER SINCE.
WHUDDD
AND THEN THERE'S THAT WHOLE LACK-OF-SPIDER-SENSE...

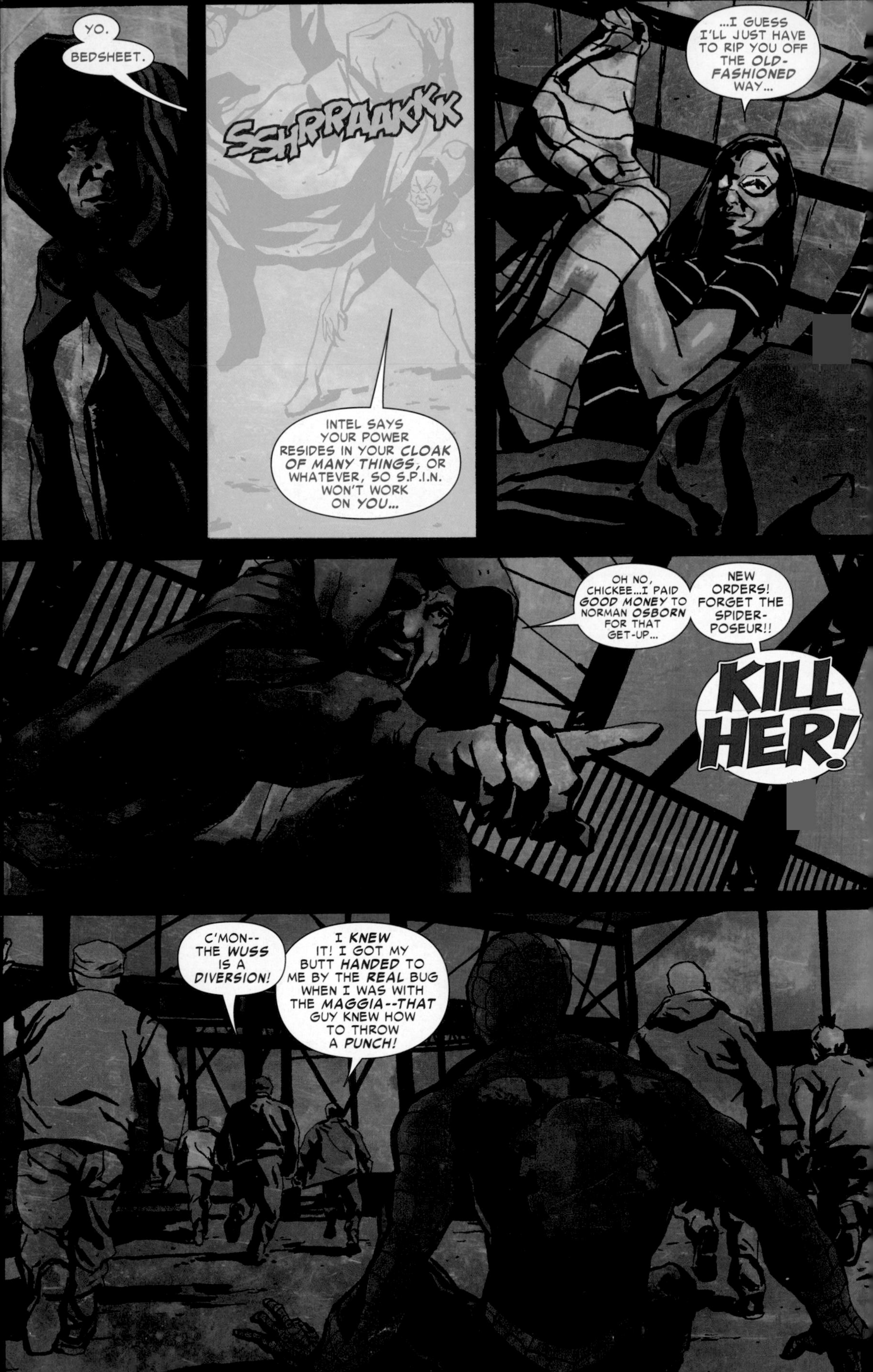
YO. BEDSHEET.
SSHRRAAKKK
INTEL SAYS YOUR POWER RESIDES IN YOUR CLOAK OF MANY THINGS, OR WHATEVER, SO S.P.I.N. WON'T WORK ON YOU...
...I GUESS I'LL JUST HAVE TO RIP YOU OFF THE OLD-FASHIONED WAY...
OH NO, CHICKEE...I PAID GOOD MONEY TO NORMAN OSBORN FOR THAT GET-UP...
NEW ORDERS! FORGET THE SPIDER-POSEUR!!
KILL HER!
C'MON-- THE WUSS IS A DIVERSION!
I KNEW IT! I GOT MY BUTT HANDED TO ME BY THE REAL BUG WHEN I WAS WITH THE MAGGIA--THAT GUY KNEW HOW TO THROW A PUNCH!

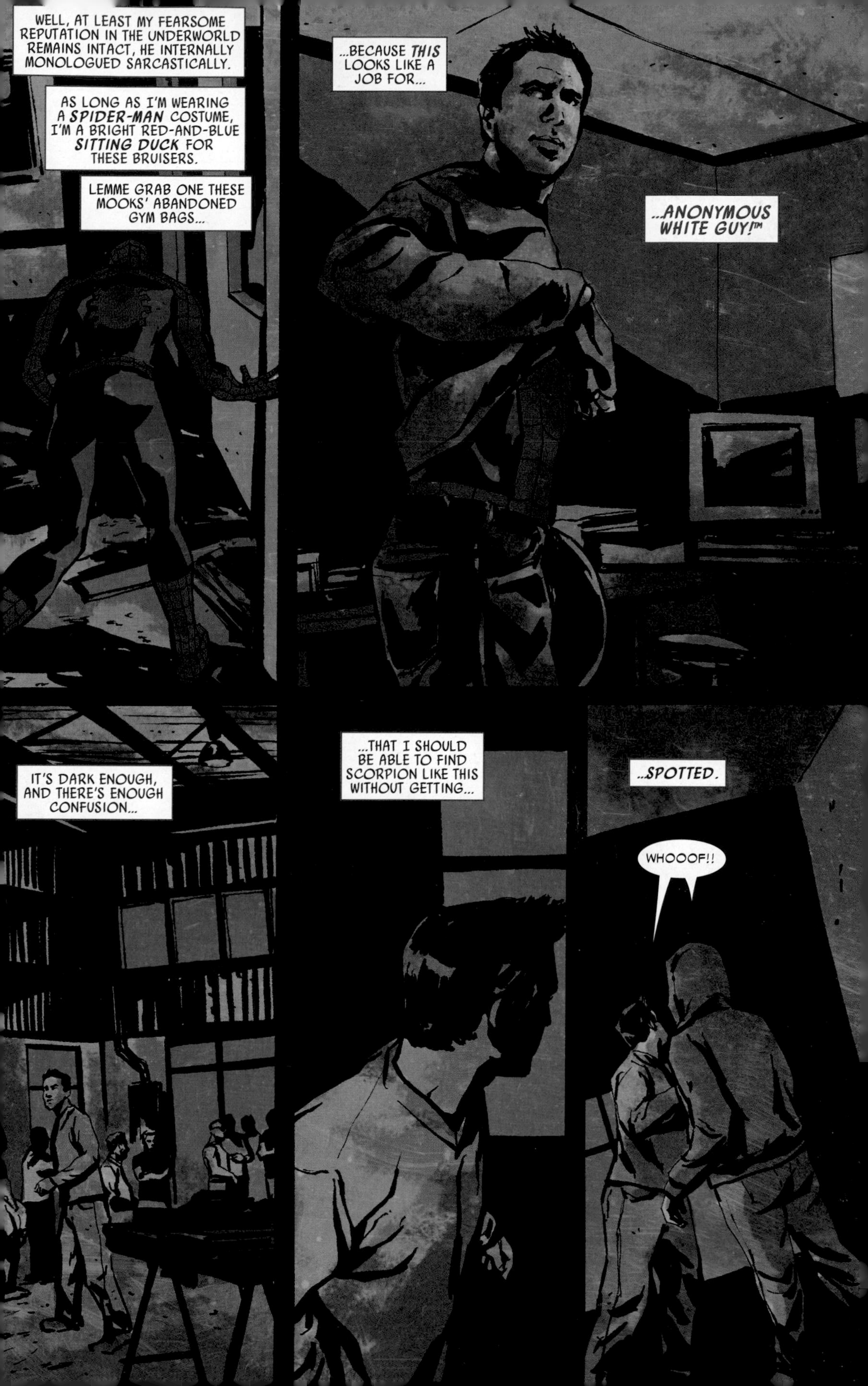
WELL, AT LEAST MY FEARSOME REPUTATION IN THE UNDERWORLD REMAINS INTACT, HE INTERNALLY MONOLOGUED SARCASTICALLY.
AS LONG AS I'M WEARING A SPIDER-MAN COSTUME, I'M A BRIGHT RED-AND-BLUE SITTING DUCK FOR THESE BRUISERS.
LEMME GRAB ONE THESE MOOKS' ABANDONED GYM BAGS...
...BECAUSE THIS LOOKS LIKE A JOB FOR...
...ANONYMOUS WHITE GUY!™
IT'S DARK ENOUGH, AND THERE'S ENOUGH CONFUSION...
...THAT I SHOULD BE ABLE TO FIND SCORPION LIKE THIS WITHOUT GETTING...
...SPOTTED.
WHOOOF!!

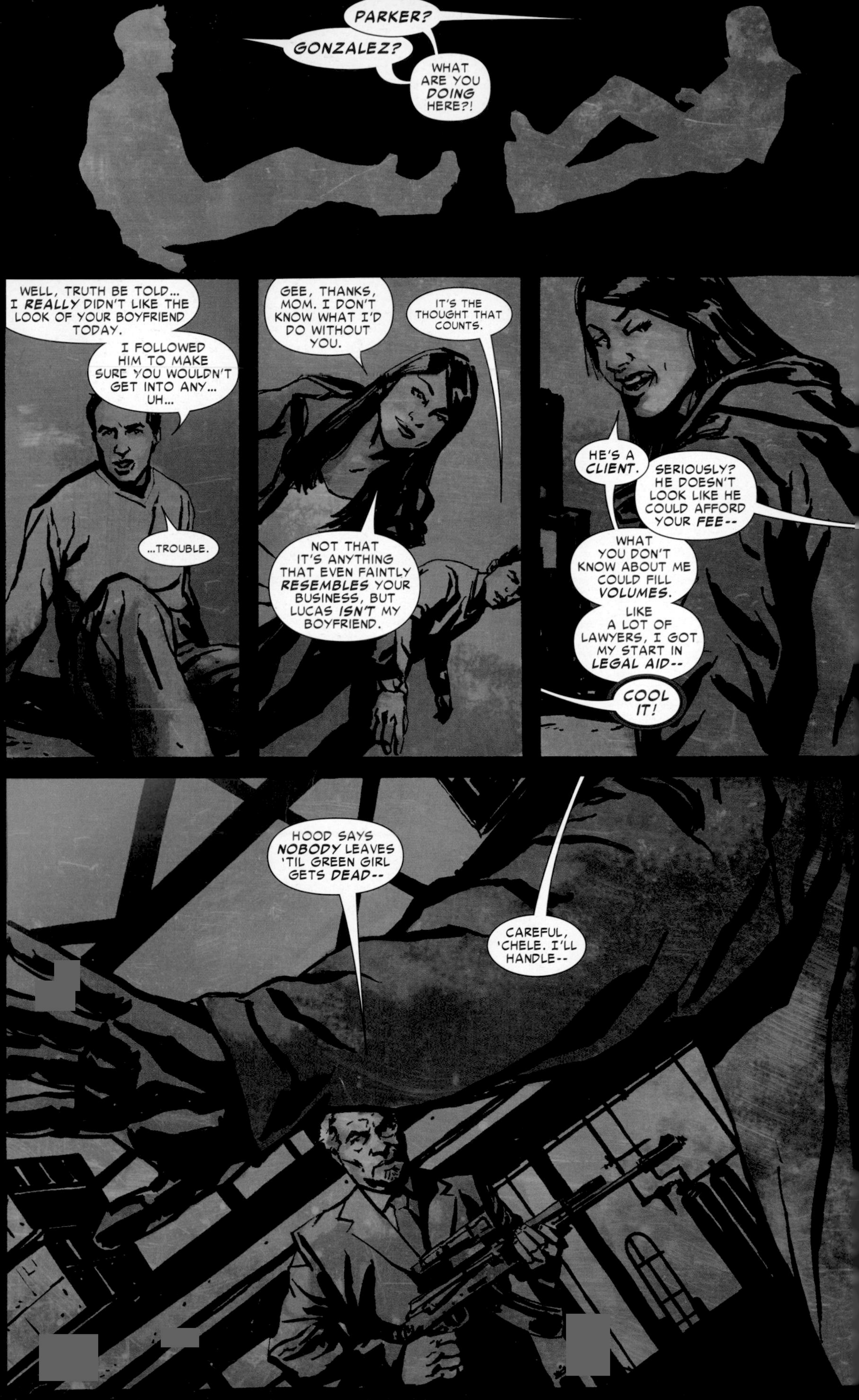
PARKER?
GONZALEZ?
WHAT ARE YOU DOING HERE?!
WELL, TRUTH BE TOLD... I REALLY DIDN'T LIKE THE LOOK OF YOUR BOYFRIEND TODAY.
I FOLLOWED HIM TO MAKE SURE YOU WOULDN'T GET INTO ANY... UH...
...TROUBLE.
GEE, THANKS, MOM. I DON'T KNOW WHAT I'D DO WITHOUT YOU.
IT'S THE THOUGHT THAT COUNTS.
NOT THAT IT'S ANYTHING THAT EVEN FAINTLY RESEMBLES YOUR BUSINESS, BUT LUCAS ISN'T MY BOYFRIEND.
HE'S A CLIENT.
SERIOUSLY? HE DOESN'T LOOK LIKE HE COULD AFFORD YOUR FEE--
WHAT YOU DON'T KNOW ABOUT ME COULD FILL VOLUMES.
LIKE A LOT OF LAWYERS, I GOT MY START IN LEGAL AID--
COOL IT!
HOOD SAYS NOBODY LEAVES 'TIL GREEN GIRL GETS DEAD--
CAREFUL, 'CHELE. I'LL HANDLE--

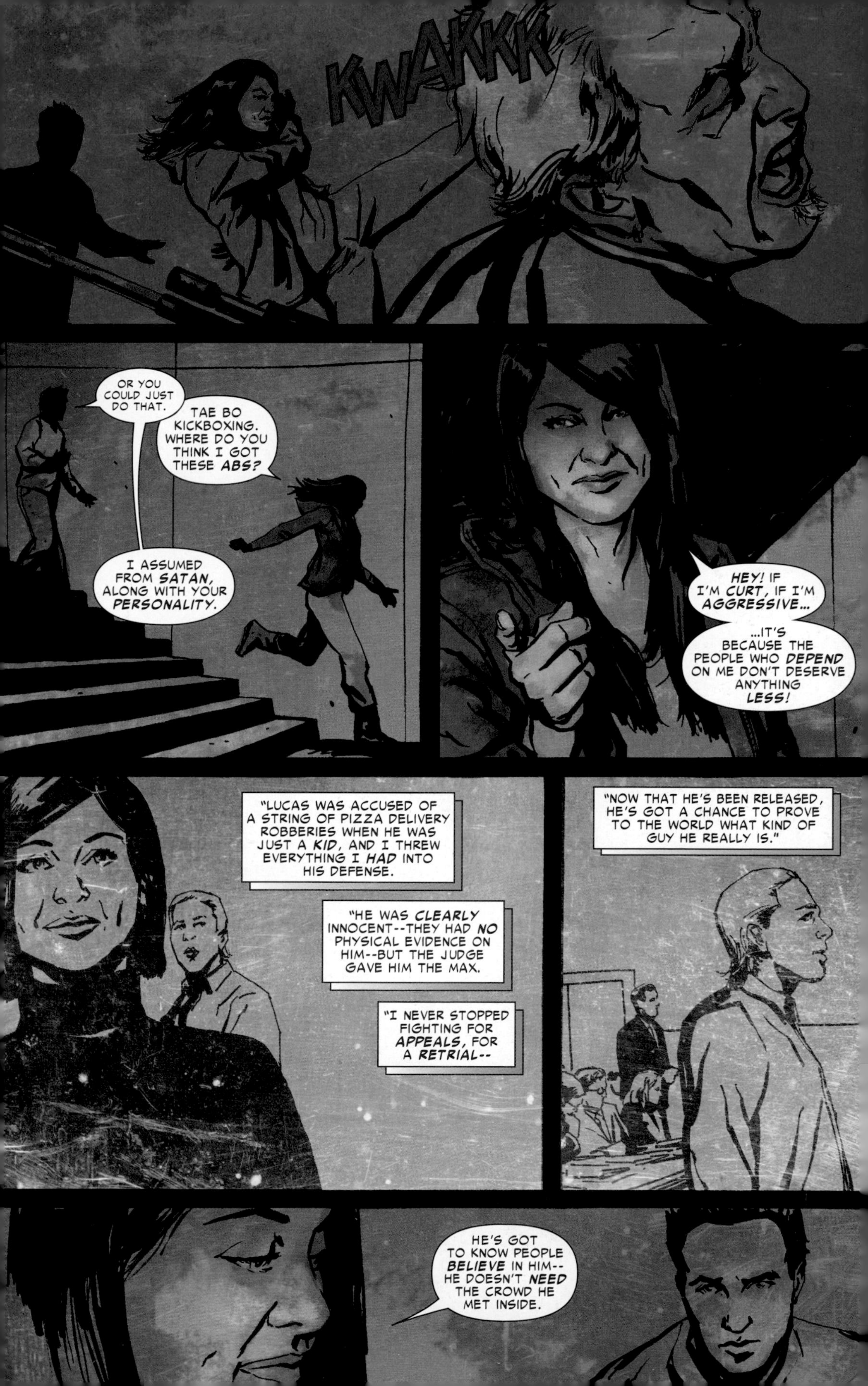
KWAKKK
OR YOU COULD JUST DO THAT.
TAE BO KICKBOXING. WHERE DO YOU THINK I GOT THESE ABS?
I ASSUMED FROM SATAN, ALONG WITH YOUR PERSONALITY.
HEY! IF I'M CURT, IF I'M AGGRESSIVE...
...IT'S BECAUSE THE PEOPLE WHO DEPEND ON ME DON'T DESERVE ANYTHING LESS!
"LUCAS WAS ACCUSED OF A STRING OF PIZZA DELIVERY ROBBERIES WHEN HE WAS JUST A KID, AND I THREW EVERYTHING I HAD INTO HIS DEFENSE.
"HE WAS CLEARLY INNOCENT--THEY HAD NO PHYSICAL EVIDENCE ON HIM--BUT THE JUDGE GAVE HIM THE MAX.
"I NEVER STOPPED FIGHTING FOR APPEALS, FOR A RETRIAL--
"NOW THAT HE'S BEEN RELEASED, HE'S GOT A CHANCE TO PROVE TO THE WORLD WHAT KIND OF GUY HE REALLY IS."
HE'S GOT TO KNOW PEOPLE BELIEVE IN HIM--HE DOESN'T NEED THE CROWD HE MET INSIDE.

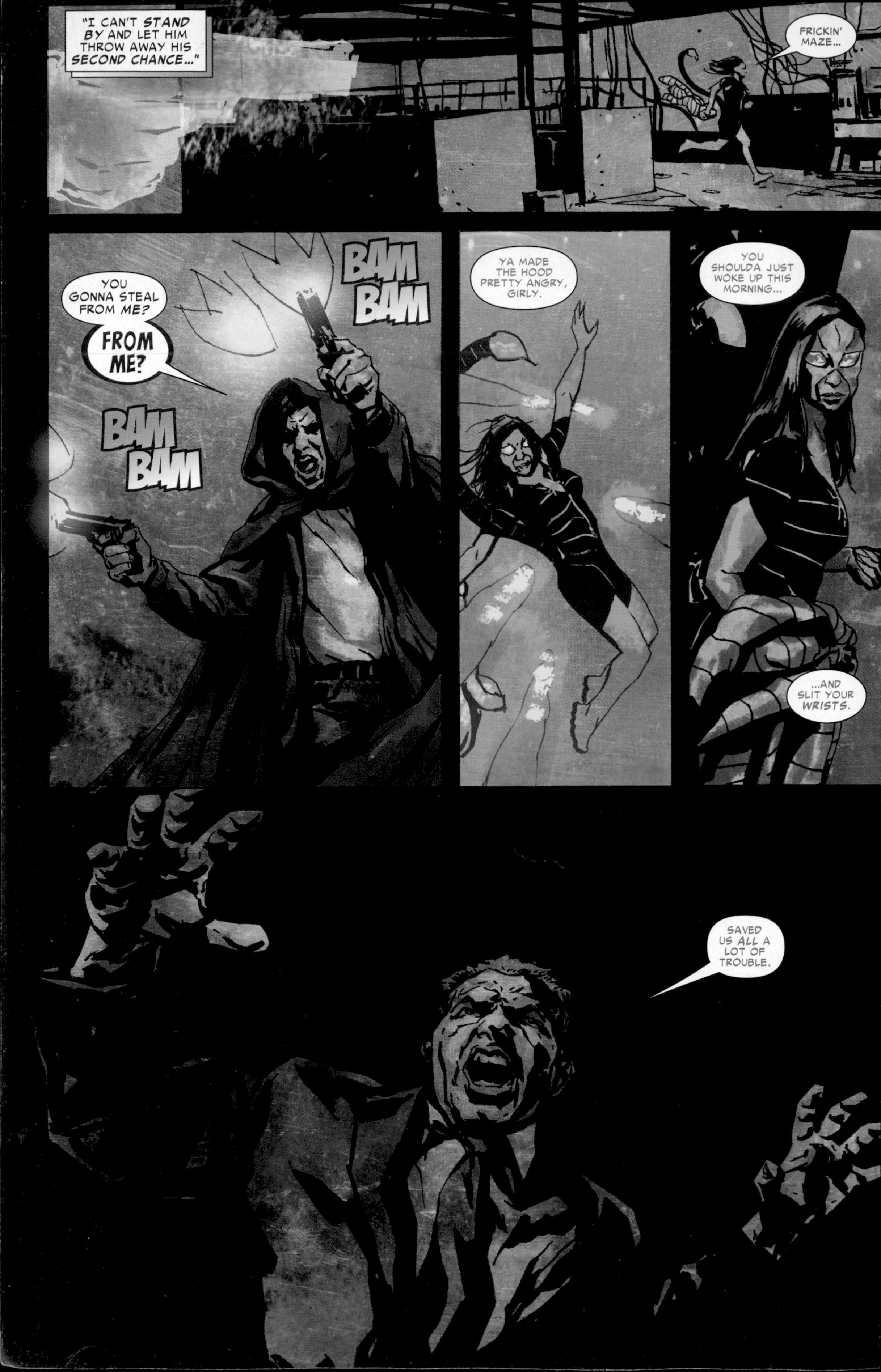
"I CAN'T STAND BY AND LET HIM THROW AWAY HIS SECOND CHANCE..."
FRICKIN' MAZE...
YOU GONNA STEAL FROM ME?
FROM ME?
BAM BAM
BAM BAM
YA MADE THE HOOD PRETTY ANGRY, GIRLY.
YOU SHOULDA JUST WOKE UP THIS MORNING...
...AND SLIT YOUR WRISTS.
SAVED US ALL A LOT OF TROUBLE.

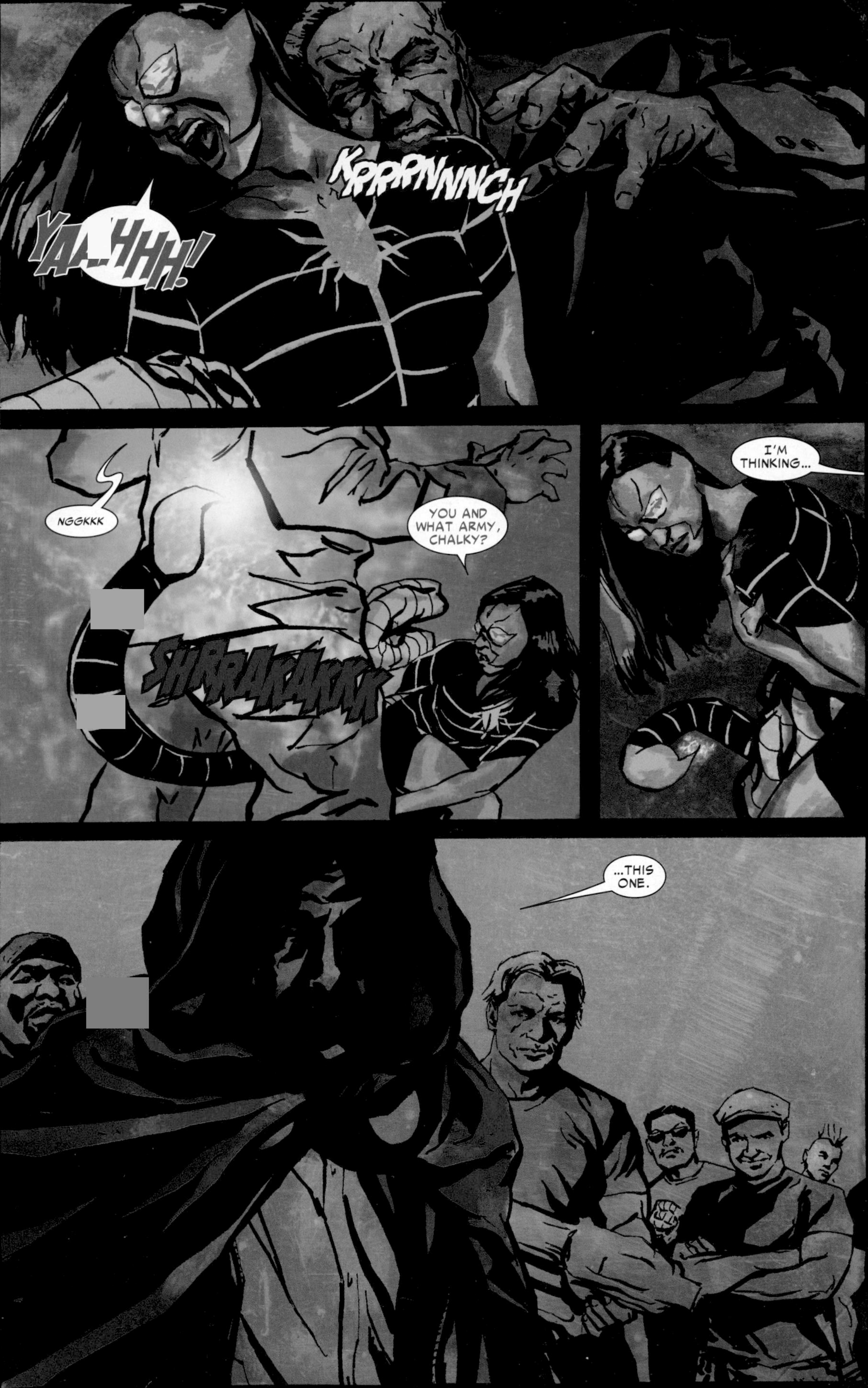
KRRRNNNCH
YAAHHH!
NGGKKK
YOU AND WHAT ARMY, CHALKY?
SHRRAKAKKK
I'M THINKING...
...THIS ONE.

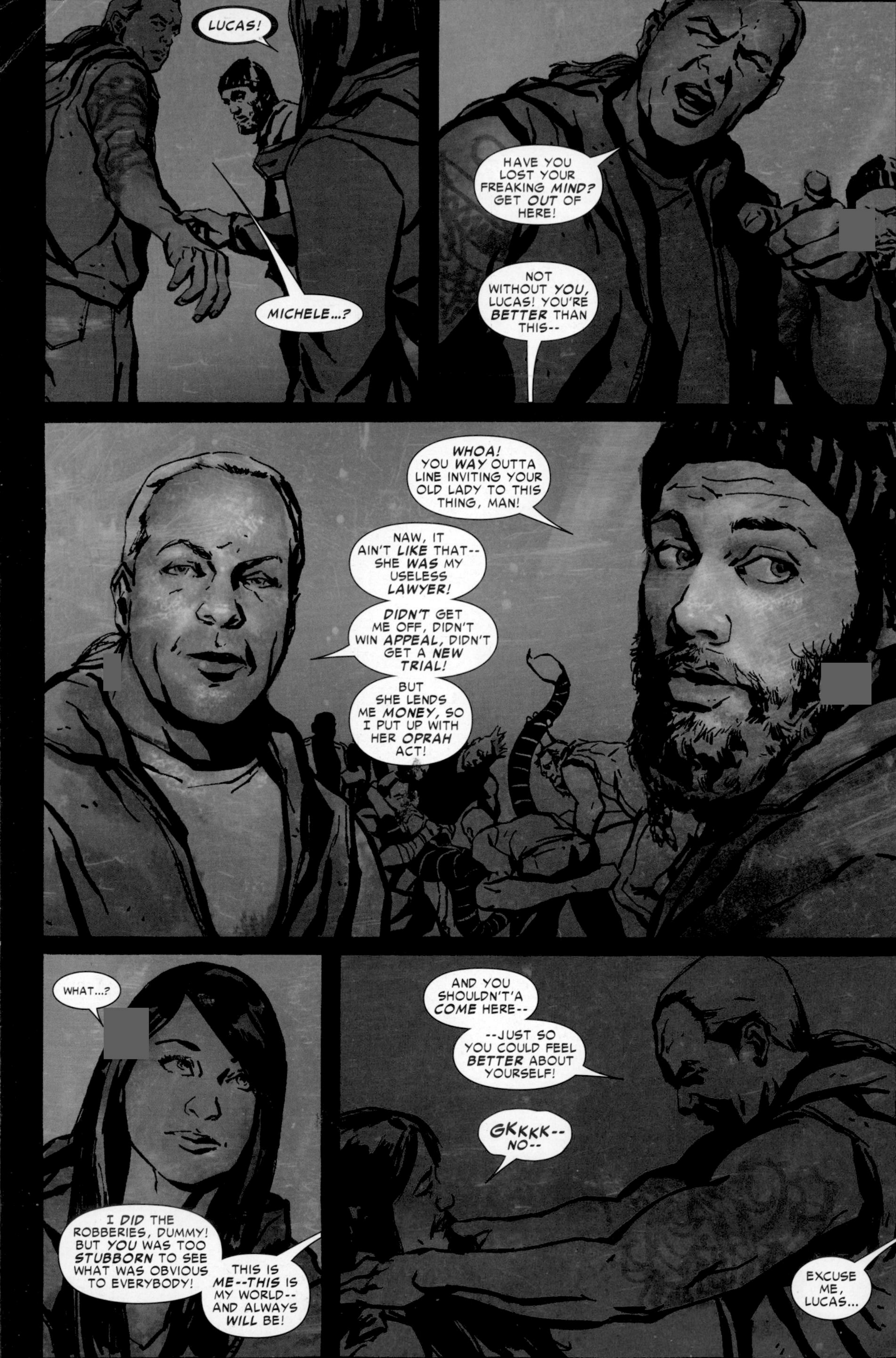
LUCAS!
MICHELE...?
HAVE YOU LOST YOUR FREAKING MIND? GET OUT OF HERE!
NOT WITHOUT YOU, LUCAS! YOU'RE BETTER THAN THIS--
WHOA! YOU WAY OUTTA LINE INVITING YOUR OLD LADY TO THIS THING, MAN!
NAW, IT AIN'T LIKE THAT-- SHE WAS MY USELESS LAWYER!
DIDN'T GET ME OFF, DIDN'T WIN APPEAL, DIDN'T GET A NEW TRIAL!
BUT SHE LENDS ME MONEY, SO I PUT UP WITH HER OPRAH ACT!
WHAT...?
I DID THE ROBBERIES, DUMMY! BUT YOU WAS TOO STUBBORN TO SEE WHAT WAS OBVIOUS TO EVERYBODY!
THIS IS ME--THIS IS MY WORLD-- AND ALWAYS WILL BE!
AND YOU SHOULDN'T'A COME HERE--
--JUST SO YOU COULD FEEL BETTER ABOUT YOURSELF!
GKKKK-- NO--
EXCUSE ME, LUCAS...

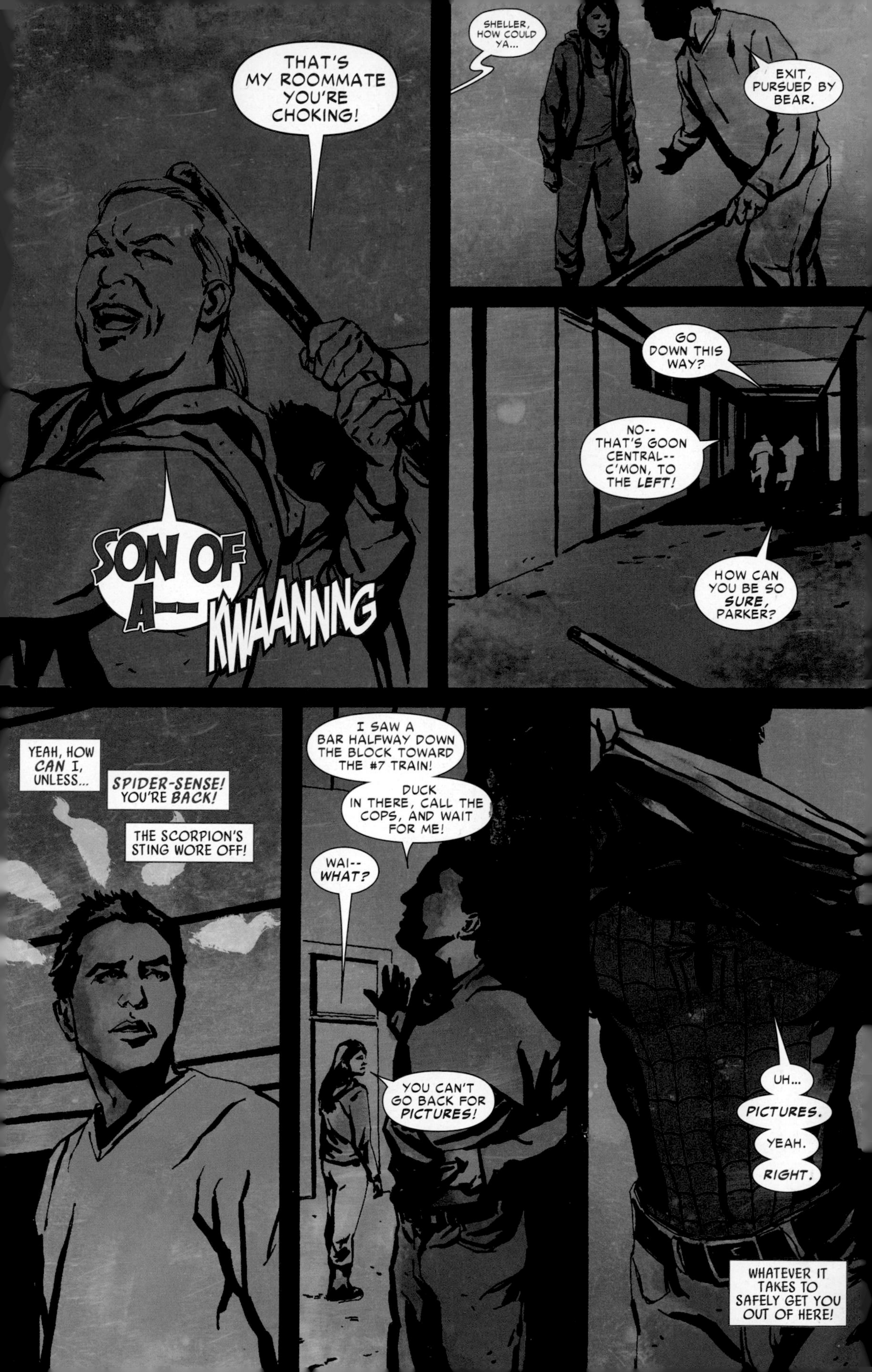
THAT'S MY ROOMMATE YOU'RE CHOKING!
SON OF A--
KWAANNNG
SHELLER, HOW COULD YA...
EXIT, PURSUED BY BEAR.
GO DOWN THIS WAY?
NO-- THAT'S GOON CENTRAL-- C'MON, TO THE LEFT!
HOW CAN YOU BE SO SURE, PARKER?
YEAH, HOW CAN I, UNLESS...
SPIDER-SENSE! YOU'RE BACK!
THE SCORPION'S STING WORE OFF!
I SAW A BAR HALFWAY DOWN THE BLOCK TOWARD THE #7 TRAIN!
DUCK IN THERE, CALL THE COPS, AND WAIT FOR ME!
WAI-- WHAT?
YOU CAN'T GO BACK FOR PICTURES!
UH...
PICTURES.
YEAH.
RIGHT.
WHATEVER IT TAKES TO SAFELY GET YOU OUT OF HERE!

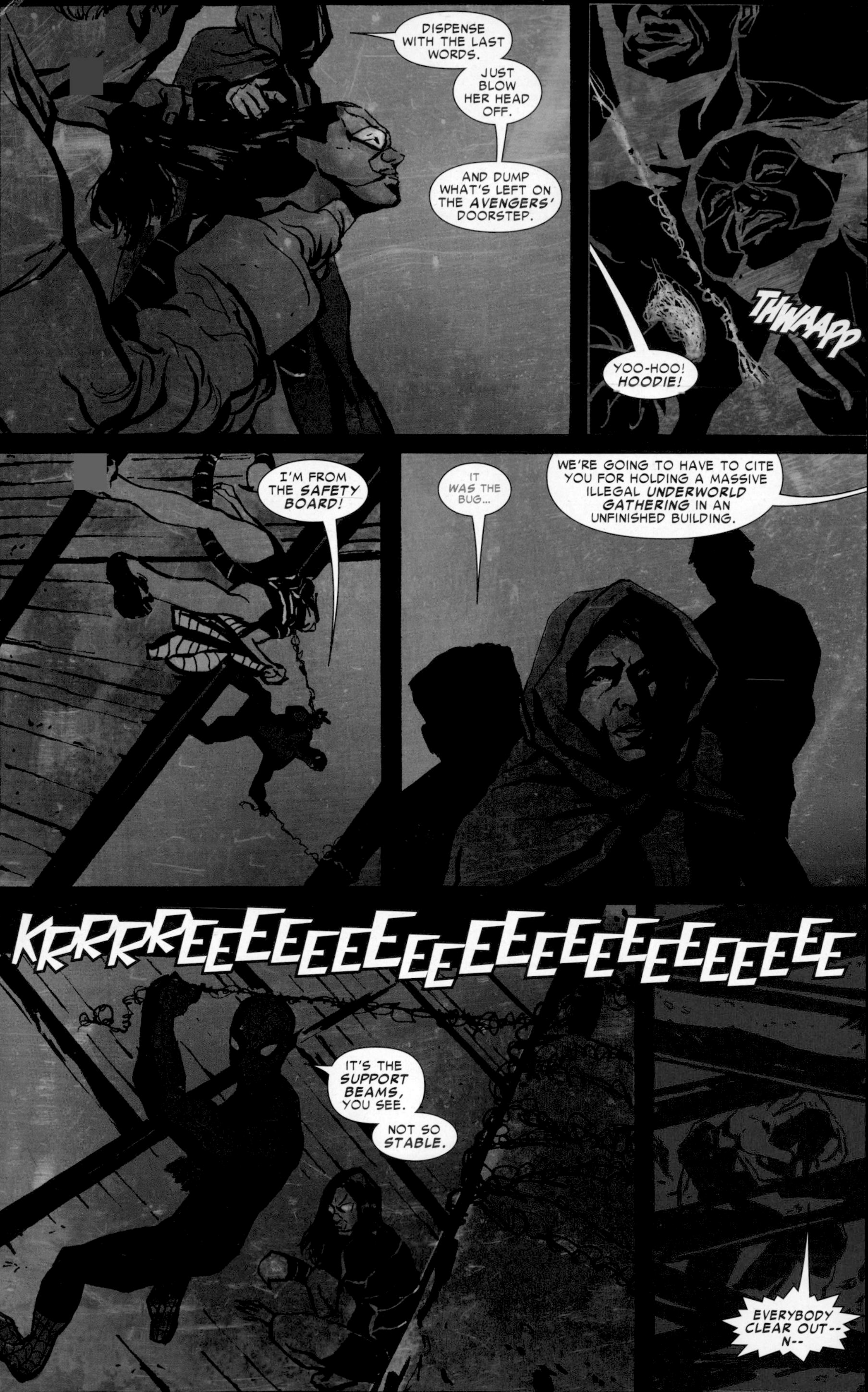
DISPENSE WITH THE LAST WORDS.
JUST BLOW HER HEAD OFF.
AND DUMP WHAT'S LEFT ON THE AVENGERS' DOORSTEP.
THWAAPP
YOO-HOO! HOODIE!
I'M FROM THE SAFETY BOARD!
IT WAS THE BUG...
WE'RE GOING TO HAVE TO CITE YOU FOR HOLDING A MASSIVE ILLEGAL UNDERWORLD GATHERING IN AN UNFINISHED BUILDING.
KRRRREEEEEEEEEEEEEEEEEEEEEEE
IT'S THE SUPPORT BEAMS, YOU SEE.
NOT SO STABLE.
EVERYBODY CLEAR OUT-- N--

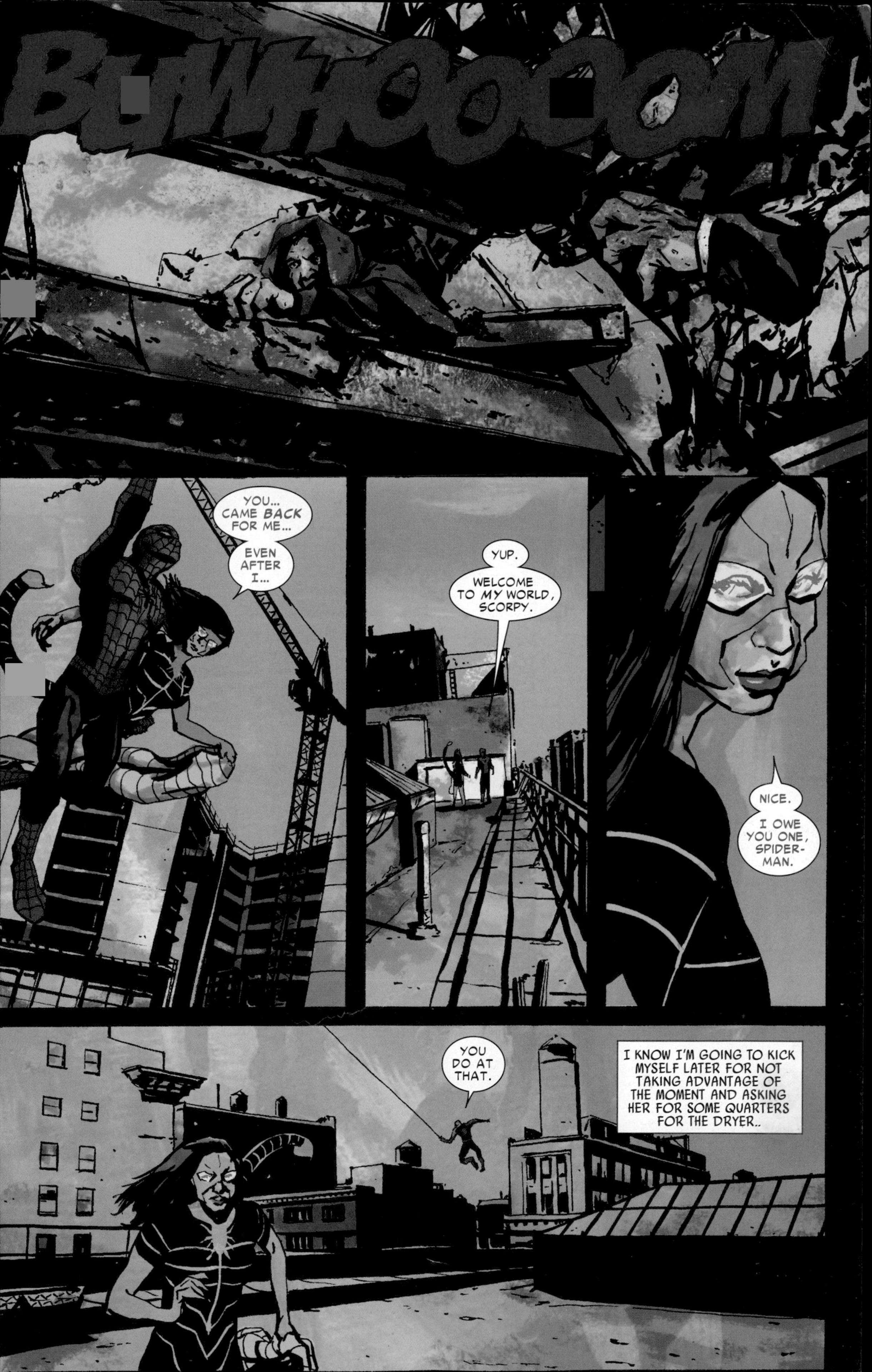

YOU... CAME BACK FOR ME...
EVEN AFTER I...
YUP.
WELCOME TO MY WORLD, SCORPY.
NICE.
I OWE YOU ONE, SPIDER-MAN.
YOU DO AT THAT.
I KNOW I'M GOING TO KICK MYSELF LATER FOR NOT TAKING ADVANTAGE OF THE MOMENT AND ASKING HER FOR SOME QUARTERS FOR THE DRYER..

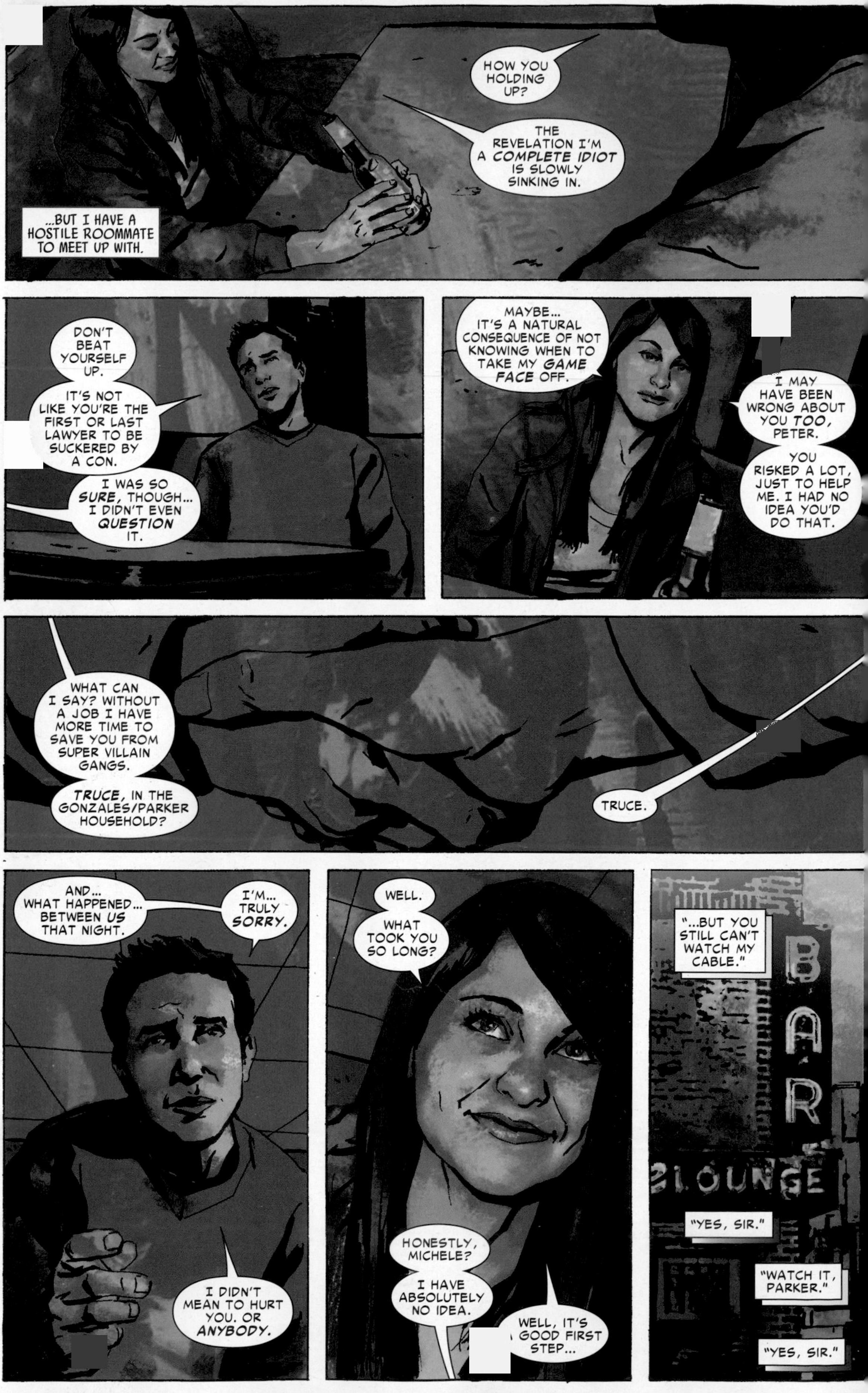
...BUT I HAVE A HOSTILE ROOMMATE TO MEET UP WITH.
HOW YOU HOLDING UP?
THE REVELATION I'M A *COMPLETE IDIOT* IS SLOWLY SINKING IN.
DON'T BEAT YOURSELF UP.
IT'S NOT LIKE YOU'RE THE FIRST OR LAST LAWYER TO BE SUCKERED BY A CON.
I WAS SO *SURE*, THOUGH... I DIDN'T EVEN *QUESTION* IT.
MAYBE... IT'S A NATURAL CONSEQUENCE OF NOT KNOWING WHEN TO TAKE MY *GAME FACE* OFF.
I MAY HAVE BEEN WRONG ABOUT YOU *TOO,* PETER.
YOU RISKED A LOT, JUST TO HELP ME. I HAD NO IDEA YOU'D DO THAT.
WHAT CAN I SAY? WITHOUT A JOB I HAVE MORE TIME TO SAVE YOU FROM SUPER VILLAIN GANGS.
TRUCE, IN THE GONZALES/PARKER HOUSEHOLD?
TRUCE.
AND... WHAT HAPPENED... BETWEEN *US* THAT NIGHT.
I'M... TRULY *SORRY.*
I DIDN'T MEAN TO HURT YOU. OR *ANYBODY.*
WELL.
WHAT TOOK YOU SO LONG?
HONESTLY, MICHELE?
I HAVE ABSOLUTELY NO IDEA.
WELL, IT'S GOOD FIRST STEP...
"...BUT YOU STILL CAN'T WATCH MY CABLE."
BAR
LOUNGE
"YES, SIR."
"WATCH IT, PARKER."
"YES, SIR."

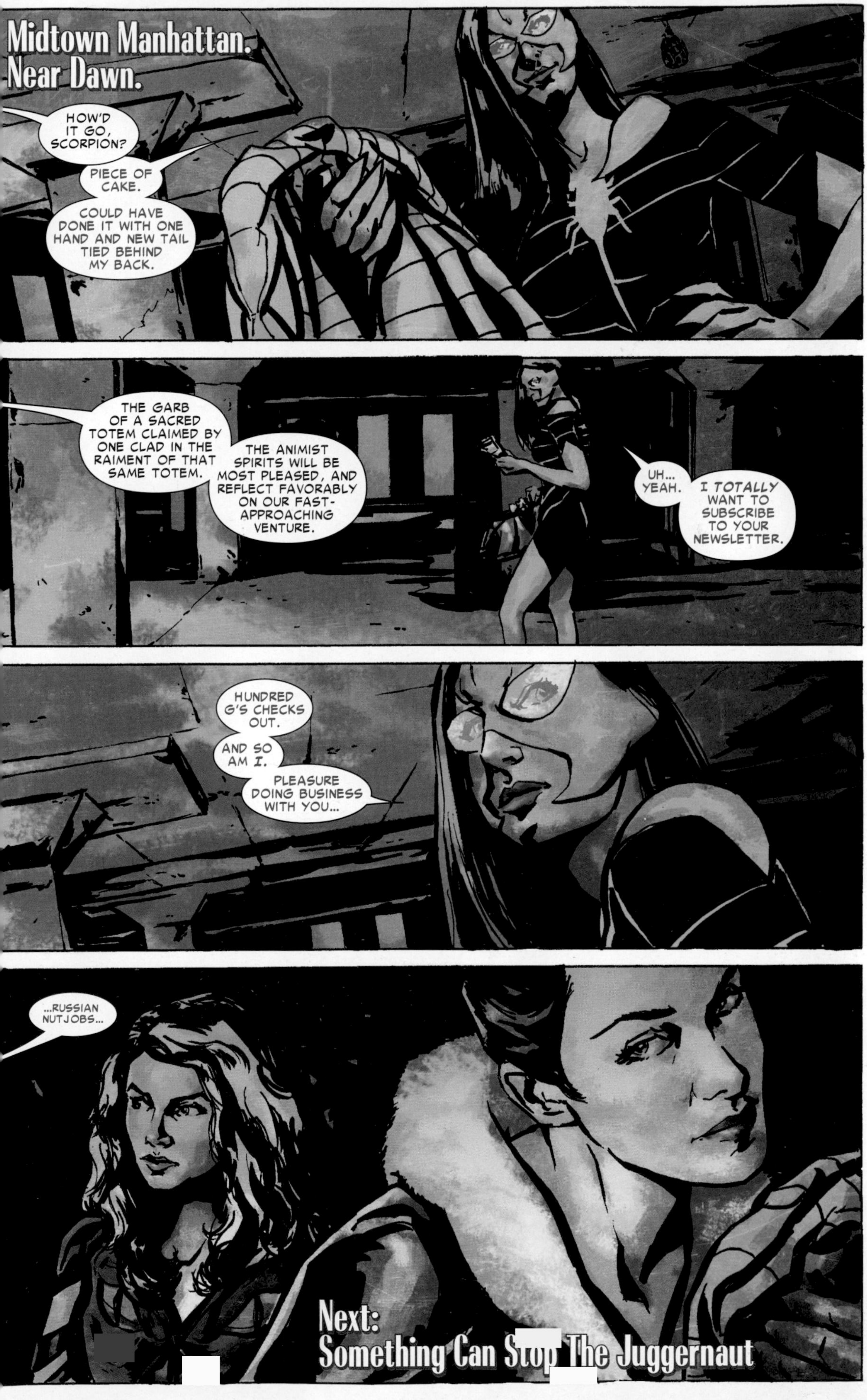
Midtown Manhattan. Near Dawn.
HOW'D IT GO, SCORPION?
PIECE OF CAKE.
COULD HAVE DONE IT WITH ONE HAND AND NEW TAIL TIED BEHIND MY BACK.
THE GARB OF A SACRED TOTEM CLAIMED BY ONE CLAD IN THE RAIMENT OF THAT SAME TOTEM.
THE ANIMIST SPIRITS WILL BE MOST PLEASED, AND REFLECT FAVORABLY ON OUR FAST-APPROACHING VENTURE.
UH... YEAH.
I TOTALLY WANT TO SUBSCRIBE TO YOUR NEWSLETTER.
HUNDRED G'S CHECKS OUT.
AND SO AM I.
PLEASURE DOING BUSINESS WITH YOU...
...RUSSIAN NUTJOBS...
Next:
Something Can Stop The Juggernaut

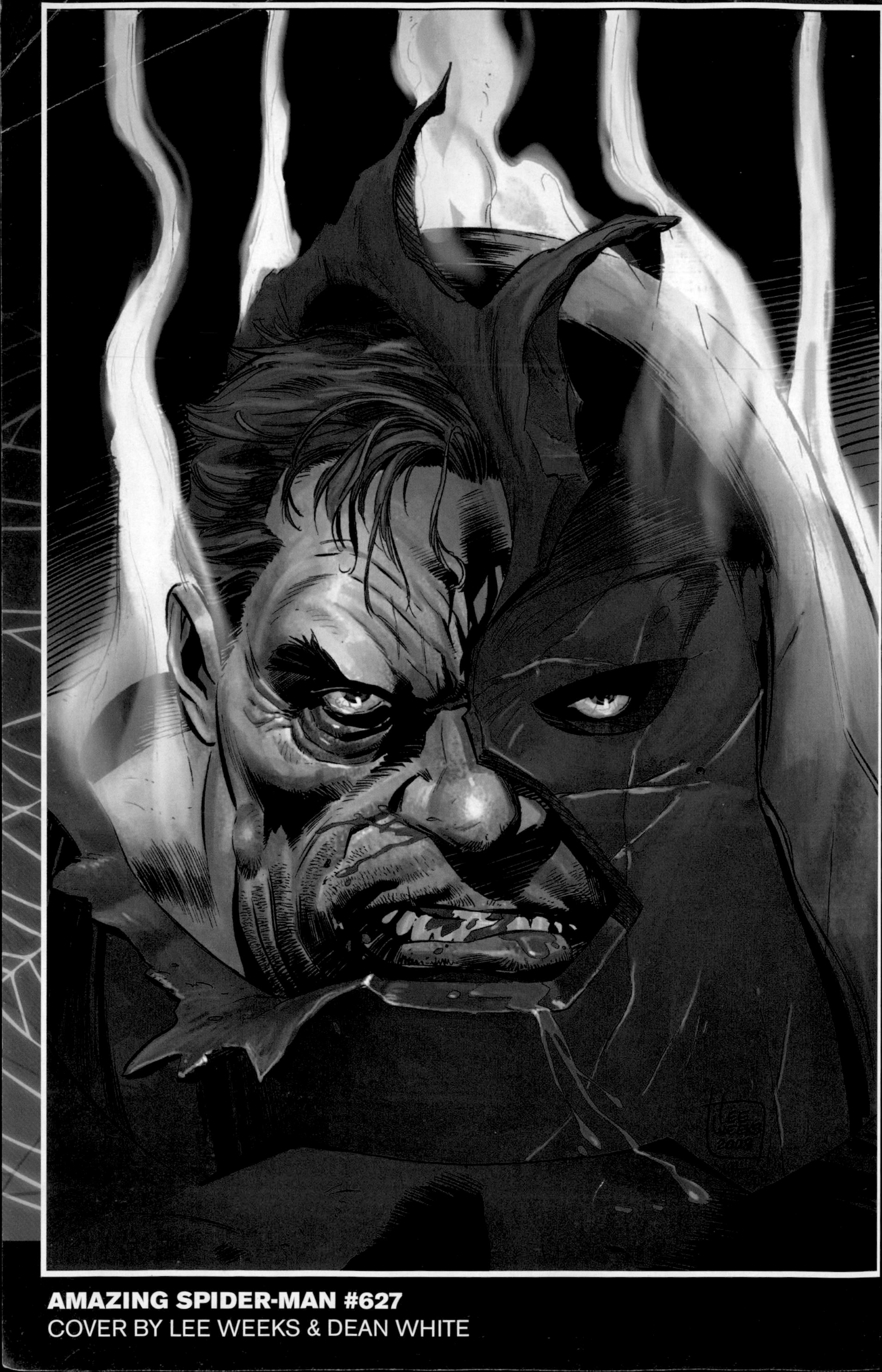

AMAZING SPIDER-MAN #627
COVER BY LEE WEEKS & DEAN WHITE

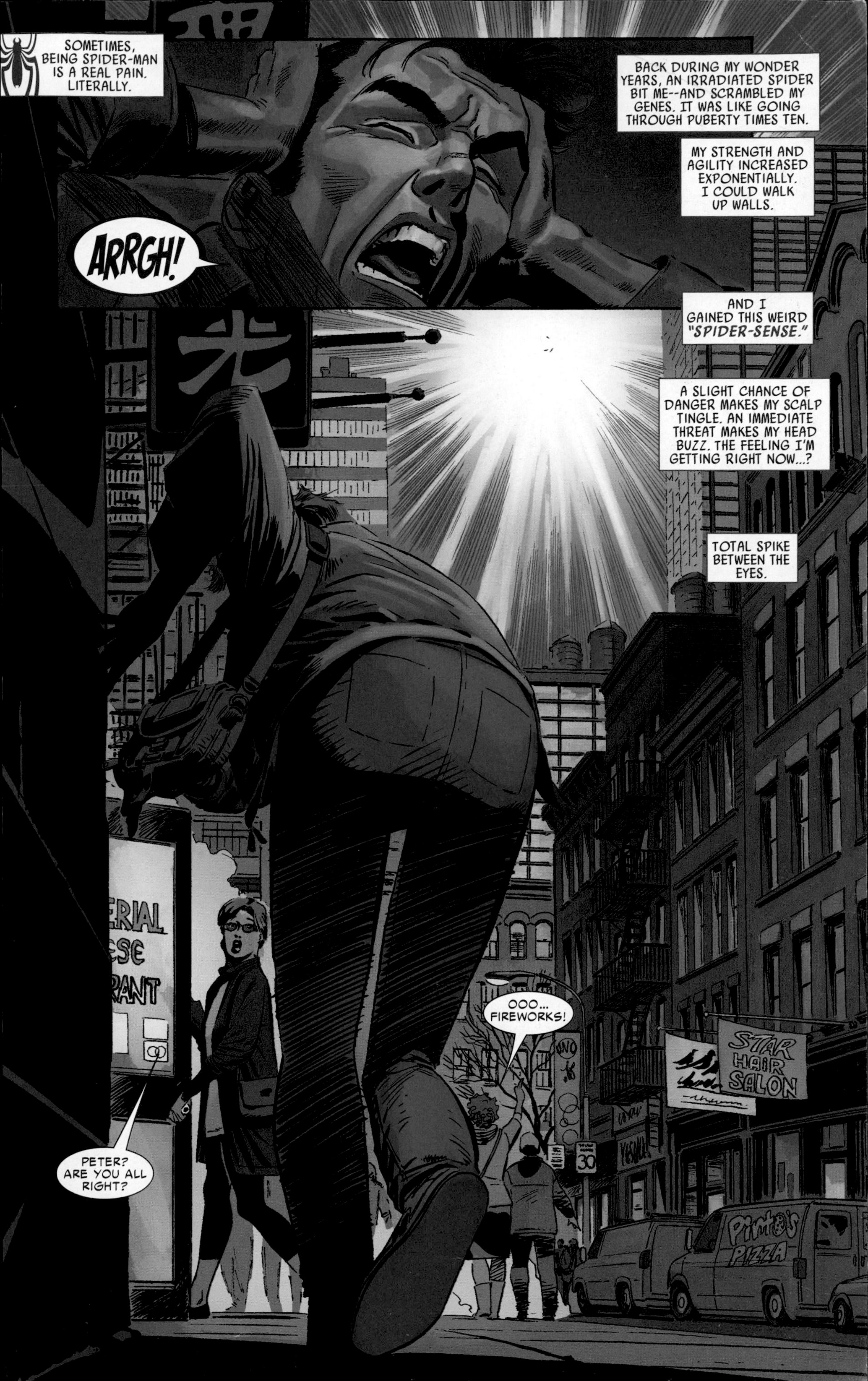
SOMETIMES, BEING SPIDER-MAN IS A REAL PAIN. LITERALLY.
BACK DURING MY WONDER YEARS, AN IRRADIATED SPIDER BIT ME--AND SCRAMBLED MY GENES. IT WAS LIKE GOING THROUGH PUBERTY TIMES TEN.
MY STRENGTH AND AGILITY INCREASED EXPONENTIALLY. I COULD WALK UP WALLS.
ARRGH!
AND I GAINED THIS WEIRD "SPIDER-SENSE."
A SLIGHT CHANCE OF DANGER MAKES MY SCALP TINGLE. AN IMMEDIATE THREAT MAKES MY HEAD BUZZ. THE FEELING I'M GETTING RIGHT NOW...?
TOTAL SPIKE BETWEEN THE EYES.
OOO... FIREWORKS!
PETER? ARE YOU ALL RIGHT?
STAR HAIR SALON
Pinto's PIZZA
30

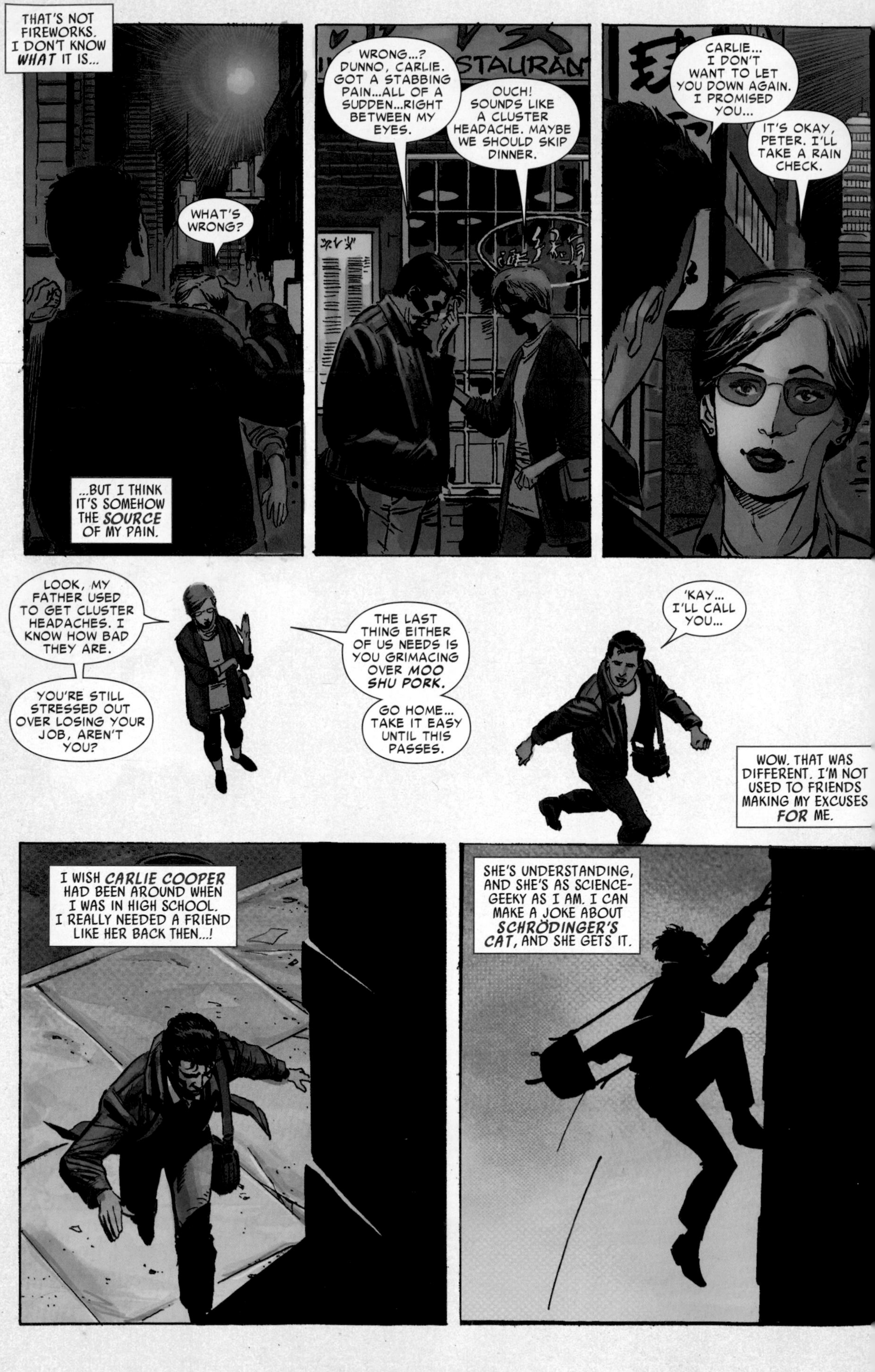
THAT'S NOT FIREWORKS. I DON'T KNOW WHAT IT IS...
WHAT'S WRONG?
...BUT I THINK IT'S SOMEHOW THE SOURCE OF MY PAIN.
STAURAN
WRONG...? DUNNO, CARLIE. GOT A STABBING PAIN...ALL OF A SUDDEN...RIGHT BETWEEN MY EYES.
OUCH! SOUNDS LIKE A CLUSTER HEADACHE. MAYBE WE SHOULD SKIP DINNER.
CARLIE... I DON'T WANT TO LET YOU DOWN AGAIN. I PROMISED YOU...
IT'S OKAY, PETER. I'LL TAKE A RAIN CHECK.
LOOK, MY FATHER USED TO GET CLUSTER HEADACHES. I KNOW HOW BAD THEY ARE.
YOU'RE STILL STRESSED OUT OVER LOSING YOUR JOB, AREN'T YOU?
THE LAST THING EITHER OF US NEEDS IS YOU GRIMACING OVER MOO SHU PORK.
GO HOME... TAKE IT EASY UNTIL THIS PASSES.
'KAY... I'LL CALL YOU...
WOW. THAT WAS DIFFERENT. I'M NOT USED TO FRIENDS MAKING MY EXCUSES FOR ME.
I WISH CARLIE COOPER HAD BEEN AROUND WHEN I WAS IN HIGH SCHOOL. I REALLY NEEDED A FRIEND LIKE HER BACK THEN...!
SHE'S UNDERSTANDING, AND SHE'S AS SCIENCE-GEEKY AS I AM. I CAN MAKE A JOKE ABOUT SCHRÖDINGER'S CAT, AND SHE GETS IT.

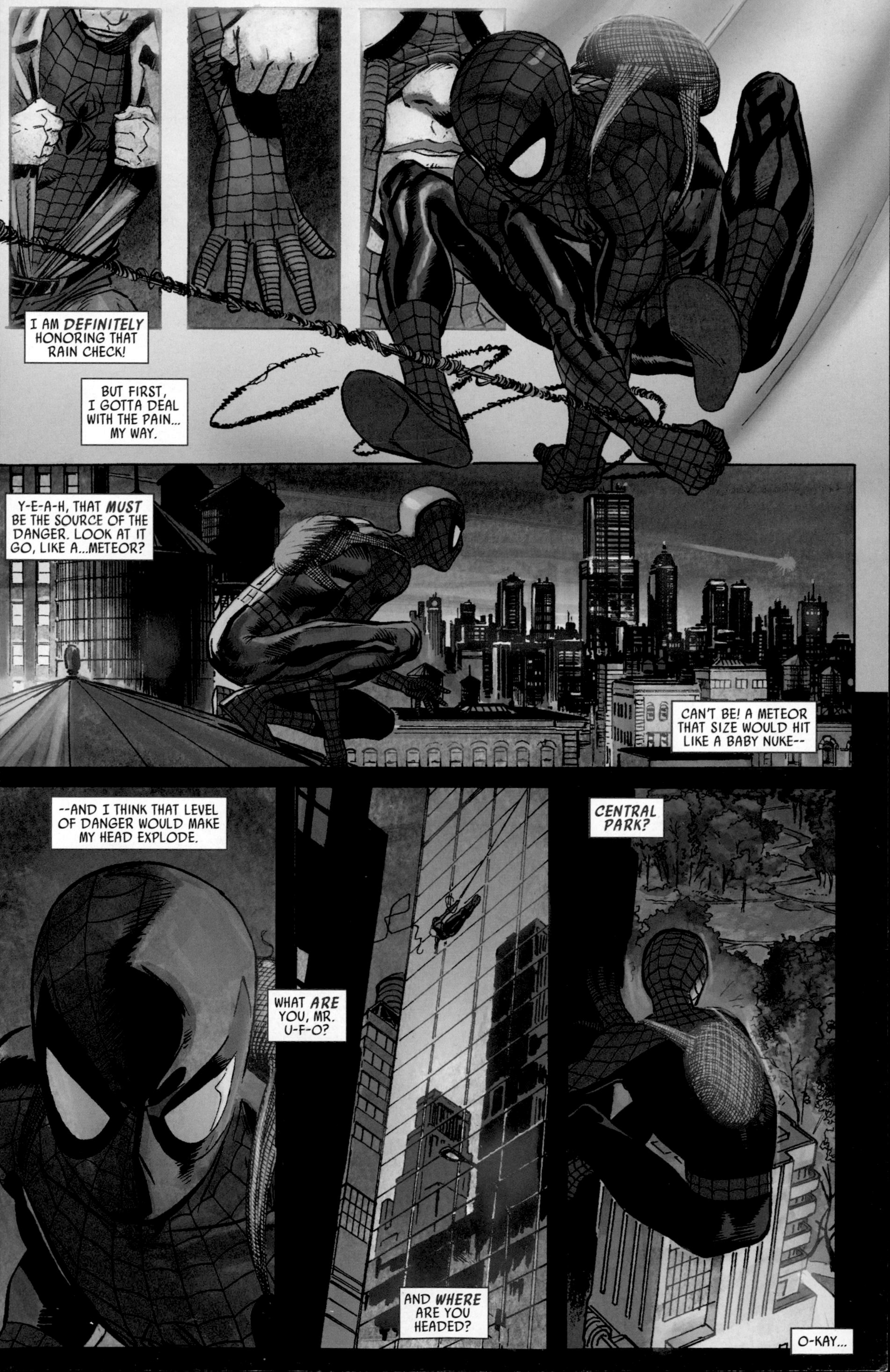
I AM DEFINITELY HONORING THAT RAIN CHECK!
BUT FIRST, I GOTTA DEAL WITH THE PAIN... MY WAY.
Y-E-A-H, THAT MUST BE THE SOURCE OF THE DANGER. LOOK AT IT GO, LIKE A...METEOR?
CAN'T BE! A METEOR THAT SIZE WOULD HIT LIKE A BABY NUKE--
--AND I THINK THAT LEVEL OF DANGER WOULD MAKE MY HEAD EXPLODE.
WHAT ARE YOU, MR. U-F-O?
AND WHERE ARE YOU HEADED?
CENTRAL PARK?
O-KAY...

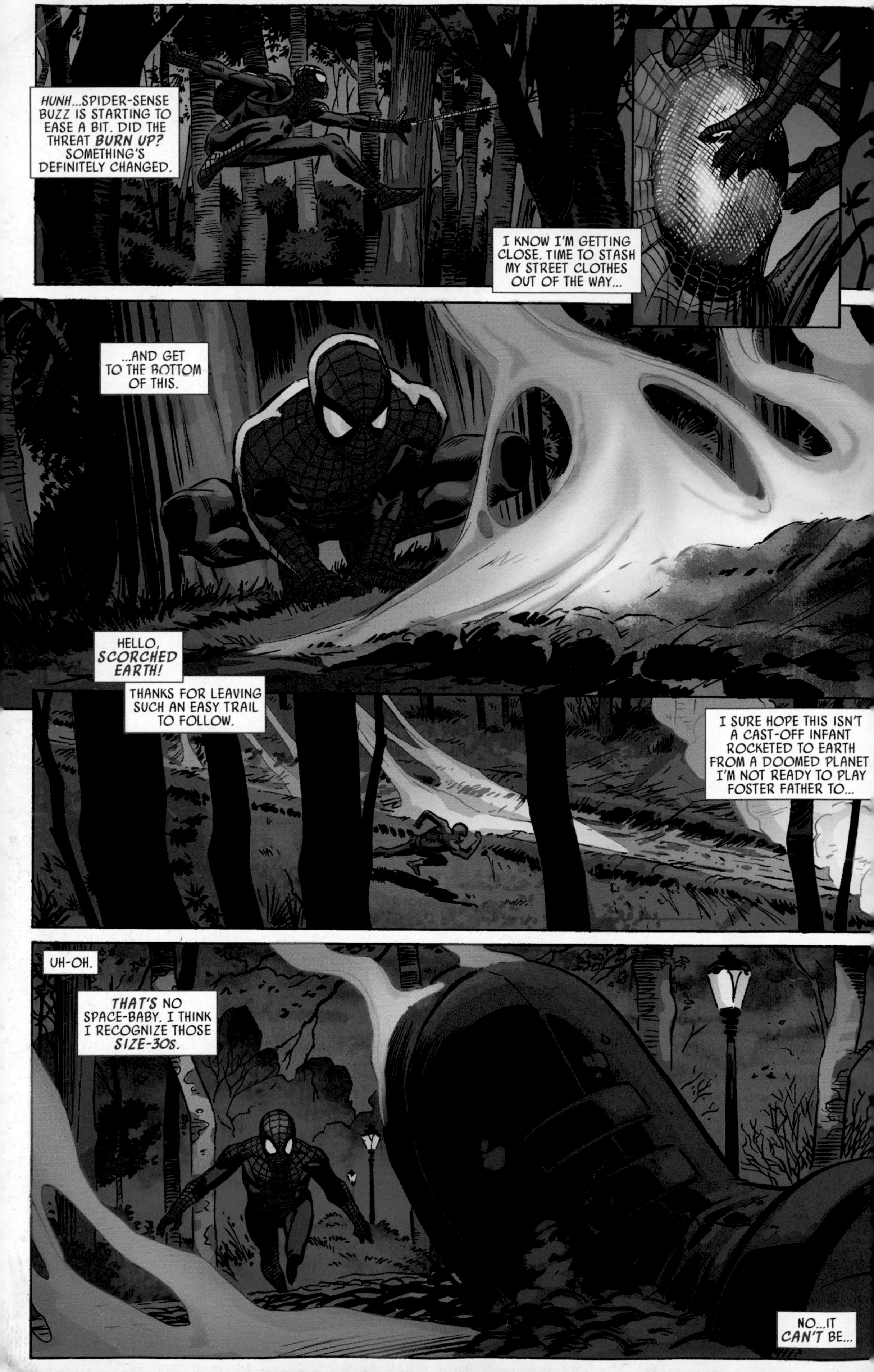

HUNH...SPIDER-SENSE BUZZ IS STARTING TO EASE A BIT. DID THE THREAT BURN UP? SOMETHING'S DEFINITELY CHANGED.
I KNOW I'M GETTING CLOSE. TIME TO STASH MY STREET CLOTHES OUT OF THE WAY...
...AND GET TO THE BOTTOM OF THIS.
HELLO, SCORCHED EARTH!
THANKS FOR LEAVING SUCH AN EASY TRAIL TO FOLLOW.
I SURE HOPE THIS ISN'T A CAST-OFF INFANT ROCKETED TO EARTH FROM A DOOMED PLANET I'M NOT READY TO PLAY FOSTER FATHER TO...
UH-OH.
THAT'S NO SPACE-BABY. I THINK I RECOGNIZE THOSE SIZE-30S.
NO...IT CAN'T BE...

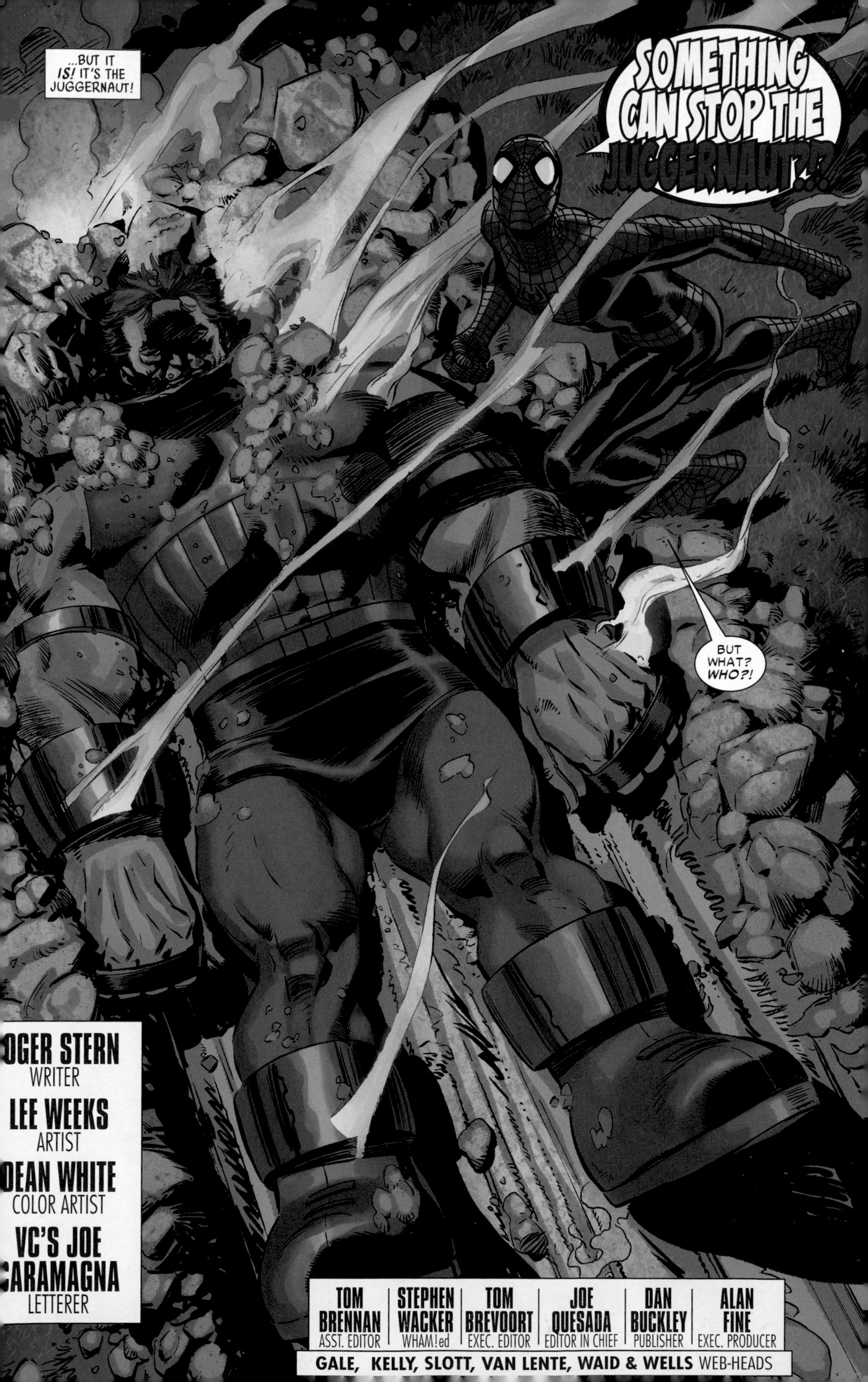
...BUT IT IS! IT'S THE JUGGERNAUT!
SOMETHING CAN STOP THE JUGGERNAUT?!?
BUT WHAT? WHO?!
OGER STERN WRITER
LEE WEEKS ARTIST
DEAN WHITE COLOR ARTIST
VC'S JOE ARAMAGNA LETTERER
TOM BRENNAN ASST. EDITOR
STEPHEN WACKER WHAM!ed
TOM BREVOORT EXEC. EDITOR
JOE QUESADA EDITOR IN CHIEF
DAN BUCKLEY PUBLISHER
ALAN FINE EXEC. PRODUCER
GALE, KELLY, SLOTT, VAN LENTE, WAID & WELLS WEB-HEADS

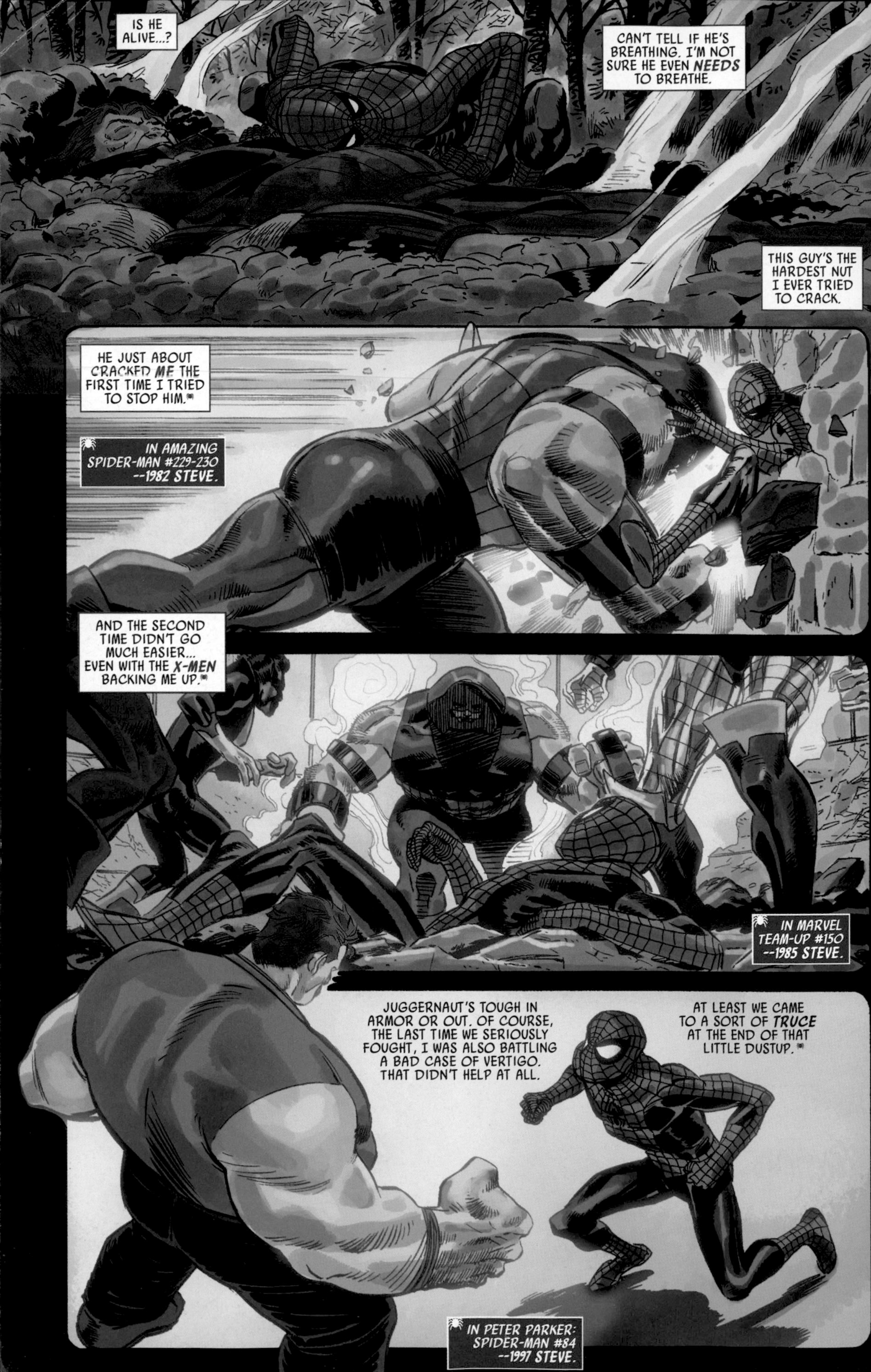
IS HE ALIVE...?
CAN'T TELL IF HE'S BREATHING. I'M NOT SURE HE EVEN NEEDS TO BREATHE.
THIS GUY'S THE HARDEST NUT I EVER TRIED TO CRACK.
HE JUST ABOUT CRACKED ME THE FIRST TIME I TRIED TO STOP HIM.*
IN AMAZING SPIDER-MAN #229-230 --1982 STEVE.
AND THE SECOND TIME DIDN'T GO MUCH EASIER... EVEN WITH THE X-MEN BACKING ME UP.*
IN MARVEL TEAM-UP #150 --1985 STEVE.
JUGGERNAUT'S TOUGH IN ARMOR OR OUT. OF COURSE, THE LAST TIME WE SERIOUSLY FOUGHT, I WAS ALSO BATTLING A BAD CASE OF VERTIGO. THAT DIDN'T HELP AT ALL.
AT LEAST WE CAME TO A SORT OF TRUCE AT THE END OF THAT LITTLE DUSTUP.*
IN PETER PARKER: SPIDER-MAN #84 --1997 STEVE.

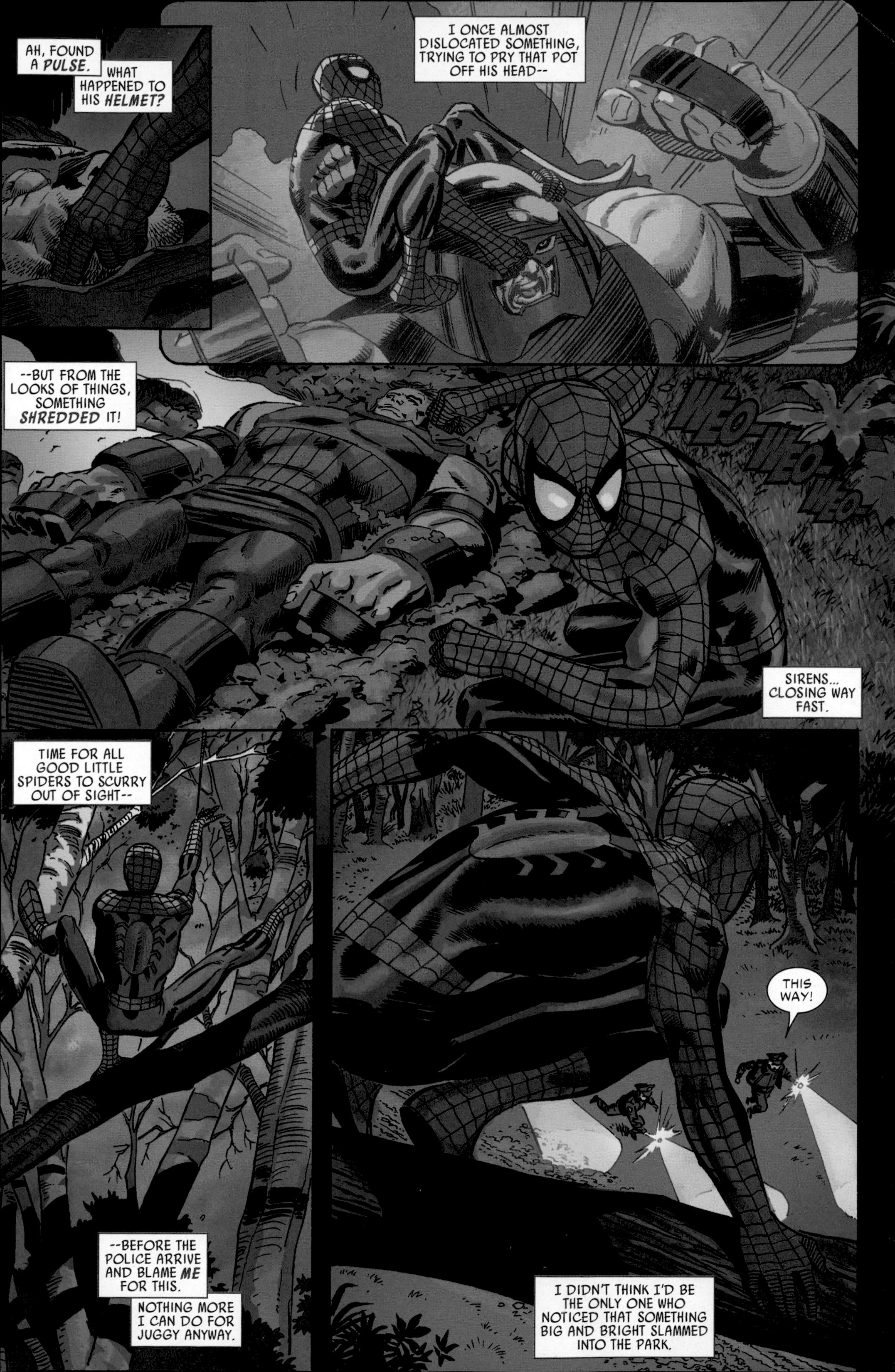
AH, FOUND A *PULSE*.
WHAT HAPPENED TO HIS *HELMET*?
I ONCE ALMOST DISLOCATED SOMETHING, TRYING TO PRY THAT POT OFF HIS HEAD--
--BUT FROM THE LOOKS OF THINGS, SOMETHING *SHREDDED* IT!
WEO-WEO-WEO-
SIRENS... CLOSING WAY FAST.
TIME FOR ALL GOOD LITTLE SPIDERS TO SCURRY OUT OF SIGHT--
--BEFORE THE POLICE ARRIVE AND BLAME *ME* FOR THIS.
NOTHING MORE I CAN DO FOR JUGGY ANYWAY.
THIS WAY!
I DIDN'T THINK I'D BE THE ONLY ONE WHO NOTICED THAT SOMETHING BIG AND BRIGHT SLAMMED INTO THE PARK.

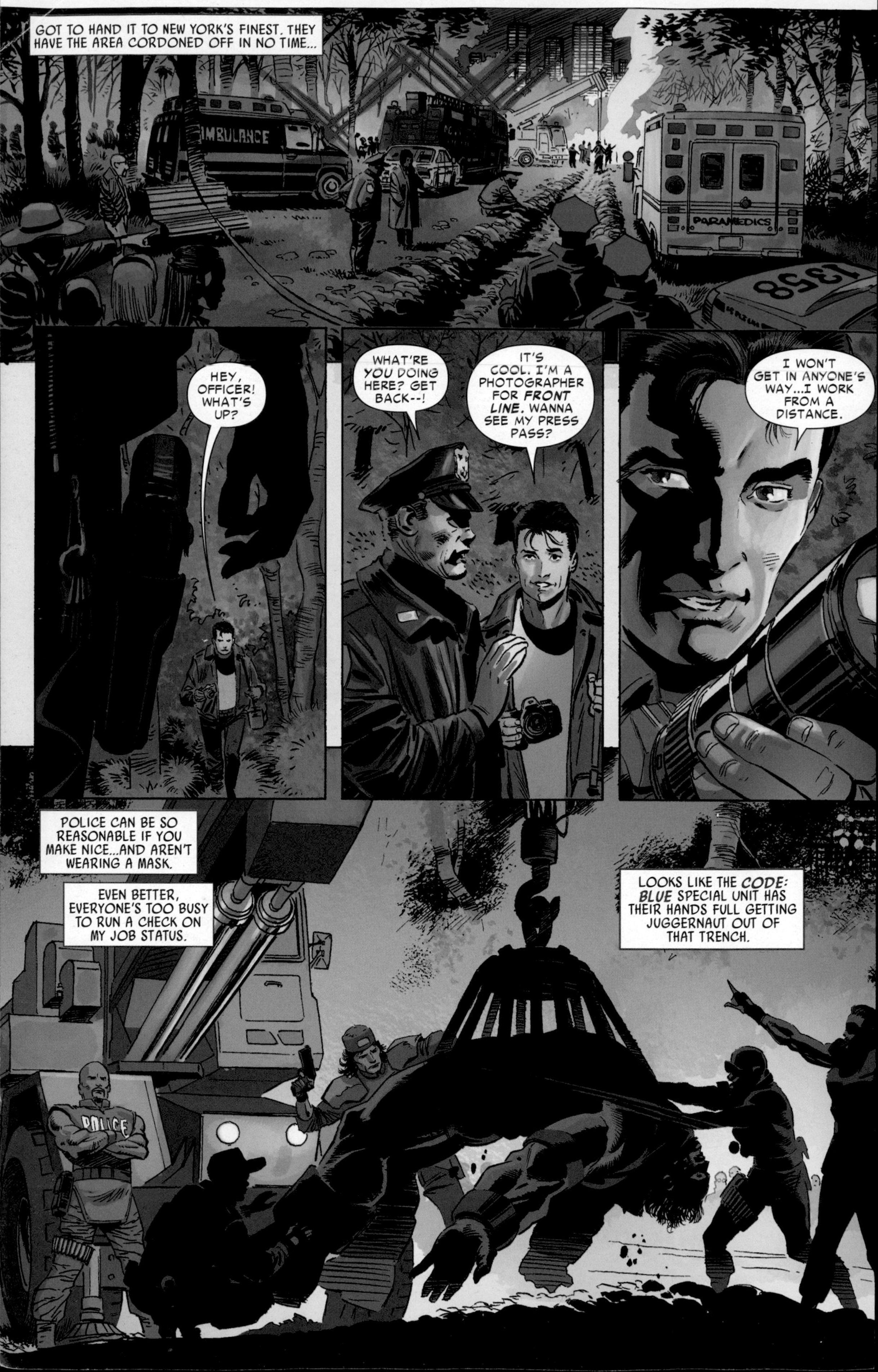
GOT TO HAND IT TO NEW YORK'S FINEST. THEY HAVE THE AREA CORDONED OFF IN NO TIME...
AMBULANCE
PARAMEDICS
1358
HEY, OFFICER! WHAT'S UP?
WHAT'RE *YOU* DOING HERE? GET BACK--!
IT'S COOL. I'M A PHOTOGRAPHER FOR *FRONT LINE.* WANNA SEE MY PRESS PASS?
I WON'T GET IN ANYONE'S WAY...I WORK FROM A DISTANCE.
POLICE CAN BE SO REASONABLE IF YOU MAKE NICE...AND AREN'T WEARING A MASK.
EVEN BETTER, EVERYONE'S TOO BUSY TO RUN A CHECK ON MY JOB STATUS.
LOOKS LIKE THE *CODE: BLUE* SPECIAL UNIT HAS THEIR HANDS FULL GETTING JUGGERNAUT OUT OF THAT TRENCH.
POLICE

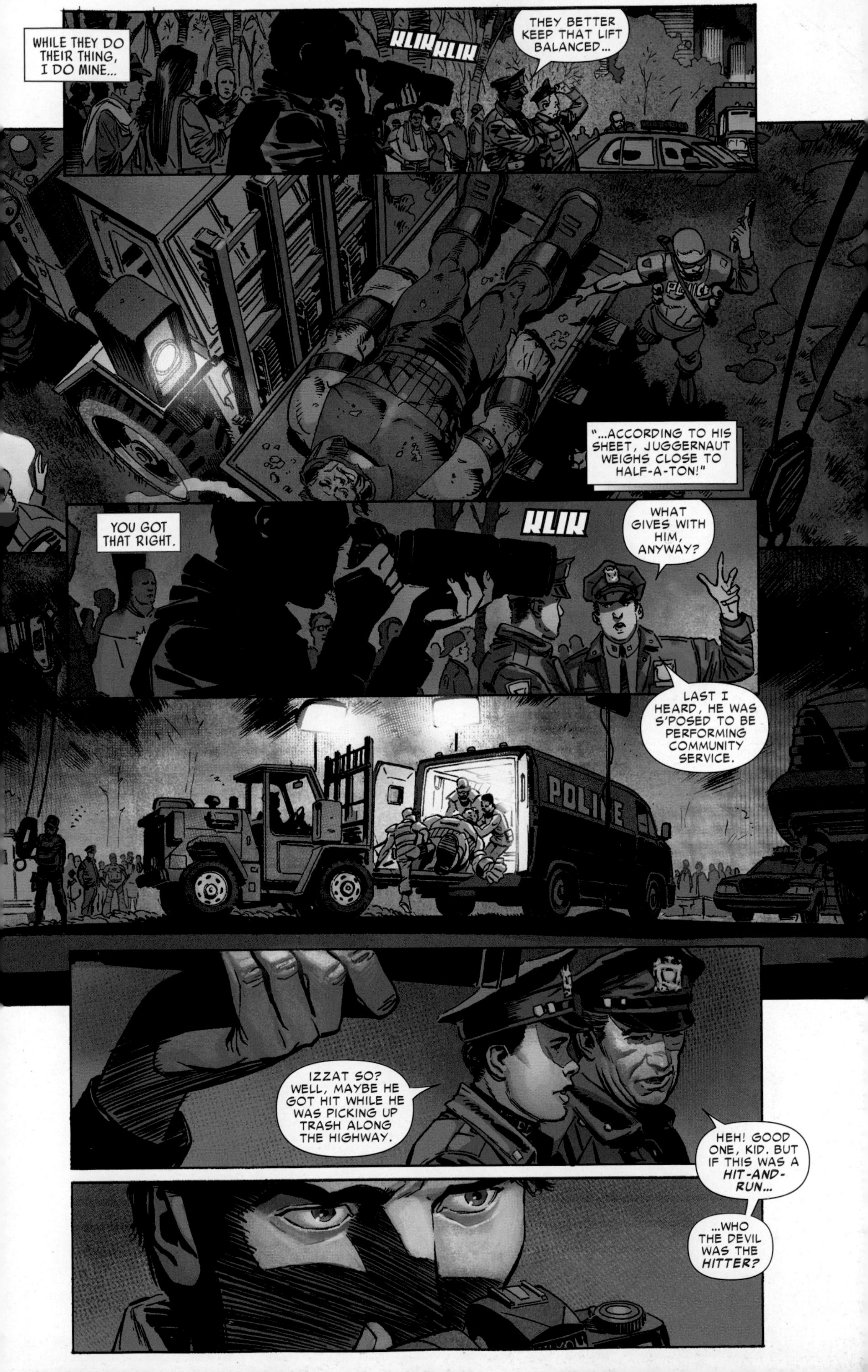

WHILE THEY DO THEIR THING, I DO MINE...
KLIK KLIK
THEY BETTER KEEP THAT LIFT BALANCED...
"...ACCORDING TO HIS SHEET, JUGGERNAUT WEIGHS CLOSE TO HALF-A-TON!"
YOU GOT THAT RIGHT.
KLIK
WHAT GIVES WITH HIM, ANYWAY?
LAST I HEARD, HE WAS S'POSED TO BE PERFORMING COMMUNITY SERVICE.
POLICE
IZZAT SO? WELL, MAYBE HE GOT HIT WHILE HE WAS PICKING UP TRASH ALONG THE HIGHWAY.
HEH! GOOD ONE, KID. BUT IF THIS WAS A *HIT-AND-RUN*...
...WHO THE DEVIL WAS THE *HITTER?*

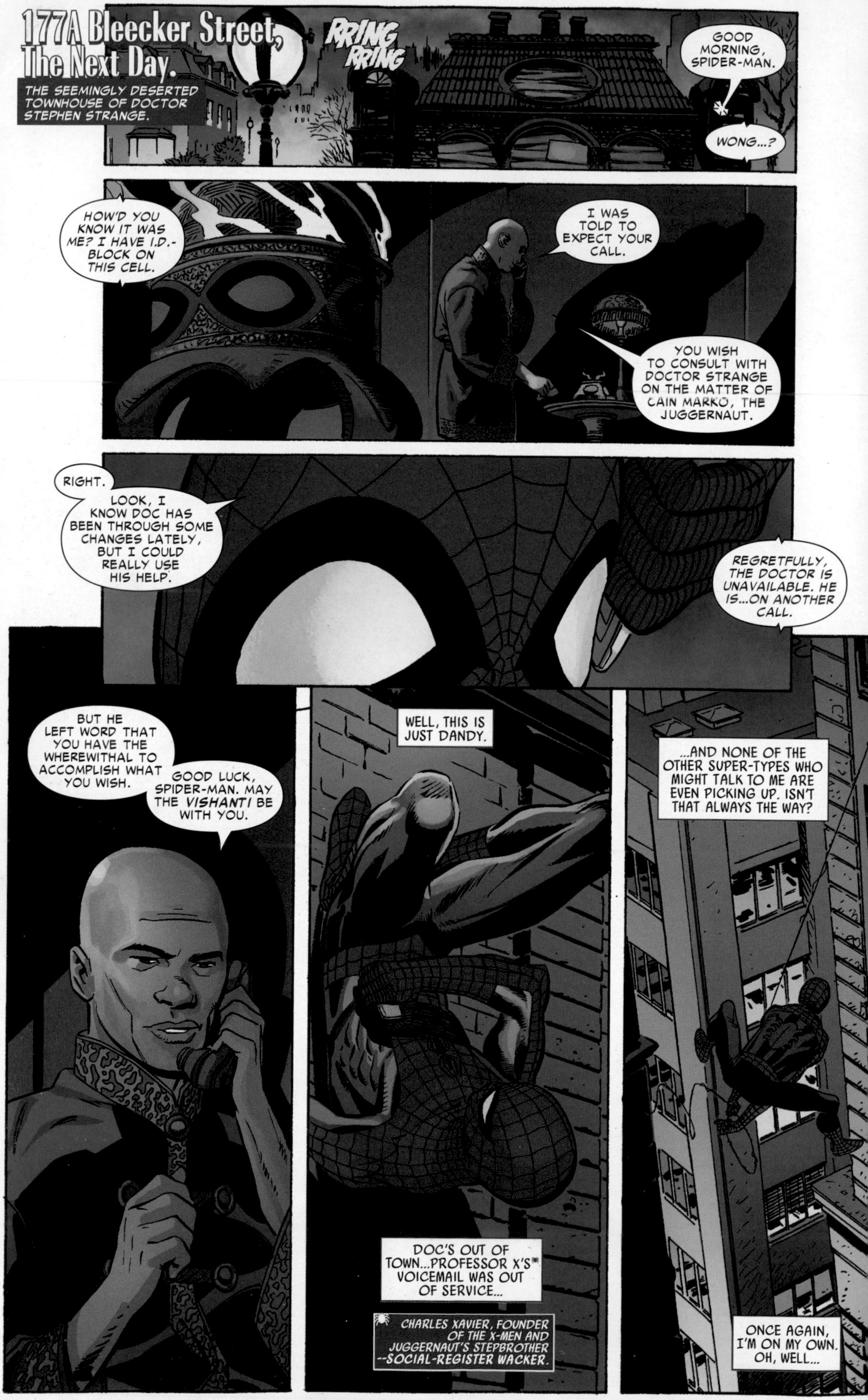
177A Bleecker Street, The Next Day.
THE SEEMINGLY DESERTED TOWNHOUSE OF DOCTOR STEPHEN STRANGE.
RRING RRING
GOOD MORNING, SPIDER-MAN.
WONG...?
HOW'D YOU KNOW IT WAS ME? I HAVE I.D.-BLOCK ON THIS CELL.
I WAS TOLD TO EXPECT YOUR CALL.
YOU WISH TO CONSULT WITH DOCTOR STRANGE ON THE MATTER OF CAIN MARKO, THE JUGGERNAUT.
RIGHT.
LOOK, I KNOW DOC HAS BEEN THROUGH SOME CHANGES LATELY, BUT I COULD REALLY USE HIS HELP.
REGRETFULLY, THE DOCTOR IS UNAVAILABLE. HE IS...ON ANOTHER CALL.
BUT HE LEFT WORD THAT YOU HAVE THE WHEREWITHAL TO ACCOMPLISH WHAT YOU WISH.
GOOD LUCK, SPIDER-MAN. MAY THE VISHANTI BE WITH YOU.
WELL, THIS IS JUST DANDY.
DOC'S OUT OF TOWN...PROFESSOR X'S* VOICEMAIL WAS OUT OF SERVICE...
*CHARLES XAVIER, FOUNDER OF THE X-MEN AND JUGGERNAUT'S STEPBROTHER --SOCIAL-REGISTER WACKER.
...AND NONE OF THE OTHER SUPER-TYPES WHO MIGHT TALK TO ME ARE EVEN PICKING UP. ISN'T THAT ALWAYS THE WAY?
ONCE AGAIN, I'M ON MY OWN. OH, WELL...

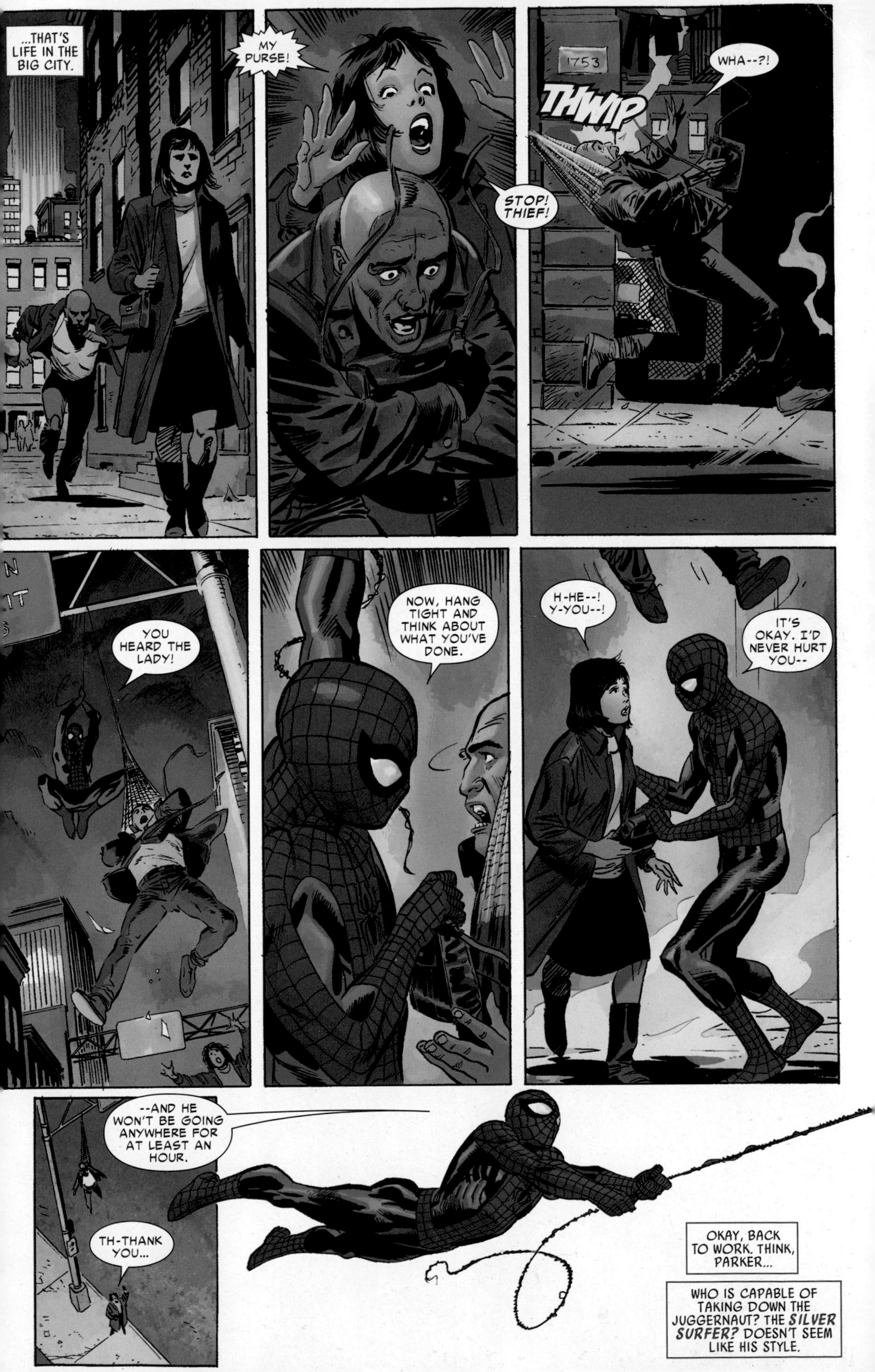
...THAT'S LIFE IN THE BIG CITY.
MY PURSE!
STOP! THIEF!
1753
THWIP
WHA--?!
YOU HEARD THE LADY!
NOW, HANG TIGHT AND THINK ABOUT WHAT YOU'VE DONE.
H-HE--! Y-YOU--!
IT'S OKAY. I'D NEVER HURT YOU--
--AND HE WON'T BE GOING ANYWHERE FOR AT LEAST AN HOUR.
TH-THANK YOU...
OKAY, BACK TO WORK. THINK, PARKER...
WHO IS CAPABLE OF TAKING DOWN THE JUGGERNAUT? THE SILVER SURFER? DOESN'T SEEM LIKE HIS STYLE.

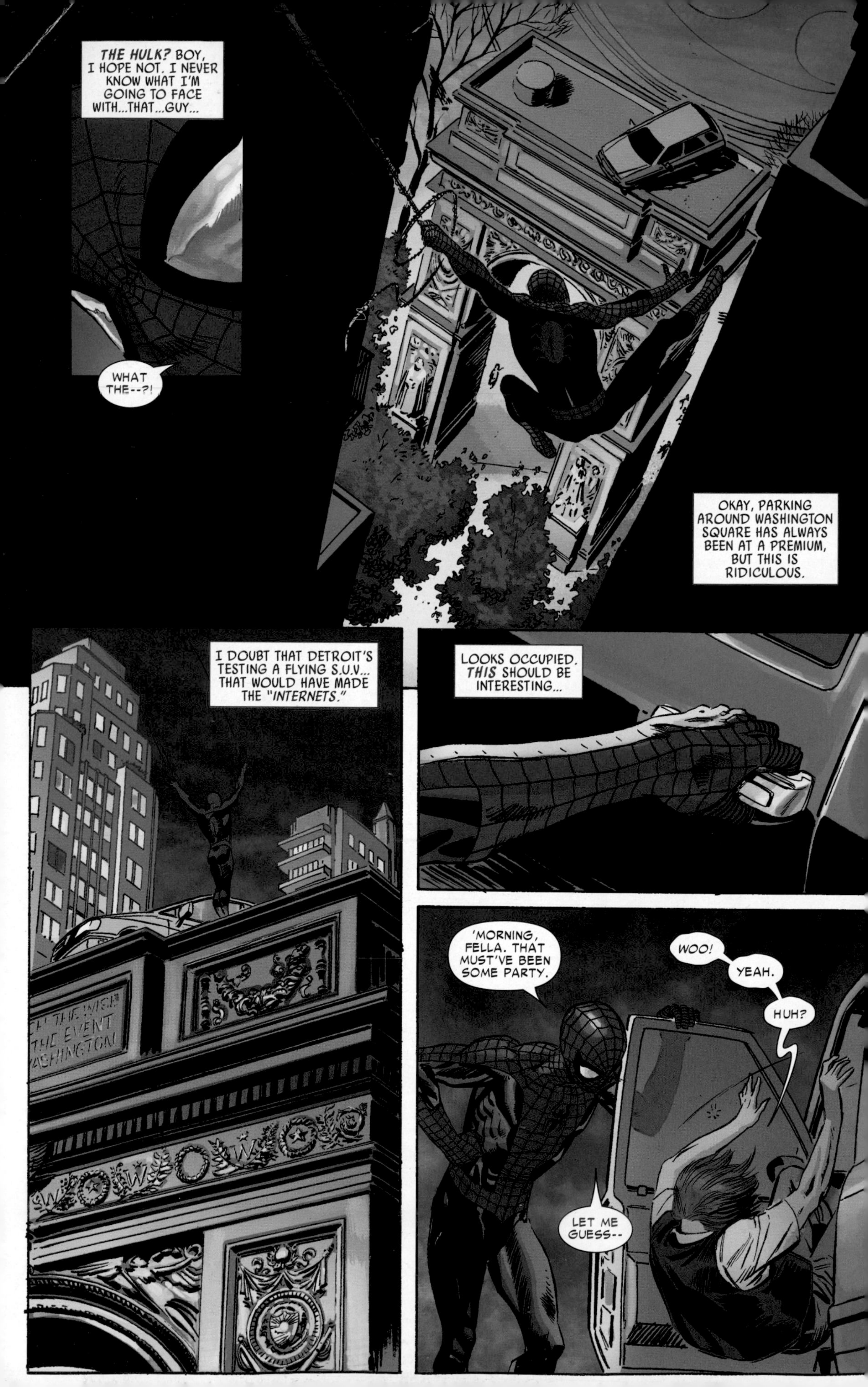
THE HULK? BOY, I HOPE NOT. I NEVER KNOW WHAT I'M GOING TO FACE WITH...THAT...GUY...
WHAT THE--?!
OKAY, PARKING AROUND WASHINGTON SQUARE HAS ALWAYS BEEN AT A PREMIUM, BUT THIS IS RIDICULOUS.
I DOUBT THAT DETROIT'S TESTING A FLYING S.U.V... THAT WOULD HAVE MADE THE "INTERNETS."
LOOKS OCCUPIED. THIS SHOULD BE INTERESTING...
'MORNING, FELLA. THAT MUST'VE BEEN SOME PARTY.
WOO!
YEAH.
HUH?
LET ME GUESS--

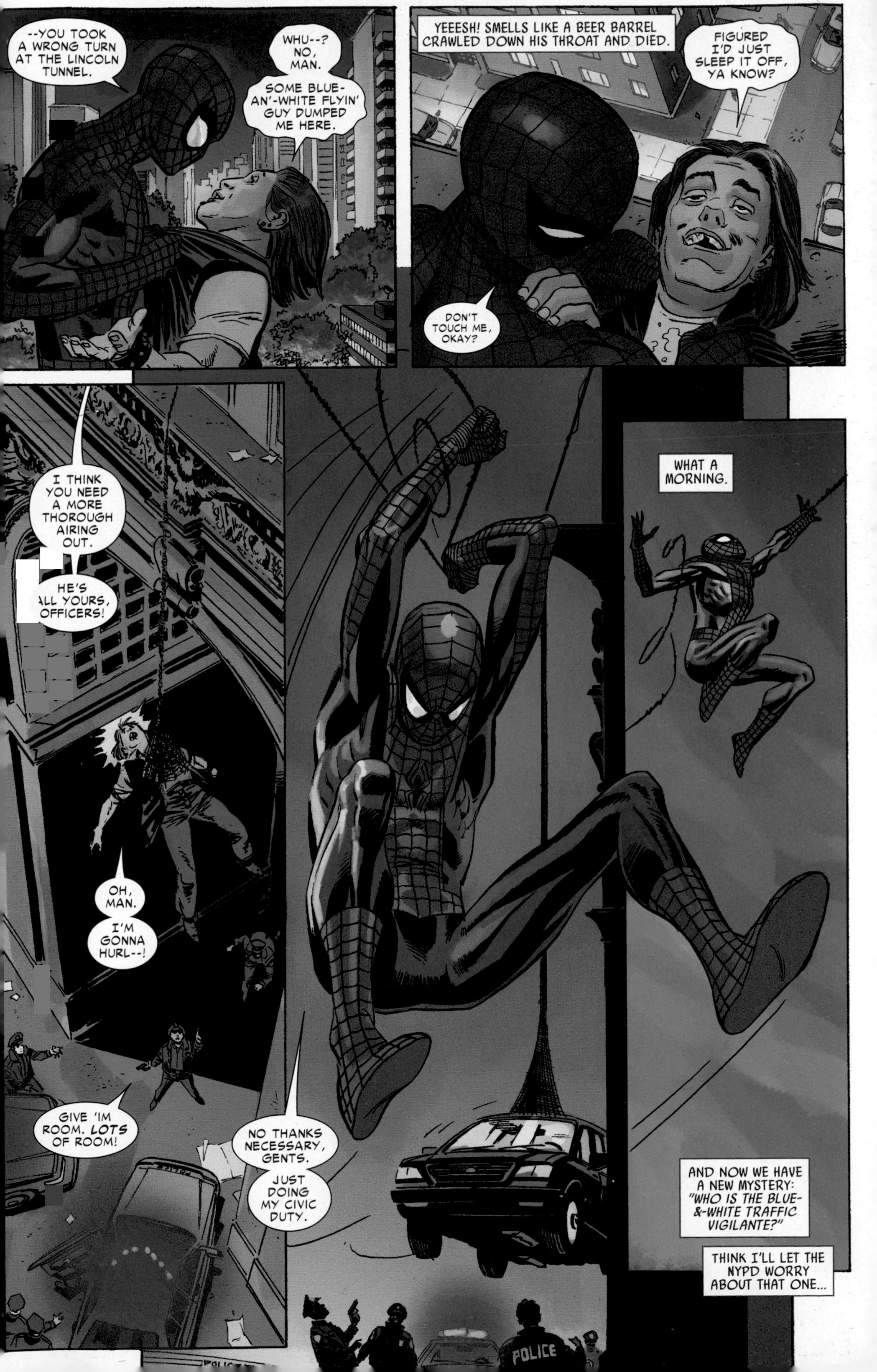
--YOU TOOK A WRONG TURN AT THE LINCOLN TUNNEL.
WHU--? NO, MAN.
SOME BLUE-AN'-WHITE FLYIN' GUY DUMPED ME HERE.
YEEESH! SMELLS LIKE A BEER BARREL CRAWLED DOWN HIS THROAT AND DIED.
FIGURED I'D JUST SLEEP IT OFF, YA KNOW?
DON'T TOUCH ME, OKAY?
I THINK YOU NEED A MORE THOROUGH AIRING OUT.
HE'S ALL YOURS, OFFICERS!
OH, MAN.
I'M GONNA HURL--!
GIVE 'IM ROOM. LOTS OF ROOM!
NO THANKS NECESSARY, GENTS.
JUST DOING MY CIVIC DUTY.
WHAT A MORNING.
AND NOW WE HAVE A NEW MYSTERY: "WHO IS THE BLUE-&-WHITE TRAFFIC VIGILANTE?"
THINK I'LL LET THE NYPD WORRY ABOUT THAT ONE...
POLICE

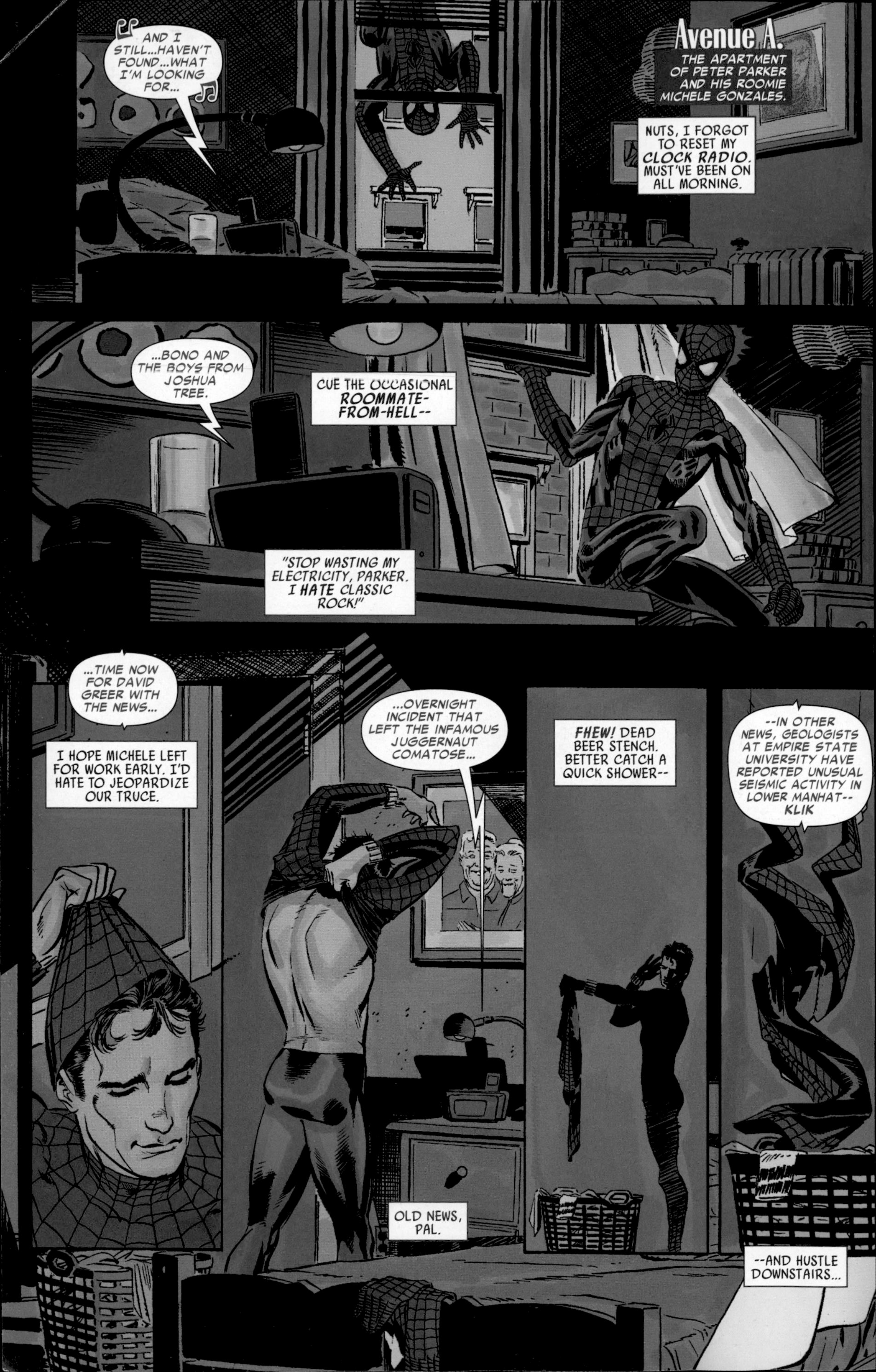
AND I STILL...HAVEN'T FOUND...WHAT I'M LOOKING FOR...
Avenue A.
THE APARTMENT OF PETER PARKER AND HIS ROOMIE MICHELE GONZALES.
NUTS, I FORGOT TO RESET MY CLOCK RADIO. MUST'VE BEEN ON ALL MORNING.
...BONO AND THE BOYS FROM JOSHUA TREE.
CUE THE OCCASIONAL ROOMMATE-FROM-HELL--
"STOP WASTING MY ELECTRICITY, PARKER. I HATE CLASSIC ROCK!"
...TIME NOW FOR DAVID GREER WITH THE NEWS...
I HOPE MICHELE LEFT FOR WORK EARLY. I'D HATE TO JEOPARDIZE OUR TRUCE.
...OVERNIGHT INCIDENT THAT LEFT THE INFAMOUS JUGGERNAUT COMATOSE...
OLD NEWS, PAL.
FHEW! DEAD BEER STENCH. BETTER CATCH A QUICK SHOWER--
--IN OTHER NEWS, GEOLOGISTS AT EMPIRE STATE UNIVERSITY HAVE REPORTED UNUSUAL SEISMIC ACTIVITY IN LOWER MANHAT-- KLIK
--AND HUSTLE DOWNSTAIRS...

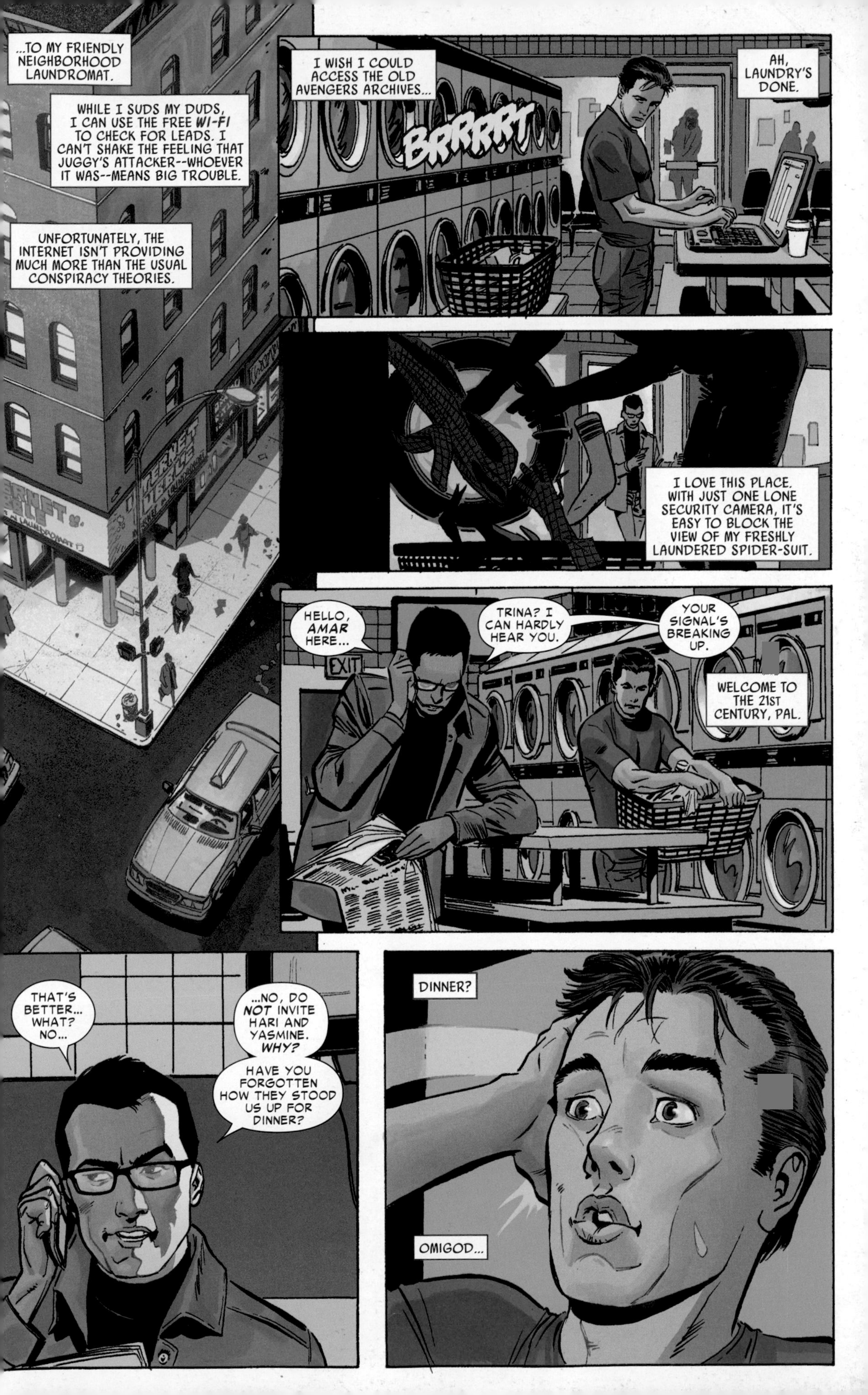
...TO MY FRIENDLY NEIGHBORHOOD LAUNDROMAT.
WHILE I SUDS MY DUDS, I CAN USE THE FREE WI-FI TO CHECK FOR LEADS. I CAN'T SHAKE THE FEELING THAT JUGGY'S ATTACKER--WHOEVER IT WAS--MEANS BIG TROUBLE.
UNFORTUNATELY, THE INTERNET ISN'T PROVIDING MUCH MORE THAN THE USUAL CONSPIRACY THEORIES.
I WISH I COULD ACCESS THE OLD AVENGERS ARCHIVES...
BRRRRT
AH, LAUNDRY'S DONE.
I LOVE THIS PLACE. WITH JUST ONE LONE SECURITY CAMERA, IT'S EASY TO BLOCK THE VIEW OF MY FRESHLY LAUNDERED SPIDER-SUIT.
HELLO, AMAR HERE...
TRINA? I CAN HARDLY HEAR YOU.
YOUR SIGNAL'S BREAKING UP.
EXIT
WELCOME TO THE 21ST CENTURY, PAL.
THAT'S BETTER... WHAT? NO...
...NO, DO NOT INVITE HARI AND YASMINE. WHY?
HAVE YOU FORGOTTEN HOW THEY STOOD US UP FOR DINNER?
DINNER?
OMIGOD...

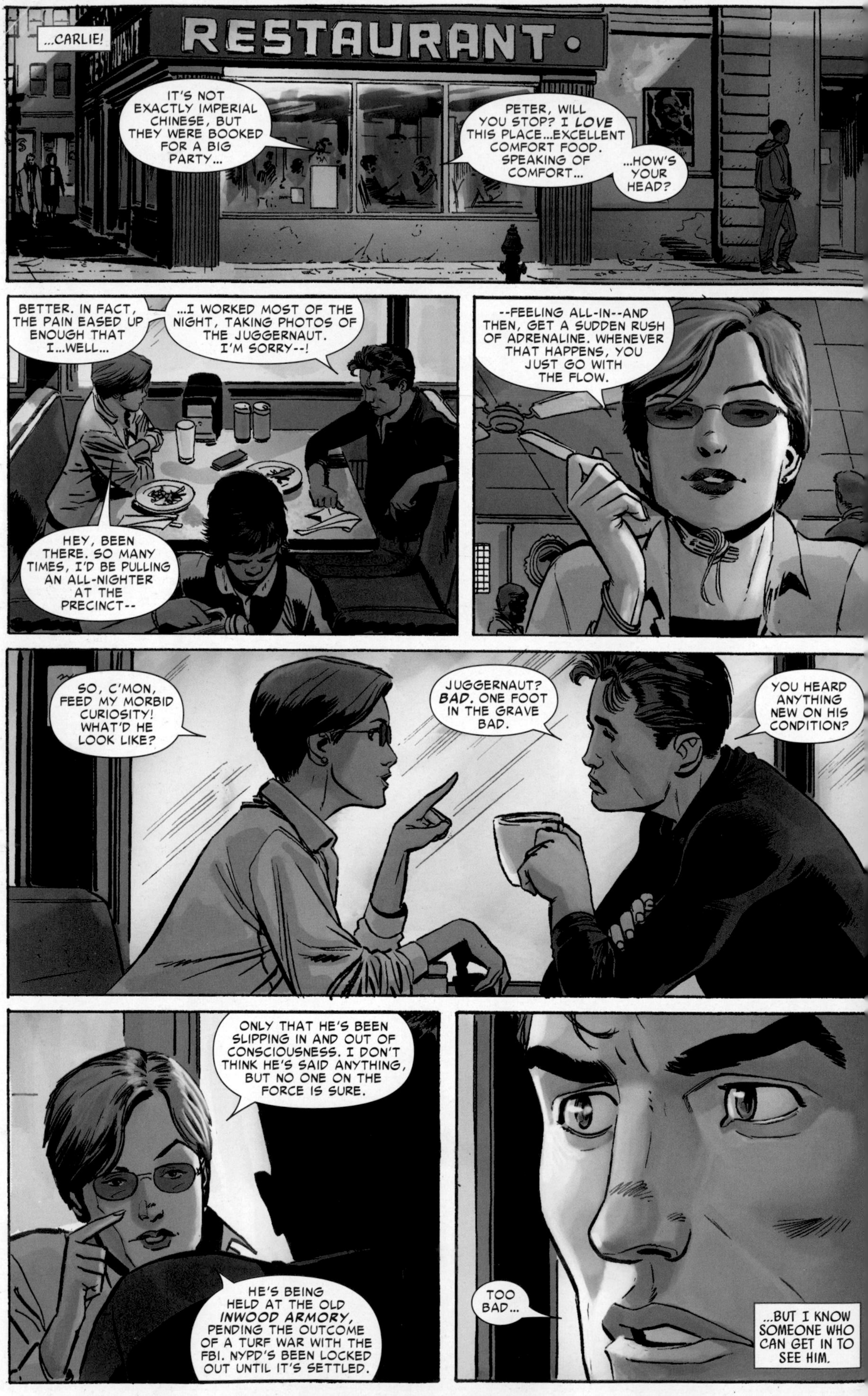
...CARLIE!
RESTAURANT
IT'S NOT EXACTLY IMPERIAL CHINESE, BUT THEY WERE BOOKED FOR A BIG PARTY...
PETER, WILL YOU STOP? I LOVE THIS PLACE...EXCELLENT COMFORT FOOD. SPEAKING OF COMFORT...
...HOW'S YOUR HEAD?
BETTER. IN FACT, THE PAIN EASED UP ENOUGH THAT I...WELL...
...I WORKED MOST OF THE NIGHT, TAKING PHOTOS OF THE JUGGERNAUT. I'M SORRY--!
HEY, BEEN THERE. SO MANY TIMES, I'D BE PULLING AN ALL-NIGHTER AT THE PRECINCT--
--FEELING ALL-IN--AND THEN, GET A SUDDEN RUSH OF ADRENALINE. WHENEVER THAT HAPPENS, YOU JUST GO WITH THE FLOW.
SO, C'MON, FEED MY MORBID CURIOSITY! WHAT'D HE LOOK LIKE?
JUGGERNAUT? BAD. ONE FOOT IN THE GRAVE BAD.
YOU HEARD ANYTHING NEW ON HIS CONDITION?
ONLY THAT HE'S BEEN SLIPPING IN AND OUT OF CONSCIOUSNESS. I DON'T THINK HE'S SAID ANYTHING, BUT NO ONE ON THE FORCE IS SURE.
HE'S BEING HELD AT THE OLD INWOOD ARMORY, PENDING THE OUTCOME OF A TURF WAR WITH THE FBI. NYPD'S BEEN LOCKED OUT UNTIL IT'S SETTLED.
TOO BAD...
...BUT I KNOW SOMEONE WHO CAN GET IN TO SEE HIM.

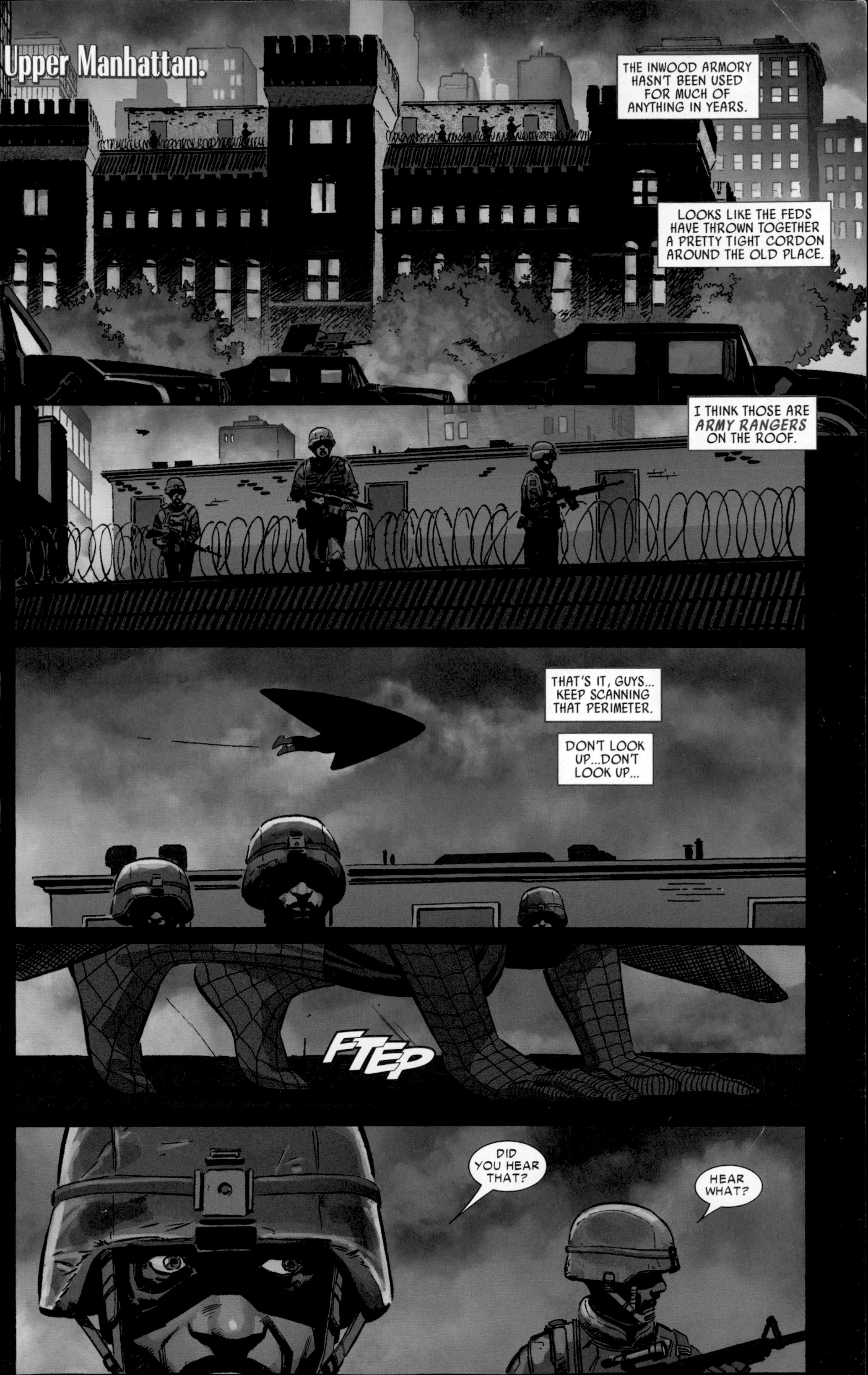
Upper Manhattan.
THE INWOOD ARMORY HASN'T BEEN USED FOR MUCH OF ANYTHING IN YEARS.
LOOKS LIKE THE FEDS HAVE THROWN TOGETHER A PRETTY TIGHT CORDON AROUND THE OLD PLACE.
I THINK THOSE ARE ARMY RANGERS ON THE ROOF.
THAT'S IT, GUYS... KEEP SCANNING THAT PERIMETER.
DON'T LOOK UP...DON'T LOOK UP...
FTEP
DID YOU HEAR THAT?
HEAR WHAT?

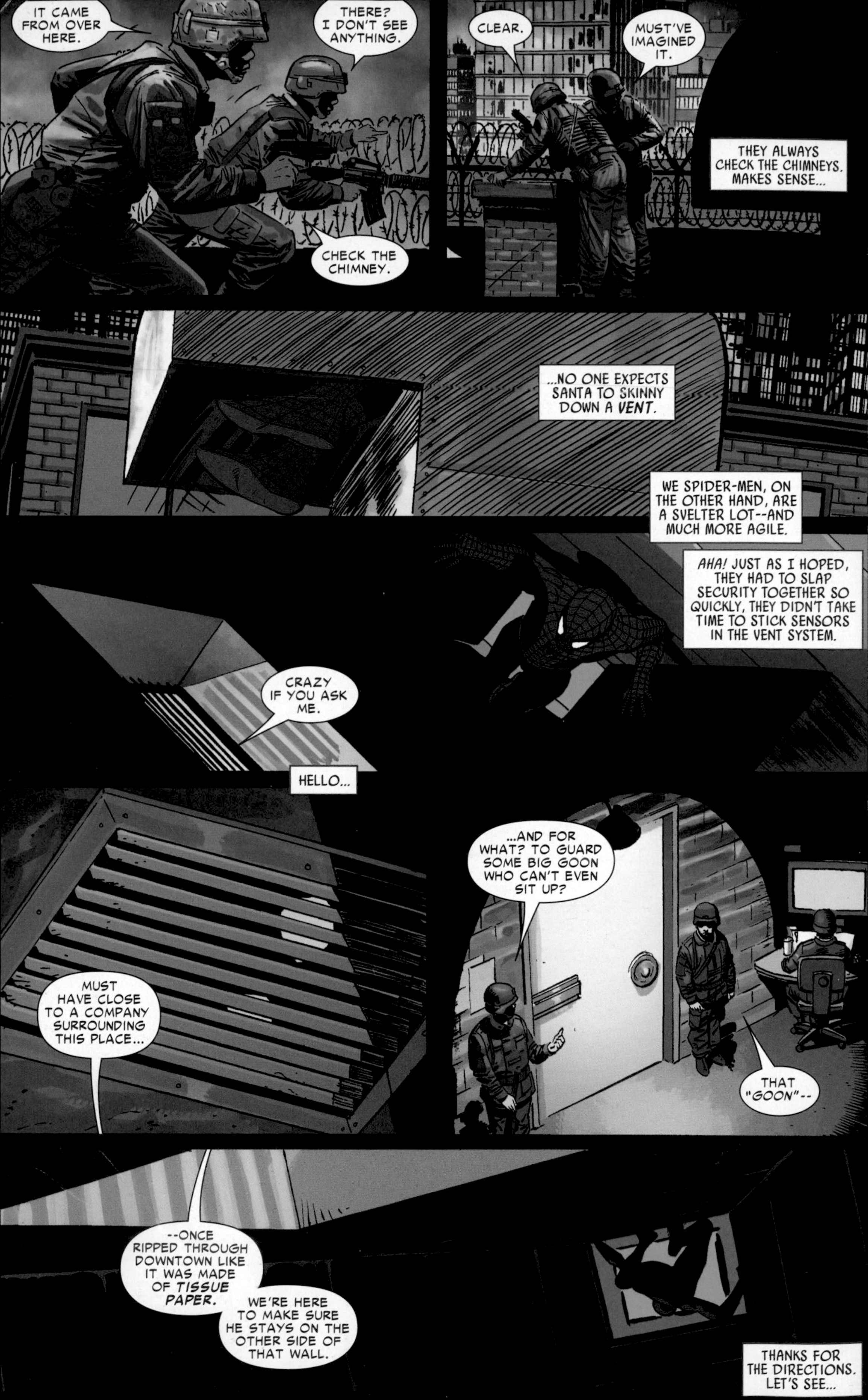
IT CAME FROM OVER HERE.
THERE? I DON'T SEE ANYTHING.
CHECK THE CHIMNEY.
CLEAR.
MUST'VE IMAGINED IT.
THEY ALWAYS CHECK THE CHIMNEYS. MAKES SENSE...
...NO ONE EXPECTS SANTA TO SKINNY DOWN A VENT.
WE SPIDER-MEN, ON THE OTHER HAND, ARE A SVELTER LOT--AND MUCH MORE AGILE.
AHA! JUST AS I HOPED, THEY HAD TO SLAP SECURITY TOGETHER SO QUICKLY, THEY DIDN'T TAKE TIME TO STICK SENSORS IN THE VENT SYSTEM.
CRAZY IF YOU ASK ME.
HELLO...
MUST HAVE CLOSE TO A COMPANY SURROUNDING THIS PLACE...
...AND FOR WHAT? TO GUARD SOME BIG GOON WHO CAN'T EVEN SIT UP?
THAT "GOON"--
--ONCE RIPPED THROUGH DOWNTOWN LIKE IT WAS MADE OF TISSUE PAPER.
WE'RE HERE TO MAKE SURE HE STAYS ON THE OTHER SIDE OF THAT WALL.
THANKS FOR THE DIRECTIONS. LET'S SEE...

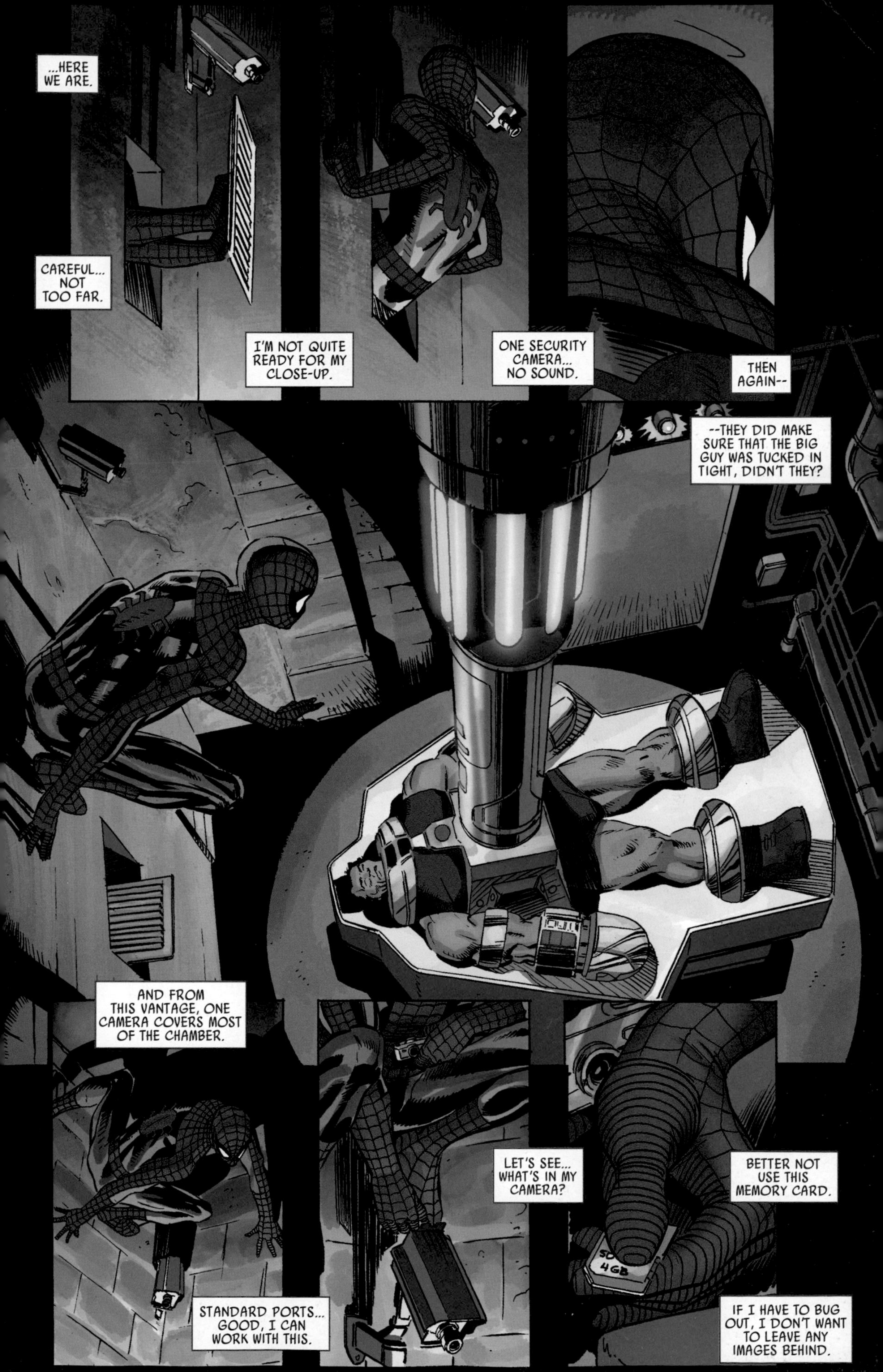
...HERE WE ARE.
CAREFUL... NOT TOO FAR.
I'M NOT QUITE READY FOR MY CLOSE-UP.
ONE SECURITY CAMERA... NO SOUND.
THEN AGAIN--
--THEY DID MAKE SURE THAT THE BIG GUY WAS TUCKED IN TIGHT, DIDN'T THEY?
AND FROM THIS VANTAGE, ONE CAMERA COVERS MOST OF THE CHAMBER.
STANDARD PORTS... GOOD, I CAN WORK WITH THIS.
LET'S SEE... WHAT'S IN MY CAMERA?
BETTER NOT USE THIS MEMORY CARD.
4GB
IF I HAVE TO BUG OUT, I DON'T WANT TO LEAVE ANY IMAGES BEHIND.

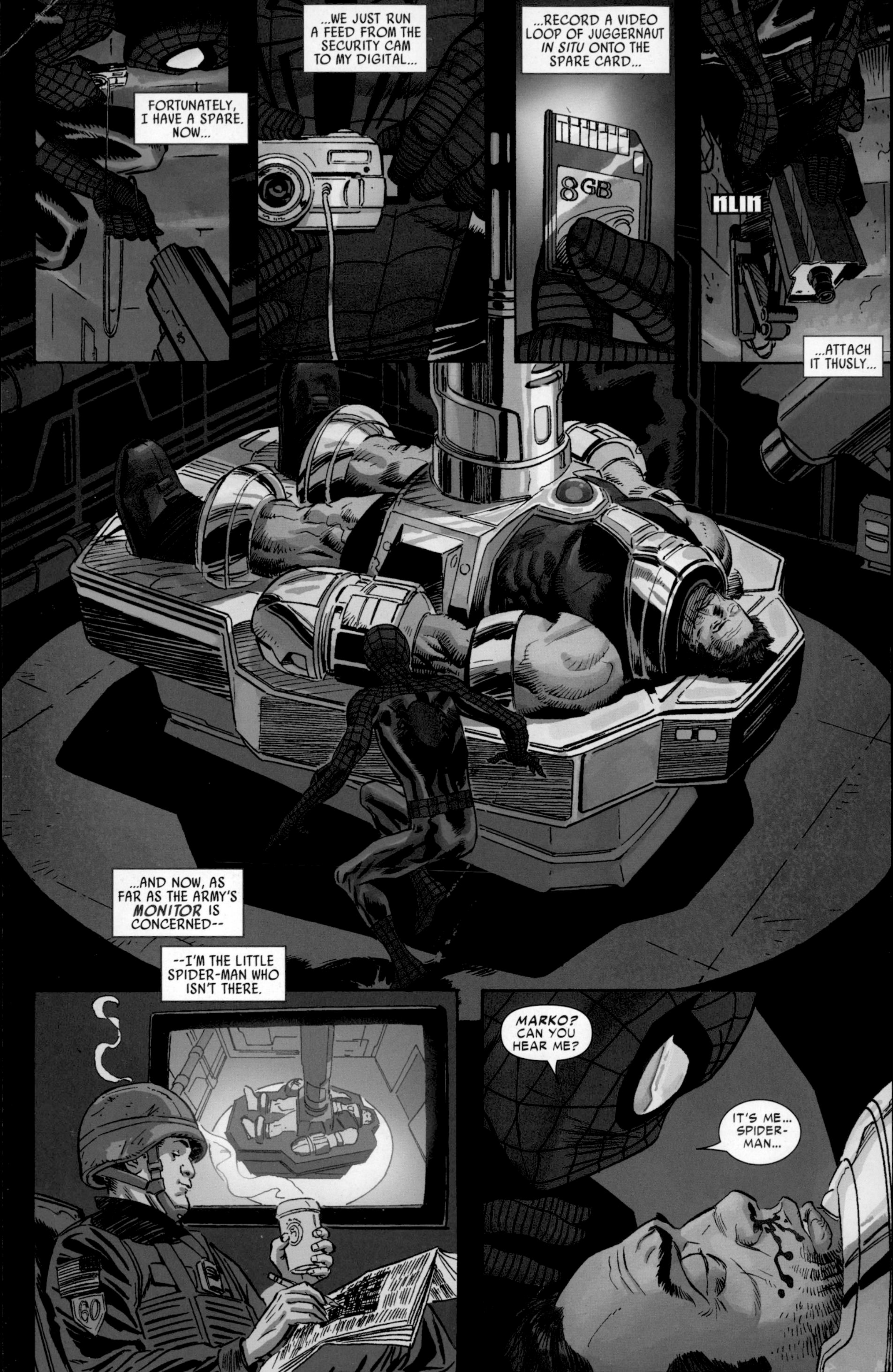
FORTUNATELY, I HAVE A SPARE. NOW...
...WE JUST RUN A FEED FROM THE SECURITY CAM TO MY DIGITAL...
...RECORD A VIDEO LOOP OF JUGGERNAUT IN SITU ONTO THE SPARE CARD...
8GB
KLIK
...ATTACH IT THUSLY...
...AND NOW, AS FAR AS THE ARMY'S MONITOR IS CONCERNED--
--I'M THE LITTLE SPIDER-MAN WHO ISN'T THERE.
60
MARKO? CAN YOU HEAR ME?
IT'S ME... SPIDER-MAN...

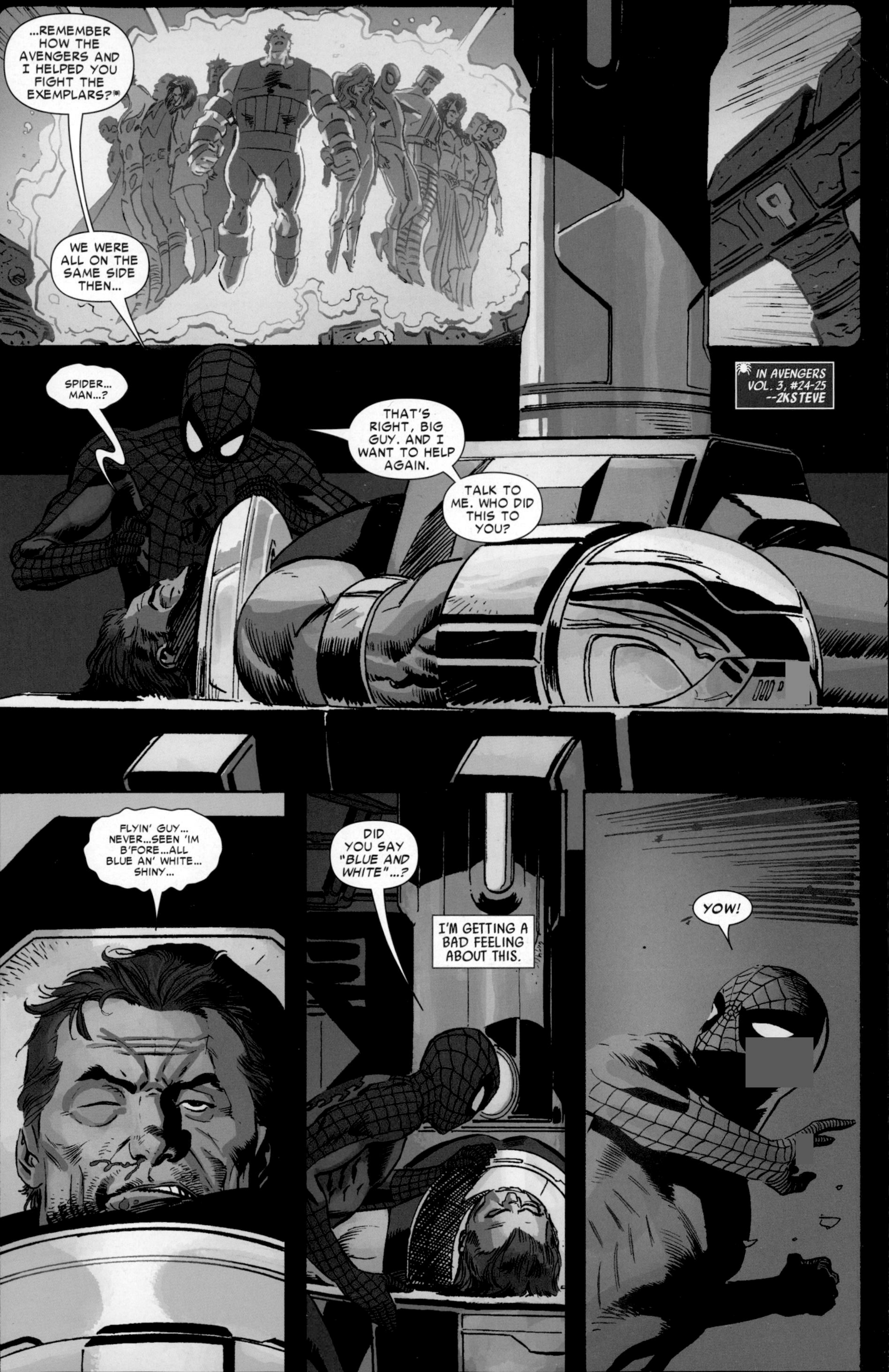
...REMEMBER HOW THE AVENGERS AND I HELPED YOU FIGHT THE EXEMPLARS?*
WE WERE ALL ON THE SAME SIDE THEN...
*IN AVENGERS VOL. 3, #24-25 --2KSTEVE
SPIDER... MAN...?
THAT'S RIGHT, BIG GUY. AND I WANT TO HELP AGAIN.
TALK TO ME. WHO DID THIS TO YOU?
FLYIN' GUY... NEVER...SEEN 'IM B'FORE...ALL BLUE AN' WHITE... SHINY...
DID YOU SAY "BLUE AND WHITE"...?
I'M GETTING A BAD FEELING ABOUT THIS.
YOW!

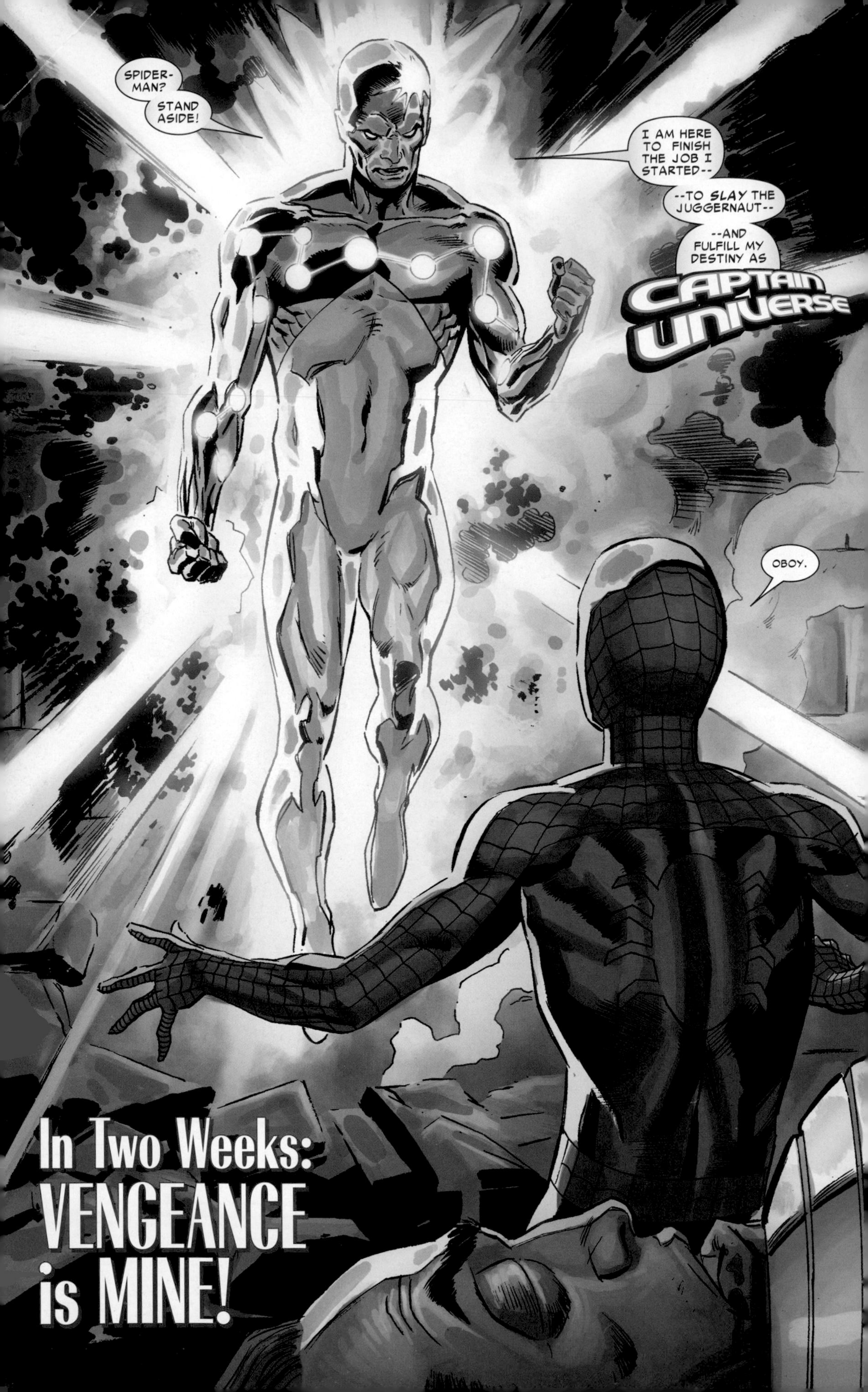
SPIDER-MAN? STAND ASIDE!
I AM HERE TO FINISH THE JOB I STARTED--
--TO SLAY THE JUGGERNAUT--
--AND FULFILL MY DESTINY AS
CAPTAIN UNIVERSE
OBOY.
In Two Weeks: VENGEANCE is MINE!

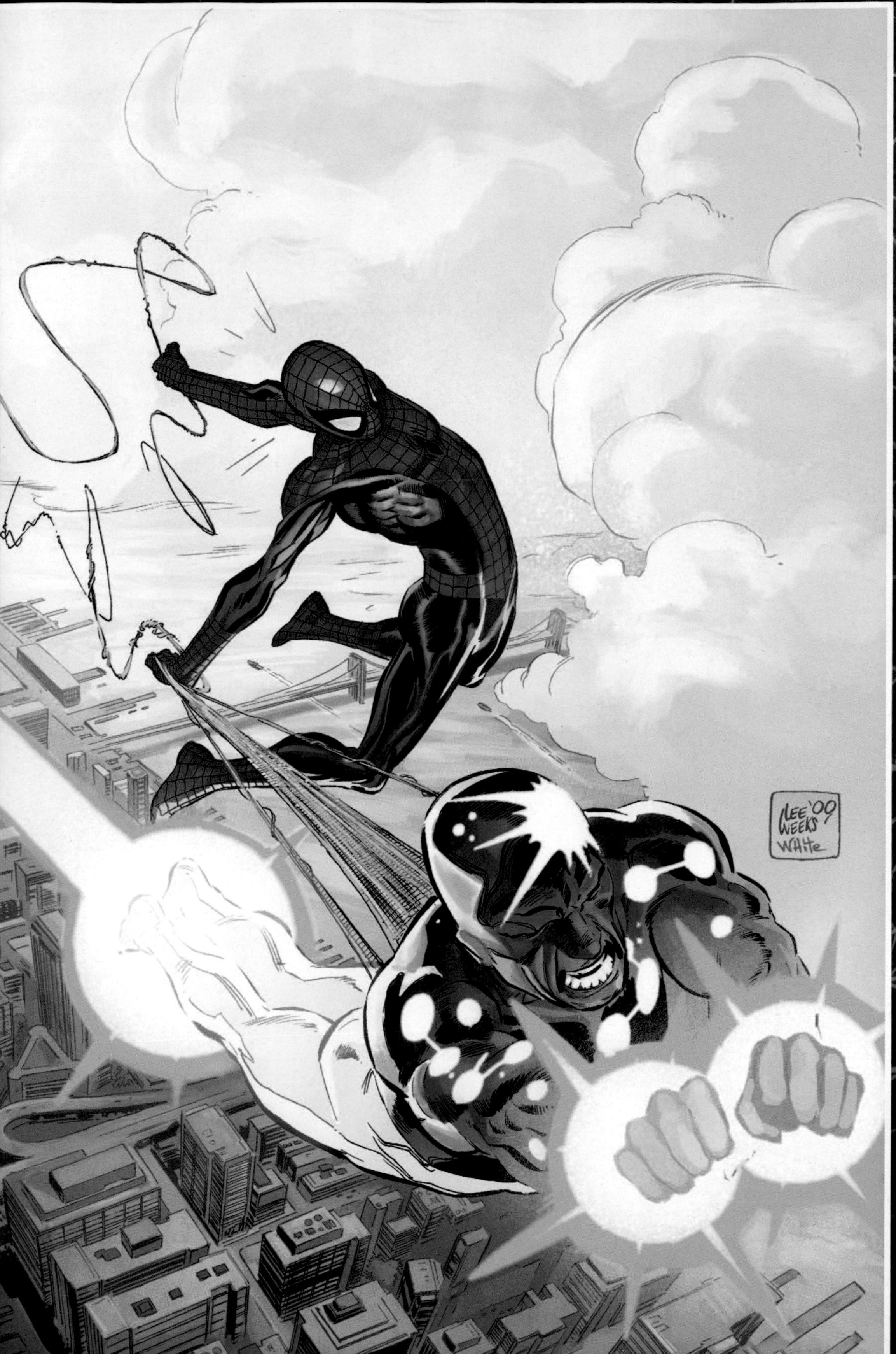
LEE '09
WEEKS
WHITE

AMAZING SPIDER-MAN #628
COVER BY LEE WEEKS & DEAN WHITE

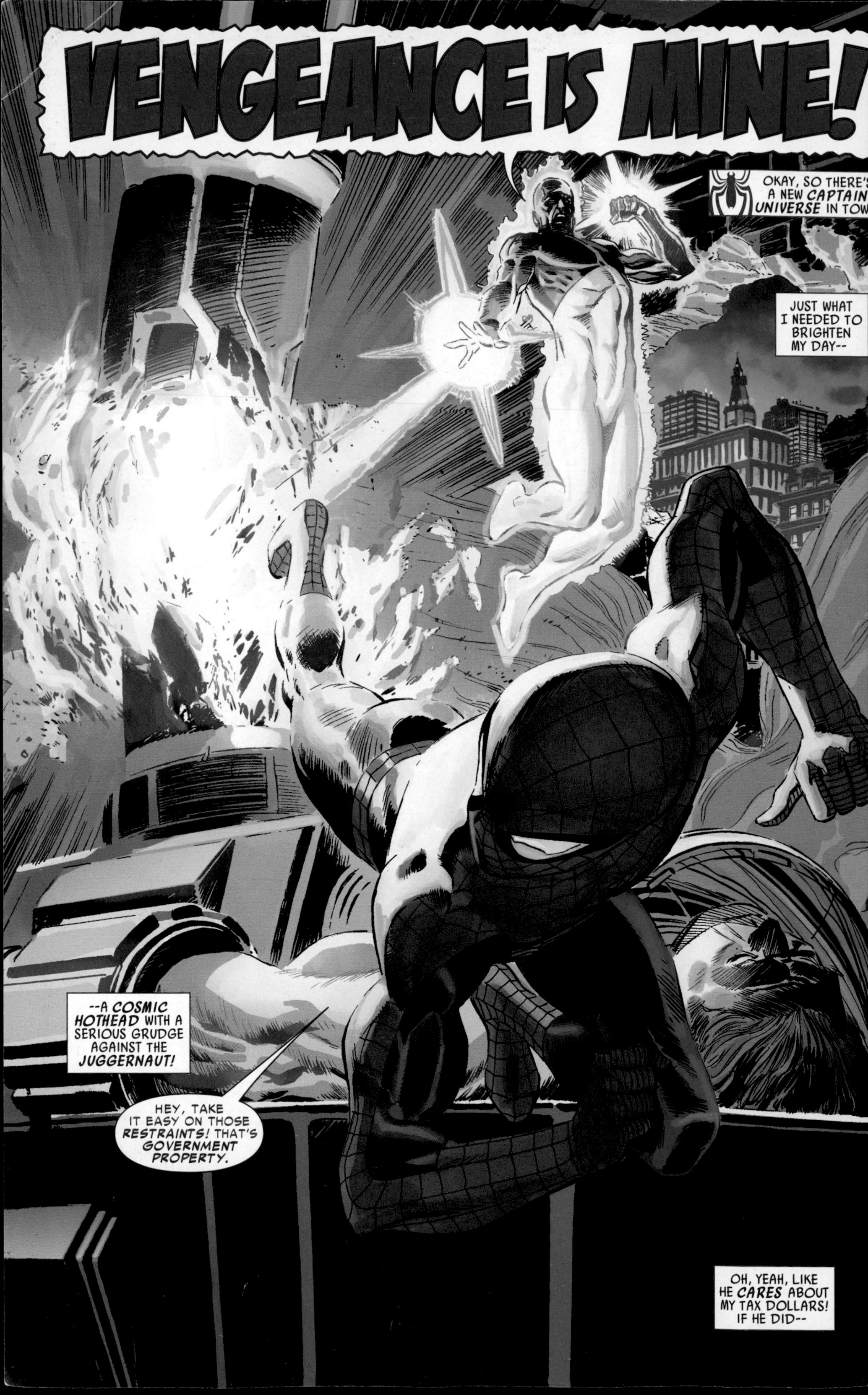
VENGEANCE IS MINE!
OKAY, SO THERE'S A NEW CAPTAIN UNIVERSE IN TOW
JUST WHAT I NEEDED TO BRIGHTEN MY DAY--
--A COSMIC HOTHEAD WITH A SERIOUS GRUDGE AGAINST THE JUGGERNAUT!
HEY, TAKE IT EASY ON THOSE RESTRAINTS! THAT'S GOVERNMENT PROPERTY.
OH, YEAH, LIKE HE CARES ABOUT MY TAX DOLLARS! IF HE DID--

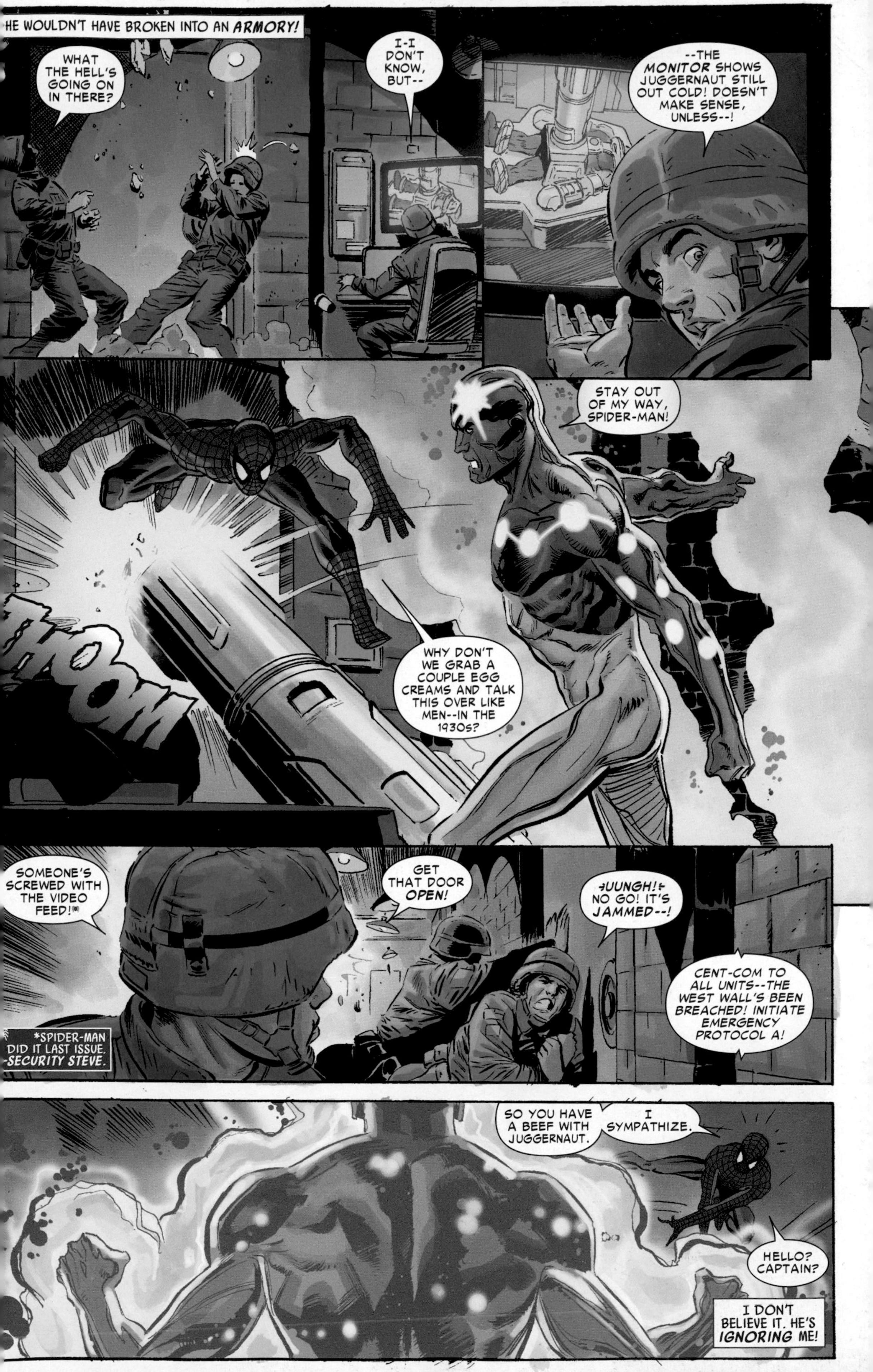
HE WOULDN'T HAVE BROKEN INTO AN ARMORY!
WHAT THE HELL'S GOING ON IN THERE?
I-I DON'T KNOW, BUT--
--THE MONITOR SHOWS JUGGERNAUT STILL OUT COLD! DOESN'T MAKE SENSE, UNLESS--!
STAY OUT OF MY WAY, SPIDER-MAN!
THOOM
WHY DON'T WE GRAB A COUPLE EGG CREAMS AND TALK THIS OVER LIKE MEN--IN THE 1930s?
SOMEONE'S SCREWED WITH THE VIDEO FEED!*
GET THAT DOOR OPEN!
UUNGH! NO GO! IT'S JAMMED--!
CENT-COM TO ALL UNITS--THE WEST WALL'S BEEN BREACHED! INITIATE EMERGENCY PROTOCOL A!
*SPIDER-MAN DID IT LAST ISSUE. --SECURITY STEVE.
SO YOU HAVE A BEEF WITH JUGGERNAUT.
I SYMPATHIZE.
HELLO? CAPTAIN?
I DON'T BELIEVE IT. HE'S IGNORING ME!

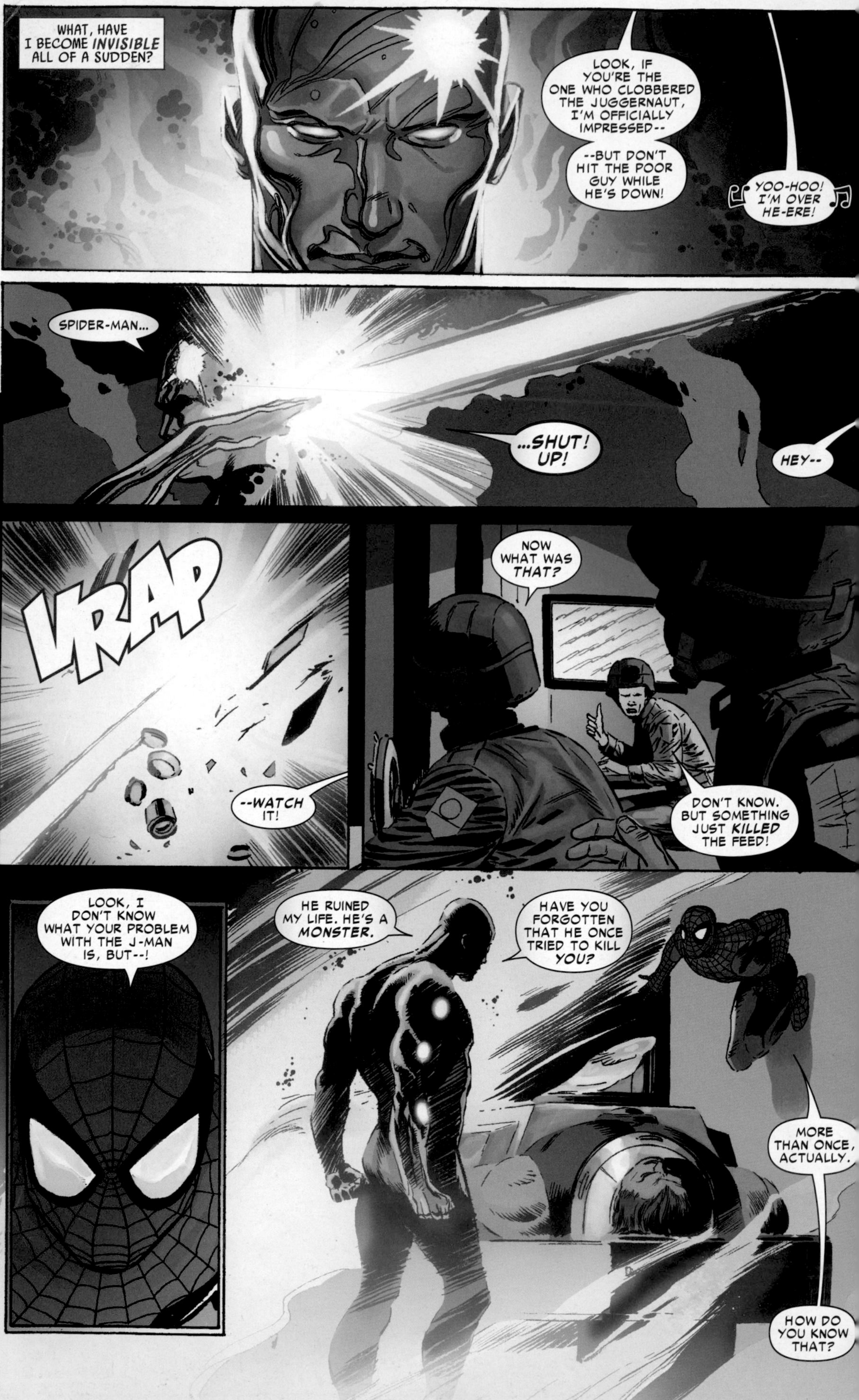
WHAT, HAVE I BECOME *INVISIBLE* ALL OF A SUDDEN?
LOOK, IF YOU'RE THE ONE WHO CLOBBERED THE JUGGERNAUT, I'M OFFICIALLY IMPRESSED--
--BUT DON'T HIT THE POOR GUY WHILE HE'S DOWN!
YOO-HOO! I'M OVER HE-ERE!
SPIDER-MAN...
...SHUT! UP!
HEY--
VRAP
--WATCH IT!
NOW WHAT WAS *THAT?*
DON'T KNOW. BUT SOMETHING JUST *KILLED* THE FEED!
LOOK, I DON'T KNOW WHAT YOUR PROBLEM WITH THE J-MAN IS, BUT--!
HE RUINED MY LIFE. HE'S A *MONSTER.*
HAVE YOU FORGOTTEN THAT HE ONCE TRIED TO KILL *YOU?*
MORE THAN ONCE, ACTUALLY.
HOW DO YOU KNOW THAT?

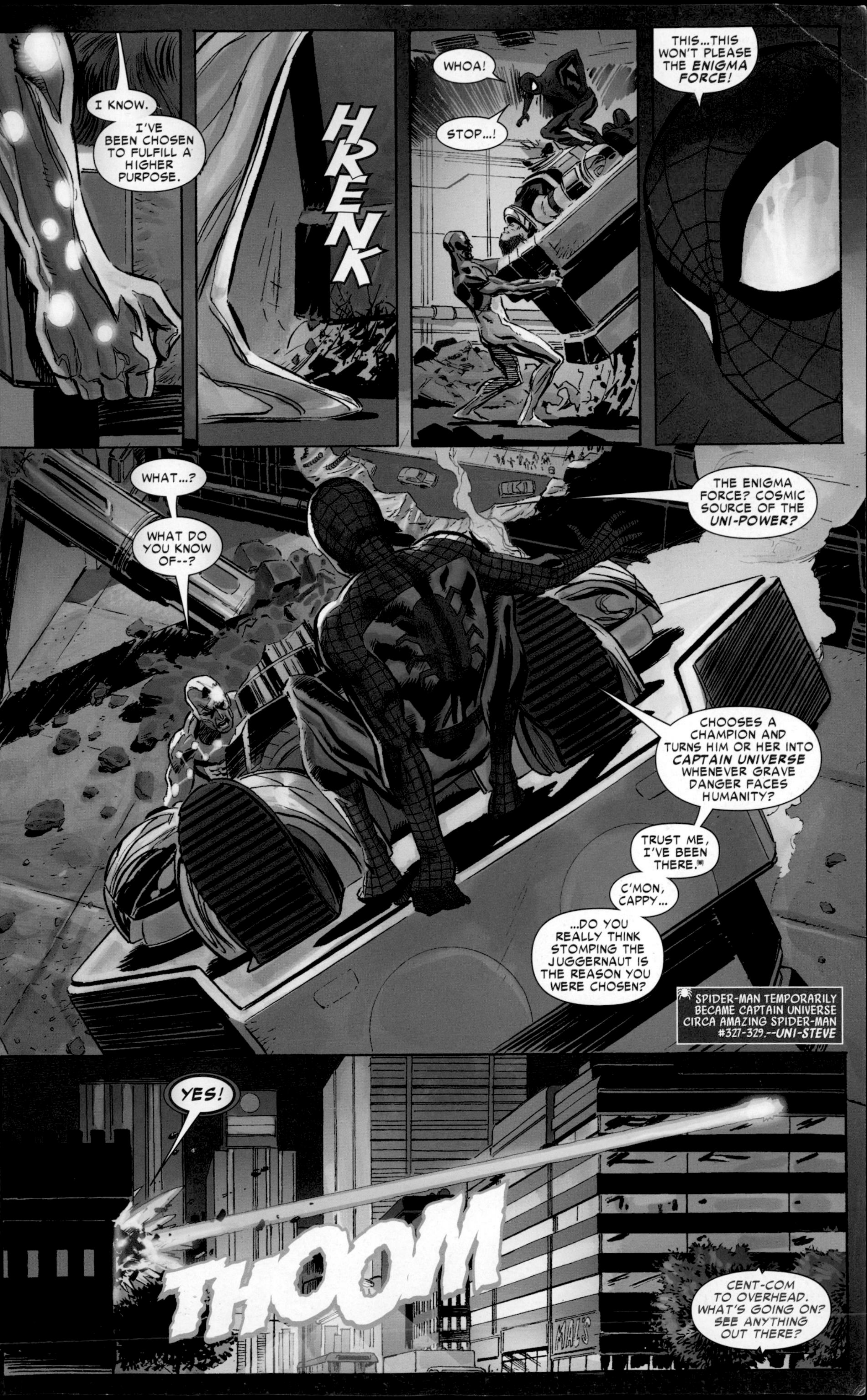
I KNOW.
I'VE BEEN CHOSEN TO FULFILL A HIGHER PURPOSE.
HRENK
WHOA!
STOP...!
THIS...THIS WON'T PLEASE THE ENIGMA FORCE!
WHAT...?
WHAT DO YOU KNOW OF--?
THE ENIGMA FORCE? COSMIC SOURCE OF THE UNI-POWER?
CHOOSES A CHAMPION AND TURNS HIM OR HER INTO CAPTAIN UNIVERSE WHENEVER GRAVE DANGER FACES HUMANITY?
TRUST ME, I'VE BEEN THERE.*
C'MON, CAPPY...
...DO YOU REALLY THINK STOMPING THE JUGGERNAUT IS THE REASON YOU WERE CHOSEN?
*SPIDER-MAN TEMPORARILY BECAME CAPTAIN UNIVERSE CIRCA AMAZING SPIDER-MAN #327-329.--UNI-STEVE
YES!
THOOM
CENT-COM TO OVERHEAD. WHAT'S GOING ON? SEE ANYTHING OUT THERE?

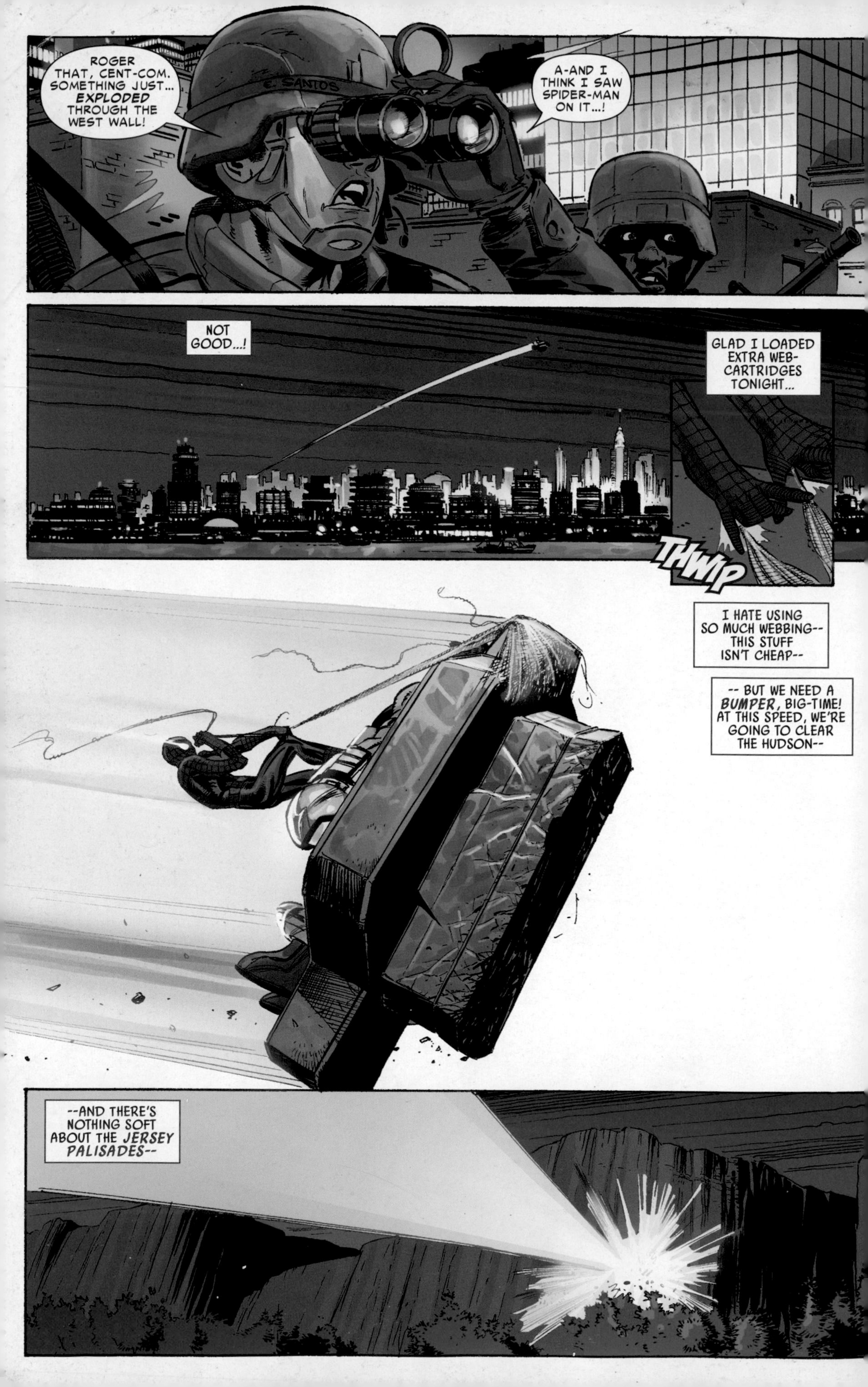

ROGER THAT, CENT-COM. SOMETHING JUST... EXPLODED THROUGH THE WEST WALL!
A-AND I THINK I SAW SPIDER-MAN ON IT...!
E. SANTOS
NOT GOOD...!
GLAD I LOADED EXTRA WEB-CARTRIDGES TONIGHT...
THWIP
I HATE USING SO MUCH WEBBING-- THIS STUFF ISN'T CHEAP--
-- BUT WE NEED A BUMPER, BIG-TIME! AT THIS SPEED, WE'RE GOING TO CLEAR THE HUDSON--
--AND THERE'S NOTHING SOFT ABOUT THE JERSEY PALISADES--

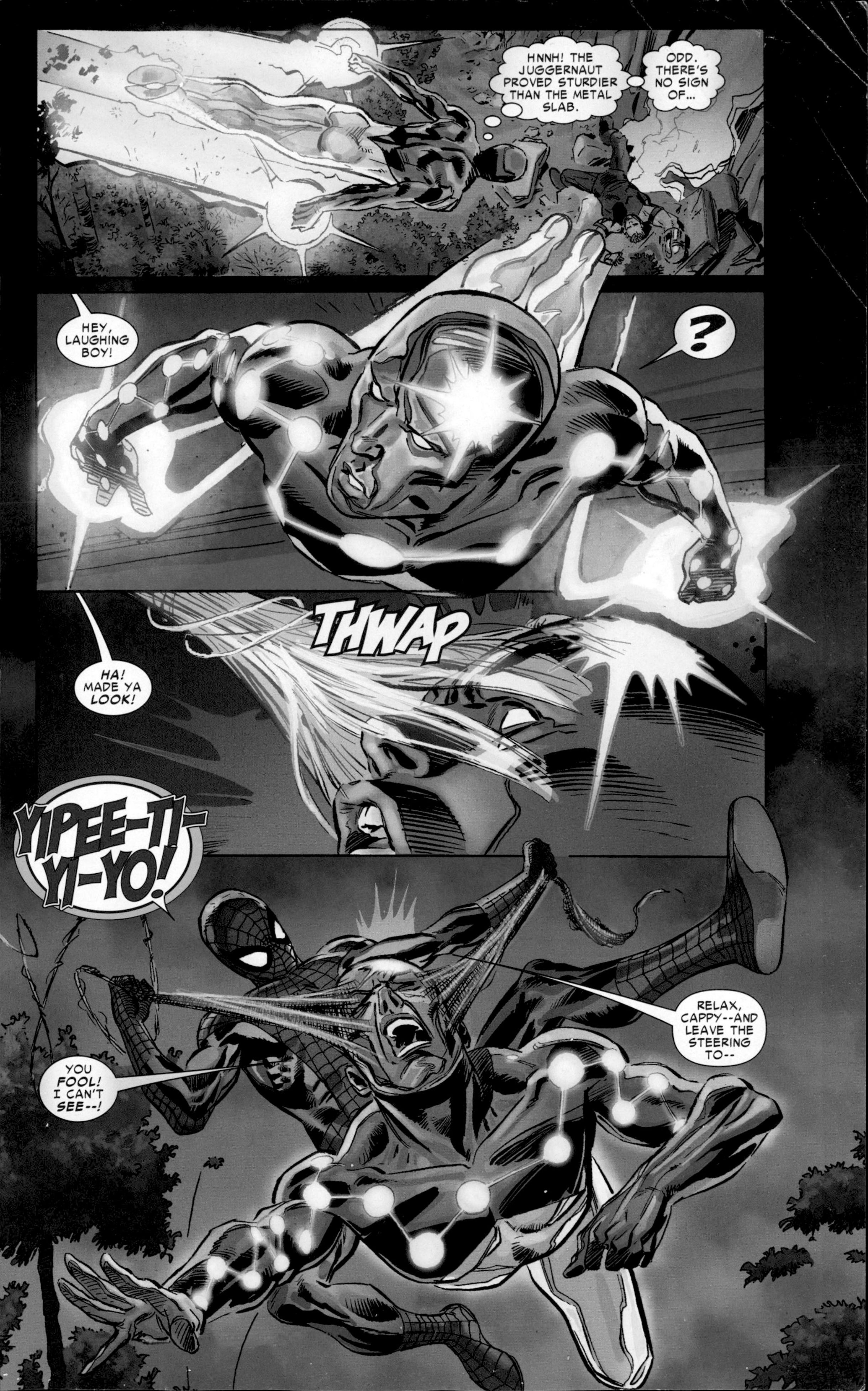

HNNH! THE JUGGERNAUT PROVED STURDIER THAN THE METAL SLAB.
ODD. THERE'S NO SIGN OF...
HEY, LAUGHING BOY!
?
THWAP
HA! MADE YA LOOK!
YIPEE-TI-YI-YO!
RELAX, CAPPY--AND LEAVE THE STEERING TO--
YOU FOOL! I CAN'T SEE--!

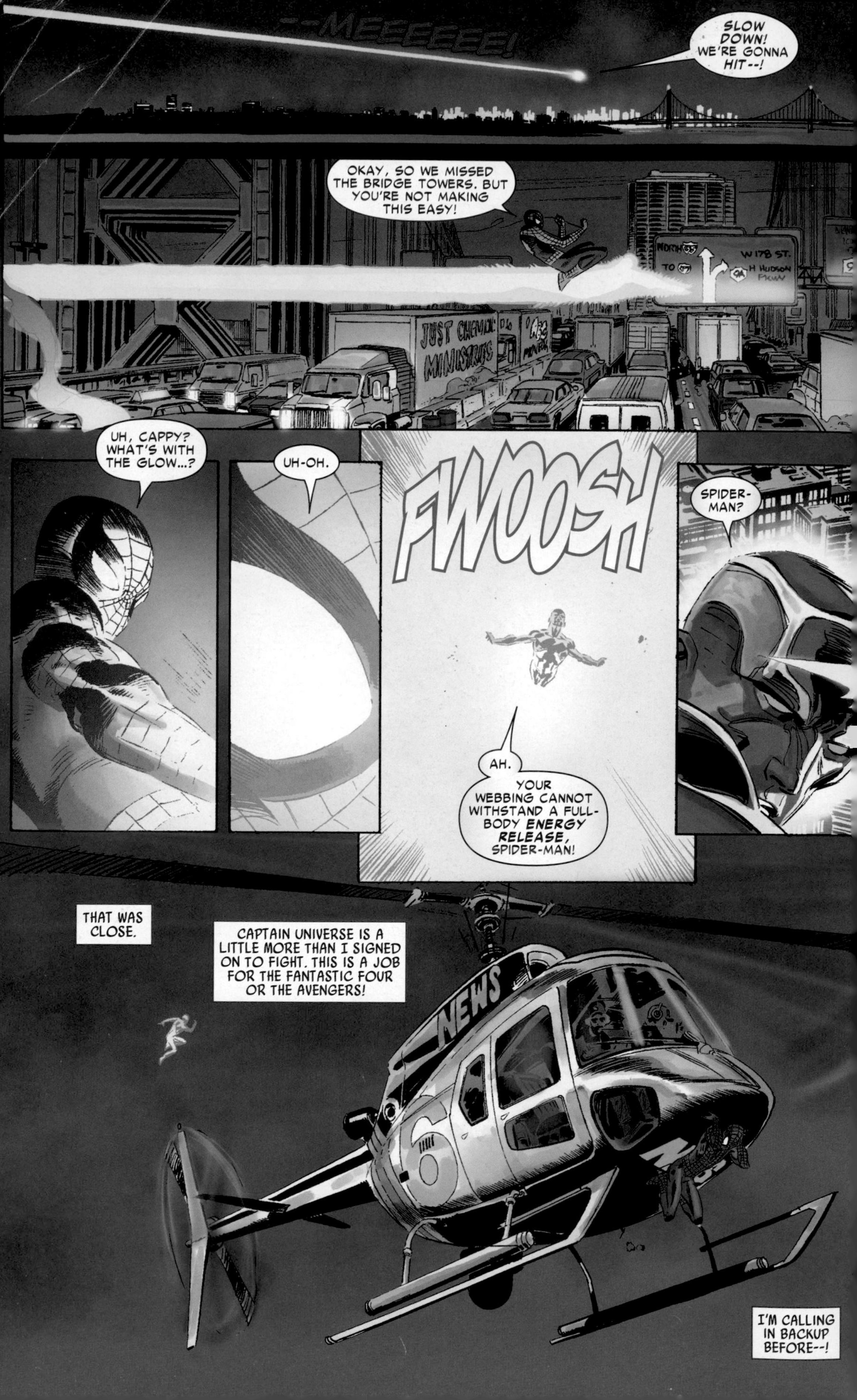
--MEEEEEEE!
SLOW DOWN! WE'RE GONNA HIT--!
OKAY, SO WE MISSED THE BRIDGE TOWERS. BUT YOU'RE NOT MAKING THIS EASY!
NORTH 95
TO 9A
W 178 ST.
H HUDSON PKWY
JUST CHEMICAL MINISTRIES
UH, CAPPY? WHAT'S WITH THE GLOW...?
UH-OH.
FWOOSH
AH.
YOUR WEBBING CANNOT WITHSTAND A FULL-BODY ENERGY RELEASE, SPIDER-MAN!
SPIDER-MAN?
THAT WAS CLOSE.
CAPTAIN UNIVERSE IS A LITTLE MORE THAN I SIGNED ON TO FIGHT. THIS IS A JOB FOR THE FANTASTIC FOUR OR THE AVENGERS!
NEWS
6
I'M CALLING IN BACKUP BEFORE--!

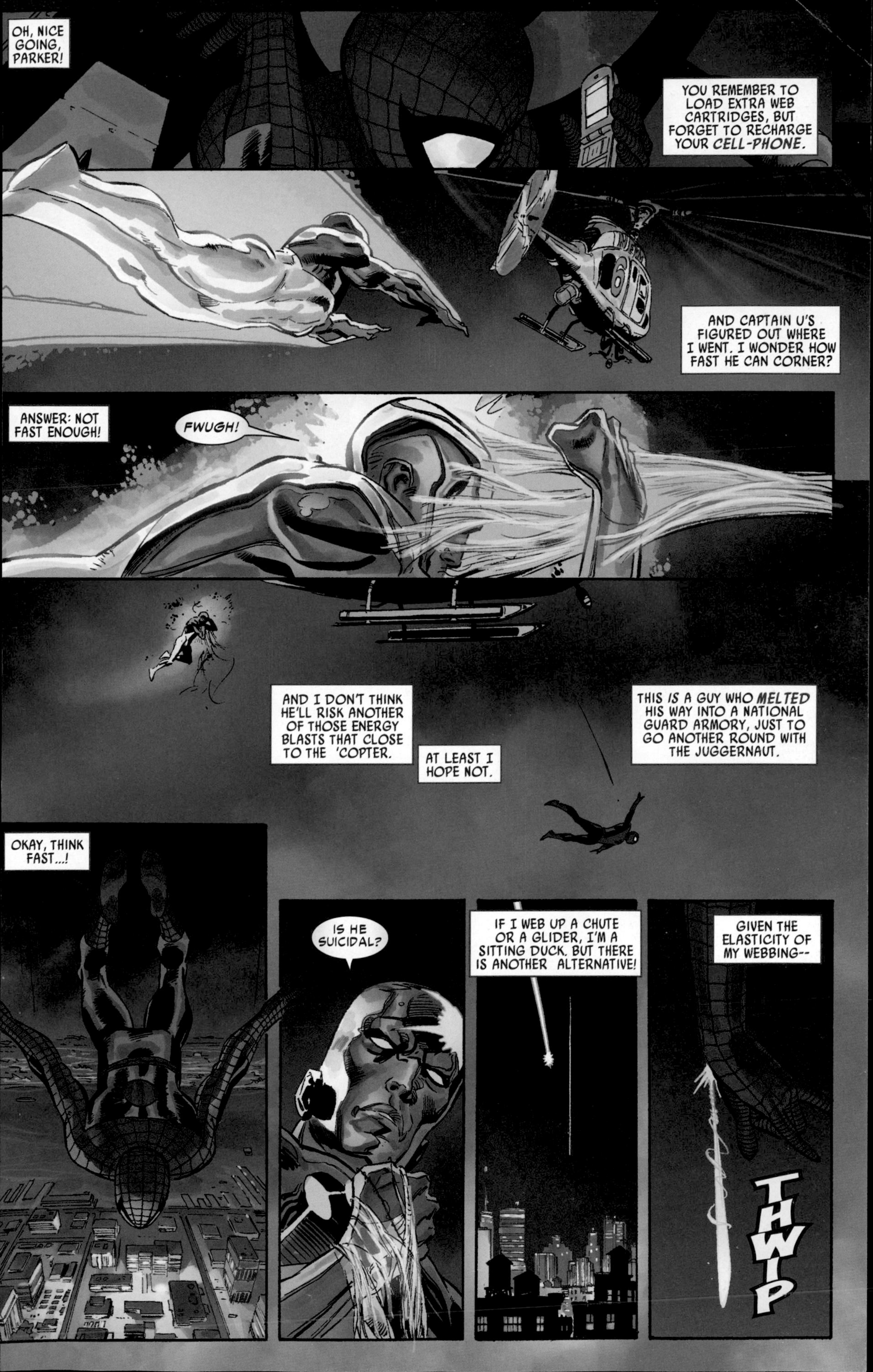

OH, NICE GOING, PARKER!
YOU REMEMBER TO LOAD EXTRA WEB CARTRIDGES, BUT FORGET TO RECHARGE YOUR CELL-PHONE.
AND CAPTAIN U'S FIGURED OUT WHERE I WENT. I WONDER HOW FAST HE CAN CORNER?
ANSWER: NOT FAST ENOUGH!
FWUGH!
AND I DON'T THINK HE'LL RISK ANOTHER OF THOSE ENERGY BLASTS THAT CLOSE TO THE 'COPTER.
AT LEAST I HOPE NOT.
THIS IS A GUY WHO MELTED HIS WAY INTO A NATIONAL GUARD ARMORY, JUST TO GO ANOTHER ROUND WITH THE JUGGERNAUT.
OKAY, THINK FAST...!
IS HE SUICIDAL?
IF I WEB UP A CHUTE OR A GLIDER, I'M A SITTING DUCK. BUT THERE IS ANOTHER ALTERNATIVE!
GIVEN THE ELASTICITY OF MY WEBBING--
THWIP

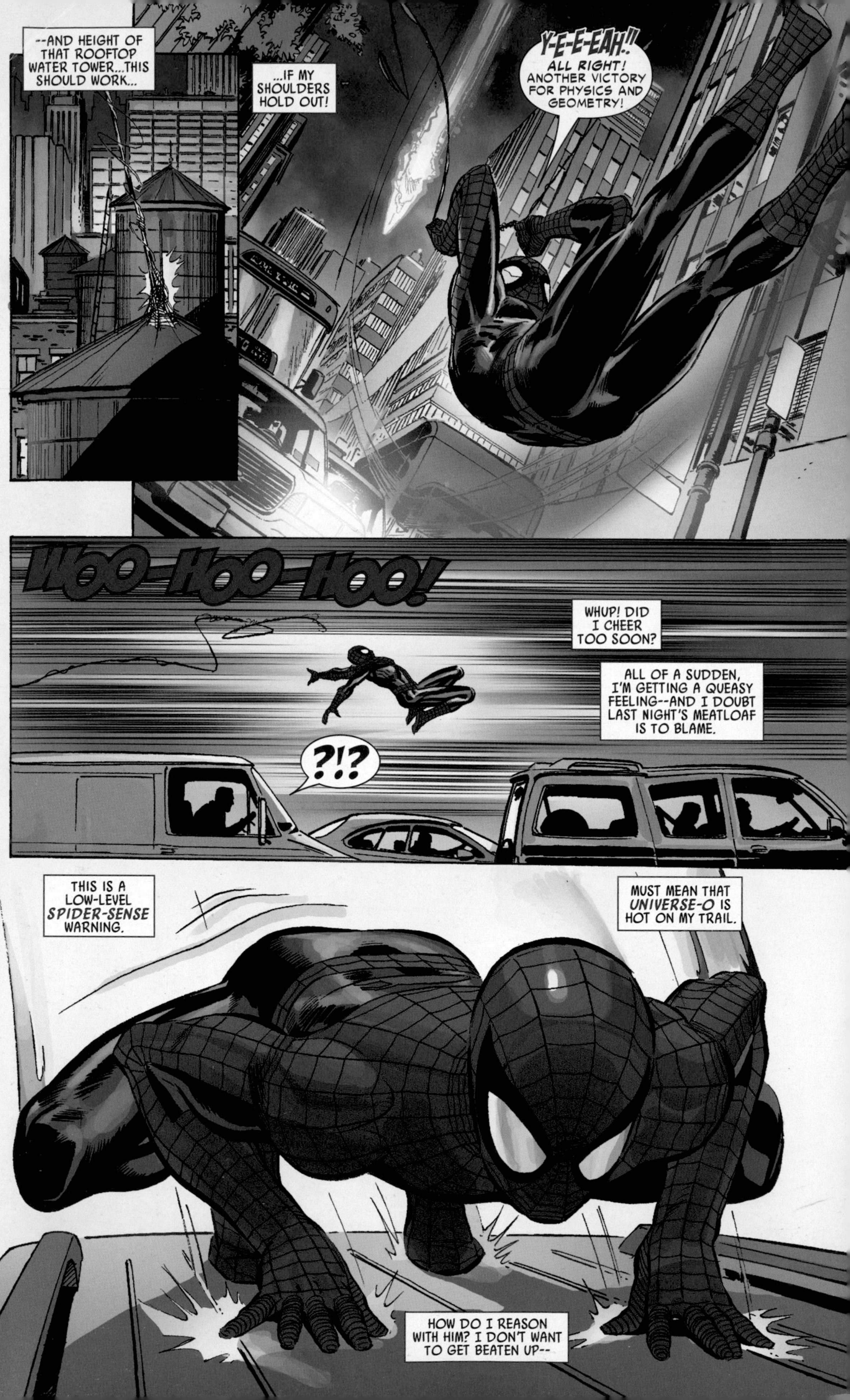
--AND HEIGHT OF THAT ROOFTOP WATER TOWER...THIS SHOULD WORK...
...IF MY SHOULDERS HOLD OUT!
Y-E-E-EAH!! ALL RIGHT! ANOTHER VICTORY FOR PHYSICS AND GEOMETRY!
WOO-HOO-HOO!
WHUP! DID I CHEER TOO SOON?
ALL OF A SUDDEN, I'M GETTING A QUEASY FEELING--AND I DOUBT LAST NIGHT'S MEATLOAF IS TO BLAME.
?!?
THIS IS A LOW-LEVEL SPIDER-SENSE WARNING.
MUST MEAN THAT UNIVERSE-O IS HOT ON MY TRAIL.
HOW DO I REASON WITH HIM? I DON'T WANT TO GET BEATEN UP--

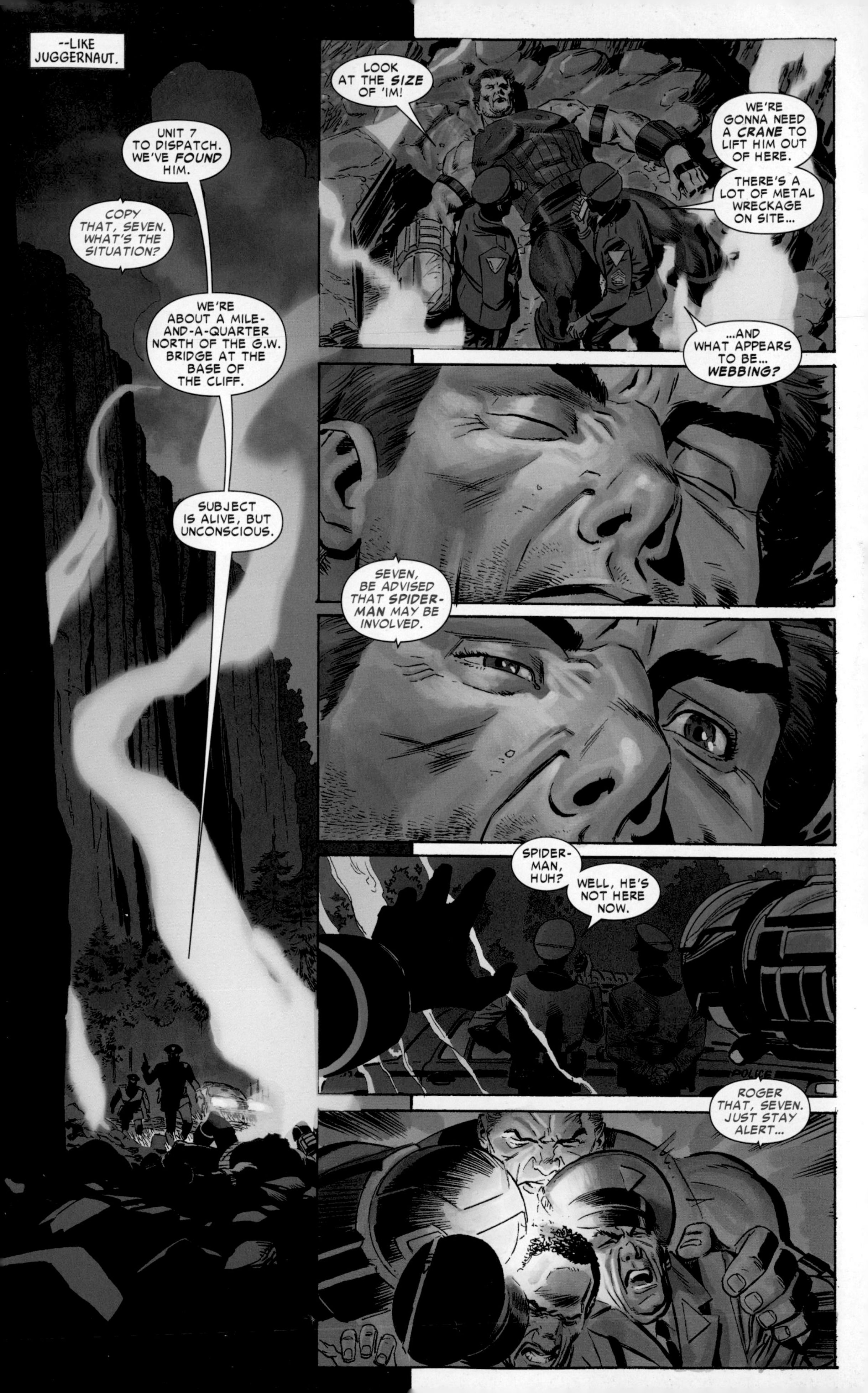
--LIKE JUGGERNAUT.
UNIT 7 TO DISPATCH. WE'VE FOUND HIM.
COPY THAT, SEVEN. WHAT'S THE SITUATION?
WE'RE ABOUT A MILE-AND-A-QUARTER NORTH OF THE G.W. BRIDGE AT THE BASE OF THE CLIFF.
SUBJECT IS ALIVE, BUT UNCONSCIOUS.
LOOK AT THE SIZE OF 'IM!
WE'RE GONNA NEED A CRANE TO LIFT HIM OUT OF HERE.
THERE'S A LOT OF METAL WRECKAGE ON SITE...
...AND WHAT APPEARS TO BE... WEBBING?
SEVEN, BE ADVISED THAT SPIDER-MAN MAY BE INVOLVED.
SPIDER-MAN, HUH?
WELL, HE'S NOT HERE NOW.
POLICE
ROGER THAT, SEVEN. JUST STAY ALERT...

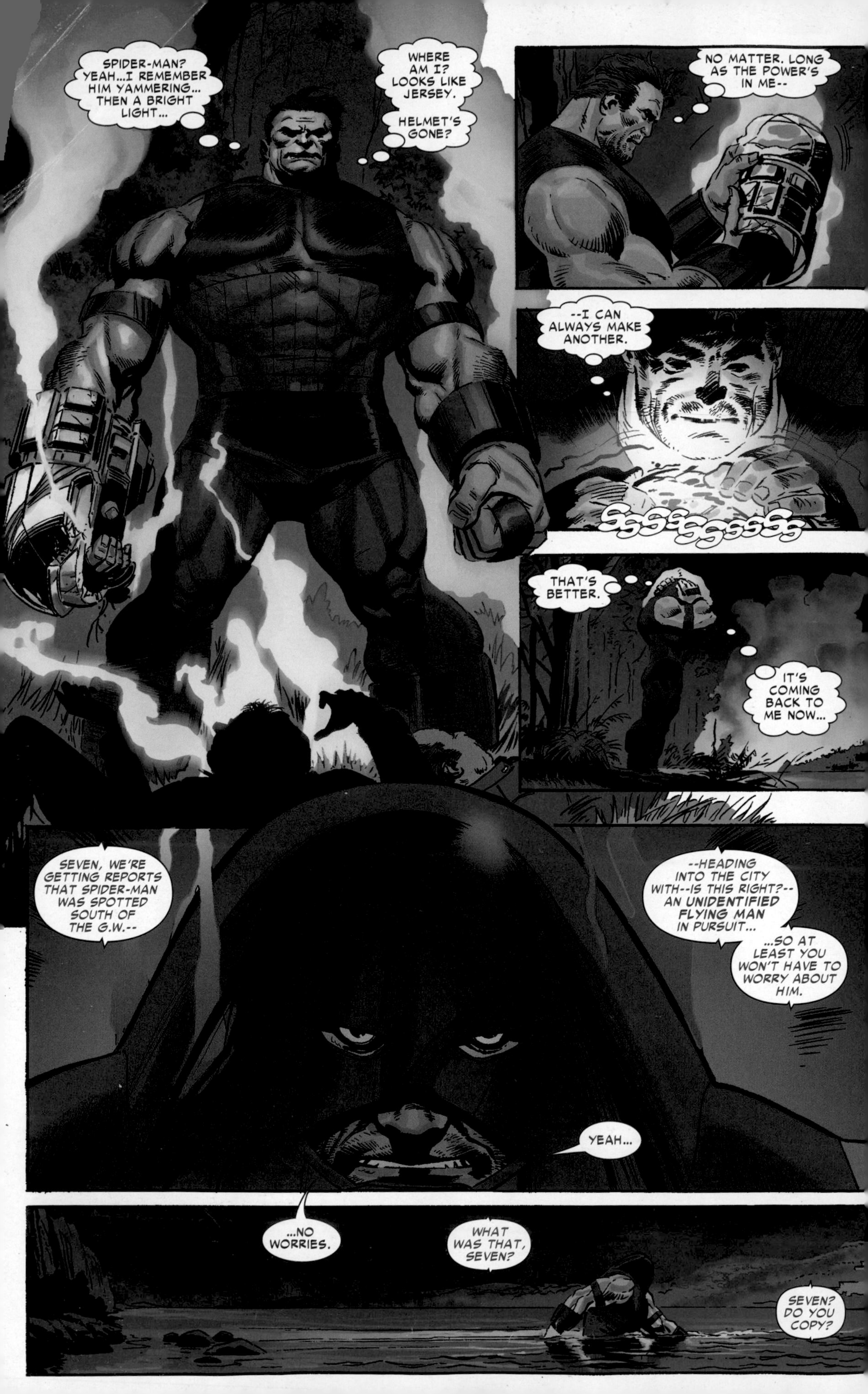
SPIDER-MAN? YEAH...I REMEMBER HIM YAMMERING... THEN A BRIGHT LIGHT...
WHERE AM I? LOOKS LIKE JERSEY.
HELMET'S GONE?
NO MATTER. LONG AS THE POWER'S IN ME--
--I CAN ALWAYS MAKE ANOTHER.
SSSSSSSSSSSS
THAT'S BETTER.
IT'S COMING BACK TO ME NOW...
SEVEN, WE'RE GETTING REPORTS THAT SPIDER-MAN WAS SPOTTED SOUTH OF THE G.W.--
--HEADING INTO THE CITY WITH--IS THIS RIGHT?--AN UNIDENTIFIED FLYING MAN IN PURSUIT...
...SO AT LEAST YOU WON'T HAVE TO WORRY ABOUT HIM.
YEAH...
...NO WORRIES.
WHAT WAS THAT, SEVEN?
SEVEN? DO YOU COPY?

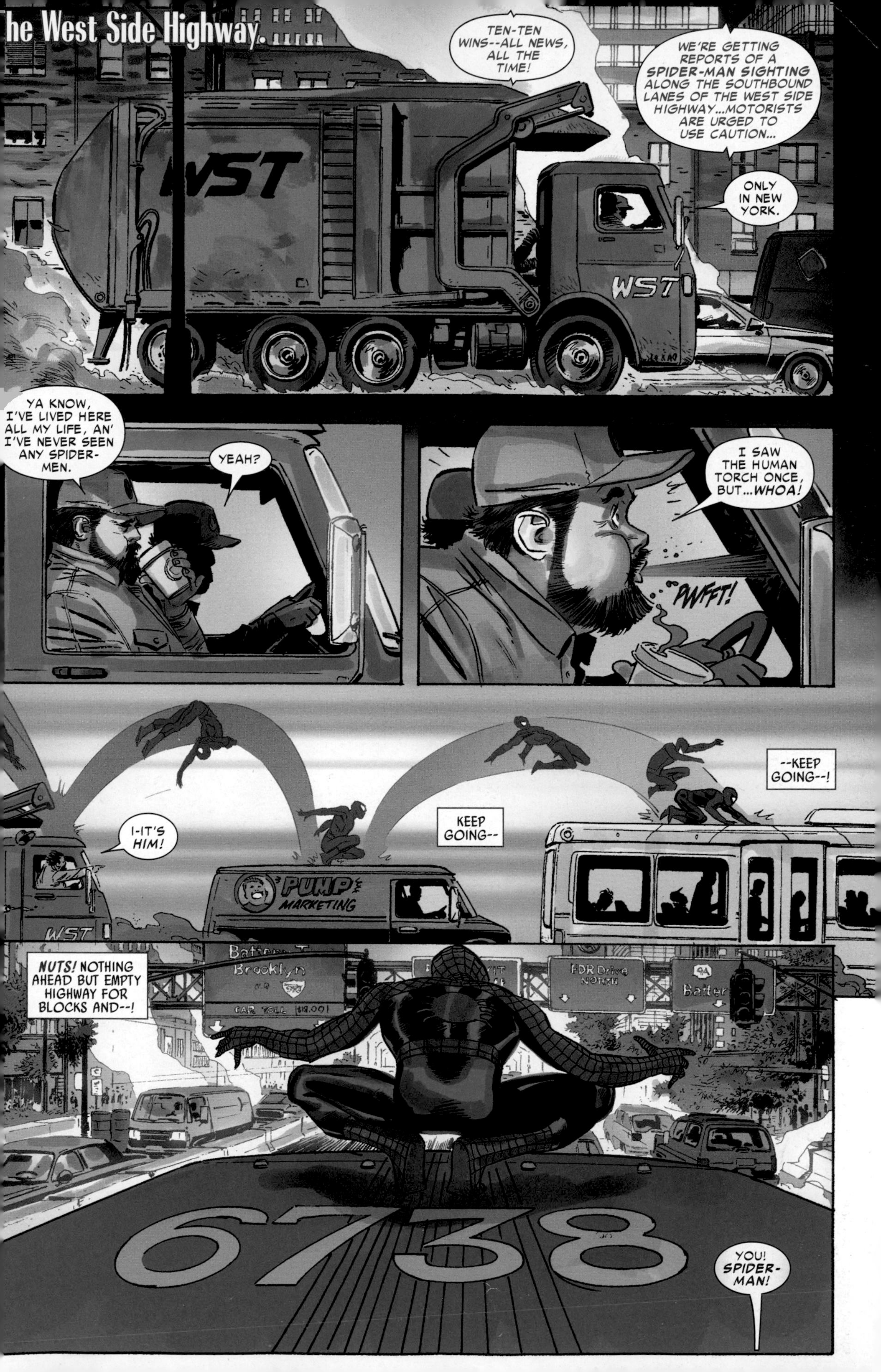

The West Side Highway.
TEN-TEN WINS--ALL NEWS, ALL THE TIME!
WE'RE GETTING REPORTS OF A SPIDER-MAN SIGHTING ALONG THE SOUTHBOUND LANES OF THE WEST SIDE HIGHWAY...MOTORISTS ARE URGED TO USE CAUTION...
ONLY IN NEW YORK.
WST
WST
YA KNOW, I'VE LIVED HERE ALL MY LIFE, AN' I'VE NEVER SEEN ANY SPIDER-MEN.
YEAH?
I SAW THE HUMAN TORCH ONCE, BUT...WHOA!
PWFFT!
I-IT'S HIM!
KEEP GOING--
--KEEP GOING--!
PUMP MARKETING
WST
NUTS! NOTHING AHEAD BUT EMPTY HIGHWAY FOR BLOCKS AND--!
Brooklyn
CAR TOLL $18.00
FDR Drive NORTH
9A
Batter
6738
YOU! SPIDER-MAN!

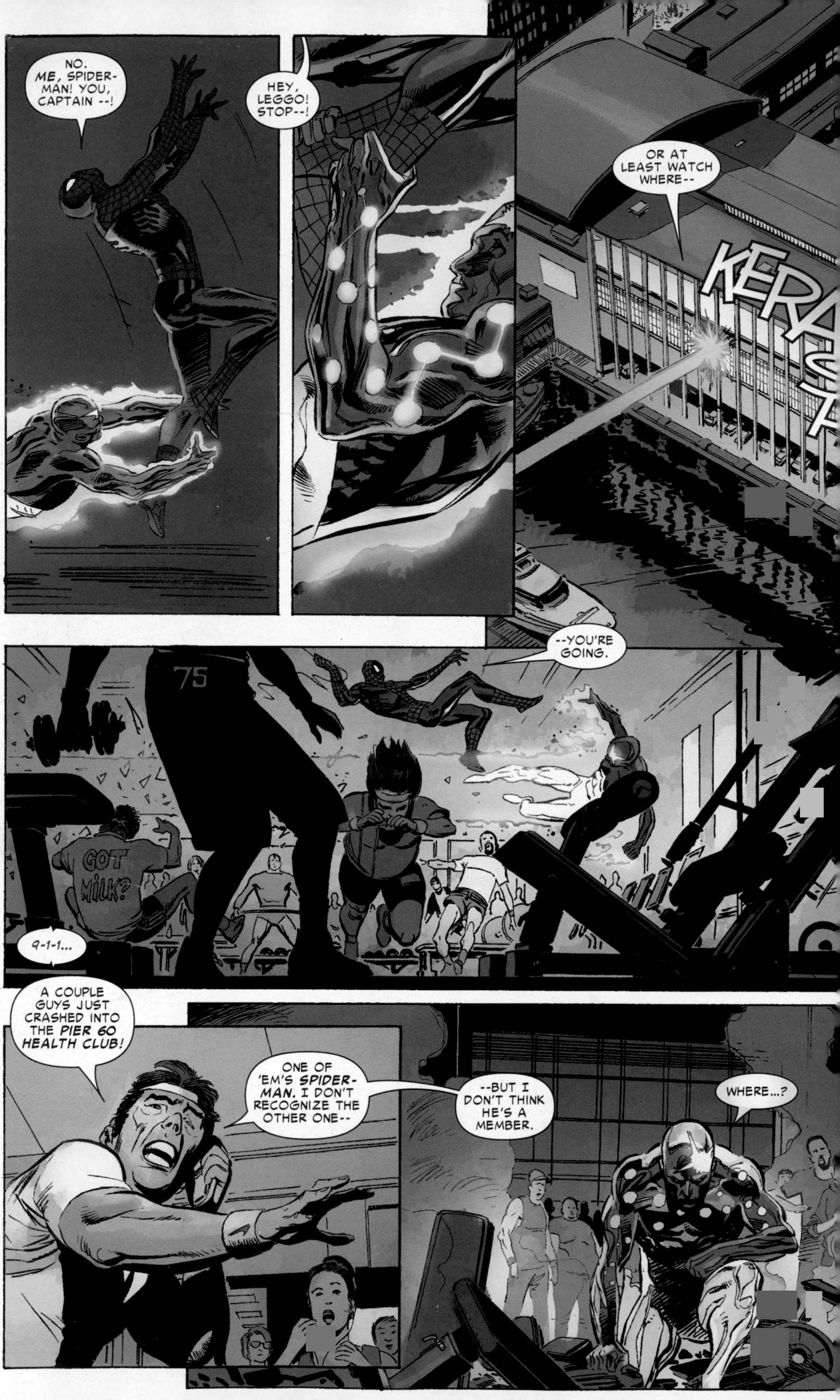
NO. ME, SPIDER-MAN! YOU, CAPTAIN --!
HEY, LEGGO! STOP--!
OR AT LEAST WATCH WHERE--
KERA
--YOU'RE GOING.
75
GOT MILK?
9-1-1...
A COUPLE GUYS JUST CRASHED INTO THE PIER 60 HEALTH CLUB!
ONE OF 'EM'S SPIDER-MAN. I DON'T RECOGNIZE THE OTHER ONE--
--BUT I DON'T THINK HE'S A MEMBER.
WHERE...?

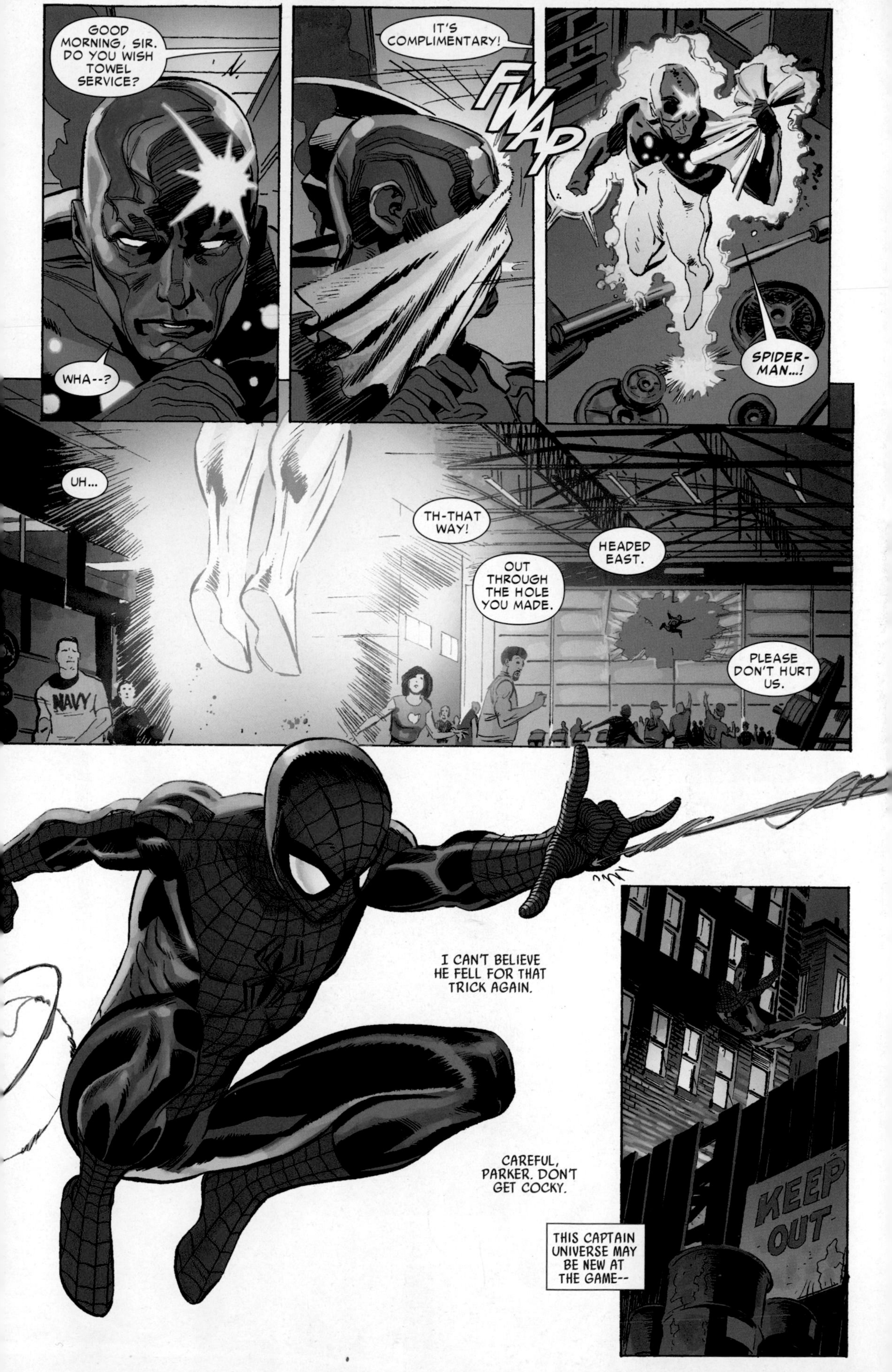
GOOD MORNING, SIR. DO YOU WISH TOWEL SERVICE?
WHA--?
IT'S COMPLIMENTARY!
FWAP
SPIDER-MAN...!
UH...
TH-THAT WAY!
OUT THROUGH THE HOLE YOU MADE.
HEADED EAST.
PLEASE DON'T HURT US.
NAVY
I CAN'T BELIEVE HE FELL FOR THAT TRICK AGAIN.
CAREFUL, PARKER. DON'T GET COCKY.
THIS CAPTAIN UNIVERSE MAY BE NEW AT THE GAME--
KEEP OUT

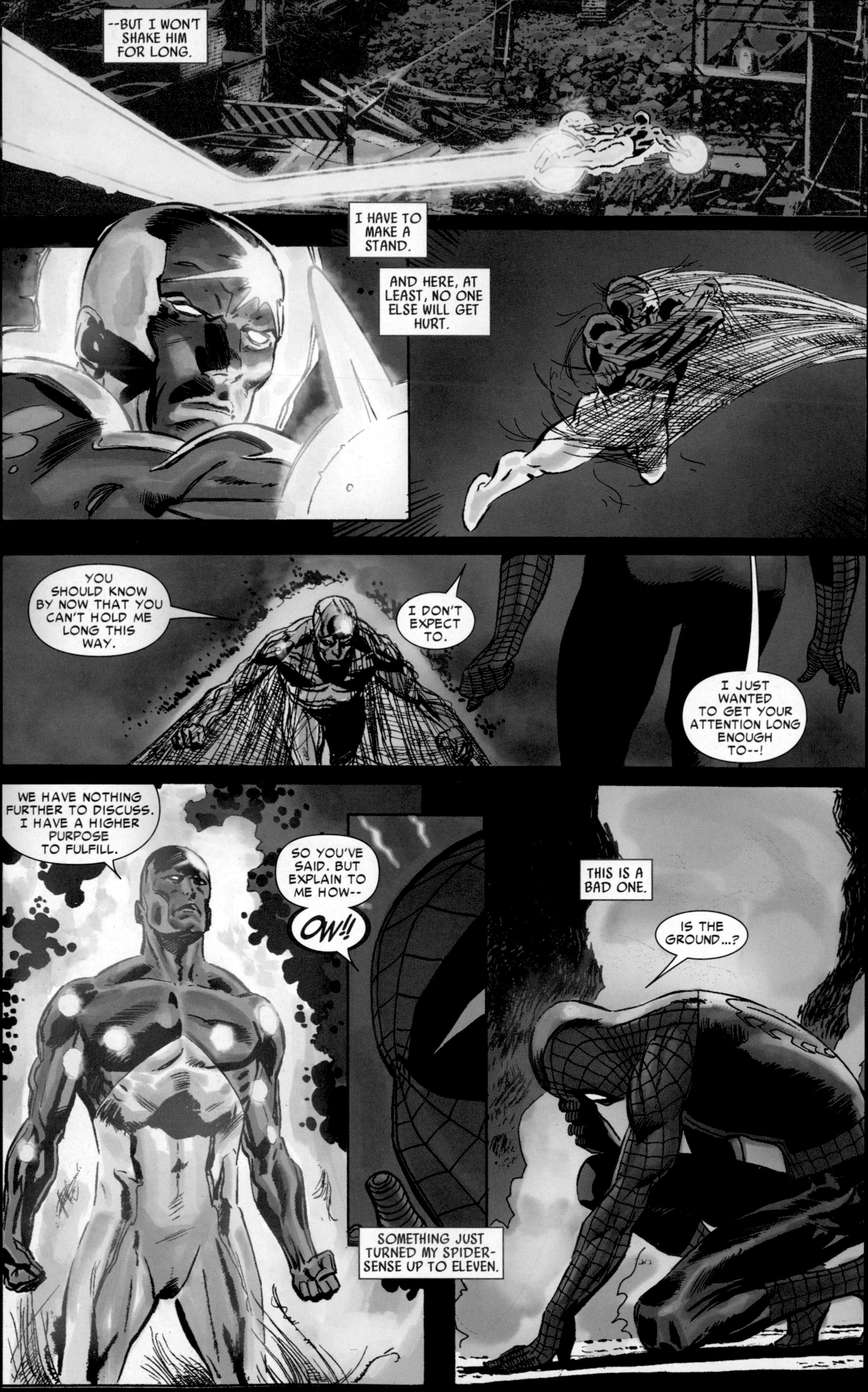
--BUT I WON'T SHAKE HIM FOR LONG.
I HAVE TO MAKE A STAND.
AND HERE, AT LEAST, NO ONE ELSE WILL GET HURT.
YOU SHOULD KNOW BY NOW THAT YOU CAN'T HOLD ME LONG THIS WAY.
I DON'T EXPECT TO.
I JUST WANTED TO GET YOUR ATTENTION LONG ENOUGH TO--!
WE HAVE NOTHING FURTHER TO DISCUSS. I HAVE A HIGHER PURPOSE TO FULFILL.
SO YOU'VE SAID. BUT EXPLAIN TO ME HOW--
OW!!
SOMETHING JUST TURNED MY SPIDER-SENSE UP TO ELEVEN.
THIS IS A BAD ONE.
IS THE GROUND...?

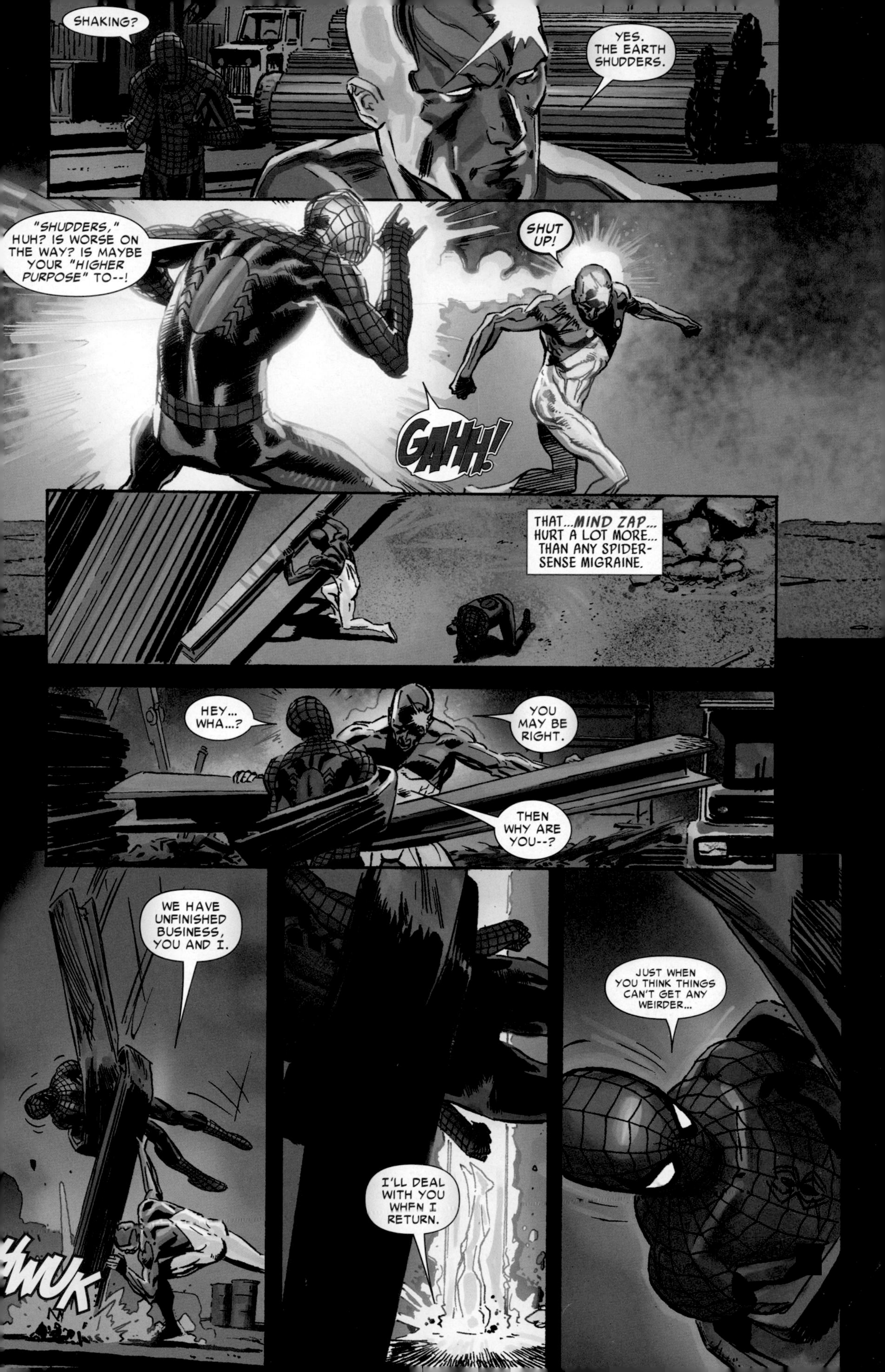
SHAKING?
YES. THE EARTH SHUDDERS.
"SHUDDERS," HUH? IS WORSE ON THE WAY? IS MAYBE YOUR "HIGHER PURPOSE" TO--!
SHUT UP!
GAHH!
THAT...MIND ZAP... HURT A LOT MORE... THAN ANY SPIDER-SENSE MIGRAINE.
HEY... WHA...?
YOU MAY BE RIGHT.
THEN WHY ARE YOU--?
WE HAVE UNFINISHED BUSINESS, YOU AND I.
HWUK
I'LL DEAL WITH YOU WHFN I RETURN.
JUST WHEN YOU THINK THINGS CAN'T GET ANY WEIRDER...

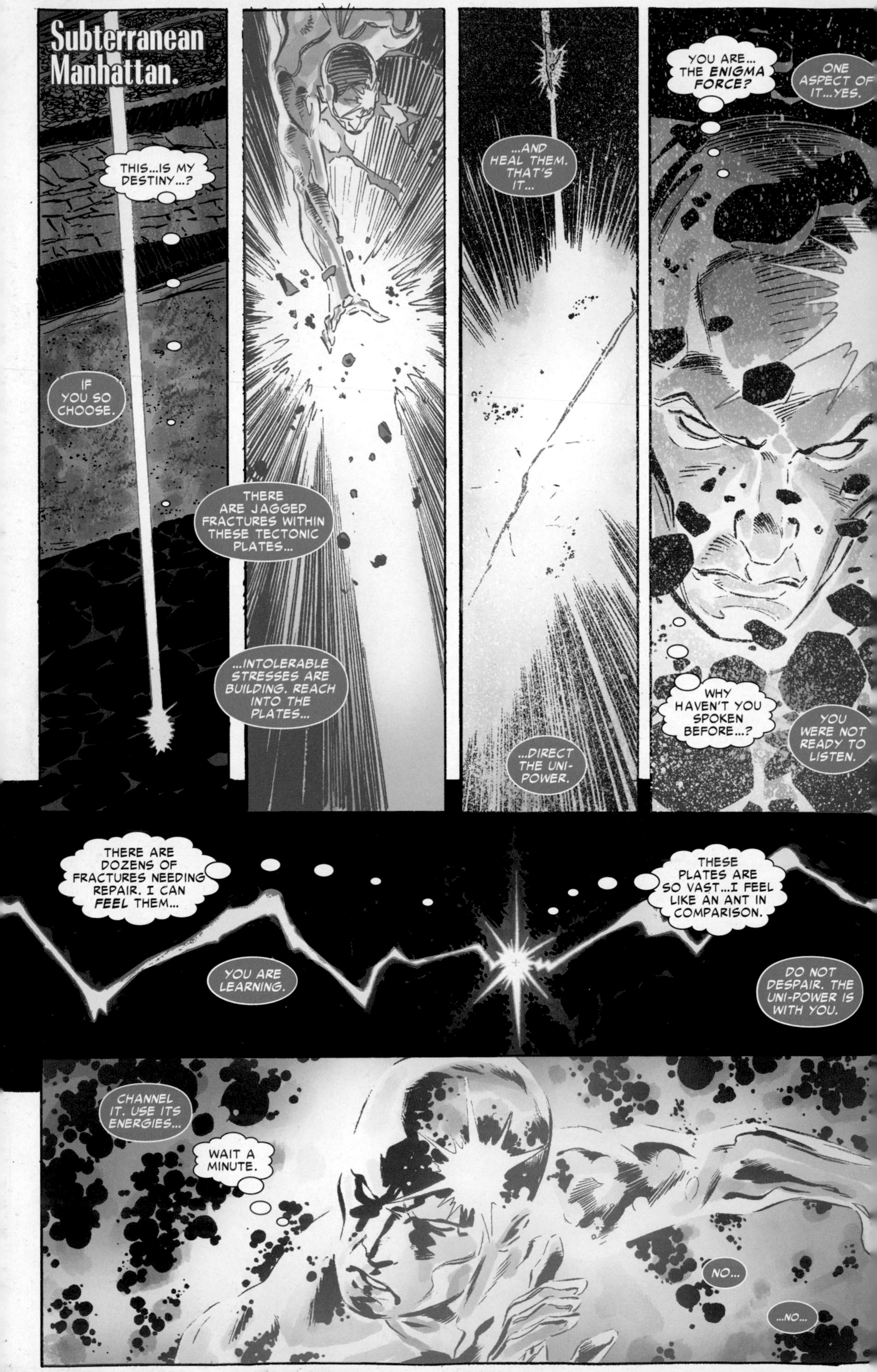
Subterranean Manhattan.
THIS...IS MY DESTINY...?
IF YOU SO CHOOSE.
THERE ARE JAGGED FRACTURES WITHIN THESE TECTONIC PLATES...
...INTOLERABLE STRESSES ARE BUILDING. REACH INTO THE PLATES...
...AND HEAL THEM. THAT'S IT...
...DIRECT THE UNI-POWER.
YOU ARE... THE ENIGMA FORCE?
ONE ASPECT OF IT...YES.
WHY HAVEN'T YOU SPOKEN BEFORE...?
YOU WERE NOT READY TO LISTEN.
THERE ARE DOZENS OF FRACTURES NEEDING REPAIR. I CAN FEEL THEM...
YOU ARE LEARNING.
THESE PLATES ARE SO VAST...I FEEL LIKE AN ANT IN COMPARISON.
DO NOT DESPAIR. THE UNI-POWER IS WITH YOU.
CHANNEL IT. USE ITS ENERGIES...
WAIT A MINUTE.
NO...
...NO...

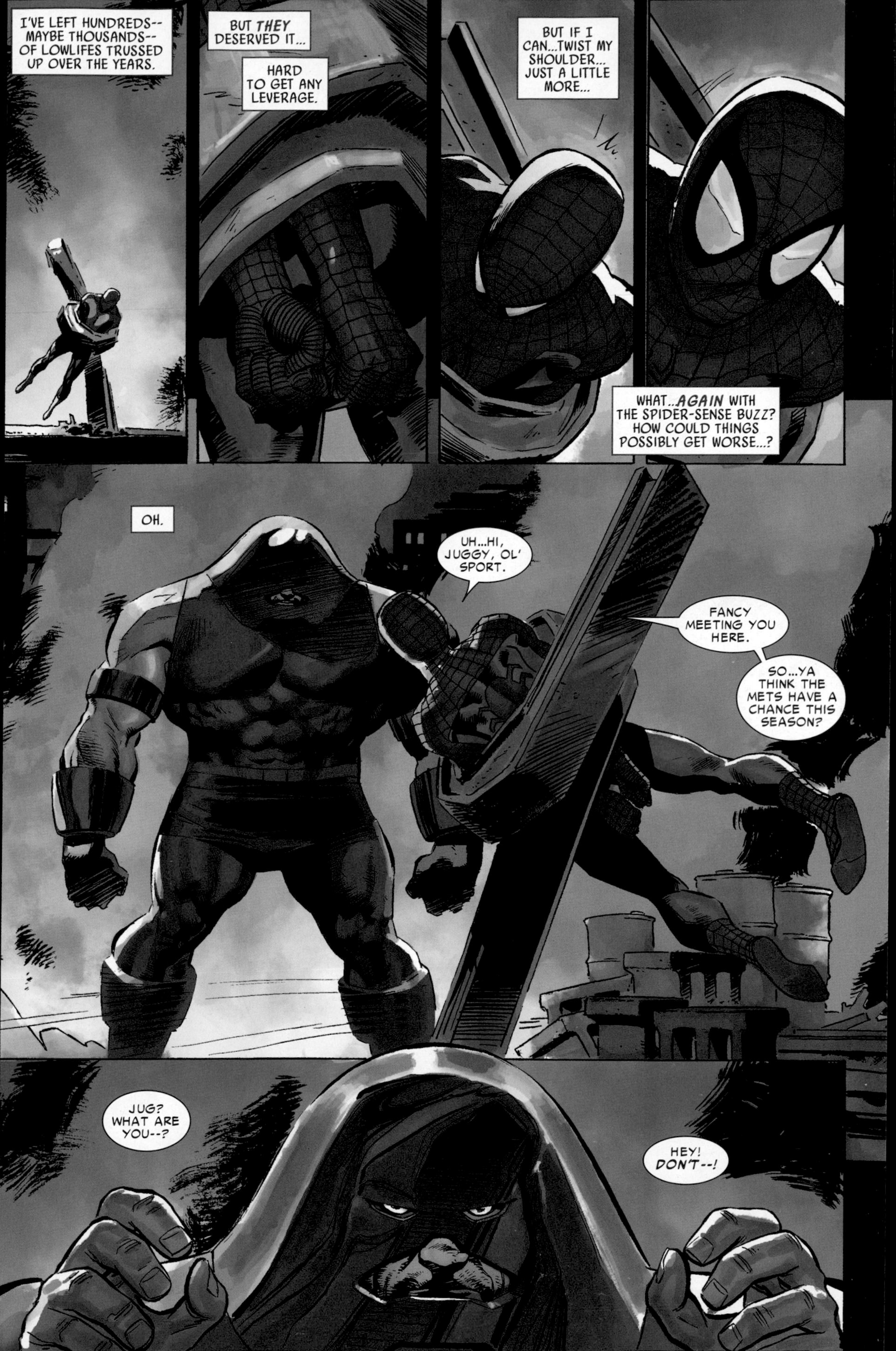
I'VE LEFT HUNDREDS-- MAYBE THOUSANDS-- OF LOWLIFES TRUSSED UP OVER THE YEARS.
BUT THEY DESERVED IT...
HARD TO GET ANY LEVERAGE.
BUT IF I CAN...TWIST MY SHOULDER... JUST A LITTLE MORE...
WHAT...AGAIN WITH THE SPIDER-SENSE BUZZ? HOW COULD THINGS POSSIBLY GET WORSE...?
OH.
UH...HI, JUGGY, OL' SPORT.
FANCY MEETING YOU HERE.
SO...YA THINK THE METS HAVE A CHANCE THIS SEASON?
JUG? WHAT ARE YOU--?
HEY! DON'T--!

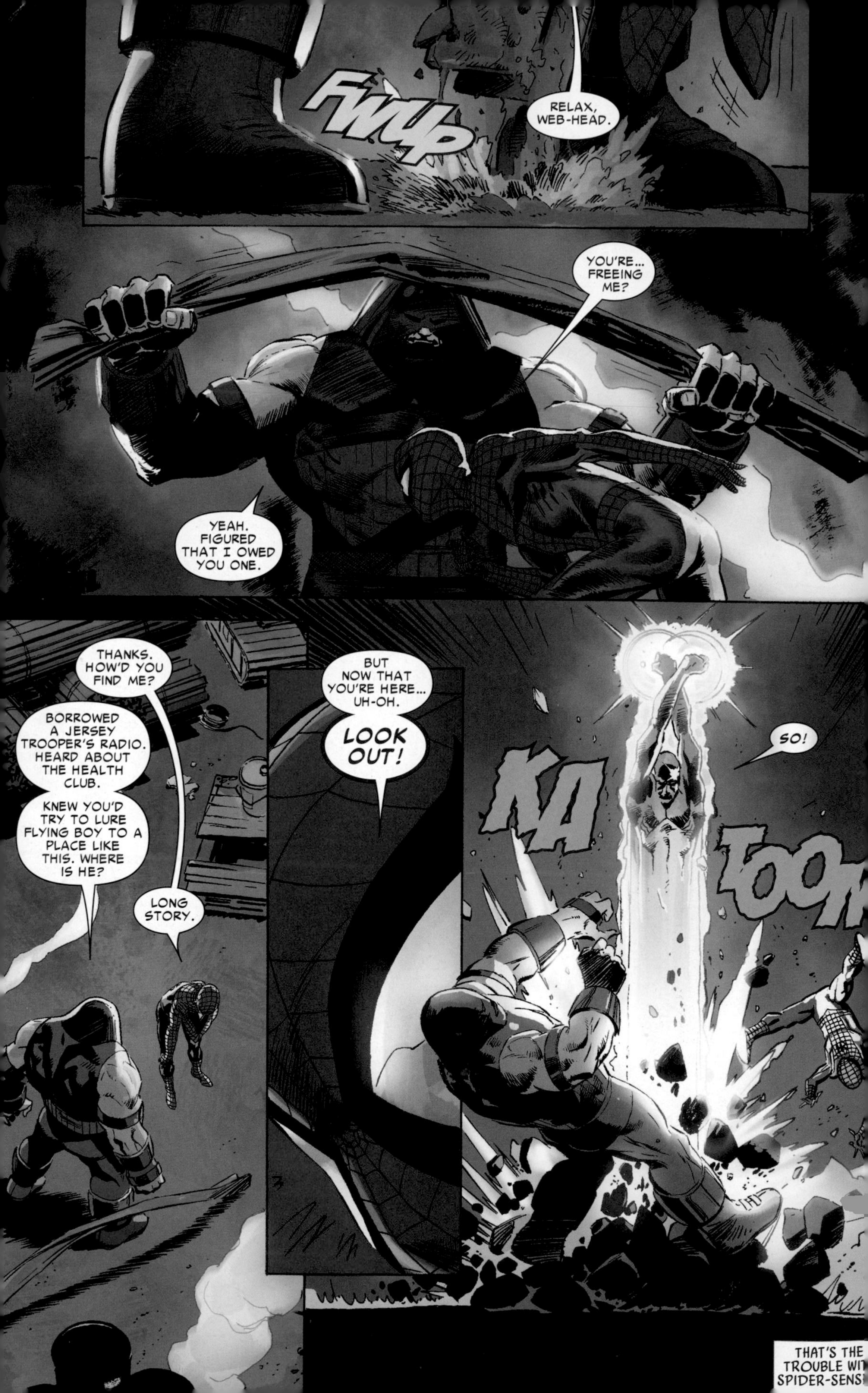
FWUP
RELAX, WEB-HEAD.
YOU'RE... FREEING ME?
YEAH. FIGURED THAT I OWED YOU ONE.
THANKS. HOW'D YOU FIND ME?
BORROWED A JERSEY TROOPER'S RADIO. HEARD ABOUT THE HEALTH CLUB.
KNEW YOU'D TRY TO LURE FLYING BOY TO A PLACE LIKE THIS. WHERE IS HE?
LONG STORY.
BUT NOW THAT YOU'RE HERE... UH-OH.
LOOK OUT!
SO!
KA
TOO
THAT'S THE TROUBLE WI
SPIDER-SENS

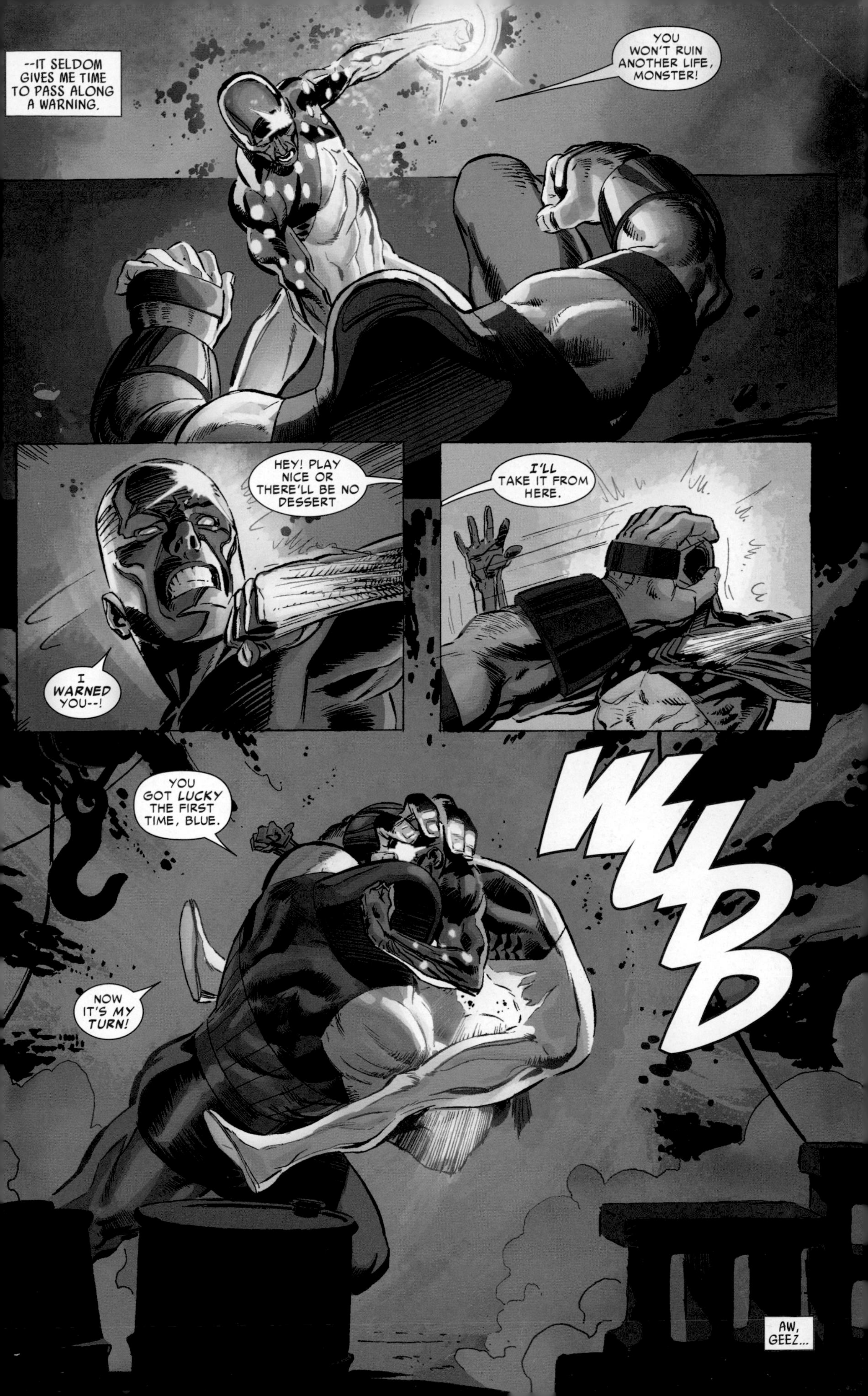
--IT SELDOM GIVES ME TIME TO PASS ALONG A WARNING.
YOU WON'T RUIN ANOTHER LIFE, MONSTER!
HEY! PLAY NICE OR THERE'LL BE NO DESSERT
I WARNED YOU--!
I'LL TAKE IT FROM HERE.
YOU GOT LUCKY THE FIRST TIME, BLUE.
NOW IT'S MY TURN!
WUD
AW, GEEZ...

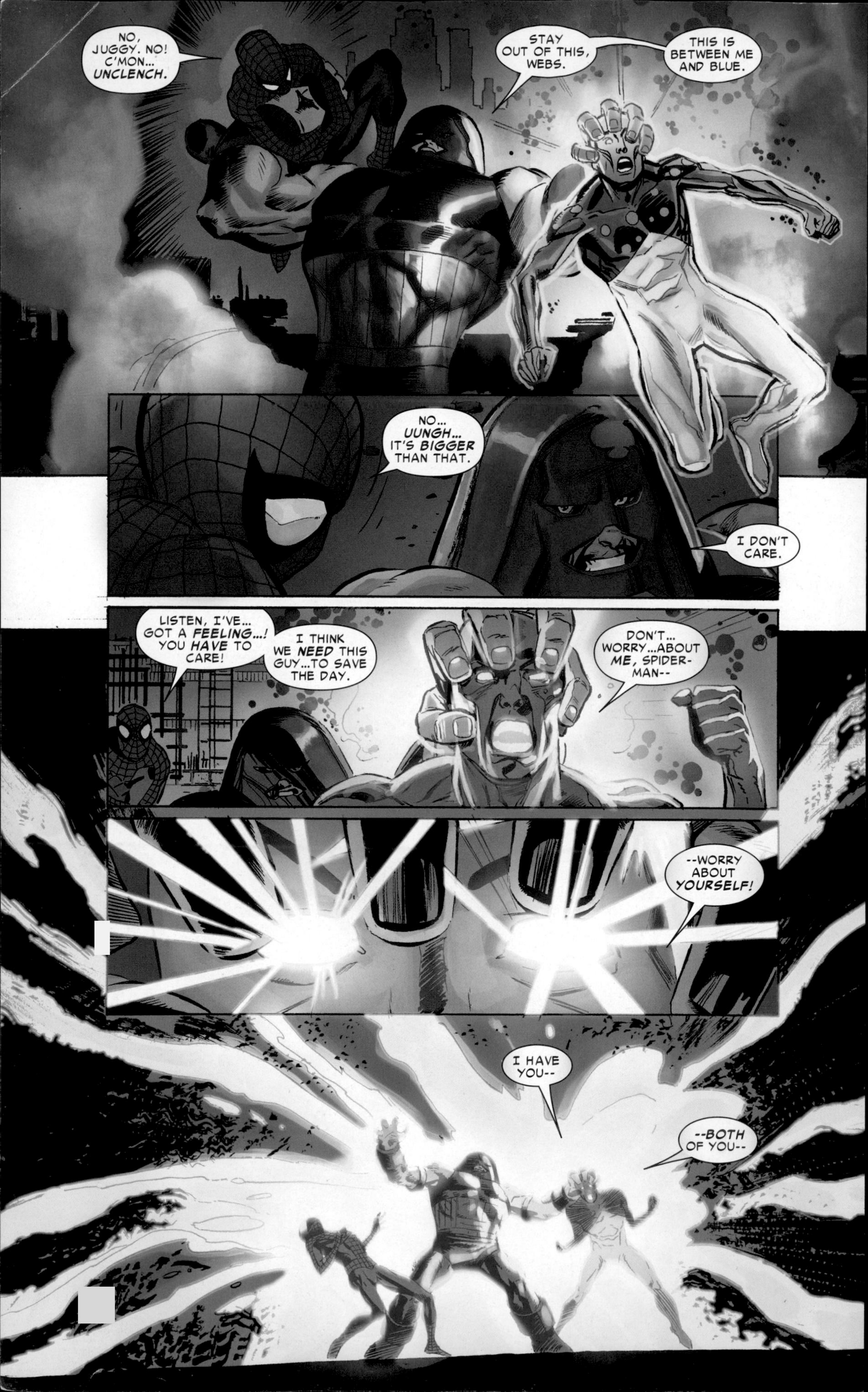
NO, JUGGY. NO! C'MON... UNCLENCH.
STAY OUT OF THIS, WEBS.
THIS IS BETWEEN ME AND BLUE.
NO... UUNGH... IT'S BIGGER THAN THAT.
I DON'T CARE.
LISTEN, I'VE... GOT A FEELING...! YOU HAVE TO CARE!
I THINK WE NEED THIS GUY...TO SAVE THE DAY.
DON'T... WORRY...ABOUT ME, SPIDER-MAN--
--WORRY ABOUT YOURSELF!
I HAVE YOU--
--BOTH OF YOU--

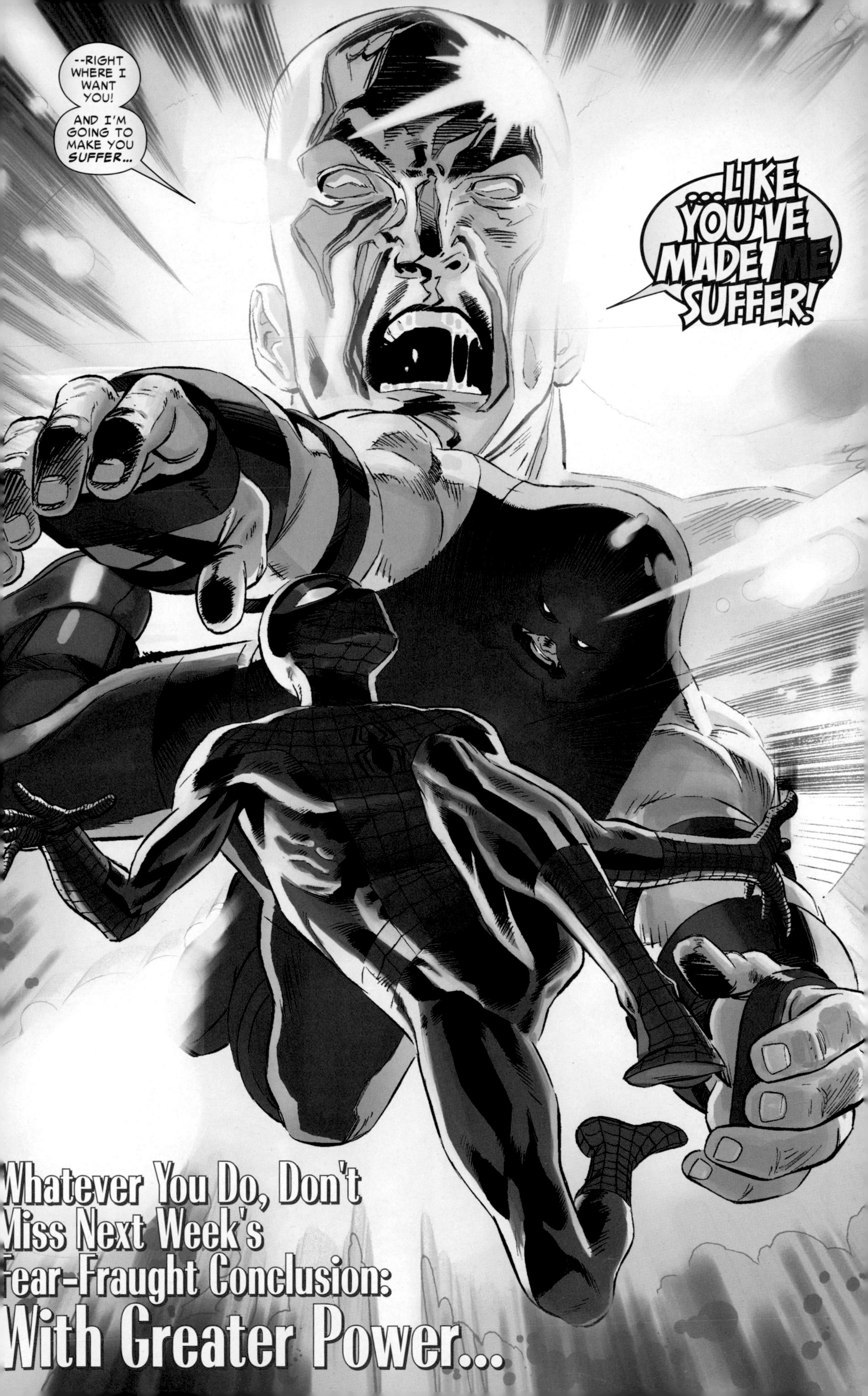
--RIGHT WHERE I WANT YOU!
AND I'M GOING TO MAKE YOU SUFFER...
...LIKE YOU'VE MADE ME SUFFER!
Whatever You Do, Don't Miss Next Week's Fear-Fraught Conclusion:
With Greater Power...

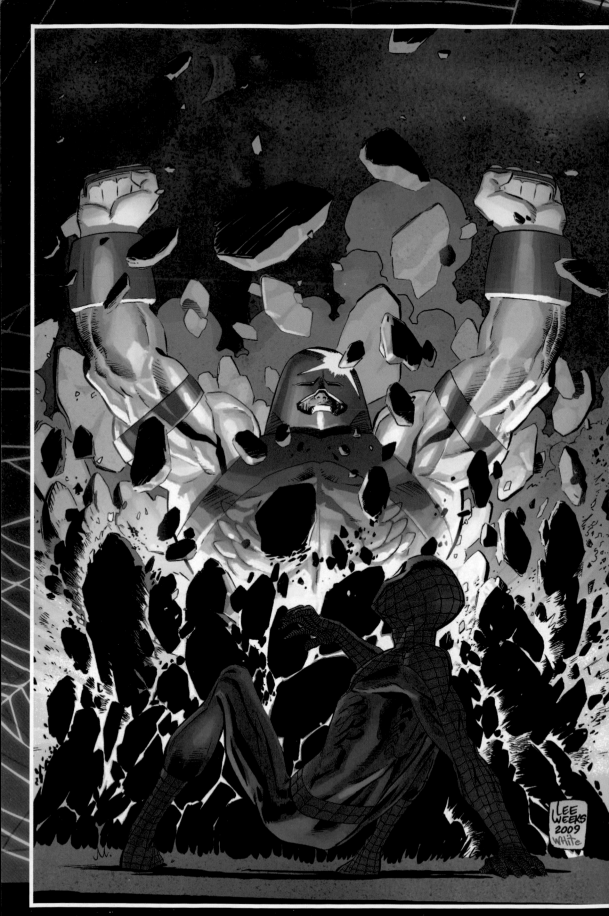

AMAZING SPIDER-MAN #629
COVER BY LEE WEEKS & DEAN WHITE

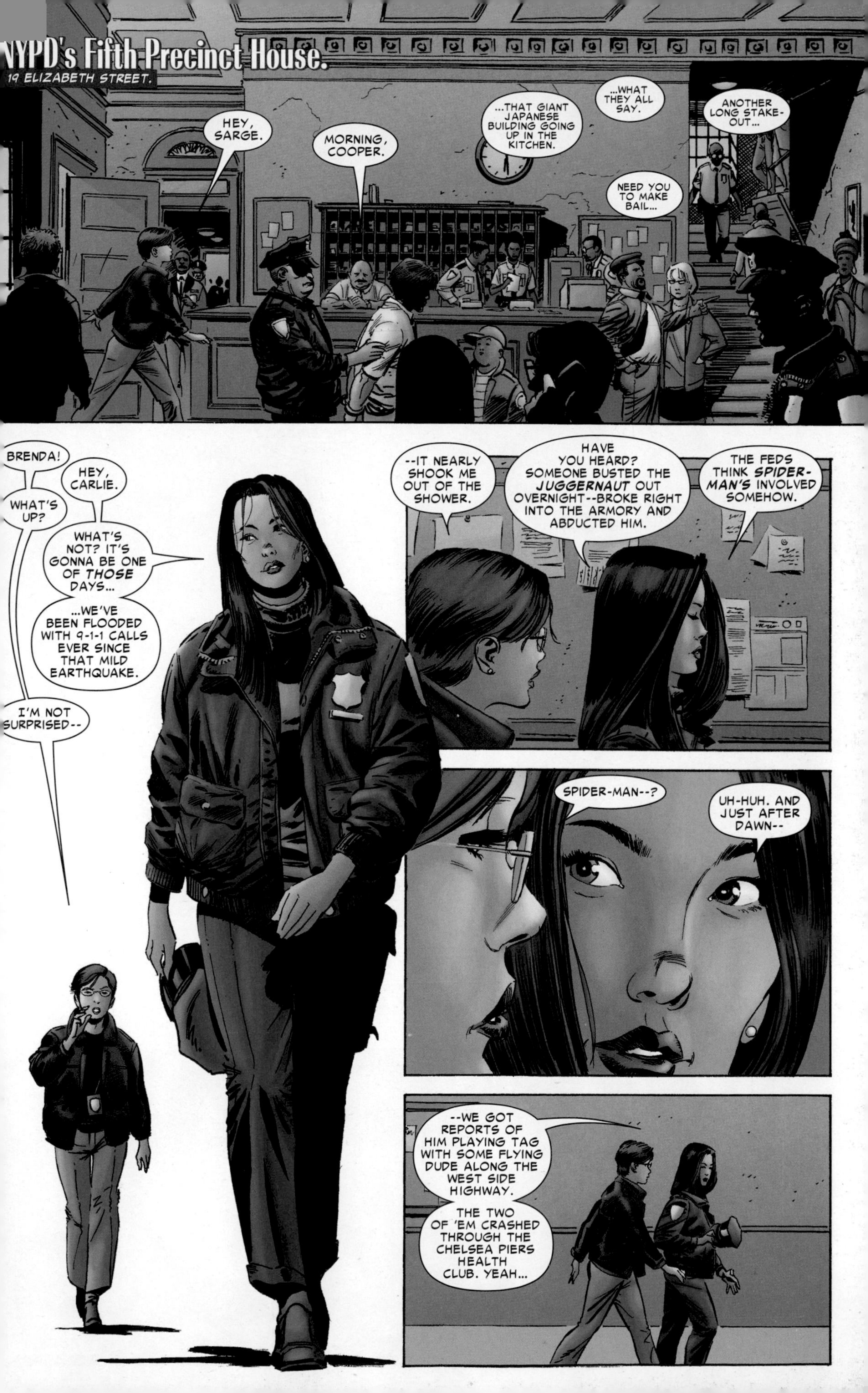

NYPD's Fifth Precinct House.
19 ELIZABETH STREET.
HEY, SARGE.
MORNING, COOPER.
...THAT GIANT JAPANESE BUILDING GOING UP IN THE KITCHEN.
...WHAT THEY ALL SAY.
NEED YOU TO MAKE BAIL...
ANOTHER LONG STAKE-OUT...
BRENDA!
HEY, CARLIE.
WHAT'S UP?
WHAT'S NOT? IT'S GONNA BE ONE OF THOSE DAYS...
...WE'VE BEEN FLOODED WITH 9-1-1 CALLS EVER SINCE THAT MILD EARTHQUAKE.
I'M NOT SURPRISED--
--IT NEARLY SHOOK ME OUT OF THE SHOWER.
HAVE YOU HEARD? SOMEONE BUSTED THE JUGGERNAUT OUT OVERNIGHT--BROKE RIGHT INTO THE ARMORY AND ABDUCTED HIM.
THE FEDS THINK SPIDER-MAN'S INVOLVED SOMEHOW.
SPIDER-MAN--?
UH-HUH. AND JUST AFTER DAWN--
--WE GOT REPORTS OF HIM PLAYING TAG WITH SOME FLYING DUDE ALONG THE WEST SIDE HIGHWAY.
THE TWO OF 'EM CRASHED THROUGH THE CHELSEA PIERS HEALTH CLUB. YEAH...

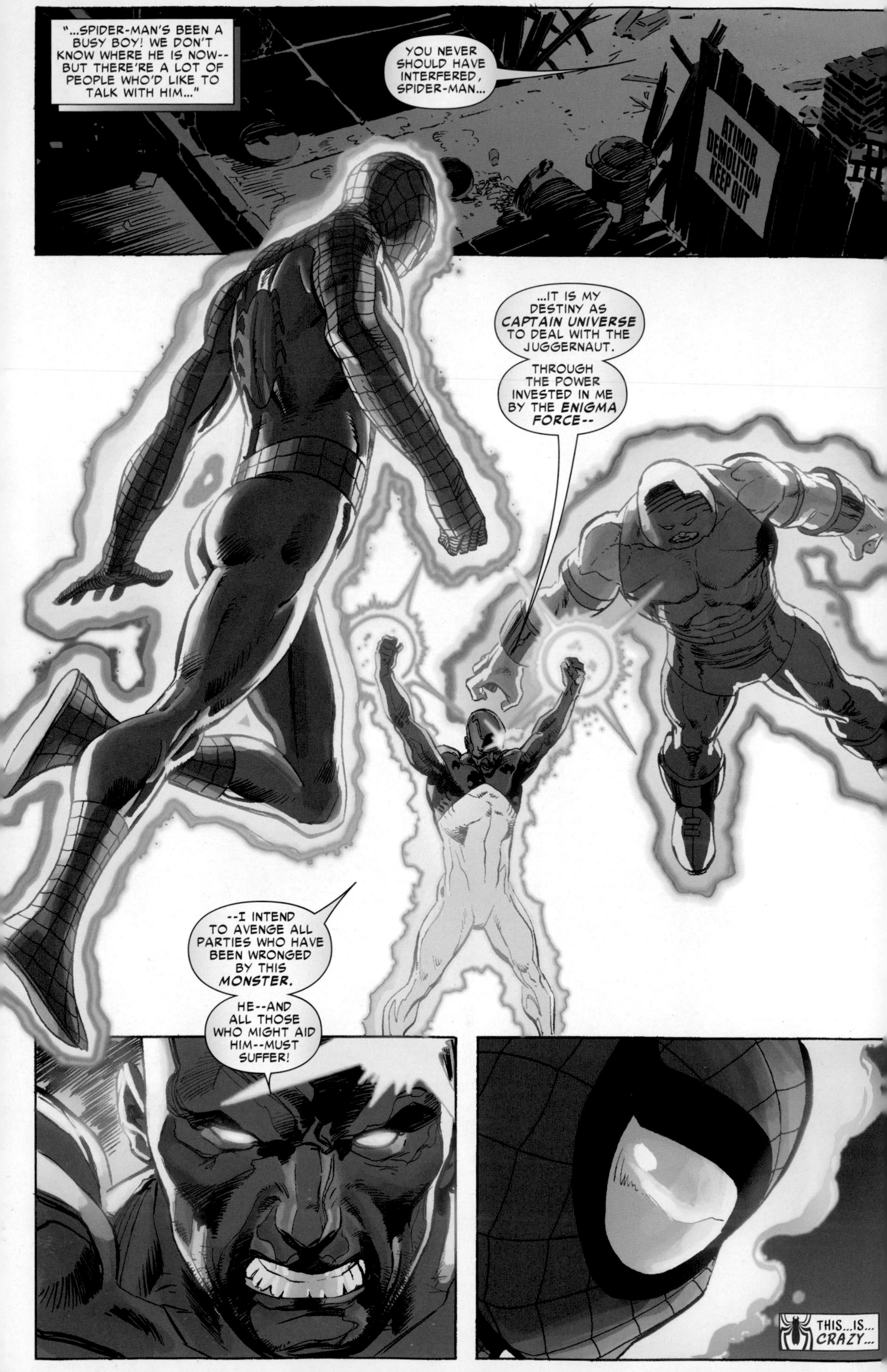
"...SPIDER-MAN'S BEEN A BUSY BOY! WE DON'T KNOW WHERE HE IS NOW--BUT THERE'RE A LOT OF PEOPLE WHO'D LIKE TO TALK WITH HIM..."
YOU NEVER SHOULD HAVE INTERFERED, SPIDER-MAN...
ATIMOR DEMOLITION KEEP OUT
...IT IS MY DESTINY AS CAPTAIN UNIVERSE TO DEAL WITH THE JUGGERNAUT.
THROUGH THE POWER INVESTED IN ME BY THE ENIGMA FORCE--
--I INTEND TO AVENGE ALL PARTIES WHO HAVE BEEN WRONGED BY THIS MONSTER.
HE--AND ALL THOSE WHO MIGHT AID HIM--MUST SUFFER!
THIS...IS... CRAZY...

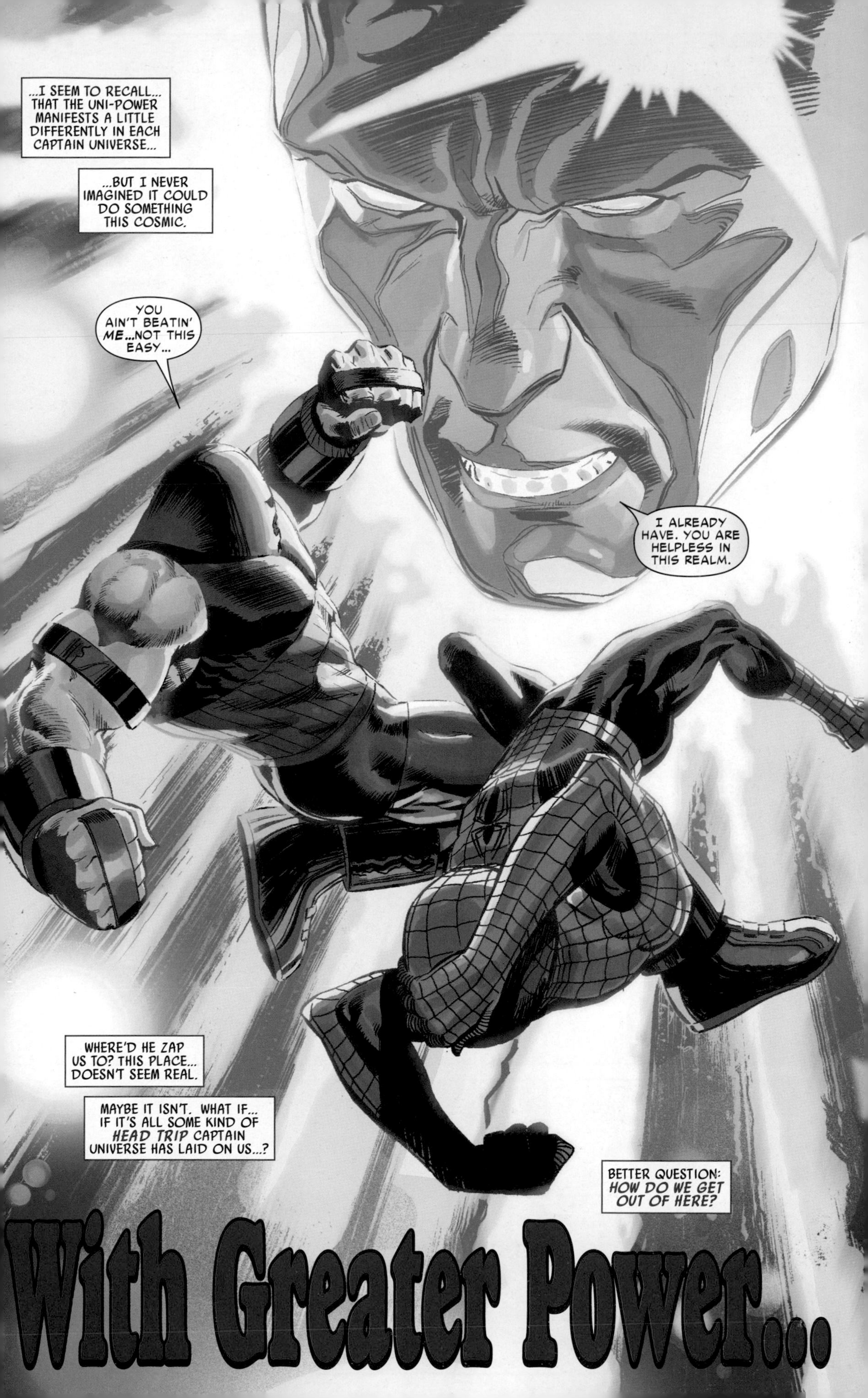
...I SEEM TO RECALL... THAT THE UNI-POWER MANIFESTS A LITTLE DIFFERENTLY IN EACH CAPTAIN UNIVERSE...
...BUT I NEVER IMAGINED IT COULD DO SOMETHING THIS COSMIC.
YOU AIN'T BEATIN' ME...NOT THIS EASY...
I ALREADY HAVE. YOU ARE HELPLESS IN THIS REALM.
WHERE'D HE ZAP US TO? THIS PLACE... DOESN'T SEEM REAL.
MAYBE IT ISN'T. WHAT IF... IF IT'S ALL SOME KIND OF HEAD TRIP CAPTAIN UNIVERSE HAS LAID ON US...?
BETTER QUESTION: HOW DO WE GET OUT OF HERE?
With Greater Power...

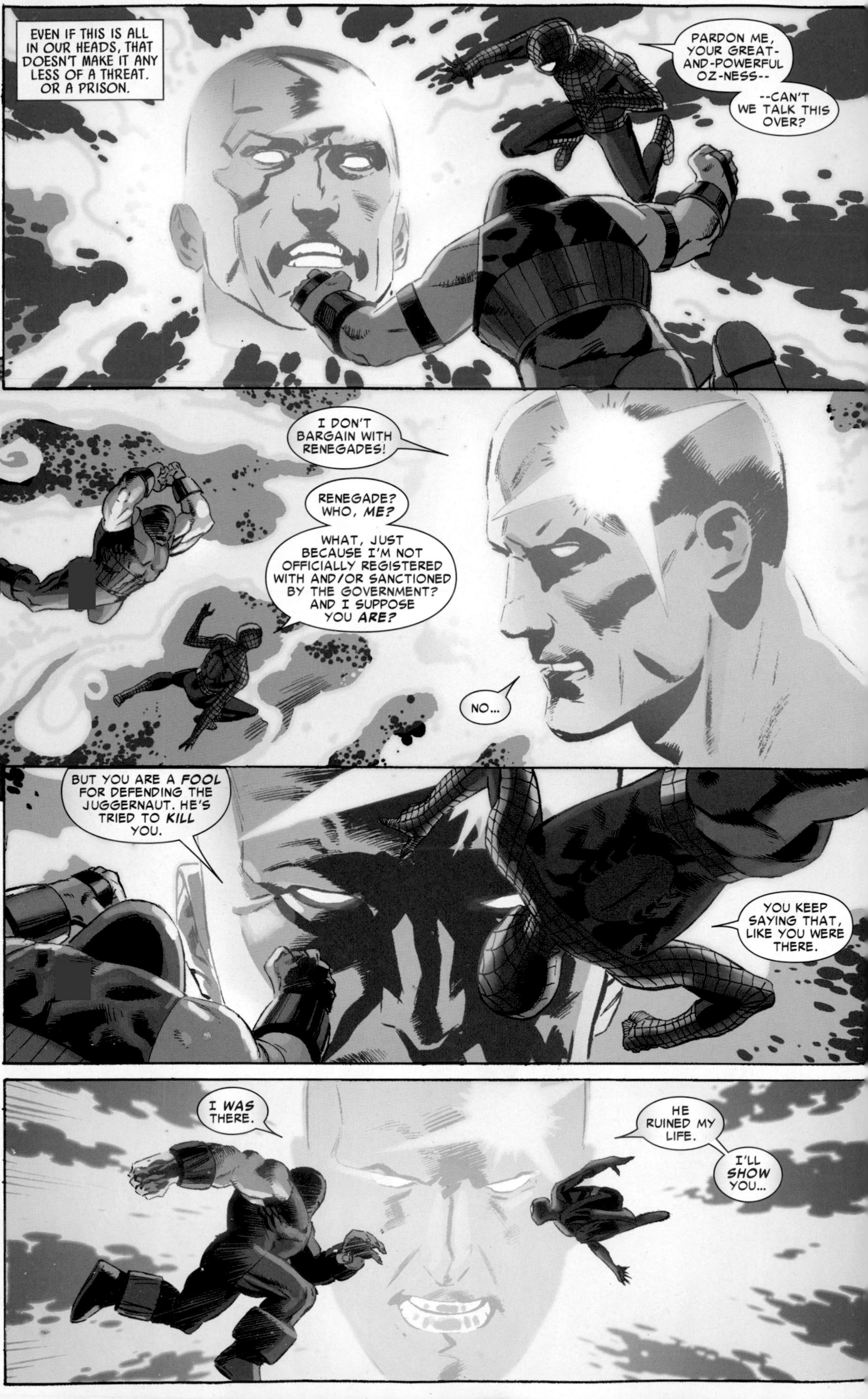
EVEN IF THIS IS ALL IN OUR HEADS, THAT DOESN'T MAKE IT ANY LESS OF A THREAT. OR A PRISON.
PARDON ME, YOUR GREAT-AND-POWERFUL OZ-NESS--
--CAN'T WE TALK THIS OVER?
I DON'T BARGAIN WITH RENEGADES!
RENEGADE? WHO, ME?
WHAT, JUST BECAUSE I'M NOT OFFICIALLY REGISTERED WITH AND/OR SANCTIONED BY THE GOVERNMENT? AND I SUPPOSE YOU ARE?
NO...
BUT YOU ARE A FOOL FOR DEFENDING THE JUGGERNAUT. HE'S TRIED TO KILL YOU.
YOU KEEP SAYING THAT, LIKE YOU WERE THERE.
I WAS THERE.
HE RUINED MY LIFE.
I'LL SHOW YOU...

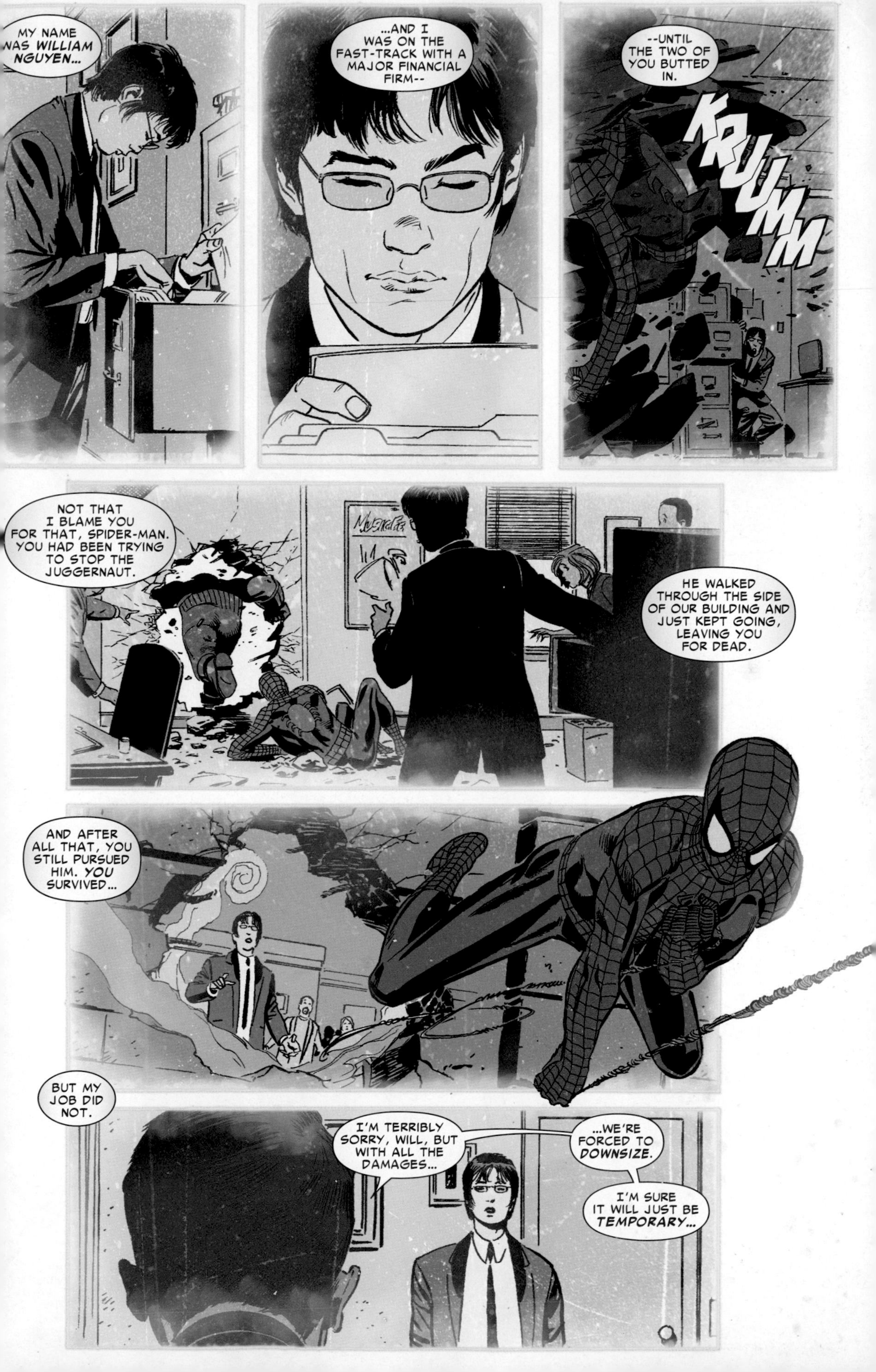
MY NAME WAS WILLIAM NGUYEN...
...AND I WAS ON THE FAST-TRACK WITH A MAJOR FINANCIAL FIRM--
--UNTIL THE TWO OF YOU BUTTED IN.
KRUMM
NOT THAT I BLAME YOU FOR THAT, SPIDER-MAN. YOU HAD BEEN TRYING TO STOP THE JUGGERNAUT.
HE WALKED THROUGH THE SIDE OF OUR BUILDING AND JUST KEPT GOING, LEAVING YOU FOR DEAD.
AND AFTER ALL THAT, YOU STILL PURSUED HIM. YOU SURVIVED...
BUT MY JOB DID NOT.
I'M TERRIBLY SORRY, WILL, BUT WITH ALL THE DAMAGES...
...WE'RE FORCED TO DOWNSIZE.
I'M SURE IT WILL JUST BE TEMPORARY...

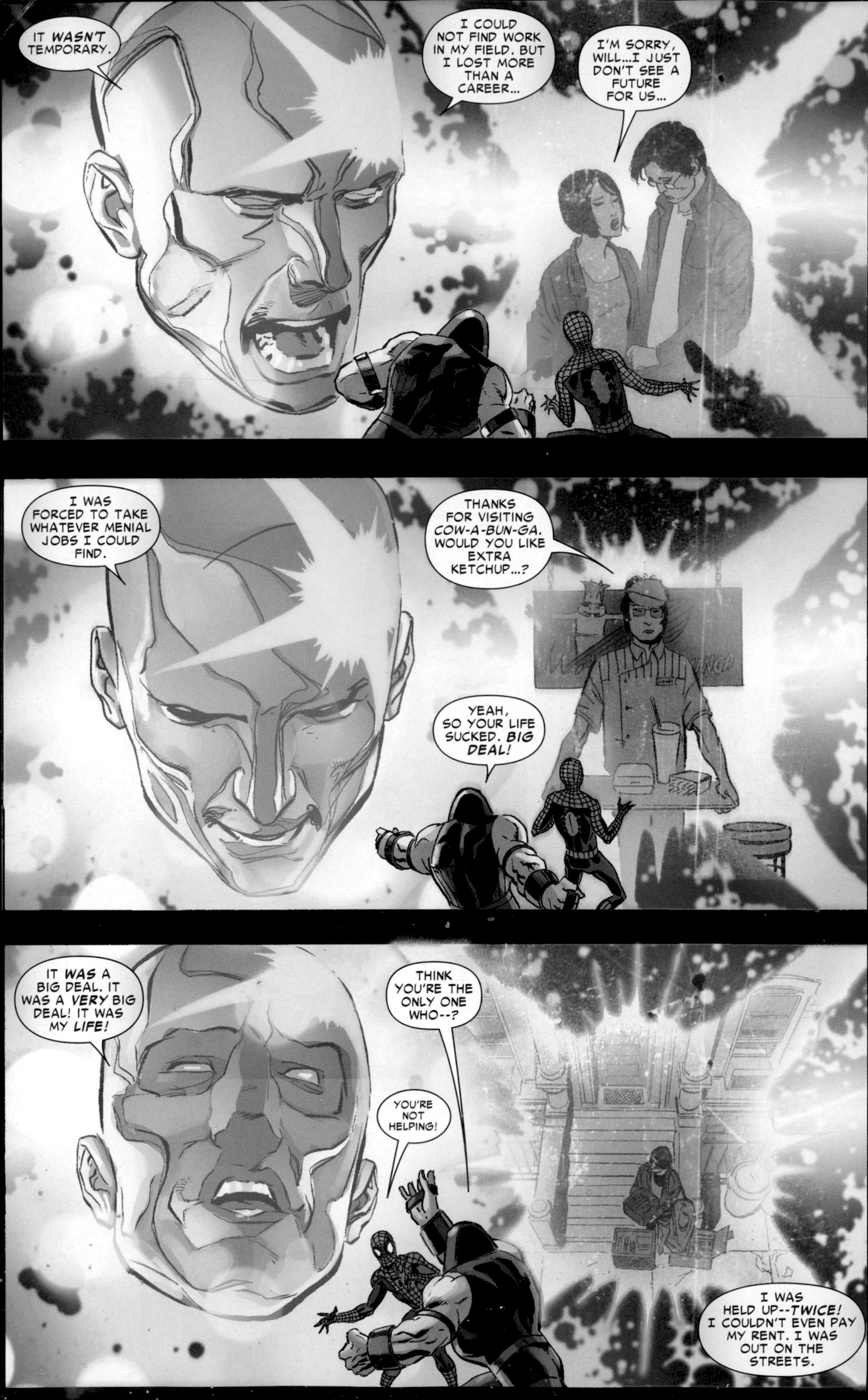
IT WASN'T TEMPORARY.
I COULD NOT FIND WORK IN MY FIELD. BUT I LOST MORE THAN A CAREER...
I'M SORRY, WILL...I JUST DON'T SEE A FUTURE FOR US...
I WAS FORCED TO TAKE WHATEVER MENIAL JOBS I COULD FIND.
THANKS FOR VISITING COW-A-BUN-GA. WOULD YOU LIKE EXTRA KETCHUP...?
YEAH, SO YOUR LIFE SUCKED. BIG DEAL!
IT WAS A BIG DEAL. IT WAS A VERY BIG DEAL! IT WAS MY LIFE!
THINK YOU'RE THE ONLY ONE WHO--?
YOU'RE NOT HELPING!
I WAS HELD UP--TWICE! I COULDN'T EVEN PAY MY RENT. I WAS OUT ON THE STREETS.

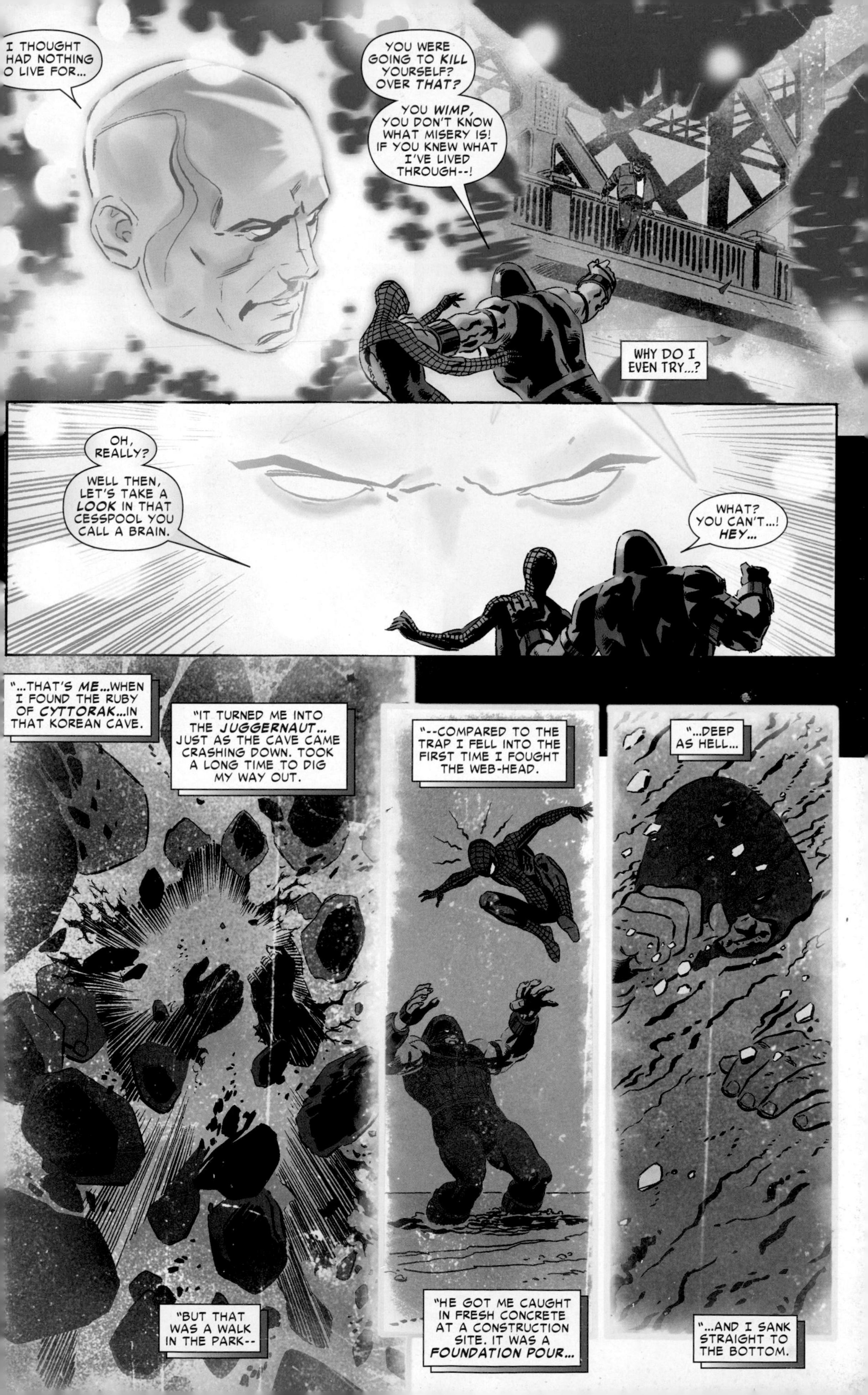
I THOUGHT
HAD NOTHING
O LIVE FOR...
YOU WERE GOING TO KILL YOURSELF? OVER THAT?
YOU WIMP, YOU DON'T KNOW WHAT MISERY IS! IF YOU KNEW WHAT I'VE LIVED THROUGH--!
WHY DO I EVEN TRY...?
OH, REALLY?
WELL THEN, LET'S TAKE A LOOK IN THAT CESSPOOL YOU CALL A BRAIN.
WHAT? YOU CAN'T...! HEY...
"...THAT'S ME...WHEN I FOUND THE RUBY OF CYTTORAK...IN THAT KOREAN CAVE.
"IT TURNED ME INTO THE JUGGERNAUT... JUST AS THE CAVE CAME CRASHING DOWN. TOOK A LONG TIME TO DIG MY WAY OUT.
"BUT THAT WAS A WALK IN THE PARK--
"--COMPARED TO THE TRAP I FELL INTO THE FIRST TIME I FOUGHT THE WEB-HEAD.
"HE GOT ME CAUGHT IN FRESH CONCRETE AT A CONSTRUCTION SITE. IT WAS A FOUNDATION POUR...
"...DEEP AS HELL...
"...AND I SANK STRAIGHT TO THE BOTTOM.

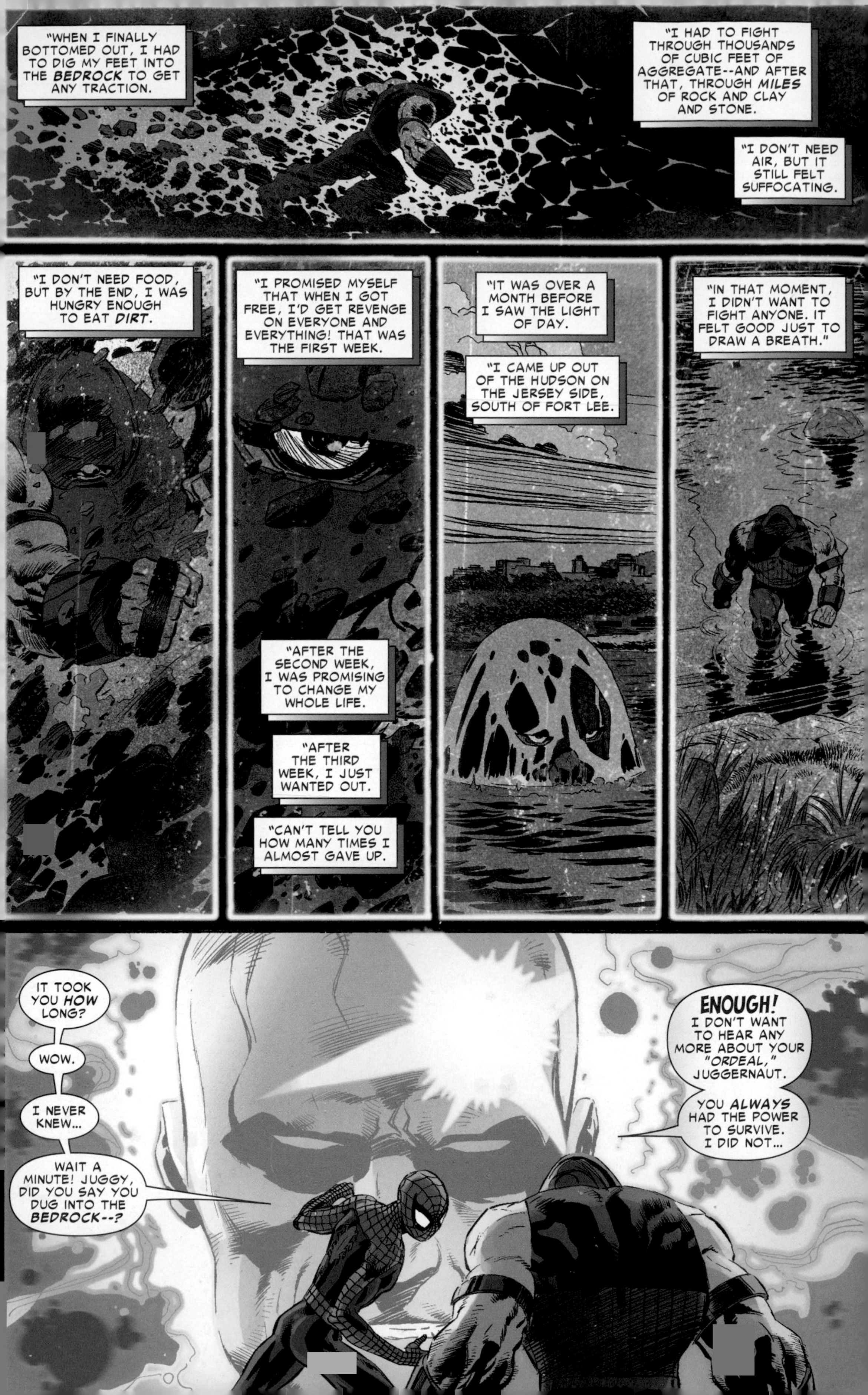

"WHEN I FINALLY BOTTOMED OUT, I HAD TO DIG MY FEET INTO THE BEDROCK TO GET ANY TRACTION.
"I HAD TO FIGHT THROUGH THOUSANDS OF CUBIC FEET OF AGGREGATE--AND AFTER THAT, THROUGH MILES OF ROCK AND CLAY AND STONE.
"I DON'T NEED AIR, BUT IT STILL FELT SUFFOCATING.
"I DON'T NEED FOOD, BUT BY THE END, I WAS HUNGRY ENOUGH TO EAT DIRT.
"I PROMISED MYSELF THAT WHEN I GOT FREE, I'D GET REVENGE ON EVERYONE AND EVERYTHING! THAT WAS THE FIRST WEEK.
"AFTER THE SECOND WEEK, I WAS PROMISING TO CHANGE MY WHOLE LIFE.
"AFTER THE THIRD WEEK, I JUST WANTED OUT.
"CAN'T TELL YOU HOW MANY TIMES I ALMOST GAVE UP.
"IT WAS OVER A MONTH BEFORE I SAW THE LIGHT OF DAY.
"I CAME UP OUT OF THE HUDSON ON THE JERSEY SIDE, SOUTH OF FORT LEE.
"IN THAT MOMENT, I DIDN'T WANT TO FIGHT ANYONE. IT FELT GOOD JUST TO DRAW A BREATH."
IT TOOK YOU HOW LONG?
WOW.
I NEVER KNEW...
WAIT A MINUTE! JUGGY, DID YOU SAY YOU DUG INTO THE BEDROCK--?
ENOUGH! I DON'T WANT TO HEAR ANY MORE ABOUT YOUR "ORDEAL," JUGGERNAUT.
YOU ALWAYS HAD THE POWER TO SURVIVE. I DID NOT...

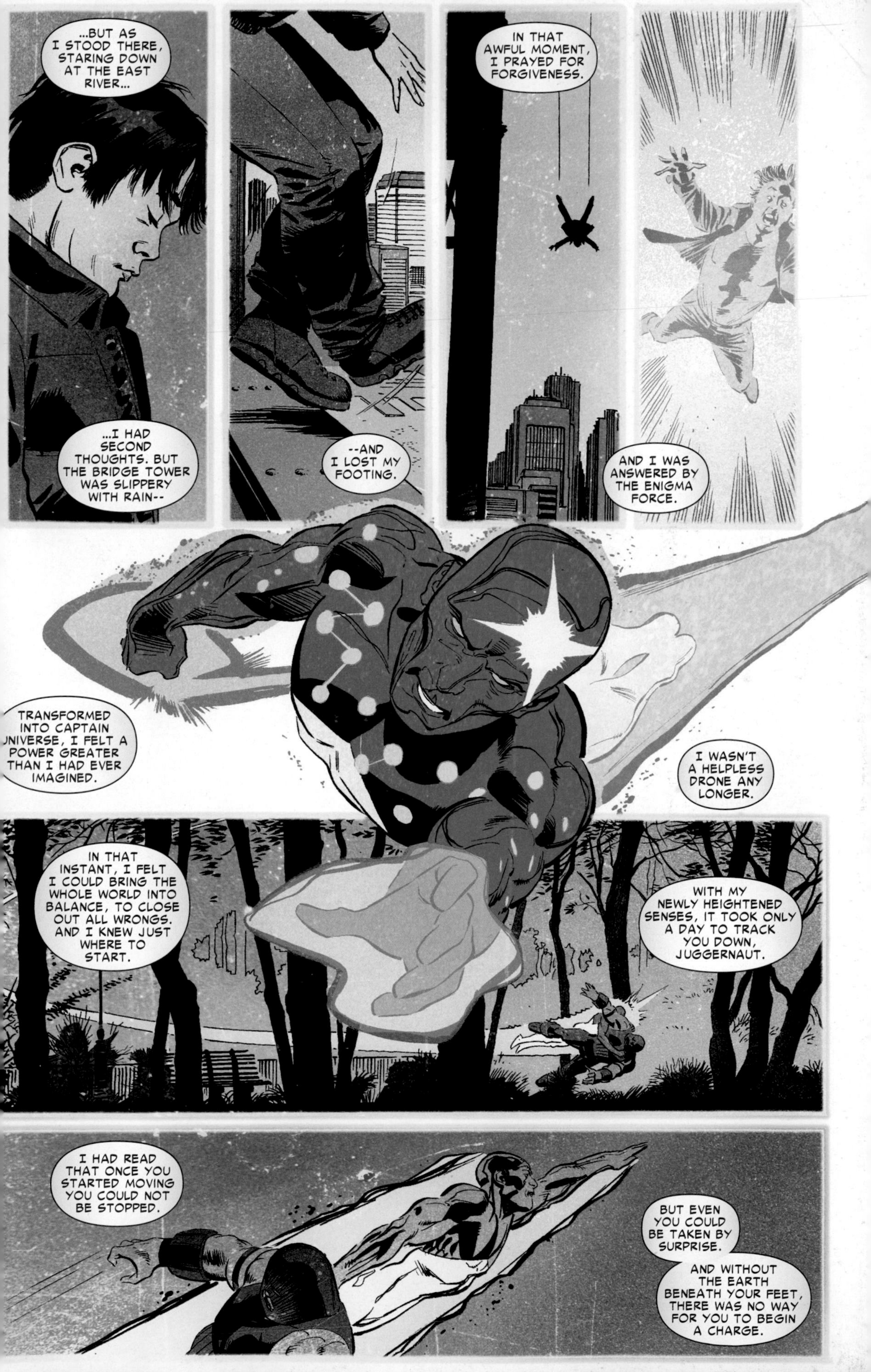
...BUT AS I STOOD THERE, STARING DOWN AT THE EAST RIVER...
...I HAD SECOND THOUGHTS. BUT THE BRIDGE TOWER WAS SLIPPERY WITH RAIN--
--AND I LOST MY FOOTING.
IN THAT AWFUL MOMENT, I PRAYED FOR FORGIVENESS.
AND I WAS ANSWERED BY THE ENIGMA FORCE.
TRANSFORMED INTO CAPTAIN UNIVERSE, I FELT A POWER GREATER THAN I HAD EVER IMAGINED.
I WASN'T A HELPLESS DRONE ANY LONGER.
IN THAT INSTANT, I FELT I COULD BRING THE WHOLE WORLD INTO BALANCE, TO CLOSE OUT ALL WRONGS. AND I KNEW JUST WHERE TO START.
WITH MY NEWLY HEIGHTENED SENSES, IT TOOK ONLY A DAY TO TRACK YOU DOWN, JUGGERNAUT.
I HAD READ THAT ONCE YOU STARTED MOVING YOU COULD NOT BE STOPPED.
BUT EVEN YOU COULD BE TAKEN BY SURPRISE.
AND WITHOUT THE EARTH BENEATH YOUR FEET, THERE WAS NO WAY FOR YOU TO BEGIN A CHARGE.

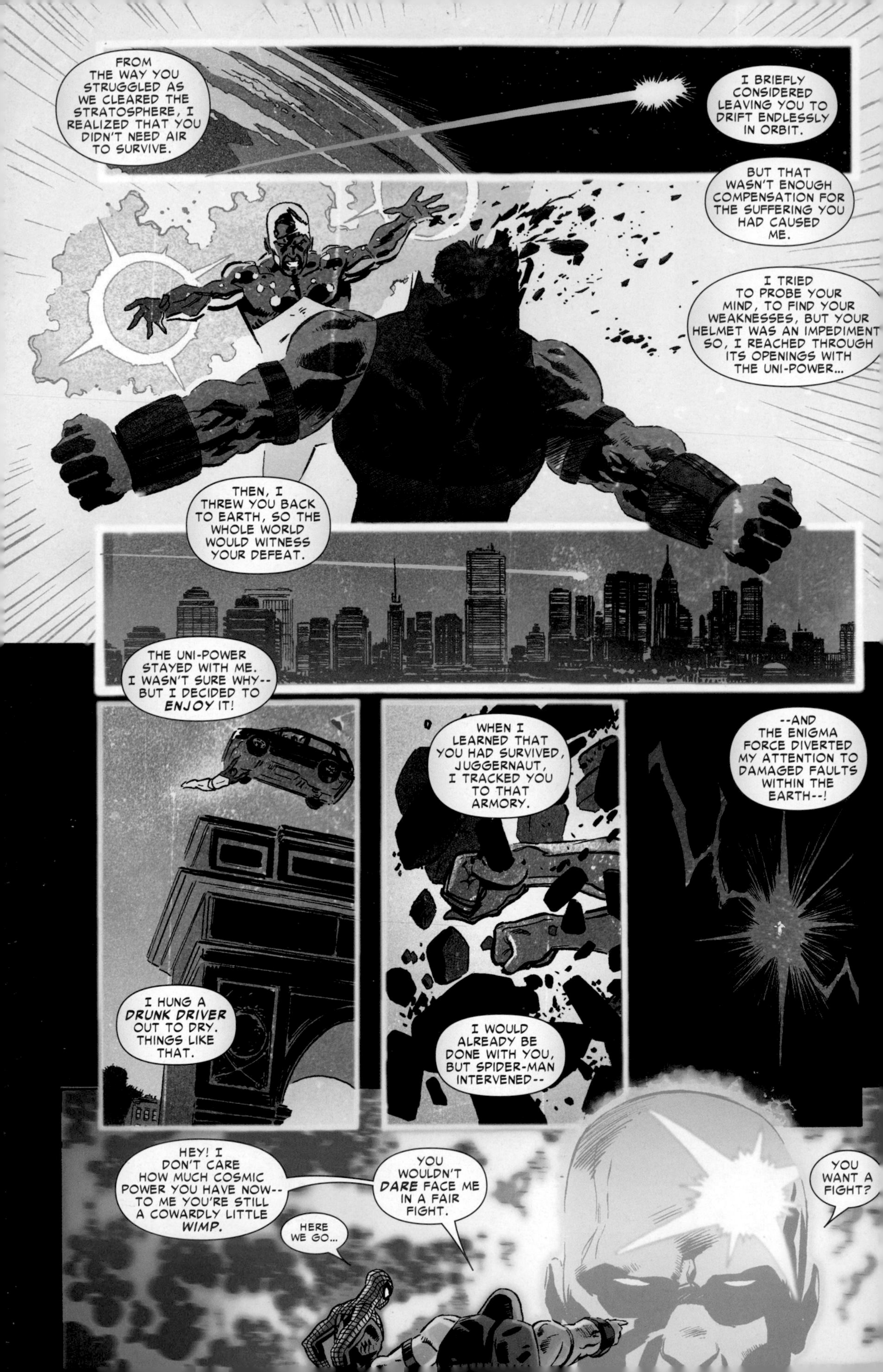
FROM THE WAY YOU STRUGGLED AS WE CLEARED THE STRATOSPHERE, I REALIZED THAT YOU DIDN'T NEED AIR TO SURVIVE.
I BRIEFLY CONSIDERED LEAVING YOU TO DRIFT ENDLESSLY IN ORBIT.
BUT THAT WASN'T ENOUGH COMPENSATION FOR THE SUFFERING YOU HAD CAUSED ME.
I TRIED TO PROBE YOUR MIND, TO FIND YOUR WEAKNESSES, BUT YOUR HELMET WAS AN IMPEDIMENT SO, I REACHED THROUGH ITS OPENINGS WITH THE UNI-POWER...
THEN, I THREW YOU BACK TO EARTH, SO THE WHOLE WORLD WOULD WITNESS YOUR DEFEAT.
THE UNI-POWER STAYED WITH ME. I WASN'T SURE WHY-- BUT I DECIDED TO *ENJOY* IT!
I HUNG A ***DRUNK DRIVER*** OUT TO DRY. THINGS LIKE THAT.
WHEN I LEARNED THAT YOU HAD SURVIVED, JUGGERNAUT, I TRACKED YOU TO THAT ARMORY.
I WOULD ALREADY BE DONE WITH YOU, BUT SPIDER-MAN INTERVENED--
--AND THE ENIGMA FORCE DIVERTED MY ATTENTION TO DAMAGED FAULTS WITHIN THE EARTH--!
HEY! I DON'T CARE HOW MUCH COSMIC POWER YOU HAVE NOW-- TO ME YOU'RE STILL A COWARDLY LITTLE ***WIMP.***
HERE WE GO...
YOU WOULDN'T ***DARE*** FACE ME IN A FAIR FIGHT.
YOU WANT A FIGHT?

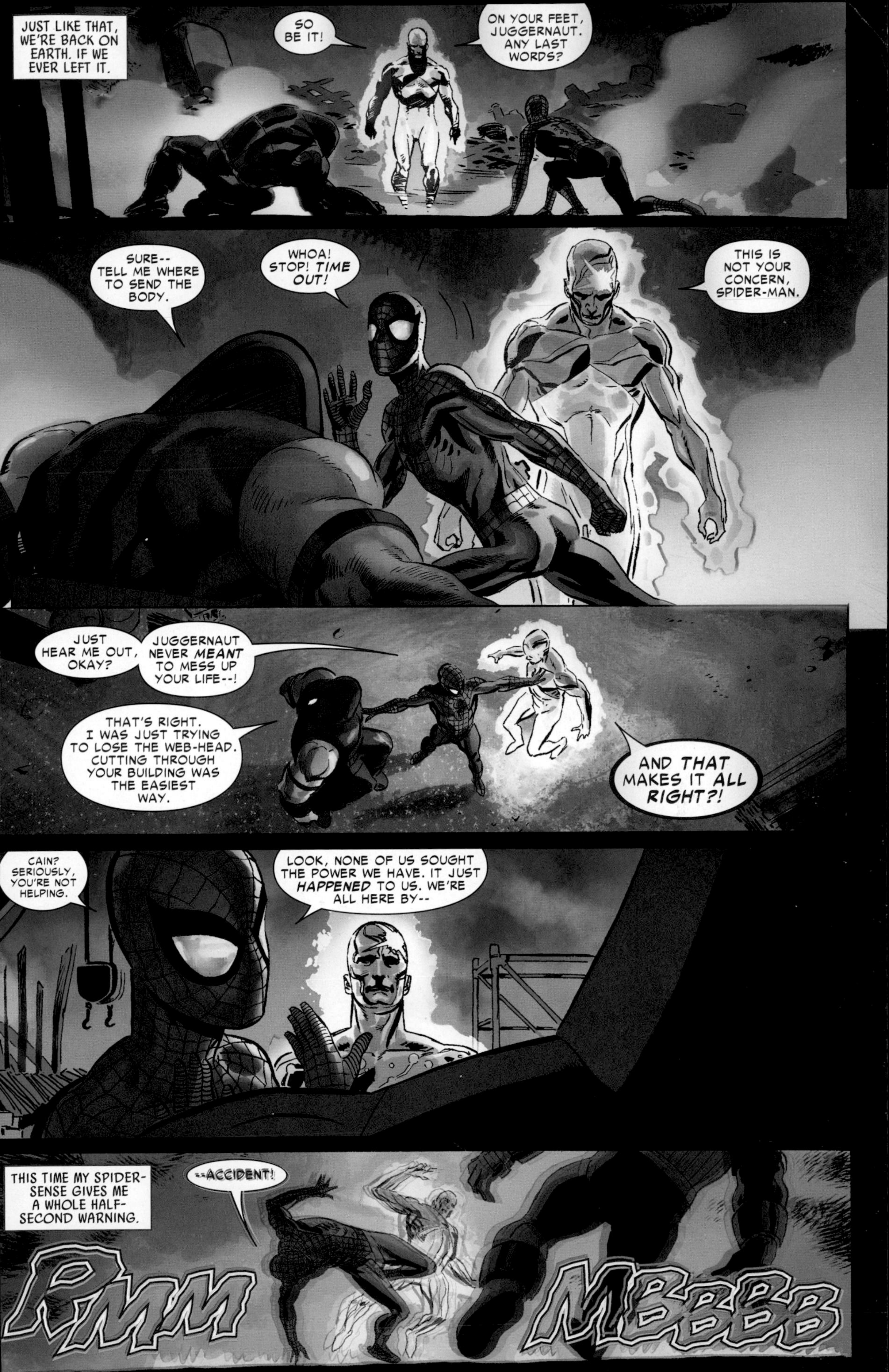
JUST LIKE THAT, WE'RE BACK ON EARTH. IF WE EVER LEFT IT.
SO BE IT!
ON YOUR FEET, JUGGERNAUT. ANY LAST WORDS?
SURE-- TELL ME WHERE TO SEND THE BODY.
WHOA! STOP! TIME OUT!
THIS IS NOT YOUR CONCERN, SPIDER-MAN.
JUST HEAR ME OUT, OKAY?
JUGGERNAUT NEVER MEANT TO MESS UP YOUR LIFE--!
THAT'S RIGHT. I WAS JUST TRYING TO LOSE THE WEB-HEAD. CUTTING THROUGH YOUR BUILDING WAS THE EASIEST WAY.
AND THAT MAKES IT ALL RIGHT?!
CAIN? SERIOUSLY, YOU'RE NOT HELPING.
LOOK, NONE OF US SOUGHT THE POWER WE HAVE. IT JUST HAPPENED TO US. WE'RE ALL HERE BY--
THIS TIME MY SPIDER-SENSE GIVES ME A WHOLE HALF-SECOND WARNING.
--ACCIDENT!

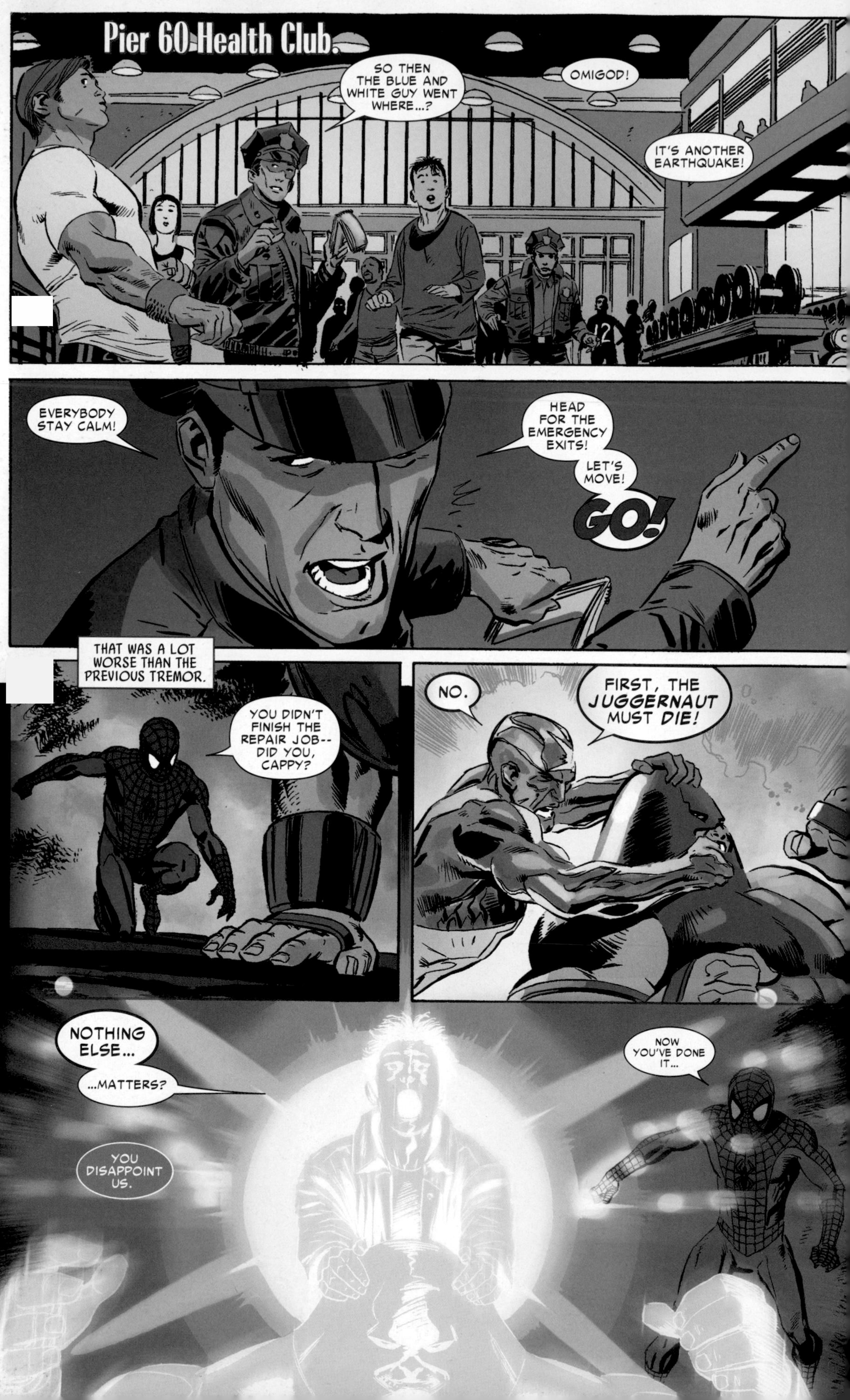
Pier 60 Health Club.
SO THEN THE BLUE AND WHITE GUY WENT WHERE...?
OMIGOD!
IT'S ANOTHER EARTHQUAKE!
EVERYBODY STAY CALM!
HEAD FOR THE EMERGENCY EXITS!
LET'S MOVE!
GO!
THAT WAS A LOT WORSE THAN THE PREVIOUS TREMOR.
YOU DIDN'T FINISH THE REPAIR JOB-- DID YOU, CAPPY?
NO.
FIRST, THE JUGGERNAUT MUST DIE!
NOTHING ELSE...
...MATTERS?
YOU DISAPPOINT US.
NOW YOU'VE DONE IT...

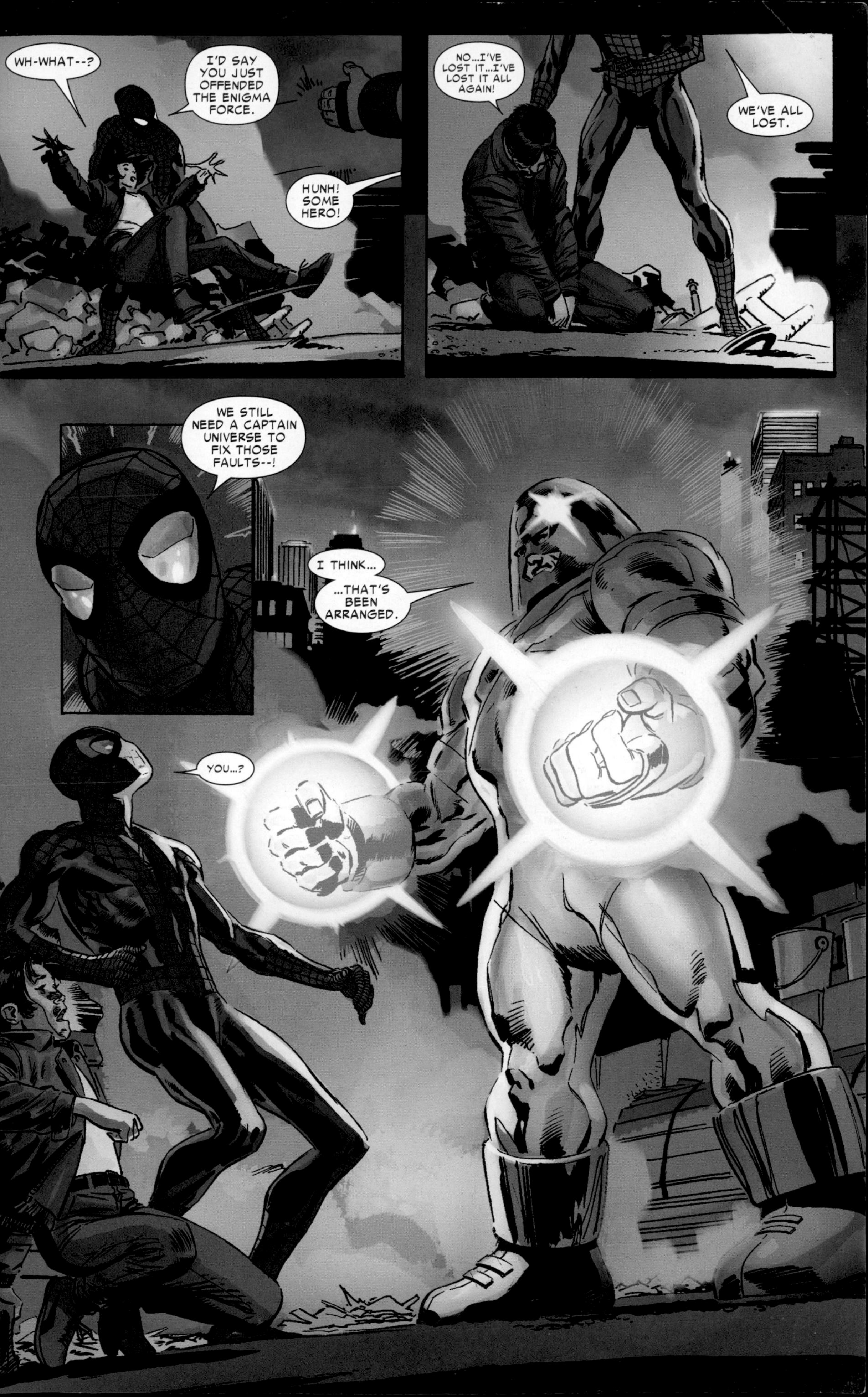
WH-WHAT--?
I'D SAY YOU JUST OFFENDED THE ENIGMA FORCE.
HUNH! SOME HERO!
NO...I'VE LOST IT...I'VE LOST IT ALL AGAIN!
WE'VE ALL LOST.
WE STILL NEED A CAPTAIN UNIVERSE TO FIX THOSE FAULTS--!
I THINK...
...THAT'S BEEN ARRANGED.
YOU...?

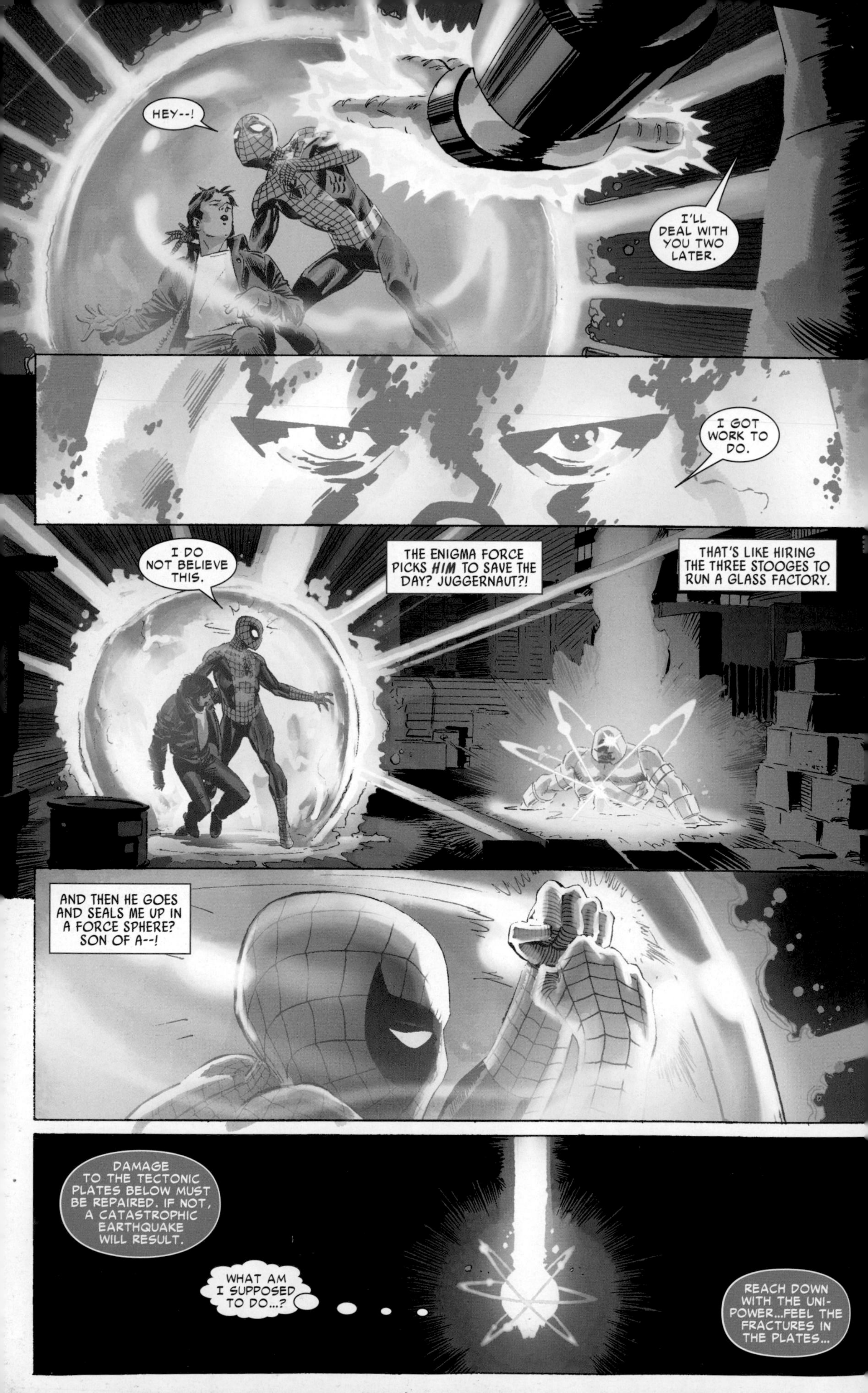
HEY--!
I'LL DEAL WITH YOU TWO LATER.
I GOT WORK TO DO.
I DO NOT BELIEVE THIS.
THE ENIGMA FORCE PICKS HIM TO SAVE THE DAY? JUGGERNAUT?!
THAT'S LIKE HIRING THE THREE STOOGES TO RUN A GLASS FACTORY.
AND THEN HE GOES AND SEALS ME UP IN A FORCE SPHERE? SON OF A--!
DAMAGE TO THE TECTONIC PLATES BELOW MUST BE REPAIRED. IF NOT, A CATASTROPHIC EARTHQUAKE WILL RESULT.
WHAT AM I SUPPOSED TO DO...?
REACH DOWN WITH THE UNI-POWER...FEEL THE FRACTURES IN THE PLATES...

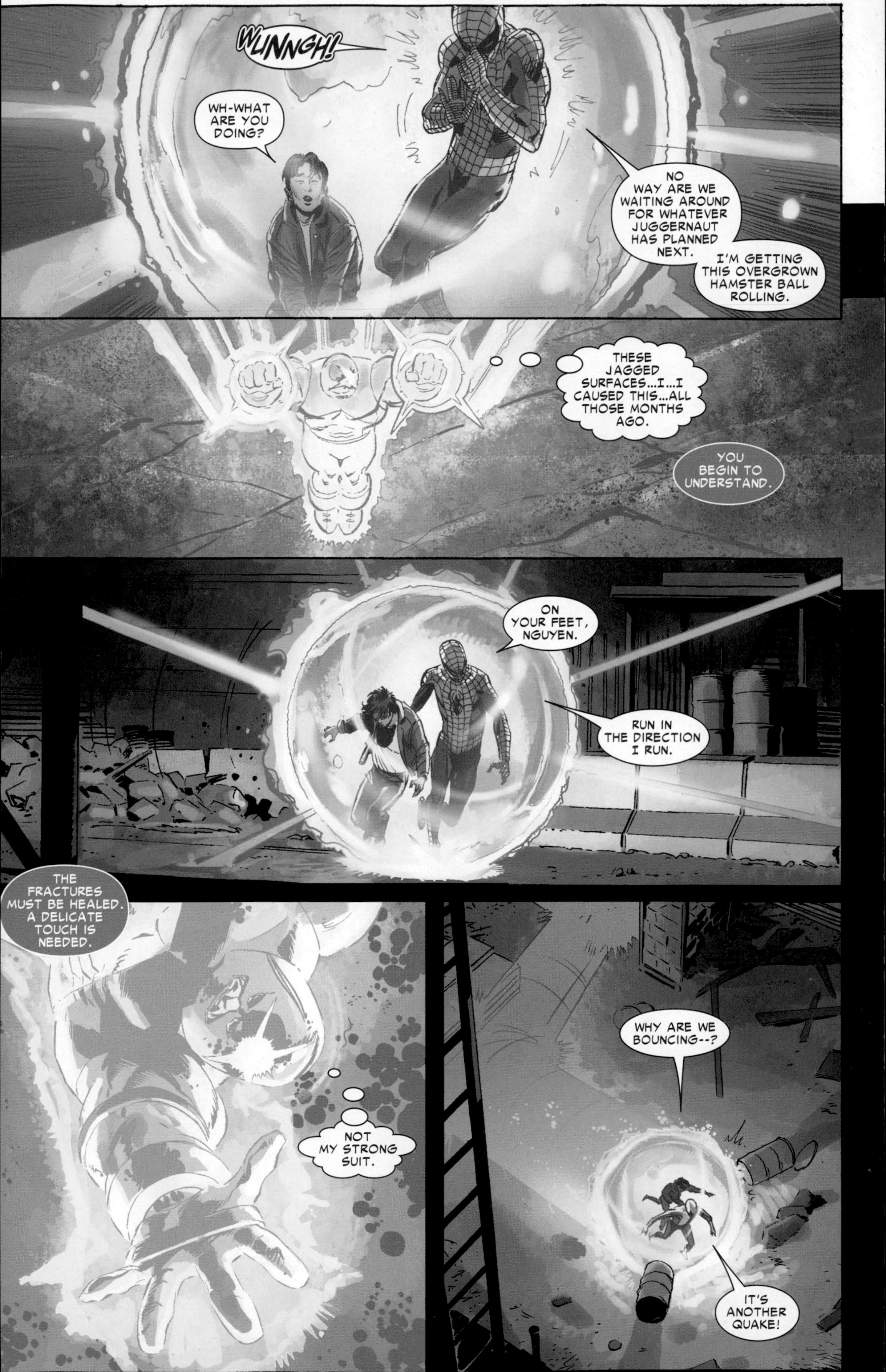

WUNNGH!
WH-WHAT ARE YOU DOING?
NO WAY ARE WE WAITING AROUND FOR WHATEVER JUGGERNAUT HAS PLANNED NEXT.
I'M GETTING THIS OVERGROWN HAMSTER BALL ROLLING.
THESE JAGGED SURFACES...I...I CAUSED THIS...ALL THOSE MONTHS AGO.
YOU BEGIN TO UNDERSTAND.
ON YOUR FEET, NGUYEN.
RUN IN THE DIRECTION I RUN.
THE FRACTURES MUST BE HEALED. A DELICATE TOUCH IS NEEDED.
NOT MY STRONG SUIT.
WHY ARE WE BOUNCING--?
IT'S ANOTHER QUAKE!

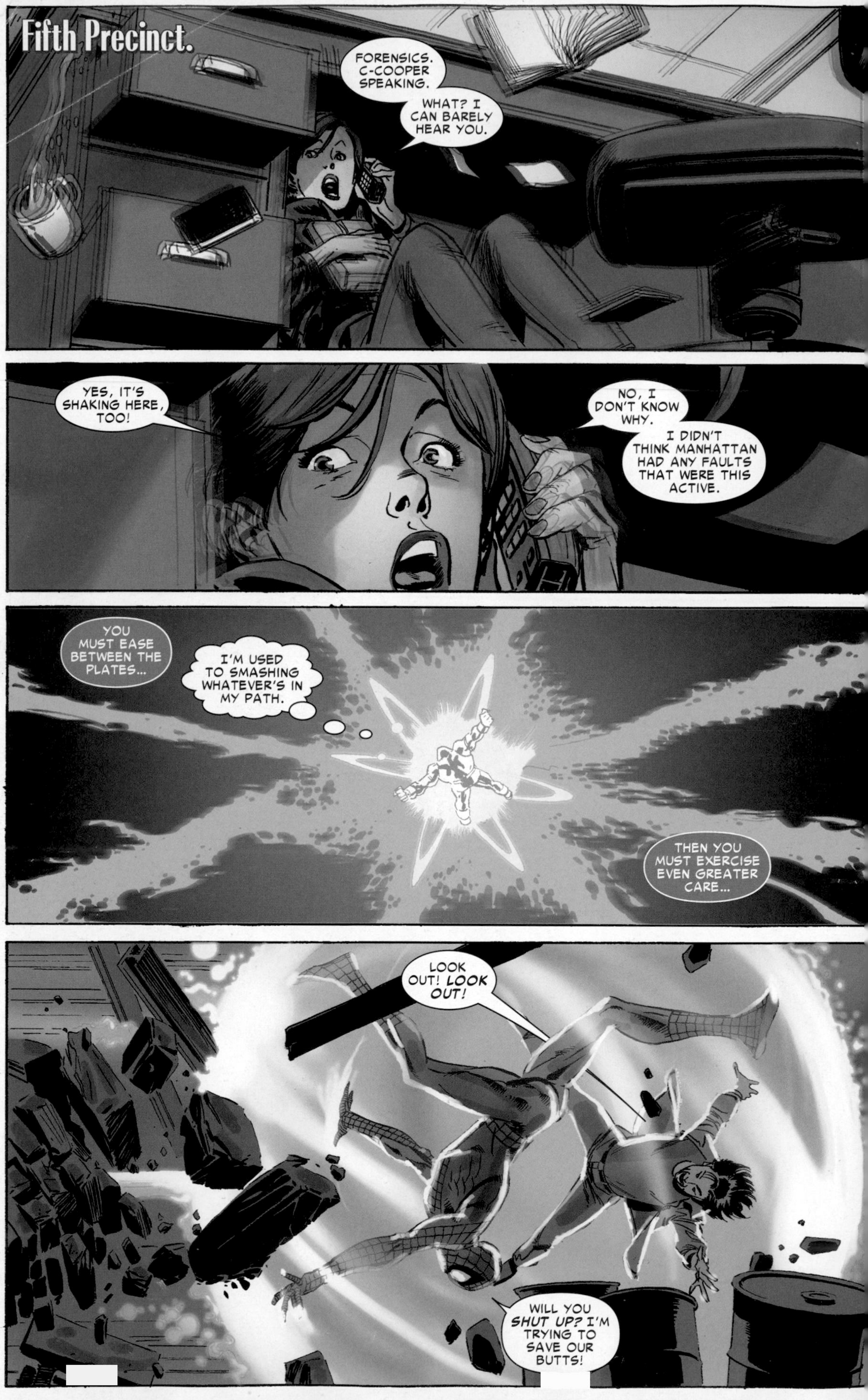
Fifth Precinct.
FORENSICS. C-COOPER SPEAKING.
WHAT? I CAN BARELY HEAR YOU.
YES, IT'S SHAKING HERE, TOO!
NO, I DON'T KNOW WHY.
I DIDN'T THINK MANHATTAN HAD ANY FAULTS THAT WERE THIS ACTIVE.
YOU MUST EASE BETWEEN THE PLATES...
I'M USED TO SMASHING WHATEVER'S IN MY PATH.
THEN YOU MUST EXERCISE EVEN GREATER CARE...
LOOK OUT! LOOK OUT!
WILL YOU SHUT UP? I'M TRYING TO SAVE OUR BUTTS!

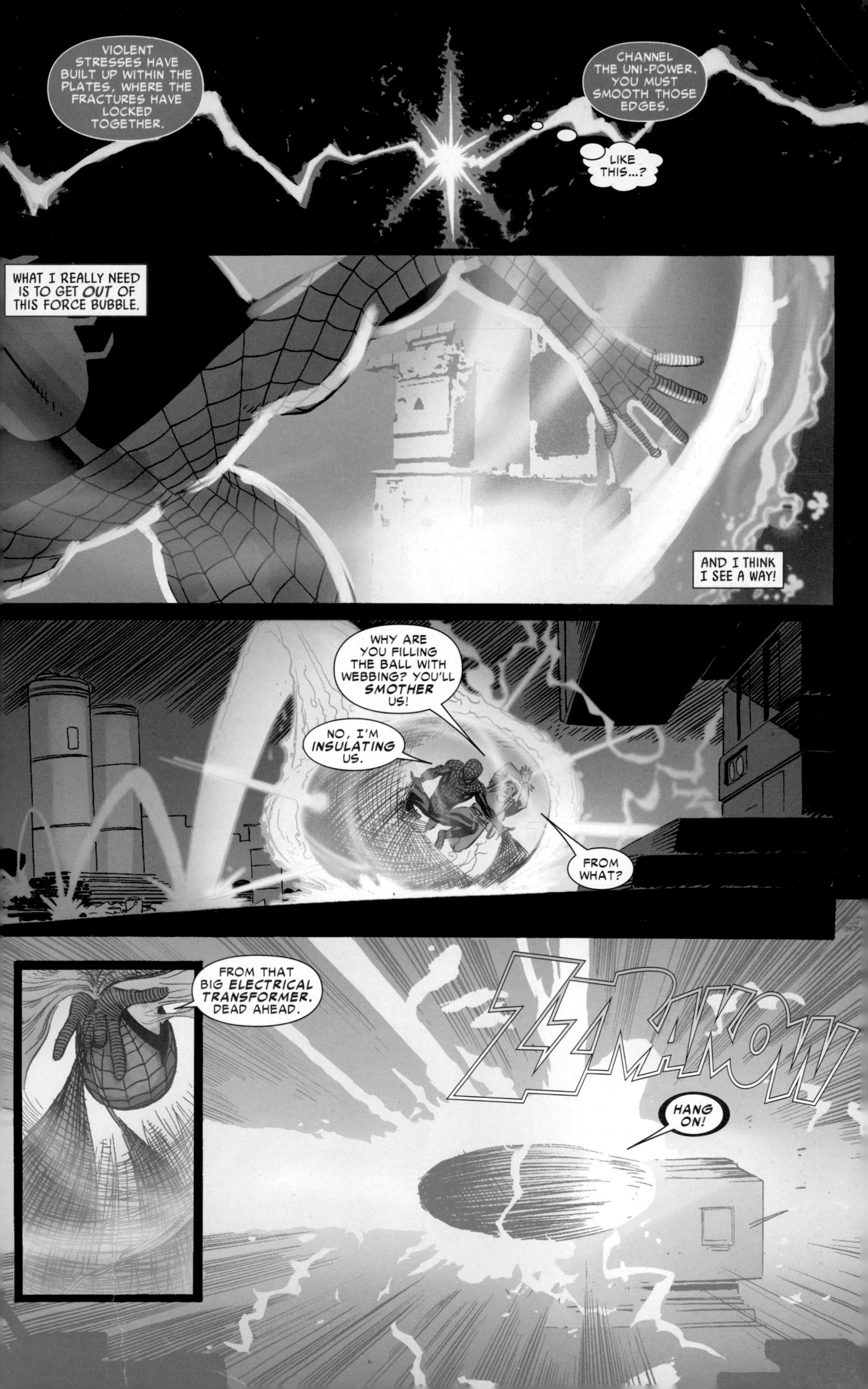
VIOLENT STRESSES HAVE BUILT UP WITHIN THE PLATES, WHERE THE FRACTURES HAVE LOCKED TOGETHER.
CHANNEL THE UNI-POWER. YOU MUST SMOOTH THOSE EDGES.
LIKE THIS...?
WHAT I REALLY NEED IS TO GET OUT OF THIS FORCE BUBBLE.
AND I THINK I SEE A WAY!
WHY ARE YOU FILLING THE BALL WITH WEBBING? YOU'LL SMOTHER US!
NO, I'M INSULATING US.
FROM WHAT?
FROM THAT BIG ELECTRICAL TRANSFORMER. DEAD AHEAD.
ZZAKOW
HANG ON!

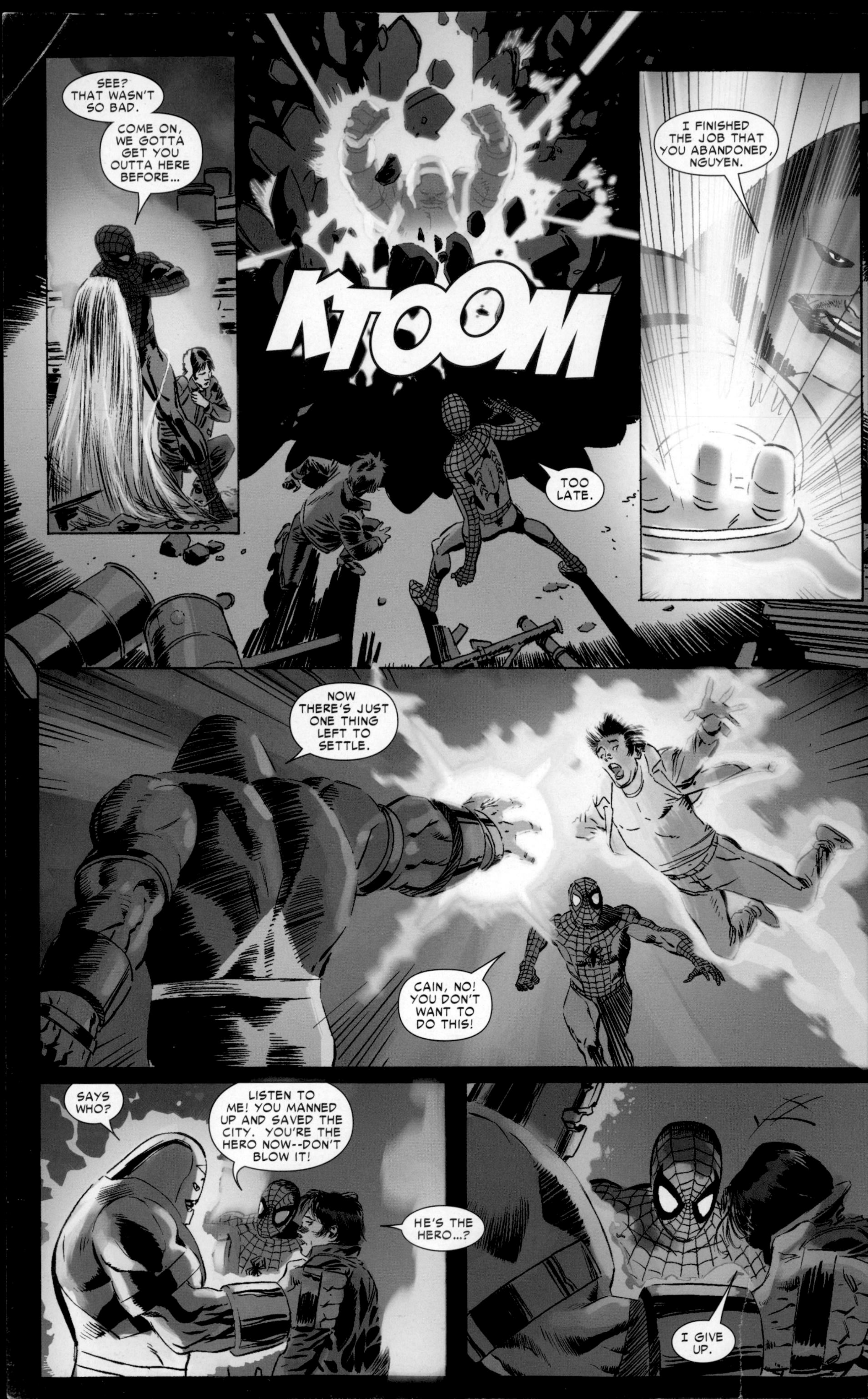
SEE? THAT WASN'T SO BAD.
COME ON, WE GOTTA GET YOU OUTTA HERE BEFORE...
KTOOM
TOO LATE.
I FINISHED THE JOB THAT YOU ABANDONED, NGUYEN.
NOW THERE'S JUST ONE THING LEFT TO SETTLE.
CAIN, NO! YOU DON'T WANT TO DO THIS!
SAYS WHO?
LISTEN TO ME! YOU MANNED UP AND SAVED THE CITY. YOU'RE THE HERO NOW--DON'T BLOW IT!
HE'S THE HERO...?
I GIVE UP.

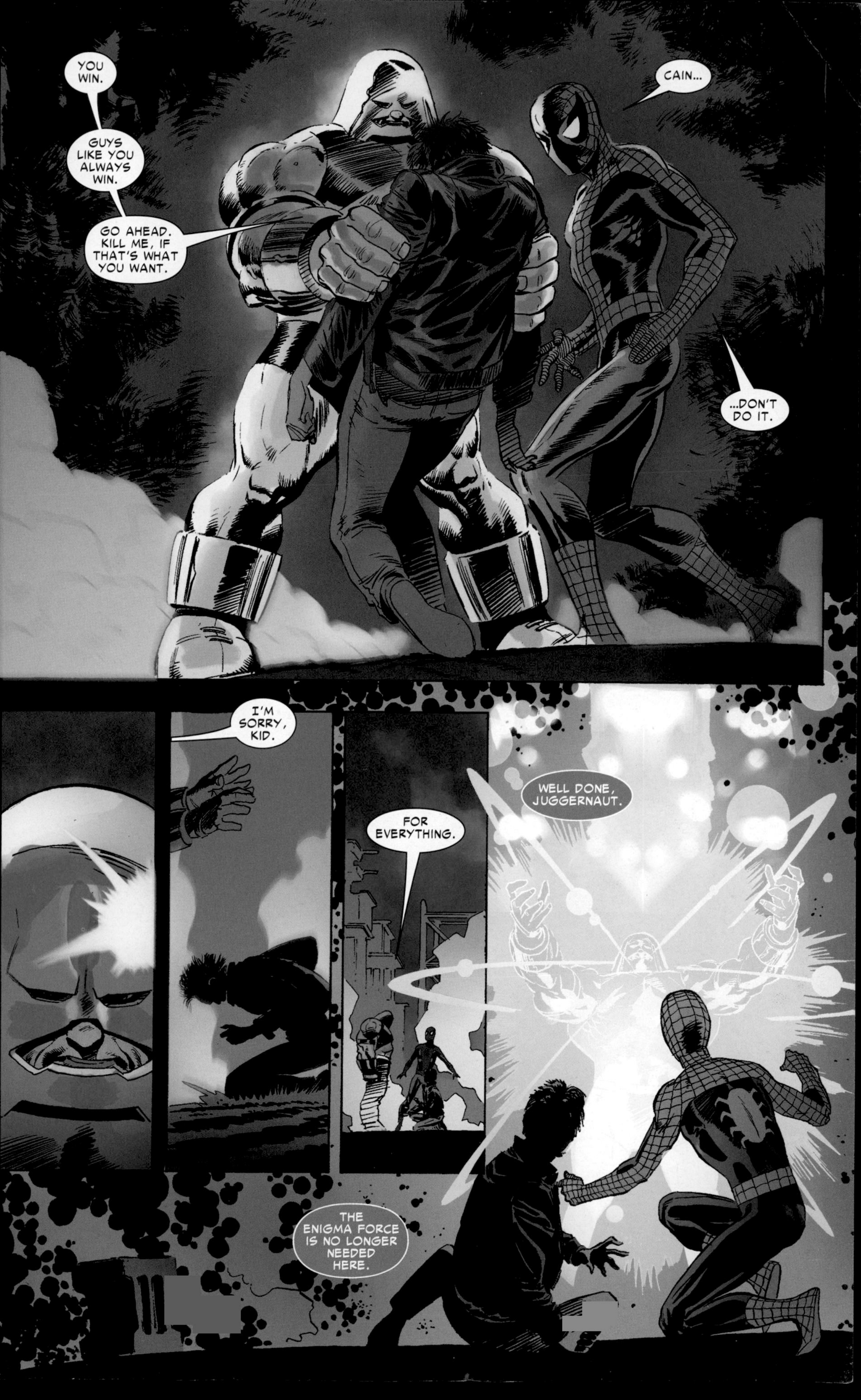
YOU WIN.
GUYS LIKE YOU ALWAYS WIN.
GO AHEAD. KILL ME, IF THAT'S WHAT YOU WANT.
CAIN...
...DON'T DO IT.
I'M SORRY, KID.
FOR EVERYTHING.
WELL DONE, JUGGERNAUT.
THE ENIGMA FORCE IS NO LONGER NEEDED HERE.

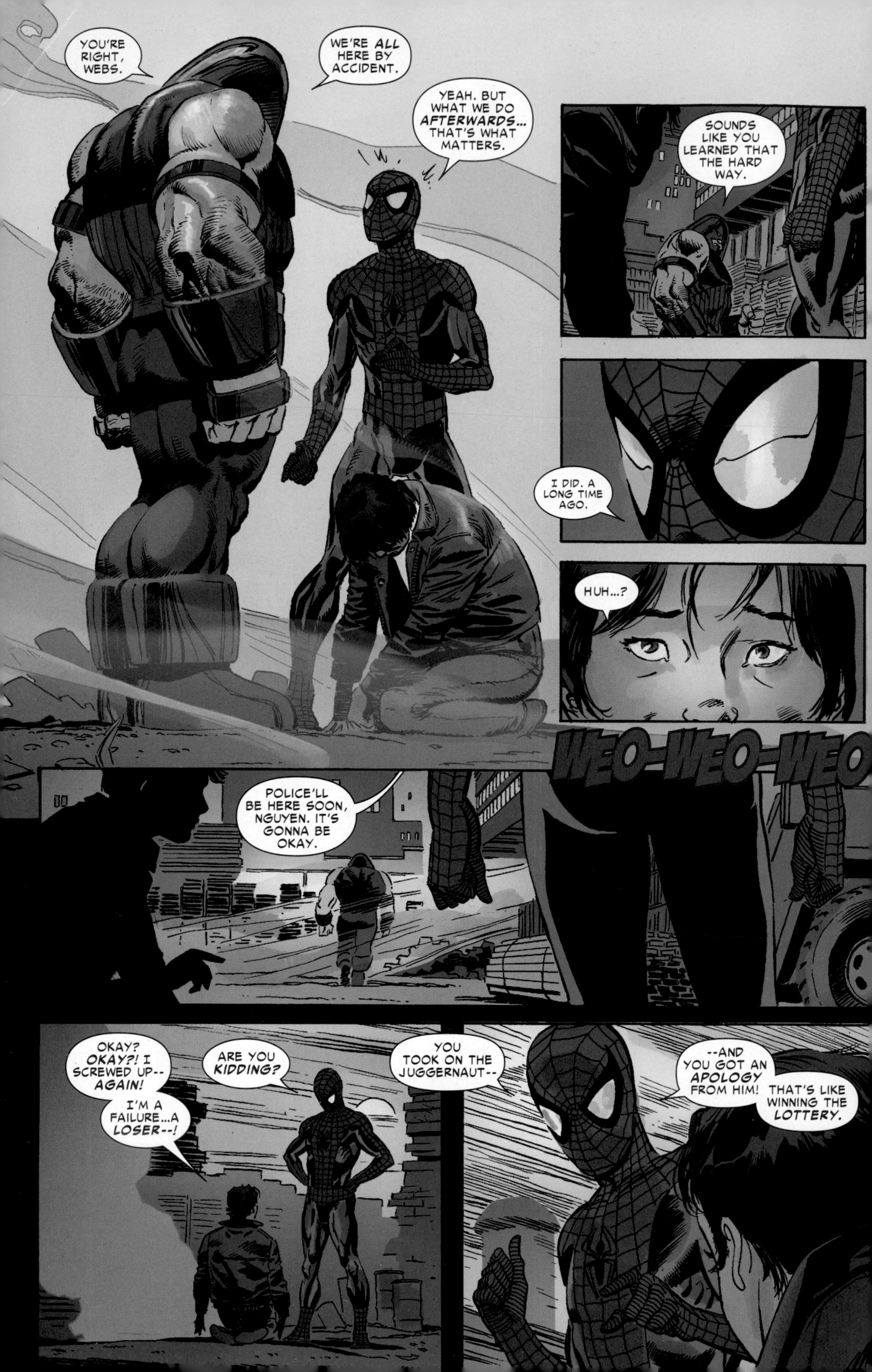
YOU'RE RIGHT, WEBS.
WE'RE ALL HERE BY ACCIDENT.
YEAH. BUT WHAT WE DO AFTERWARDS... THAT'S WHAT MATTERS.
SOUNDS LIKE YOU LEARNED THAT THE HARD WAY.
I DID. A LONG TIME AGO.
HUH...?
WEO-WEO-WEO-WEO
POLICE'LL BE HERE SOON, NGUYEN. IT'S GONNA BE OKAY.
OKAY? OKAY?! I SCREWED UP-- AGAIN!
I'M A FAILURE...A LOSER--!
ARE YOU KIDDING?
YOU TOOK ON THE JUGGERNAUT--
--AND YOU GOT AN APOLOGY FROM HIM!
THAT'S LIKE WINNING THE LOTTERY.

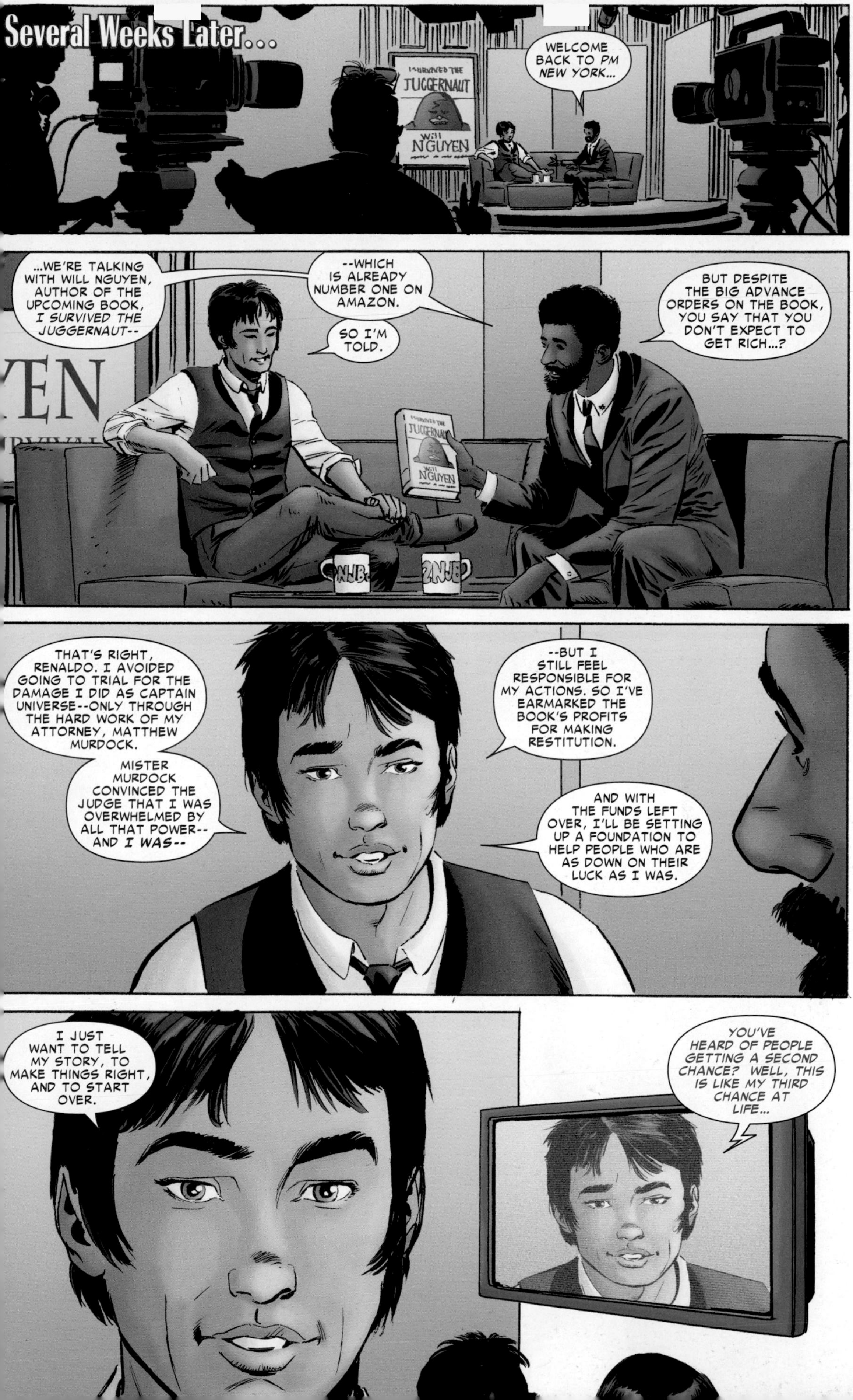
Several Weeks Later...
WELCOME BACK TO PM NEW YORK...
I SURVIVED THE JUGGERNAUT
Will NGUYEN
...WE'RE TALKING WITH WILL NGUYEN, AUTHOR OF THE UPCOMING BOOK, I SURVIVED THE JUGGERNAUT--
--WHICH IS ALREADY NUMBER ONE ON AMAZON.
SO I'M TOLD.
BUT DESPITE THE BIG ADVANCE ORDERS ON THE BOOK, YOU SAY THAT YOU DON'T EXPECT TO GET RICH...?
THAT'S RIGHT, RENALDO. I AVOIDED GOING TO TRIAL FOR THE DAMAGE I DID AS CAPTAIN UNIVERSE--ONLY THROUGH THE HARD WORK OF MY ATTORNEY, MATTHEW MURDOCK.
MISTER MURDOCK CONVINCED THE JUDGE THAT I WAS OVERWHELMED BY ALL THAT POWER--AND I WAS--
--BUT I STILL FEEL RESPONSIBLE FOR MY ACTIONS. SO I'VE EARMARKED THE BOOK'S PROFITS FOR MAKING RESTITUTION.
AND WITH THE FUNDS LEFT OVER, I'LL BE SETTING UP A FOUNDATION TO HELP PEOPLE WHO ARE AS DOWN ON THEIR LUCK AS I WAS.
I JUST WANT TO TELL MY STORY, TO MAKE THINGS RIGHT, AND TO START OVER.
YOU'VE HEARD OF PEOPLE GETTING A SECOND CHANCE? WELL, THIS IS LIKE MY THIRD CHANCE AT LIFE...

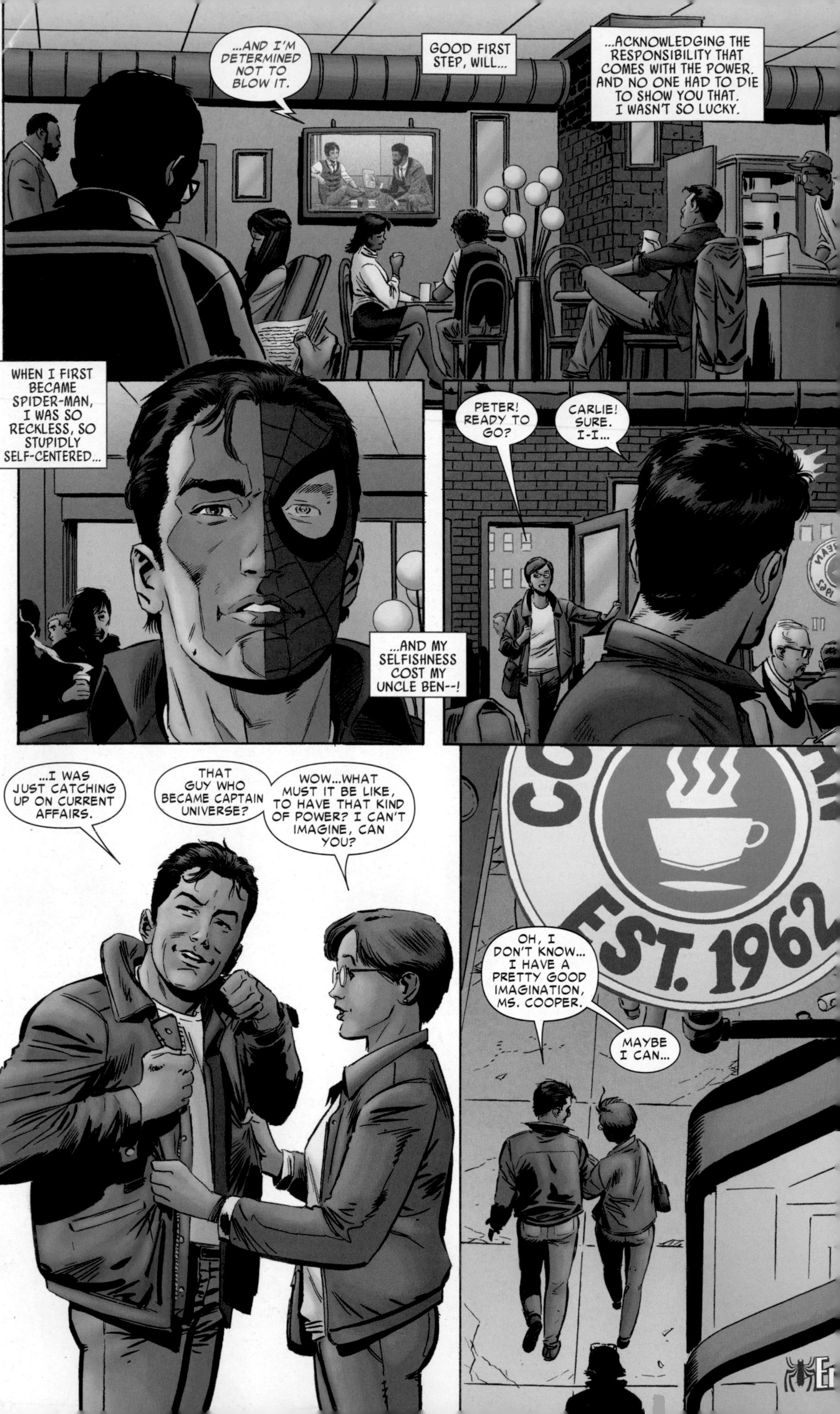
...AND I'M DETERMINED NOT TO BLOW IT.
GOOD FIRST STEP, WILL...
...ACKNOWLEDGING THE RESPONSIBILITY THAT COMES WITH THE POWER. AND NO ONE HAD TO DIE TO SHOW YOU THAT. I WASN'T SO LUCKY.
WHEN I FIRST BECAME SPIDER-MAN, I WAS SO RECKLESS, SO STUPIDLY SELF-CENTERED...
...AND MY SELFISHNESS COST MY UNCLE BEN--!
PETER! READY TO GO?
CARLIE! SURE. I-I...
...I WAS JUST CATCHING UP ON CURRENT AFFAIRS.
THAT GUY WHO BECAME CAPTAIN UNIVERSE?
WOW...WHAT MUST IT BE LIKE, TO HAVE THAT KIND OF POWER? I CAN'T IMAGINE, CAN YOU?
EST. 1962
OH, I DON'T KNOW... I HAVE A PRETTY GOOD IMAGINATION, MS. COOPER.
MAYBE I CAN...

THE UNEMPLOYED PETER PARKER IN:

Brother, Can You Spare A Crime?

MARK WAID & TOM PEYER	TODD NAUCK	ANDRES MOSSA	VC's JOE CARAMAGNA
WRITER	ARTIST	COLORIST	LETTERER

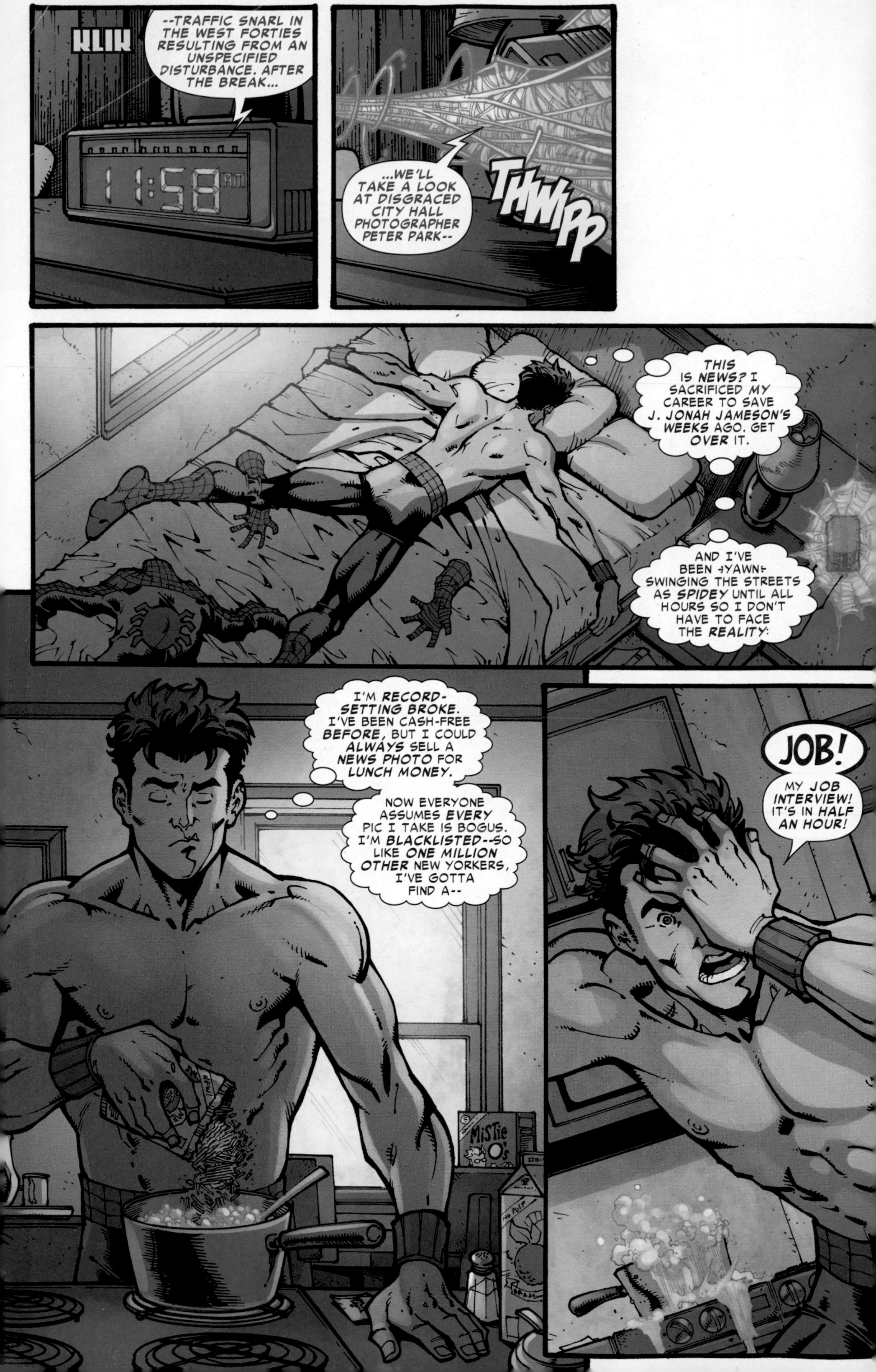
KLIK
--TRAFFIC SNARL IN THE WEST FORTIES RESULTING FROM AN UNSPECIFIED DISTURBANCE. AFTER THE BREAK...
11:58 AM
...WE'LL TAKE A LOOK AT DISGRACED CITY HALL PHOTOGRAPHER PETER PARK--
THWIPP
THIS IS NEWS? I SACRIFICED MY CAREER TO SAVE J. JONAH JAMESON'S WEEKS AGO. GET OVER IT.
AND I'VE BEEN ÷YAWN÷ SWINGING THE STREETS AS SPIDEY UNTIL ALL HOURS SO I DON'T HAVE TO FACE THE REALITY:
I'M RECORD-SETTING BROKE. I'VE BEEN CASH-FREE BEFORE, BUT I COULD ALWAYS SELL A NEWS PHOTO FOR LUNCH MONEY.
NOW EVERYONE ASSUMES EVERY PIC I TAKE IS BOGUS. I'M BLACKLISTED--SO LIKE ONE MILLION OTHER NEW YORKERS, I'VE GOTTA FIND A--
MiSTie O's
NO PULP
JOB!
MY JOB INTERVIEW! IT'S IN HALF AN HOUR!

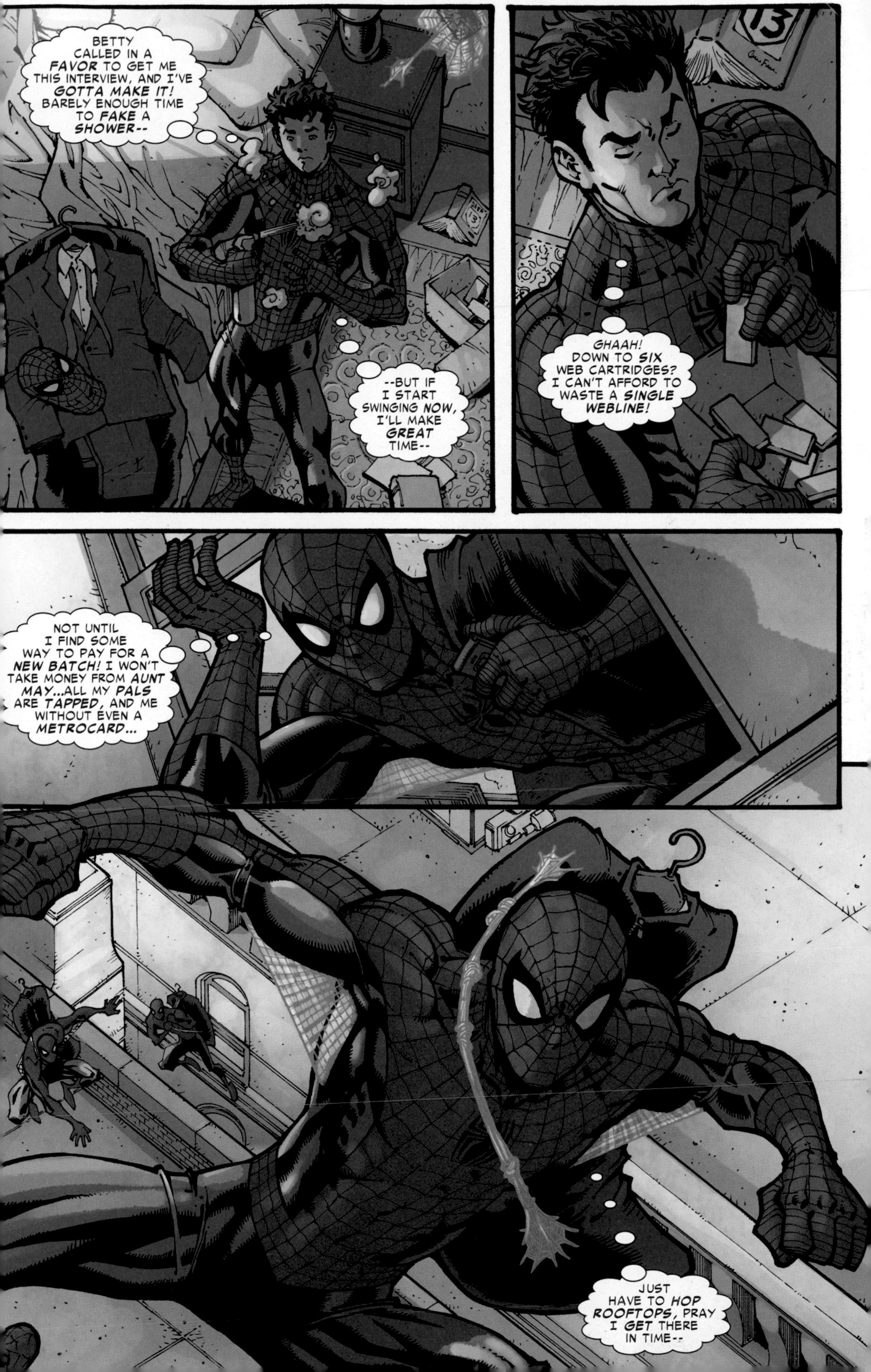
BETTY CALLED IN A FAVOR TO GET ME THIS INTERVIEW, AND I'VE GOTTA MAKE IT! BARELY ENOUGH TIME TO FAKE A SHOWER--
--BUT IF I START SWINGING NOW, I'LL MAKE GREAT TIME--
GHAAH! DOWN TO SIX WEB CARTRIDGES? I CAN'T AFFORD TO WASTE A SINGLE WEBLINE!
NOT UNTIL I FIND SOME WAY TO PAY FOR A NEW BATCH! I WON'T TAKE MONEY FROM AUNT MAY...ALL MY PALS ARE TAPPED, AND ME WITHOUT EVEN A METROCARD...
JUST HAVE TO HOP ROOFTOPS, PRAY I GET THERE IN TIME--

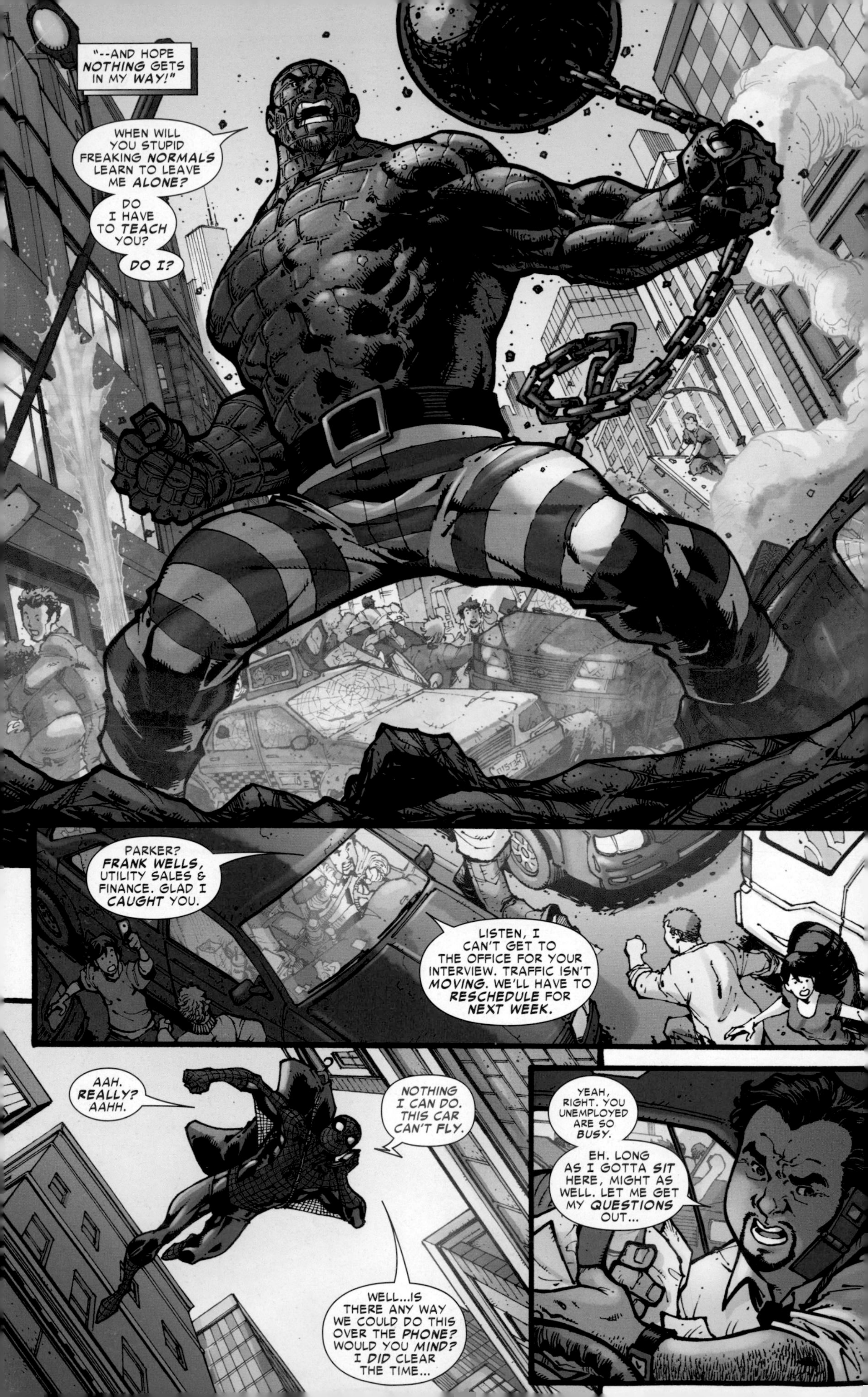
"--AND HOPE NOTHING GETS IN MY WAY!"
WHEN WILL YOU STUPID FREAKING NORMALS LEARN TO LEAVE ME ALONE?
DO I HAVE TO TEACH YOU?
DO I?
PARKER? FRANK WELLS, UTILITY SALES & FINANCE. GLAD I CAUGHT YOU.
LISTEN, I CAN'T GET TO THE OFFICE FOR YOUR INTERVIEW. TRAFFIC ISN'T MOVING. WE'LL HAVE TO RESCHEDULE FOR NEXT WEEK.
AAH. REALLY? AAHH.
NOTHING I CAN DO. THIS CAR CAN'T FLY.
WELL...IS THERE ANY WAY WE COULD DO THIS OVER THE PHONE? WOULD YOU MIND? I DID CLEAR THE TIME...
YEAH, RIGHT. YOU UNEMPLOYED ARE SO BUSY.
EH. LONG AS I GOTTA SIT HERE, MIGHT AS WELL. LET ME GET MY QUESTIONS OUT...

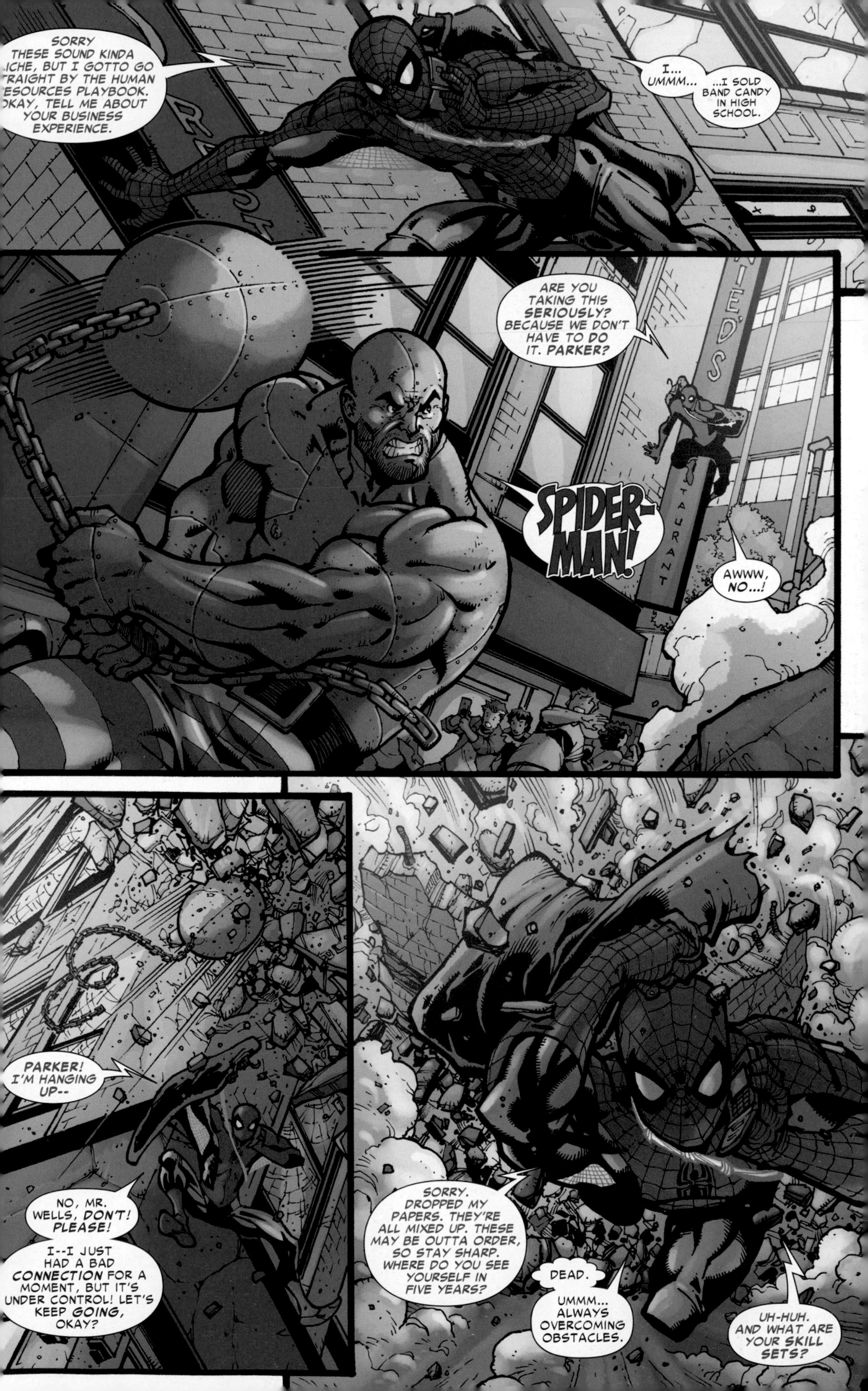

SORRY THESE SOUND KINDA LICHE, BUT I GOTTO GO TRAIGHT BY THE HUMAN ESOURCES PLAYBOOK. OKAY, TELL ME ABOUT YOUR BUSINESS EXPERIENCE.
I... UMMM...
...I SOLD BAND CANDY IN HIGH SCHOOL.
ARE YOU TAKING THIS SERIOUSLY? BECAUSE WE DON'T HAVE TO DO IT. PARKER?
SPIDER-MAN!
AWWW, NO...!
PARKER! I'M HANGING UP--
NO, MR. WELLS, DON'T! PLEASE!
I--I JUST HAD A BAD CONNECTION FOR A MOMENT, BUT IT'S UNDER CONTROL! LET'S KEEP GOING, OKAY?
SORRY. DROPPED MY PAPERS. THEY'RE ALL MIXED UP. THESE MAY BE OUTTA ORDER, SO STAY SHARP. WHERE DO YOU SEE YOURSELF IN FIVE YEARS?
DEAD.
UMMM... ALWAYS OVERCOMING OBSTACLES.
UH-HUH. AND WHAT ARE YOUR SKILL SETS?

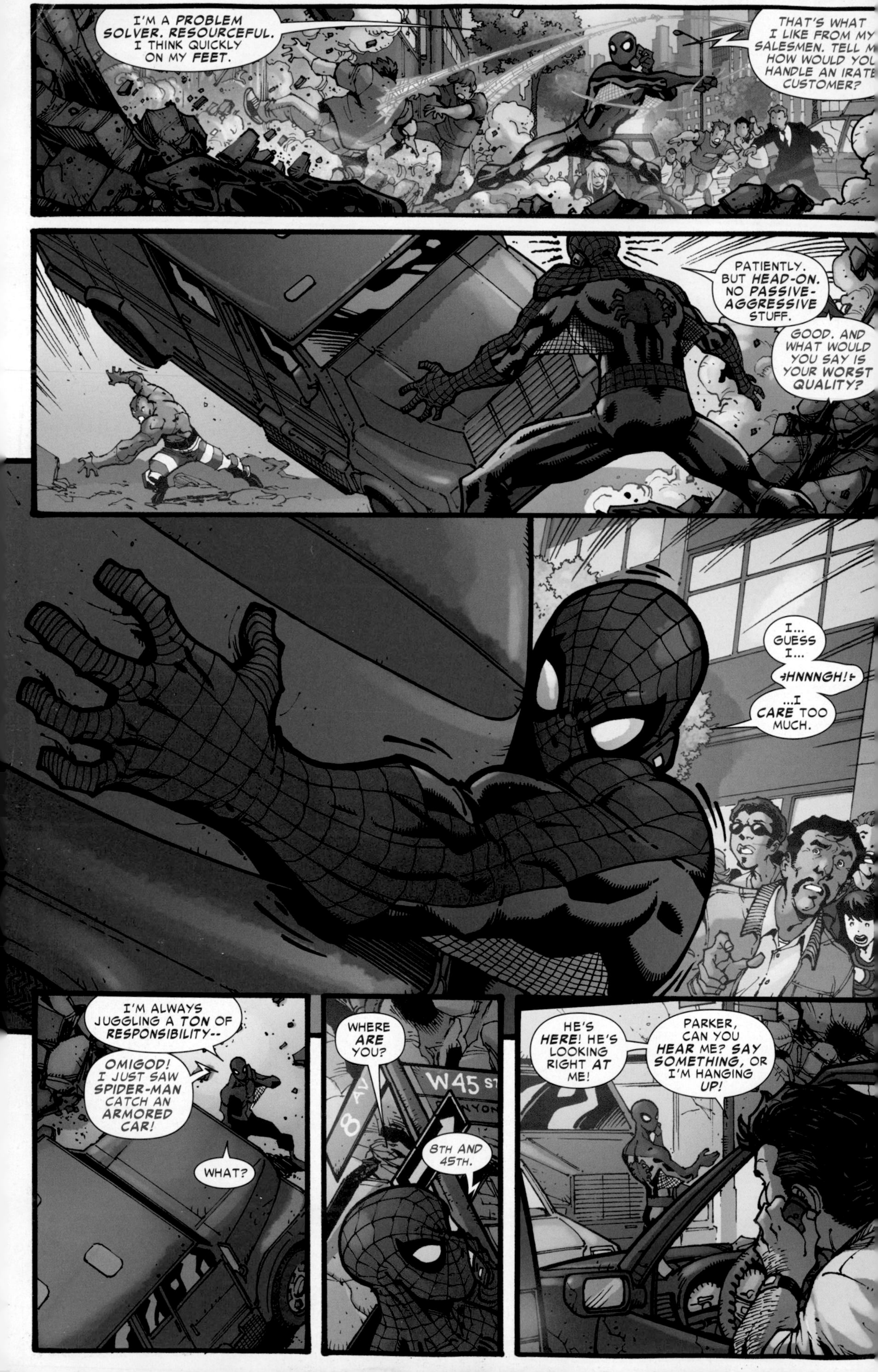
I'M A PROBLEM SOLVER. RESOURCEFUL. I THINK QUICKLY ON MY FEET.
THAT'S WHAT I LIKE FROM MY SALESMEN. TELL M HOW WOULD YOU HANDLE AN IRATE CUSTOMER?
PATIENTLY. BUT HEAD-ON. NO PASSIVE-AGGRESSIVE STUFF.
GOOD. AND WHAT WOULD YOU SAY IS YOUR WORST QUALITY?
I... GUESS I...
HNNNGH!
...I CARE TOO MUCH.
I'M ALWAYS JUGGLING A TON OF RESPONSIBILITY--
OMIGOD! I JUST SAW SPIDER-MAN CATCH AN ARMORED CAR!
WHAT?
WHERE ARE YOU?
W45 ST
8 AV
8TH AND 45TH.
HE'S HERE! HE'S LOOKING RIGHT AT ME!
PARKER, CAN YOU HEAR ME? SAY SOMETHING, OR I'M HANGING UP!

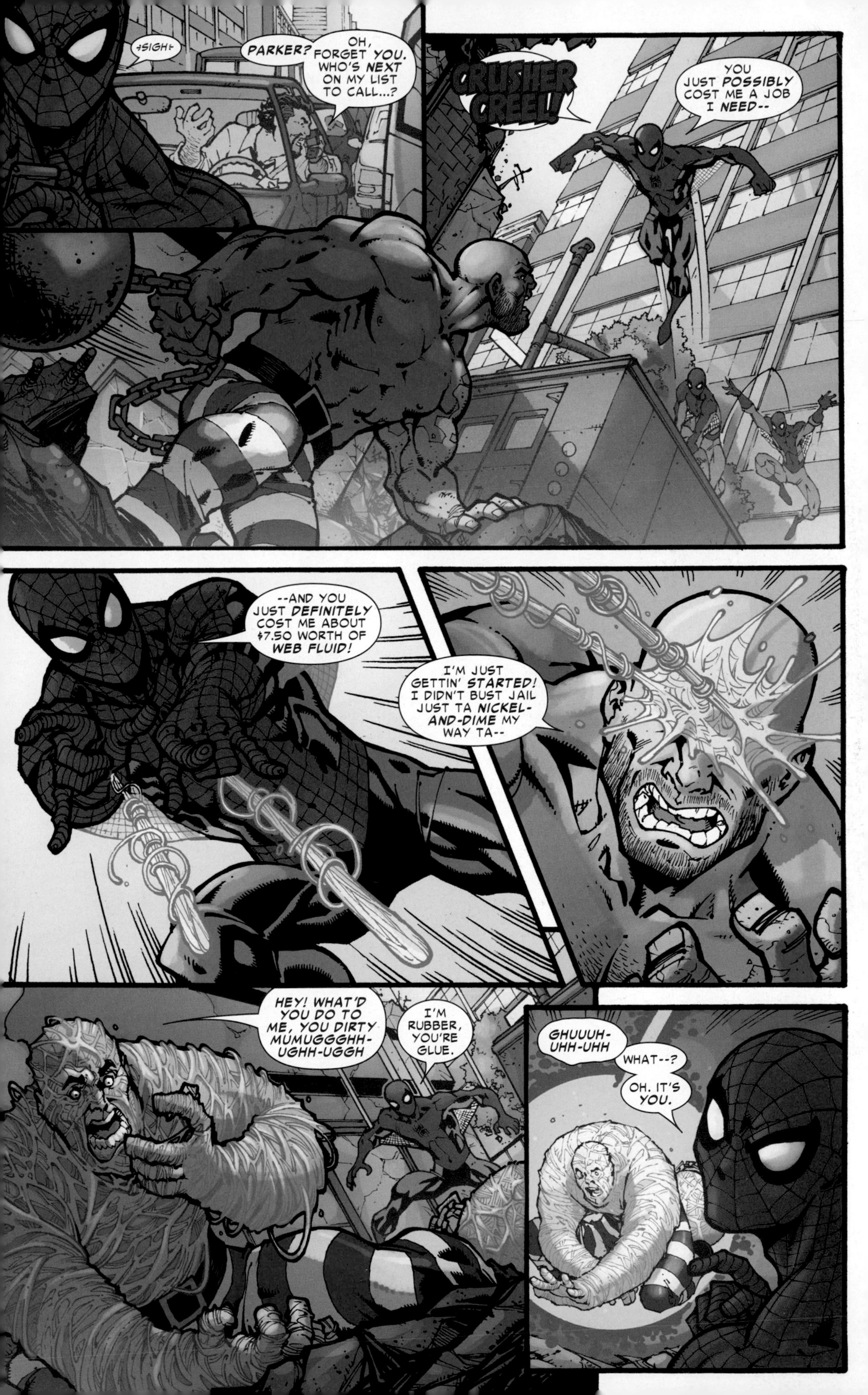

‹SIGH›
PARKER?
OH, FORGET YOU. WHO'S NEXT ON MY LIST TO CALL...?
CRUSHER CREEL!
YOU JUST POSSIBLY COST ME A JOB I NEED--
--AND YOU JUST DEFINITELY COST ME ABOUT $7.50 WORTH OF WEB FLUID!
I'M JUST GETTIN' STARTED! I DIDN'T BUST JAIL JUST TA NICKEL-AND-DIME MY WAY TA--
HEY! WHAT'D YOU DO TO ME, YOU DIRTY MUMUGGGHH-UGHH-UGGH
I'M RUBBER, YOU'RE GLUE.
GHUUUH-UHH-UHH
WHAT--?
OH. IT'S YOU.

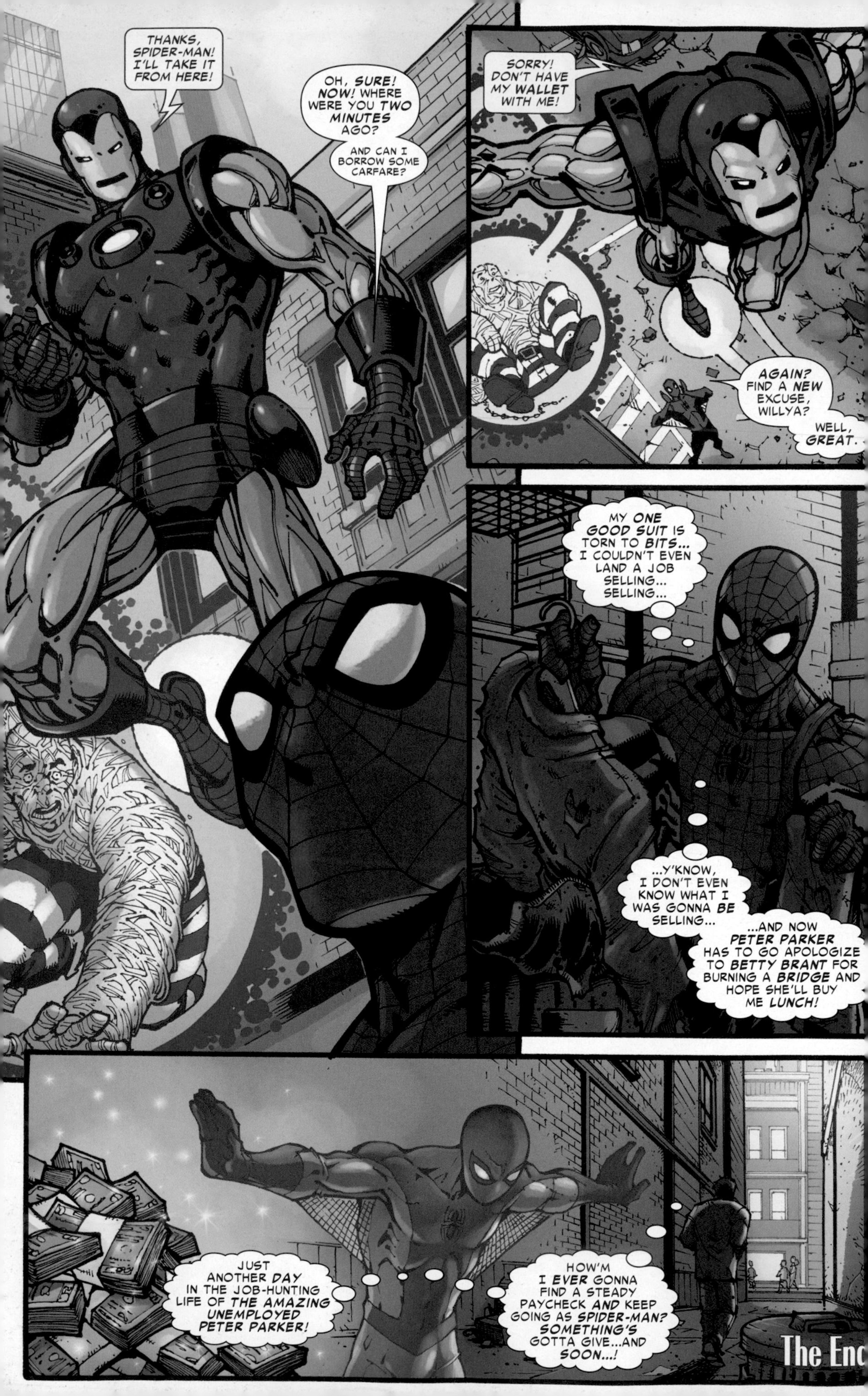
THANKS, SPIDER-MAN! I'LL TAKE IT FROM HERE!
OH, SURE! NOW! WHERE WERE YOU TWO MINUTES AGO?
AND CAN I BORROW SOME CARFARE?
SORRY! DON'T HAVE MY WALLET WITH ME!
AGAIN? FIND A NEW EXCUSE, WILLYA?
WELL, GREAT.
MY ONE GOOD SUIT IS TORN TO BITS... I COULDN'T EVEN LAND A JOB SELLING... SELLING...
...Y'KNOW, I DON'T EVEN KNOW WHAT I WAS GONNA BE SELLING...
...AND NOW PETER PARKER HAS TO GO APOLOGIZE TO BETTY BRANT FOR BURNING A BRIDGE AND HOPE SHE'LL BUY ME LUNCH!
JUST ANOTHER DAY IN THE JOB-HUNTING LIFE OF THE AMAZING UNEMPLOYED PETER PARKER!
HOW'M I EVER GONNA FIND A STEADY PAYCHECK AND KEEP GOING AS SPIDER-MAN? SOMETHING'S GOTTA GIVE...AND SOON...!
The End

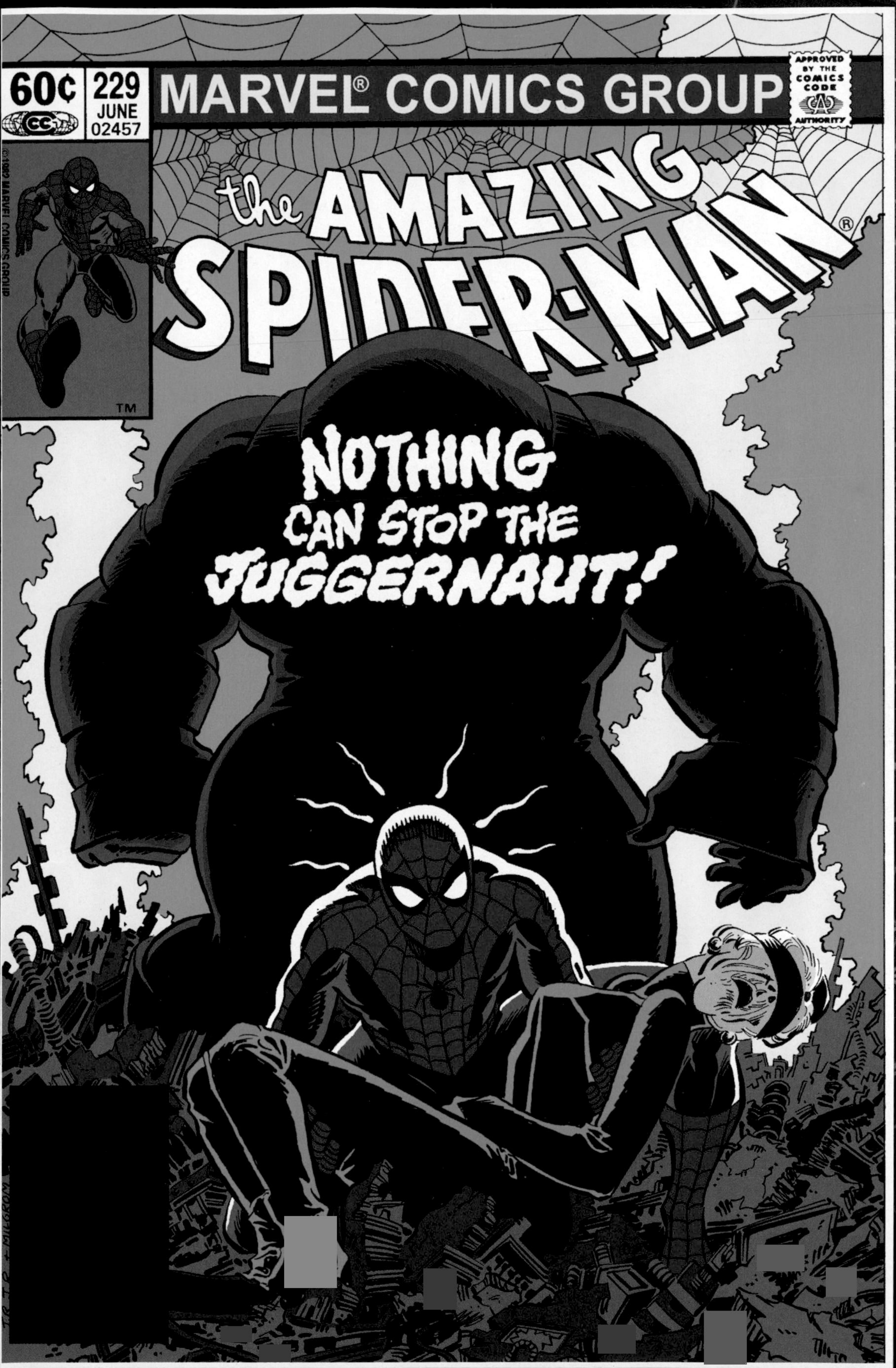
60¢
229
JUNE
02457
MARVEL® COMICS GROUP
APPROVED BY THE COMICS CODE AUTHORITY
the AMAZING SPIDER-MAN®
©1982 MARVEL COMICS GROUP
NOTHING CAN STOP THE JUGGERNAUT!

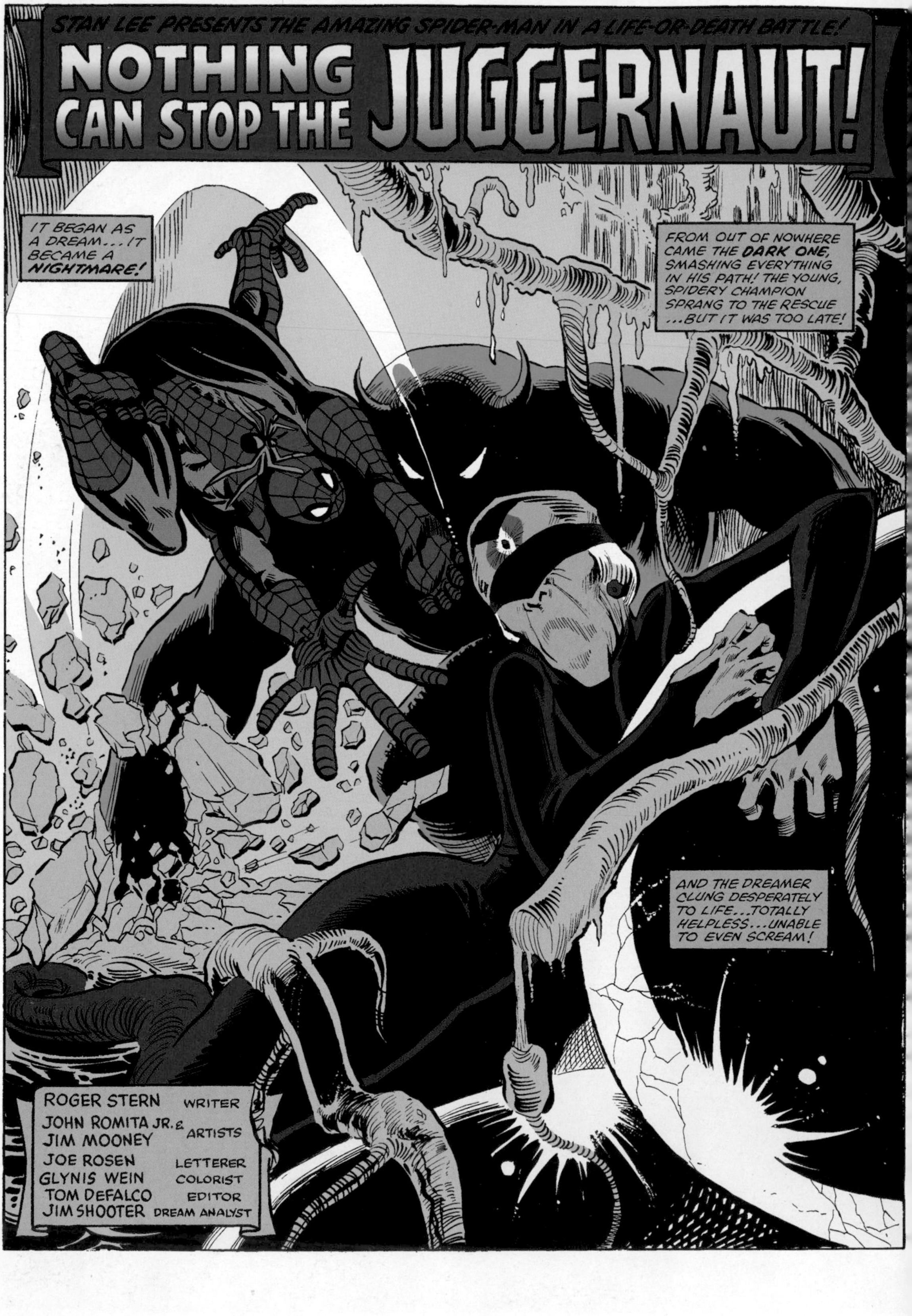
STAN LEE PRESENTS THE AMAZING SPIDER-MAN IN A LIFE-OR-DEATH BATTLE!
NOTHING CAN STOP THE JUGGERNAUT!
IT BEGAN AS A DREAM... IT BECAME A NIGHTMARE!
FROM OUT OF NOWHERE CAME THE DARK ONE, SMASHING EVERYTHING IN HIS PATH! THE YOUNG, SPIDERY CHAMPION SPRANG TO THE RESCUE ...BUT IT WAS TOO LATE!
AND THE DREAMER CLUNG DESPERATELY TO LIFE...TOTALLY HELPLESS...UNABLE TO EVEN SCREAM!
ROGER STERN WRITER
JOHN ROMITA JR. & JIM MOONEY ARTISTS
JOE ROSEN LETTERER
GLYNIS WEIN COLORIST
TOM DEFALCO EDITOR
JIM SHOOTER DREAM ANALYST

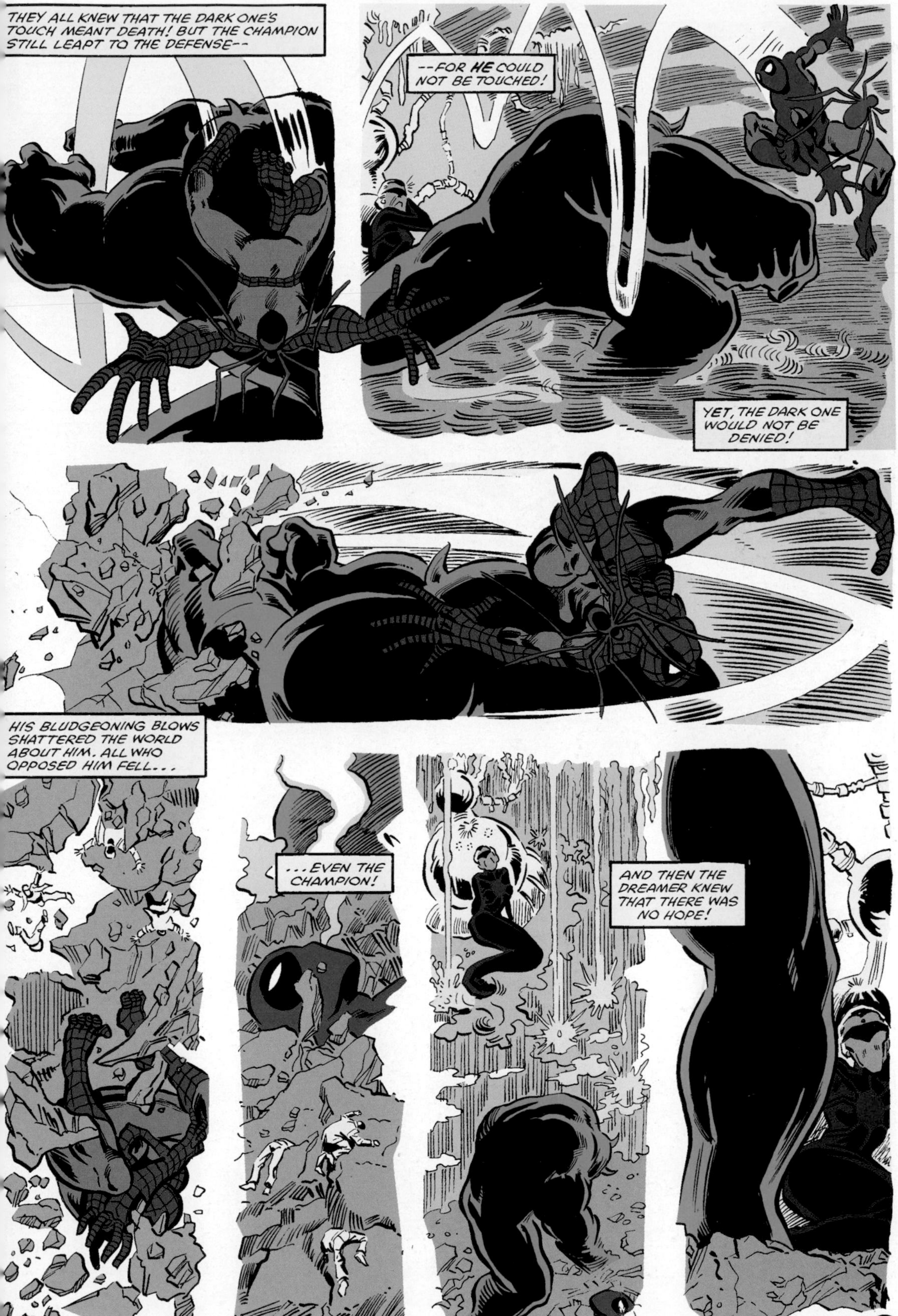

THEY ALL KNEW THAT THE DARK ONE'S TOUCH MEANT DEATH! BUT THE CHAMPION STILL LEAPT TO THE DEFENSE--
--FOR HE COULD NOT BE TOUCHED!
YET, THE DARK ONE WOULD NOT BE DENIED!
HIS BLUDGEONING BLOWS SHATTERED THE WORLD ABOUT HIM. ALL WHO OPPOSED HIM FELL...
...EVEN THE CHAMPION!
AND THEN THE DREAMER KNEW THAT THERE WAS NO HOPE!

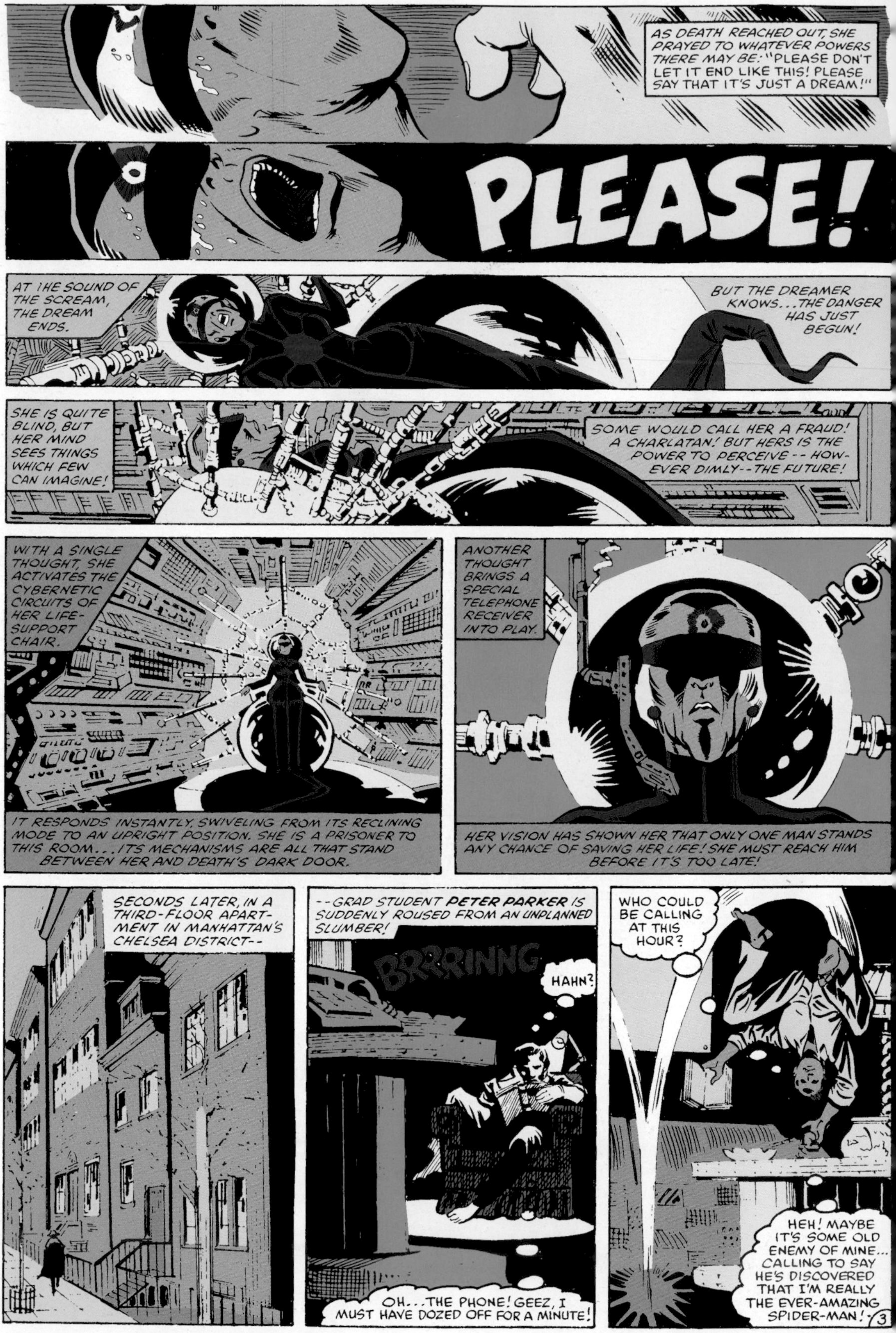

AS DEATH REACHED OUT, SHE PRAYED TO WHATEVER POWERS THERE MAY BE: "PLEASE DON'T LET IT END LIKE THIS! PLEASE SAY THAT IT'S JUST A DREAM!"
PLEASE!
AT THE SOUND OF THE SCREAM, THE DREAM ENDS.
BUT THE DREAMER KNOWS... THE DANGER HAS JUST BEGUN!
SHE IS QUITE BLIND, BUT HER MIND SEES THINGS WHICH FEW CAN IMAGINE!
SOME WOULD CALL HER A FRAUD! A CHARLATAN! BUT HERS IS THE POWER TO PERCEIVE -- HOWEVER DIMLY -- THE FUTURE!
WITH A SINGLE THOUGHT, SHE ACTIVATES THE CYBERNETIC CIRCUITS OF HER LIFE-SUPPORT CHAIR.
IT RESPONDS INSTANTLY, SWIVELING FROM ITS RECLINING MODE TO AN UPRIGHT POSITION. SHE IS A PRISONER TO THIS ROOM... ITS MECHANISMS ARE ALL THAT STAND BETWEEN HER AND DEATH'S DARK DOOR.
ANOTHER THOUGHT BRINGS A SPECIAL TELEPHONE RECEIVER INTO PLAY.
HER VISION HAS SHOWN HER THAT ONLY ONE MAN STANDS ANY CHANCE OF SAVING HER LIFE! SHE MUST REACH HIM BEFORE IT'S TOO LATE!
SECONDS LATER, IN A THIRD-FLOOR APARTMENT IN MANHATTAN'S CHELSEA DISTRICT--
--GRAD STUDENT PETER PARKER IS SUDDENLY ROUSED FROM AN UNPLANNED SLUMBER!
BRRRINNG
HAHN?
OH... THE PHONE! GEEZ, I MUST HAVE DOZED OFF FOR A MINUTE!
WHO COULD BE CALLING AT THIS HOUR?
HEH! MAYBE IT'S SOME OLD ENEMY OF MINE... CALLING TO SAY HE'S DISCOVERED THAT I'M REALLY THE EVER-AMAZING SPIDER-MAN!
3

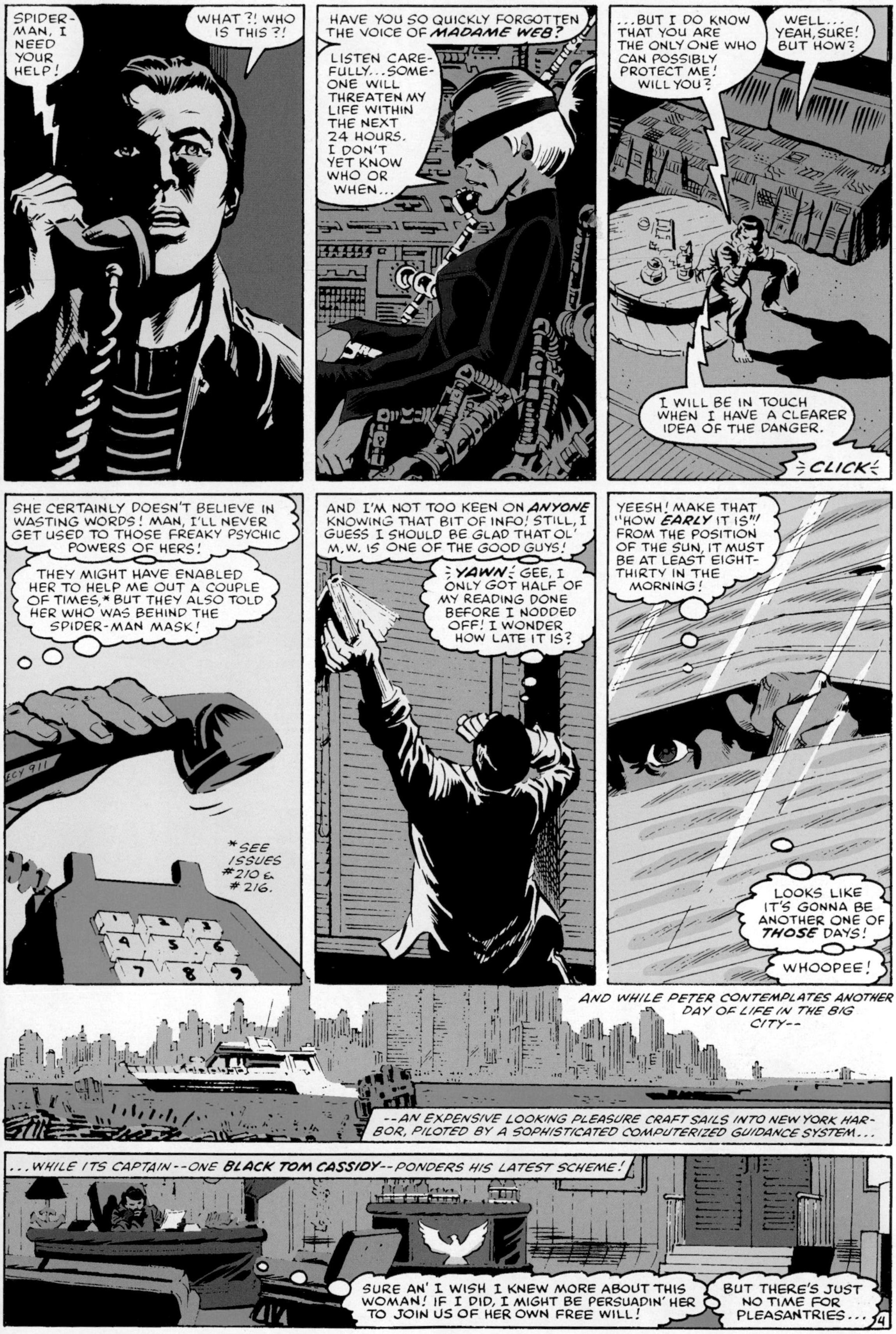
SPIDER-MAN, I NEED YOUR HELP!
WHAT?! WHO IS THIS?!
HAVE YOU SO QUICKLY FORGOTTEN THE VOICE OF MADAME WEB?
LISTEN CAREFULLY... SOMEONE WILL THREATEN MY LIFE WITHIN THE NEXT 24 HOURS. I DON'T YET KNOW WHO OR WHEN...
...BUT I DO KNOW THAT YOU ARE THE ONLY ONE WHO CAN POSSIBLY PROTECT ME! WILL YOU?
WELL... YEAH, SURE! BUT HOW?
I WILL BE IN TOUCH WHEN I HAVE A CLEARER IDEA OF THE DANGER.
CLICK
SHE CERTAINLY DOESN'T BELIEVE IN WASTING WORDS! MAN, I'LL NEVER GET USED TO THOSE FREAKY PSYCHIC POWERS OF HERS!
THEY MIGHT HAVE ENABLED HER TO HELP ME OUT A COUPLE OF TIMES,* BUT THEY ALSO TOLD HER WHO WAS BEHIND THE SPIDER-MAN MASK!
*SEE ISSUES #210 & #216.
AND I'M NOT TOO KEEN ON ANYONE KNOWING THAT BIT OF INFO! STILL, I GUESS I SHOULD BE GLAD THAT OL' M.W. IS ONE OF THE GOOD GUYS!
YAWN GEE, I ONLY GOT HALF OF MY READING DONE BEFORE I NODDED OFF! I WONDER HOW LATE IT IS?
YEESH! MAKE THAT "HOW EARLY IT IS"! FROM THE POSITION OF THE SUN, IT MUST BE AT LEAST EIGHT-THIRTY IN THE MORNING!
LOOKS LIKE IT'S GONNA BE ANOTHER ONE OF THOSE DAYS!
WHOOPEE!
AND WHILE PETER CONTEMPLATES ANOTHER DAY OF LIFE IN THE BIG CITY--
--AN EXPENSIVE LOOKING PLEASURE CRAFT SAILS INTO NEW YORK HARBOR, PILOTED BY A SOPHISTICATED COMPUTERIZED GUIDANCE SYSTEM...
...WHILE ITS CAPTAIN--ONE BLACK TOM CASSIDY--PONDERS HIS LATEST SCHEME!
SURE AN' I WISH I KNEW MORE ABOUT THIS WOMAN! IF I DID, I MIGHT BE PERSUADIN' HER TO JOIN US OF HER OWN FREE WILL!
BUT THERE'S JUST NO TIME FOR PLEASANTRIES...
4

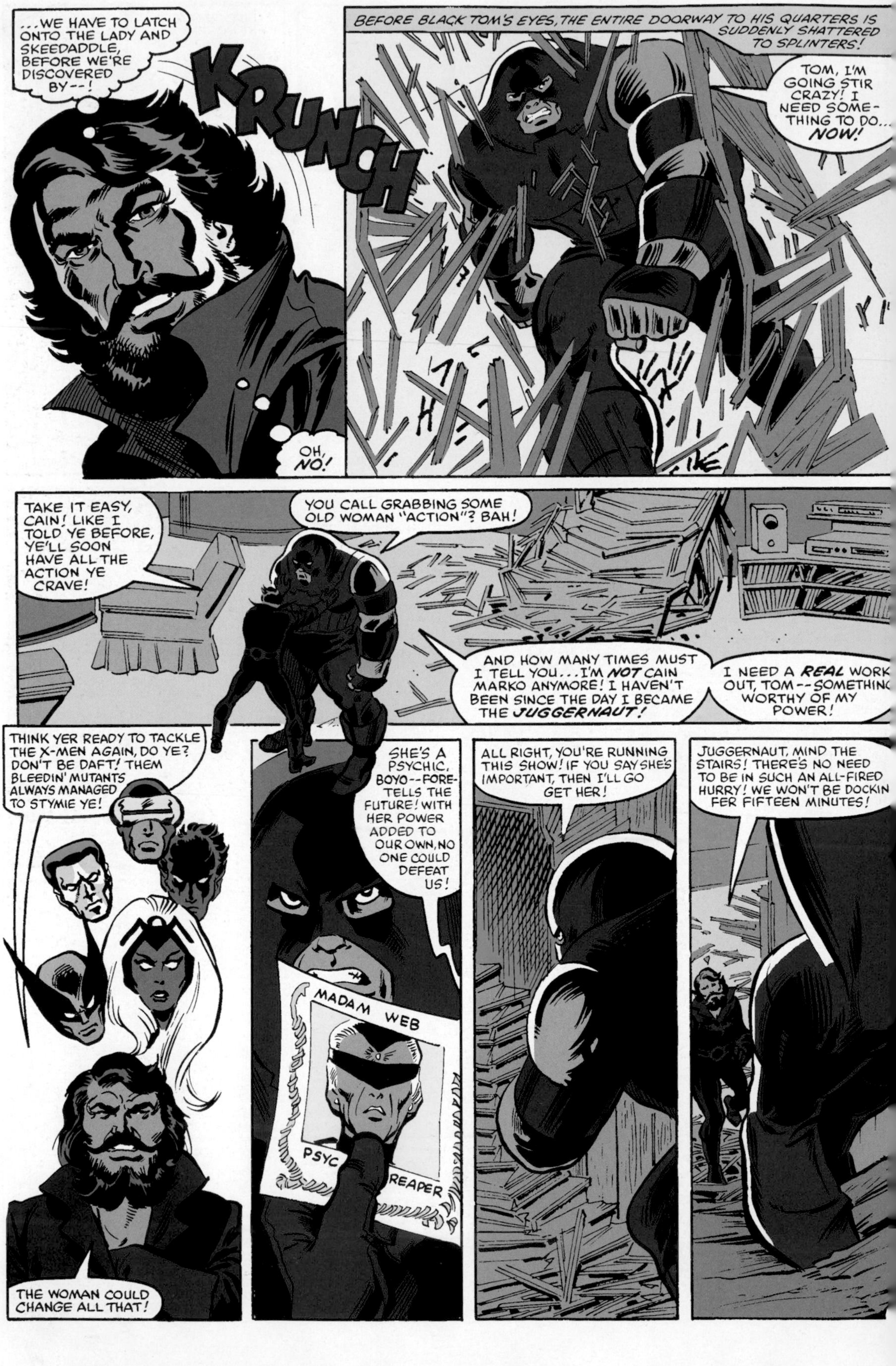
...WE HAVE TO LATCH ONTO THE LADY AND SKEEDADDLE, BEFORE WE'RE DISCOVERED BY--!
KRUNCH
OH, NO!
BEFORE BLACK TOM'S EYES, THE ENTIRE DOORWAY TO HIS QUARTERS IS SUDDENLY SHATTERED TO SPLINTERS!
TOM, I'M GOING STIR CRAZY! I NEED SOMETHING TO DO... NOW!
TAKE IT EASY, CAIN! LIKE I TOLD YE BEFORE, YE'LL SOON HAVE ALL THE ACTION YE CRAVE!
YOU CALL GRABBING SOME OLD WOMAN "ACTION"? BAH!
AND HOW MANY TIMES MUST I TELL YOU... I'M NOT CAIN MARKO ANYMORE! I HAVEN'T BEEN SINCE THE DAY I BECAME THE JUGGERNAUT!
I NEED A REAL WORKOUT, TOM--SOMETHING WORTHY OF MY POWER!
THINK YER READY TO TACKLE THE X-MEN AGAIN, DO YE? DON'T BE DAFT! THEM BLEEDIN' MUTANTS ALWAYS MANAGED TO STYMIE YE!
THE WOMAN COULD CHANGE ALL THAT!
SHE'S A PSYCHIC, BOYO--FORETELLS THE FUTURE! WITH HER POWER ADDED TO OUR OWN, NO ONE COULD DEFEAT US!
MADAM WEB
PSYC
REAPER
ALL RIGHT, YOU'RE RUNNING THIS SHOW! IF YOU SAY SHE'S IMPORTANT, THEN I'LL GO GET HER!
JUGGERNAUT, MIND THE STAIRS! THERE'S NO NEED TO BE IN SUCH AN ALL-FIRED HURRY! WE WON'T BE DOCKIN FER FIFTEEN MINUTES!

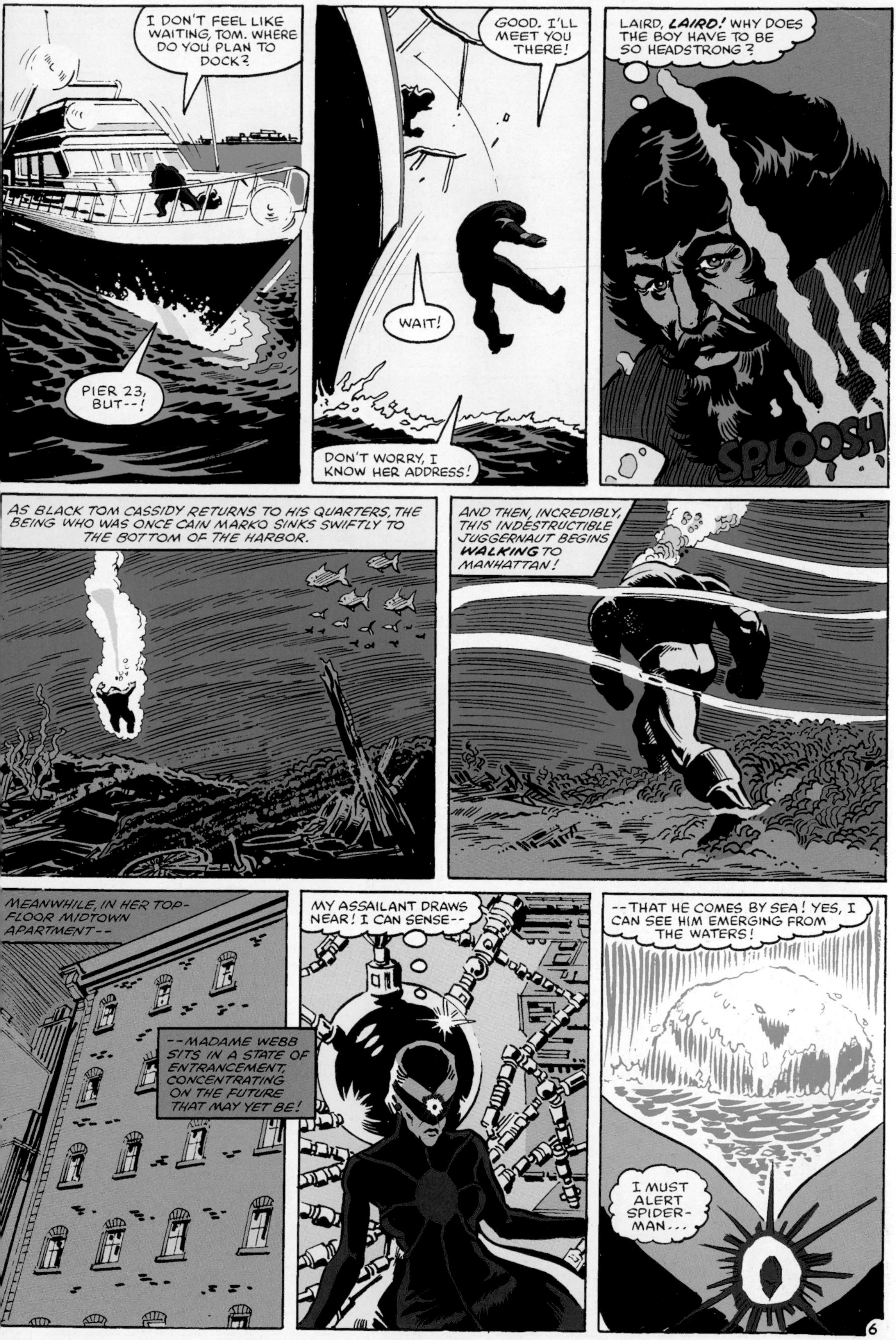

I DON'T FEEL LIKE WAITING, TOM. WHERE DO YOU PLAN TO DOCK?
PIER 23, BUT--!
GOOD. I'LL MEET YOU THERE!
WAIT!
DON'T WORRY, I KNOW HER ADDRESS!
LAIRD, LAIRD! WHY DOES THE BOY HAVE TO BE SO HEADSTRONG?
SPLOOSH
AS BLACK TOM CASSIDY RETURNS TO HIS QUARTERS, THE BEING WHO WAS ONCE CAIN MARKO SINKS SWIFTLY TO THE BOTTOM OF THE HARBOR.
AND THEN, INCREDIBLY, THIS INDESTRUCTIBLE JUGGERNAUT BEGINS WALKING TO MANHATTAN!
MEANWHILE, IN HER TOP-FLOOR MIDTOWN APARTMENT--
--MADAME WEBB SITS IN A STATE OF ENTRANCEMENT, CONCENTRATING ON THE FUTURE THAT MAY YET BE!
MY ASSAILANT DRAWS NEAR! I CAN SENSE--
--THAT HE COMES BY SEA! YES, I CAN SEE HIM EMERGING FROM THE WATERS!
I MUST ALERT SPIDER-MAN...

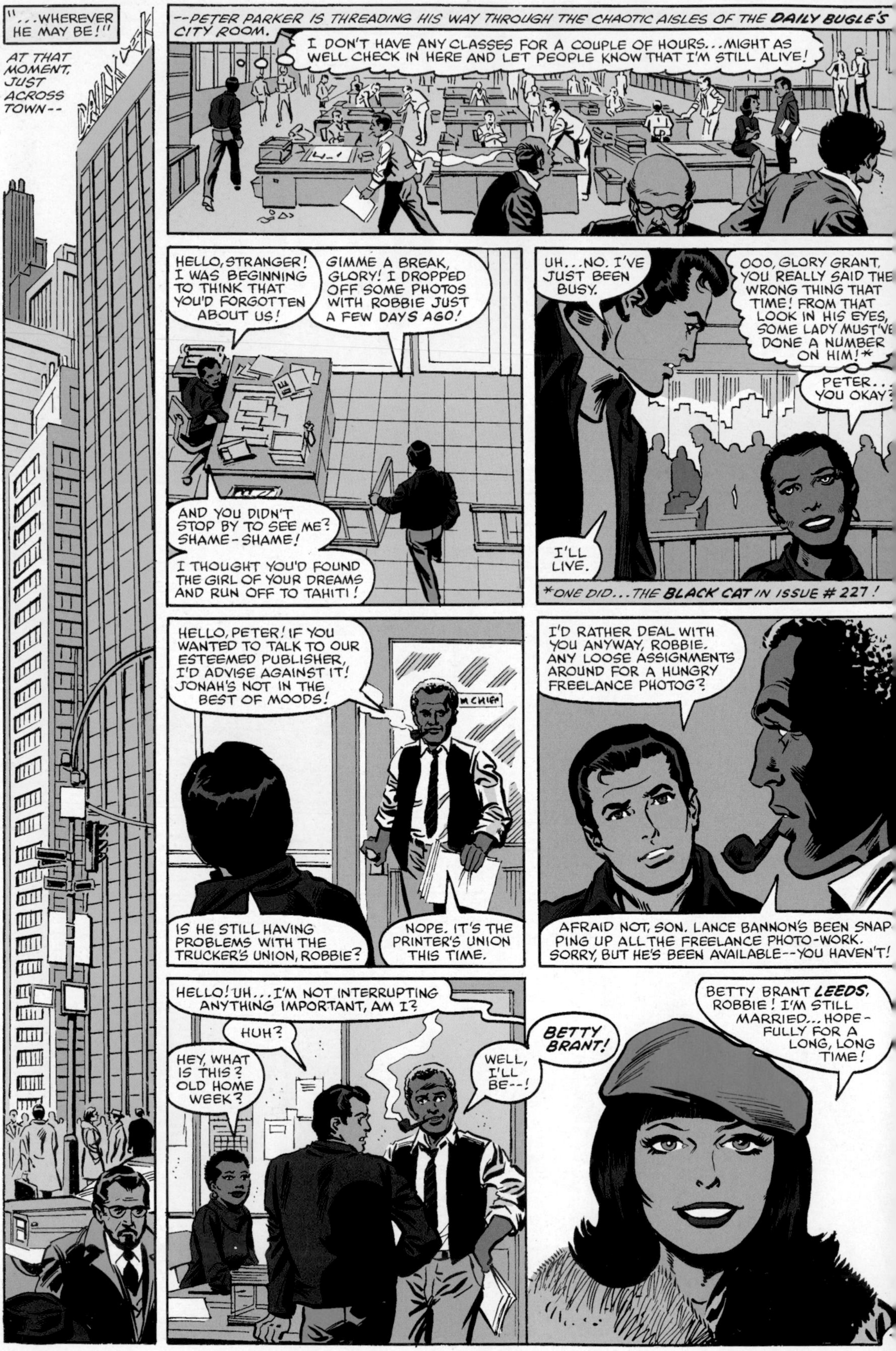
"...WHEREVER HE MAY BE!"
AT THAT MOMENT, JUST ACROSS TOWN--
--PETER PARKER IS THREADING HIS WAY THROUGH THE CHAOTIC AISLES OF THE DAILY BUGLE'S CITY ROOM.
I DON'T HAVE ANY CLASSES FOR A COUPLE OF HOURS...MIGHT AS WELL CHECK IN HERE AND LET PEOPLE KNOW THAT I'M STILL ALIVE!
HELLO, STRANGER! I WAS BEGINNING TO THINK THAT YOU'D FORGOTTEN ABOUT US!
GIMME A BREAK, GLORY! I DROPPED OFF SOME PHOTOS WITH ROBBIE JUST A FEW DAYS AGO!
AND YOU DIDN'T STOP BY TO SEE ME? SHAME-SHAME!
I THOUGHT YOU'D FOUND THE GIRL OF YOUR DREAMS AND RUN OFF TO TAHITI!
UH...NO. I'VE JUST BEEN BUSY.
OOO, GLORY GRANT, YOU REALLY SAID THE WRONG THING THAT TIME! FROM THAT LOOK IN HIS EYES, SOME LADY MUST'VE DONE A NUMBER ON HIM!*
PETER... YOU OKAY?
I'LL LIVE.
*ONE DID...THE BLACK CAT IN ISSUE #227!
HELLO, PETER! IF YOU WANTED TO TALK TO OUR ESTEEMED PUBLISHER, I'D ADVISE AGAINST IT! JONAH'S NOT IN THE BEST OF MOODS!
IS HE STILL HAVING PROBLEMS WITH THE TRUCKER'S UNION, ROBBIE?
NOPE. IT'S THE PRINTER'S UNION THIS TIME.
I'D RATHER DEAL WITH YOU ANYWAY, ROBBIE. ANY LOOSE ASSIGNMENTS AROUND FOR A HUNGRY FREELANCE PHOTOG?
AFRAID NOT, SON. LANCE BANNON'S BEEN SNAPPING UP ALL THE FREELANCE PHOTO-WORK. SORRY, BUT HE'S BEEN AVAILABLE--YOU HAVEN'T!
HELLO! UH...I'M NOT INTERRUPTING ANYTHING IMPORTANT, AM I?
HUH?
HEY, WHAT IS THIS? OLD HOME WEEK?
WELL, I'LL BE--!
BETTY BRANT!
BETTY BRANT LEEDS, ROBBIE! I'M STILL MARRIED... HOPEFULLY FOR A LONG, LONG TIME!

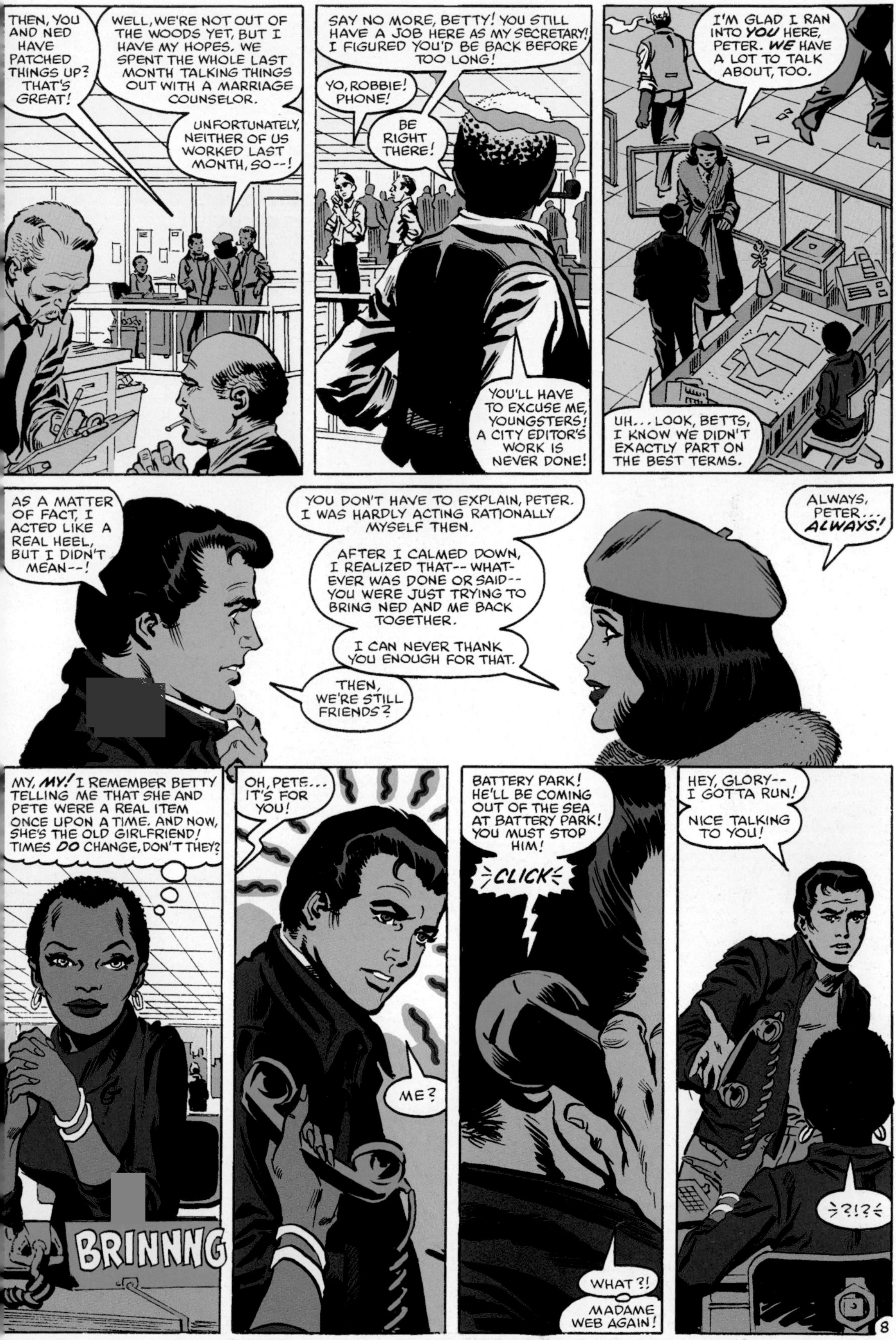

THEN, YOU AND NED HAVE PATCHED THINGS UP? THAT'S GREAT!
WELL, WE'RE NOT OUT OF THE WOODS YET, BUT I HAVE MY HOPES. WE SPENT THE WHOLE LAST MONTH TALKING THINGS OUT WITH A MARRIAGE COUNSELOR.
UNFORTUNATELY, NEITHER OF US WORKED LAST MONTH, SO--!
SAY NO MORE, BETTY! YOU STILL HAVE A JOB HERE AS MY SECRETARY! I FIGURED YOU'D BE BACK BEFORE TOO LONG!
YO, ROBBIE! PHONE!
BE RIGHT THERE!
YOU'LL HAVE TO EXCUSE ME, YOUNGSTERS! A CITY EDITOR'S WORK IS NEVER DONE!
I'M GLAD I RAN INTO YOU HERE, PETER. WE HAVE A LOT TO TALK ABOUT, TOO.
UH... LOOK, BETTS, I KNOW WE DIDN'T EXACTLY PART ON THE BEST TERMS.
AS A MATTER OF FACT, I ACTED LIKE A REAL HEEL, BUT I DIDN'T MEAN--!
YOU DON'T HAVE TO EXPLAIN, PETER. I WAS HARDLY ACTING RATIONALLY MYSELF THEN.
AFTER I CALMED DOWN, I REALIZED THAT-- WHATEVER WAS DONE OR SAID-- YOU WERE JUST TRYING TO BRING NED AND ME BACK TOGETHER.
I CAN NEVER THANK YOU ENOUGH FOR THAT.
THEN, WE'RE STILL FRIENDS?
ALWAYS, PETER... ALWAYS!
MY, MY! I REMEMBER BETTY TELLING ME THAT SHE AND PETE WERE A REAL ITEM ONCE UPON A TIME. AND NOW, SHE'S THE OLD GIRLFRIEND! TIMES DO CHANGE, DON'T THEY?
BRINNNG
OH, PETE... IT'S FOR YOU!
ME?
BATTERY PARK! HE'LL BE COMING OUT OF THE SEA AT BATTERY PARK! YOU MUST STOP HIM!
CLICK
WHAT?! MADAME WEB AGAIN!
HEY, GLORY-- I GOTTA RUN!
NICE TALKING TO YOU!
?!?

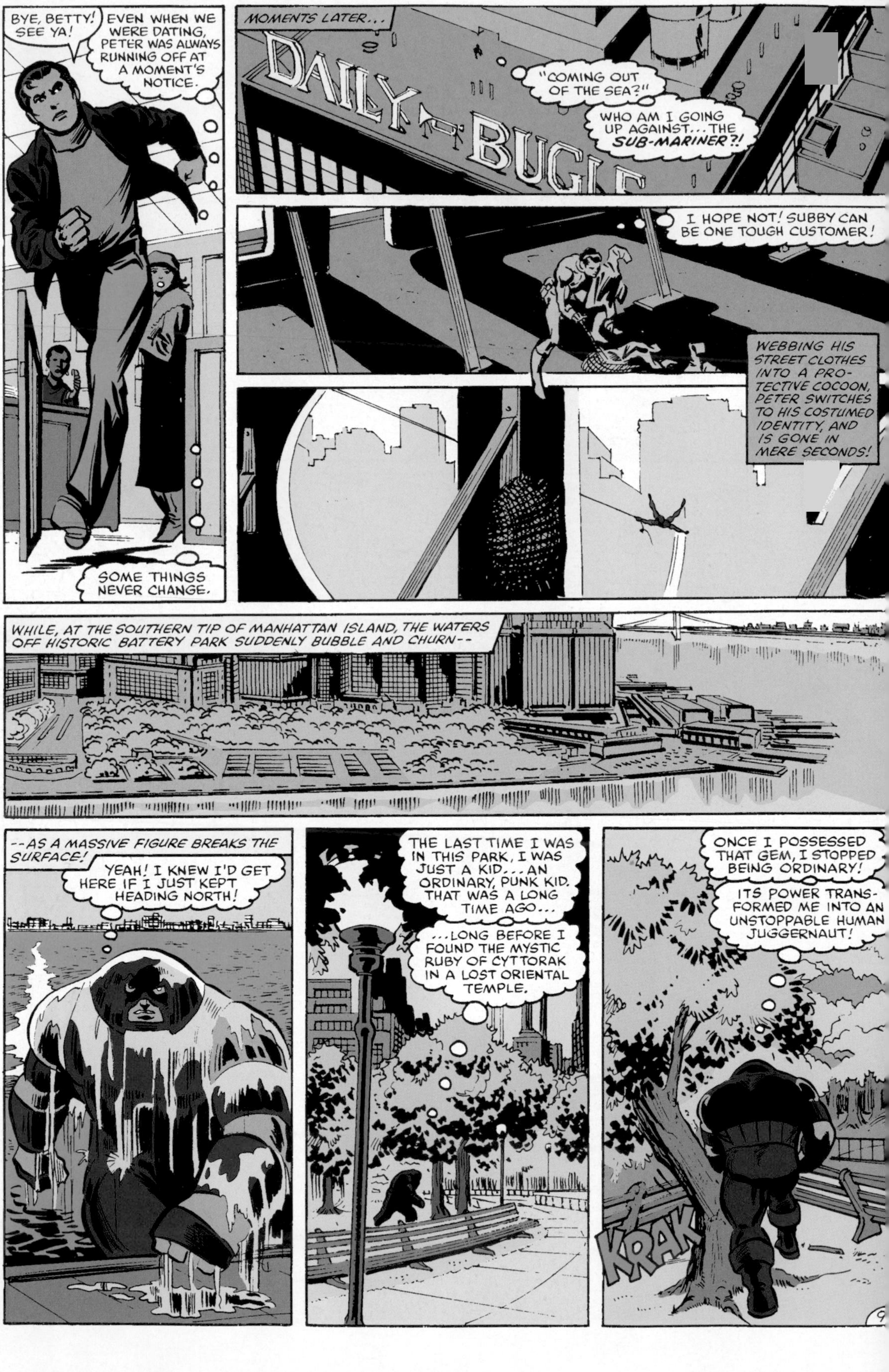
BYE, BETTY! SEE YA!
EVEN WHEN WE WERE DATING, PETER WAS ALWAYS RUNNING OFF AT A MOMENT'S NOTICE.
SOME THINGS NEVER CHANGE.
MOMENTS LATER...
DAILY BUGLE
"COMING OUT OF THE SEA?"
WHO AM I GOING UP AGAINST... THE SUB-MARINER?!
I HOPE NOT! SUBBY CAN BE ONE TOUGH CUSTOMER!
WEBBING HIS STREET CLOTHES INTO A PROTECTIVE COCOON, PETER SWITCHES TO HIS COSTUMED IDENTITY, AND IS GONE IN MERE SECONDS!
WHILE, AT THE SOUTHERN TIP OF MANHATTAN ISLAND, THE WATERS OFF HISTORIC BATTERY PARK SUDDENLY BUBBLE AND CHURN--
--AS A MASSIVE FIGURE BREAKS THE SURFACE!
YEAH! I KNEW I'D GET HERE IF I JUST KEPT HEADING NORTH!
THE LAST TIME I WAS IN THIS PARK, I WAS JUST A KID... AN ORDINARY, PUNK KID. THAT WAS A LONG TIME AGO...
...LONG BEFORE I FOUND THE MYSTIC RUBY OF CYTTORAK IN A LOST ORIENTAL TEMPLE.
ONCE I POSSESSED THAT GEM, I STOPPED BEING ORDINARY!
ITS POWER TRANSFORMED ME INTO AN UNSTOPPABLE HUMAN JUGGERNAUT!
KRAK
9

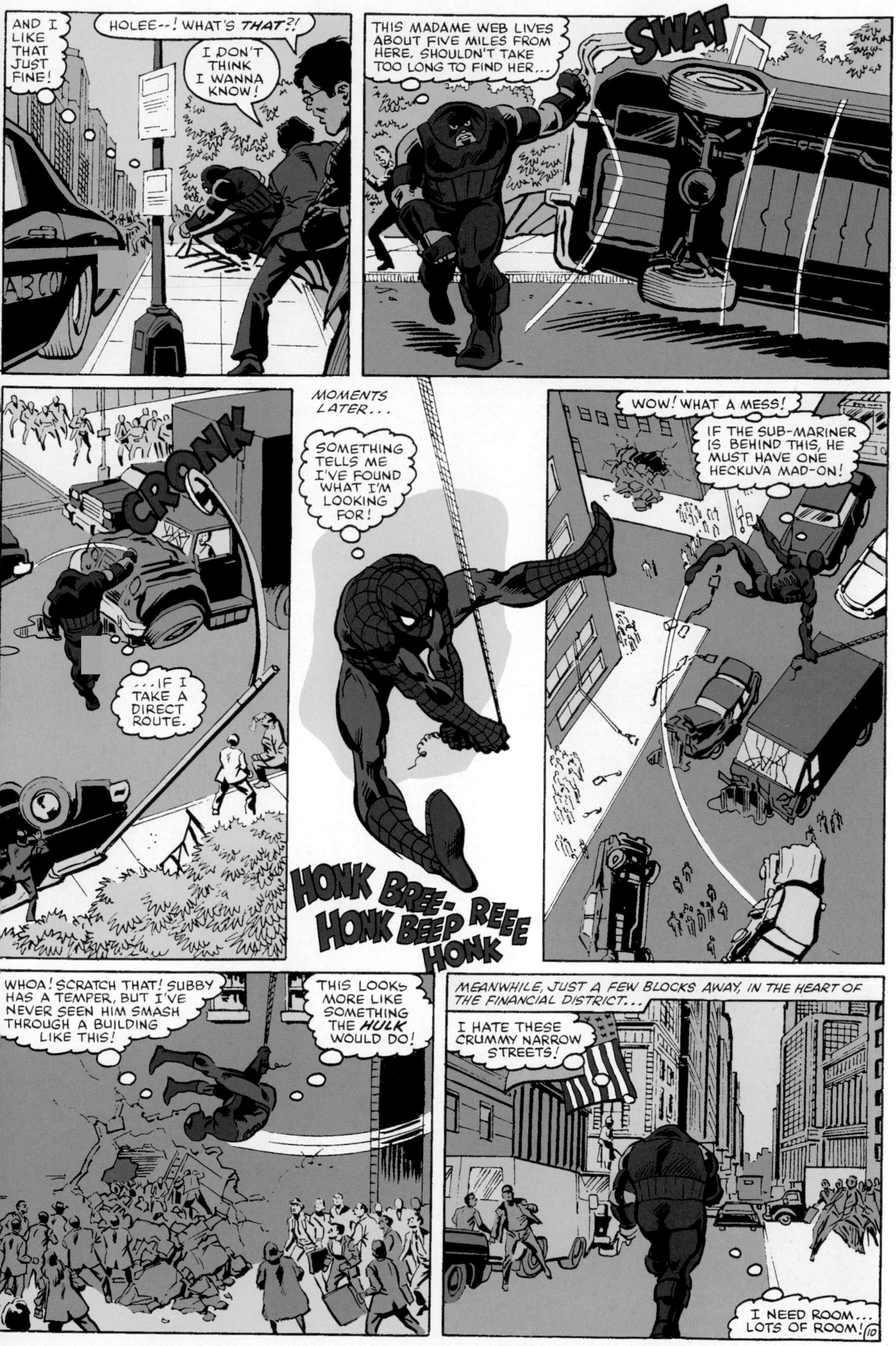
AND I LIKE THAT JUST FINE!
HOLEE--! WHAT'S THAT?!
I DON'T THINK I WANNA KNOW!
THIS MADAME WEB LIVES ABOUT FIVE MILES FROM HERE. SHOULDN'T TAKE TOO LONG TO FIND HER...
SWAT
CRONK
...IF I TAKE A DIRECT ROUTE.
MOMENTS LATER...
SOMETHING TELLS ME I'VE FOUND WHAT I'M LOOKING FOR!
HONK BREE- REEE
HONK BEEP
HONK
WOW! WHAT A MESS!
IF THE SUB-MARINER IS BEHIND THIS, HE MUST HAVE ONE HECKUVA MAD-ON!
WHOA! SCRATCH THAT! SUBBY HAS A TEMPER, BUT I'VE NEVER SEEN HIM SMASH THROUGH A BUILDING LIKE THIS!
THIS LOOKS MORE LIKE SOMETHING THE HULK WOULD DO!
MEANWHILE, JUST A FEW BLOCKS AWAY, IN THE HEART OF THE FINANCIAL DISTRICT...
I HATE THESE CRUMMY NARROW STREETS!
I NEED ROOM... LOTS OF ROOM!
10

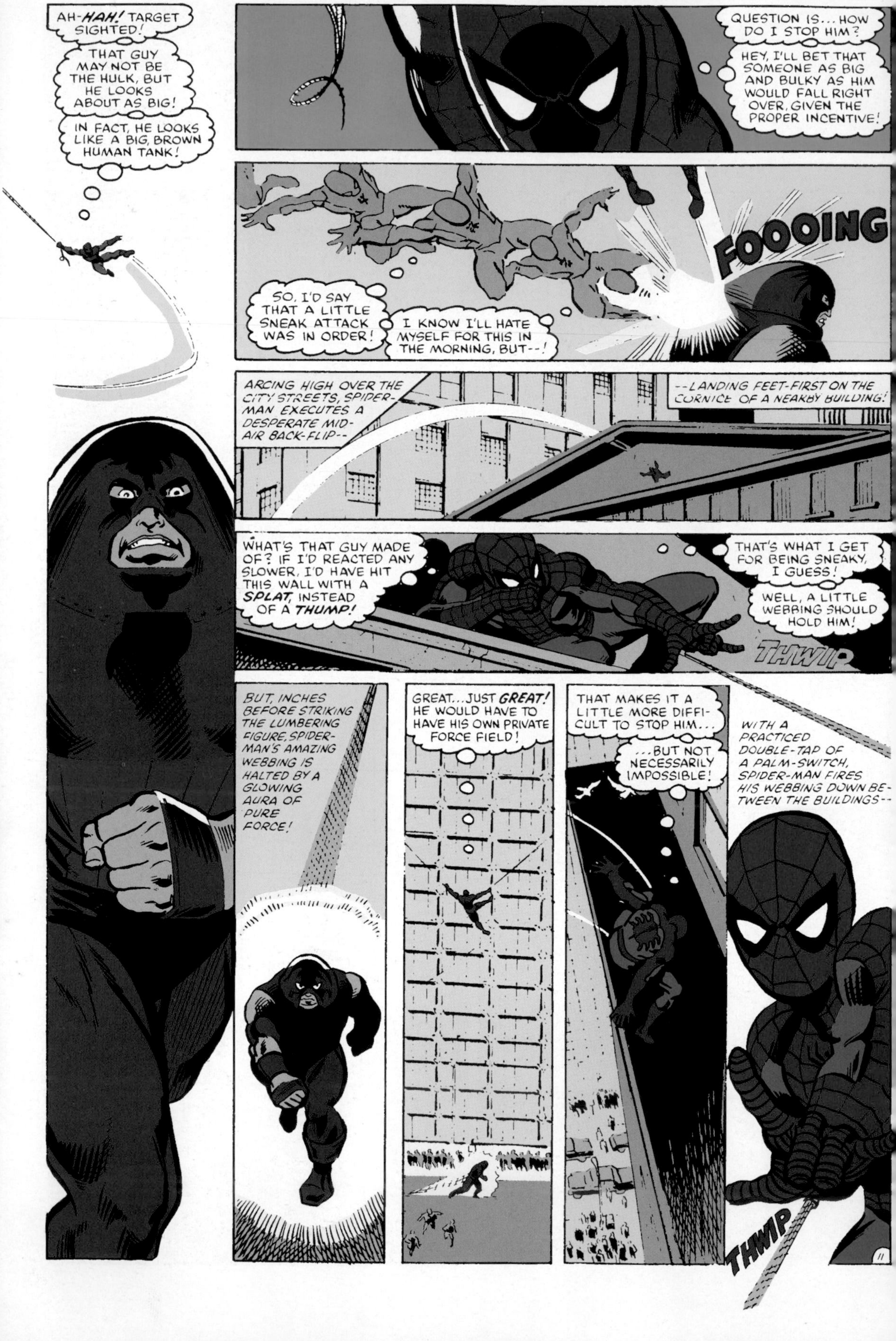

AH-HAH! TARGET SIGHTED!
THAT GUY MAY NOT BE THE HULK, BUT HE LOOKS ABOUT AS BIG!
IN FACT, HE LOOKS LIKE A BIG, BROWN HUMAN TANK!
QUESTION IS... HOW DO I STOP HIM?
HEY, I'LL BET THAT SOMEONE AS BIG AND BULKY AS HIM WOULD FALL RIGHT OVER, GIVEN THE PROPER INCENTIVE!
SO, I'D SAY THAT A LITTLE SNEAK ATTACK WAS IN ORDER!
I KNOW I'LL HATE MYSELF FOR THIS IN THE MORNING, BUT--!
FOOOING
ARCING HIGH OVER THE CITY STREETS, SPIDER-MAN EXECUTES A DESPERATE MID-AIR BACK-FLIP--
--LANDING FEET-FIRST ON THE CORNICE OF A NEARBY BUILDING!
WHAT'S THAT GUY MADE OF? IF I'D REACTED ANY SLOWER, I'D HAVE HIT THIS WALL WITH A SPLAT, INSTEAD OF A THUMP!
THAT'S WHAT I GET FOR BEING SNEAKY, I GUESS!
WELL, A LITTLE WEBBING SHOULD HOLD HIM!
THWIP
BUT, INCHES BEFORE STRIKING THE LUMBERING FIGURE, SPIDER-MAN'S AMAZING WEBBING IS HALTED BY A GLOWING AURA OF PURE FORCE!
GREAT... JUST GREAT! HE WOULD HAVE TO HAVE HIS OWN PRIVATE FORCE FIELD!
THAT MAKES IT A LITTLE MORE DIFFI-CULT TO STOP HIM...
...BUT NOT NECESSARILY IMPOSSIBLE!
WITH A PRACTICED DOUBLE-TAP OF A PALM-SWITCH, SPIDER-MAN FIRES HIS WEBBING DOWN BE-TWEEN THE BUILDINGS--
THWIP

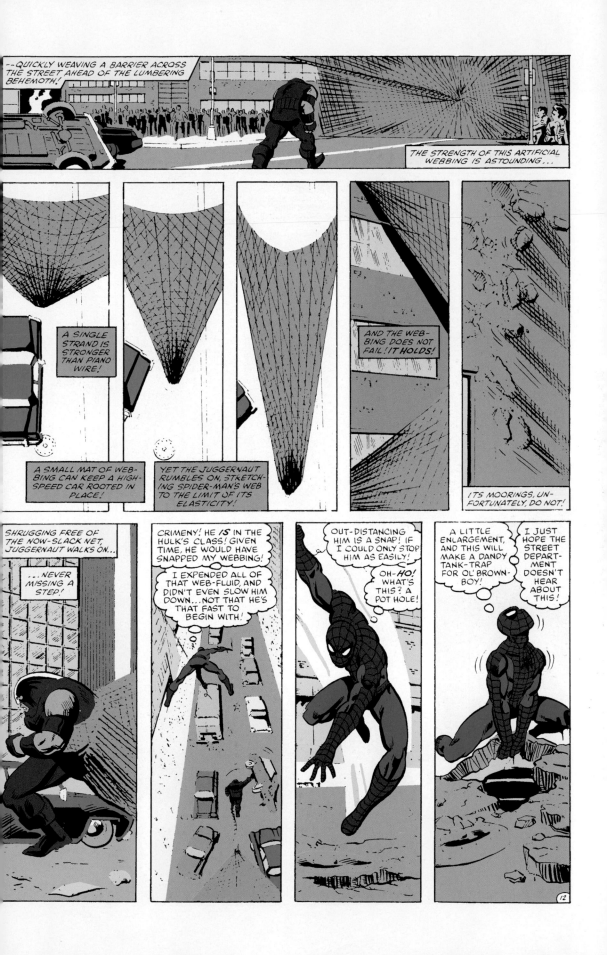

--QUICKLY WEAVING A BARRIER ACROSS THE STREET AHEAD OF THE LUMBERING BEHEMOTH!

THE STRENGTH OF THIS ARTIFICIAL WEBBING IS ASTOUNDING...

A SINGLE STRAND IS STRONGER THAN PIANO WIRE!

A SMALL MAT OF WEBBING CAN KEEP A HIGH-SPEED CAR ROOTED IN PLACE!

YET THE JUGGERNAUT RUMBLES ON, STRETCHING SPIDER-MAN'S WEB TO THE LIMIT OF ITS ELASTICITY!

AND THE WEBBING DOES NOT FAIL! IT HOLDS!

ITS MOORINGS, UNFORTUNATELY, DO NOT!

SHRUGGING FREE OF THE NOW-SLACK NET, JUGGERNAUT WALKS ON...

...NEVER MISSING A STEP!

CRIMENY! HE *IS* IN THE HULK'S CLASS! GIVEN TIME, HE WOULD HAVE SNAPPED MY WEBBING!

I EXPENDED ALL OF THAT WEB-FLUID, AND DIDN'T EVEN SLOW HIM DOWN...NOT THAT HE'S THAT FAST TO BEGIN WITH!

OUT-DISTANCING HIM IS A SNAP! IF I COULD ONLY STOP HIM AS EASILY!

OH-*HO!* WHAT'S THIS? A POT HOLE!

A LITTLE ENLARGEMENT, AND THIS WILL MAKE A DANDY TANK-TRAP FOR OL' BROWN-BOY!

I JUST HOPE THE STREET DEPARTMENT DOESN'T HEAR ABOUT THIS!

12

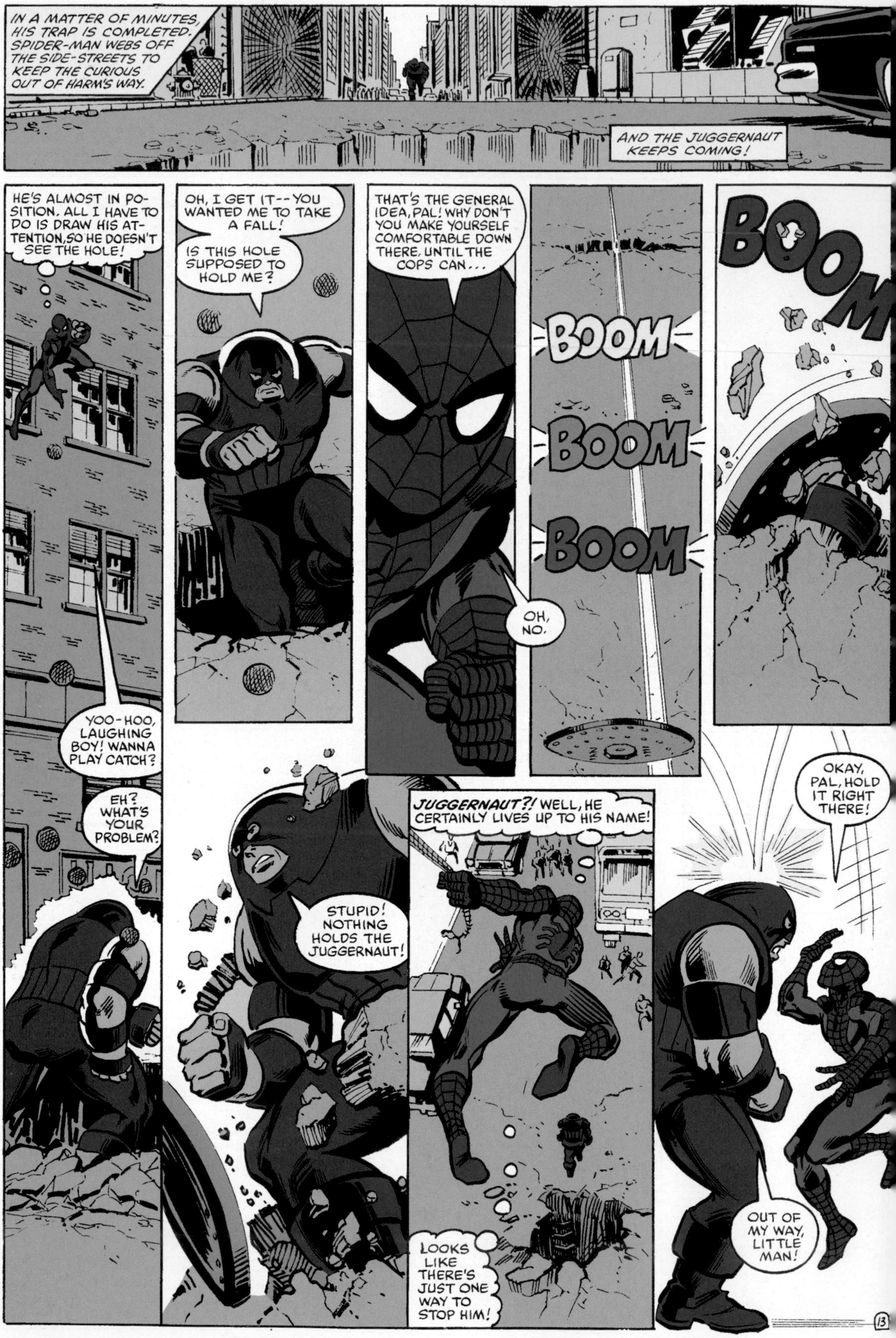

IN A MATTER OF MINUTES, HIS TRAP IS COMPLETED. SPIDER-MAN WEBS OFF THE SIDE-STREETS TO KEEP THE CURIOUS OUT OF HARM'S WAY.
AND THE JUGGERNAUT KEEPS COMING!
HE'S ALMOST IN POSITION. ALL I HAVE TO DO IS DRAW HIS ATTENTION, SO HE DOESN'T SEE THE HOLE!
YOO-HOO, LAUGHING BOY! WANNA PLAY CATCH?
EH? WHAT'S YOUR PROBLEM?
OH, I GET IT--YOU WANTED ME TO TAKE A FALL!
IS THIS HOLE SUPPOSED TO HOLD ME?
THAT'S THE GENERAL IDEA, PAL! WHY DON'T YOU MAKE YOURSELF COMFORTABLE DOWN THERE, UNTIL THE COPS CAN...
BOOM
BOOM
BOOM
OH, NO.
BOOM
STUPID! NOTHING HOLDS THE JUGGERNAUT!
JUGGERNAUT?! WELL, HE CERTAINLY LIVES UP TO HIS NAME!
LOOKS LIKE THERE'S JUST ONE WAY TO STOP HIM!
OKAY, PAL, HOLD IT RIGHT THERE!
OUT OF MY WAY, LITTLE MAN!

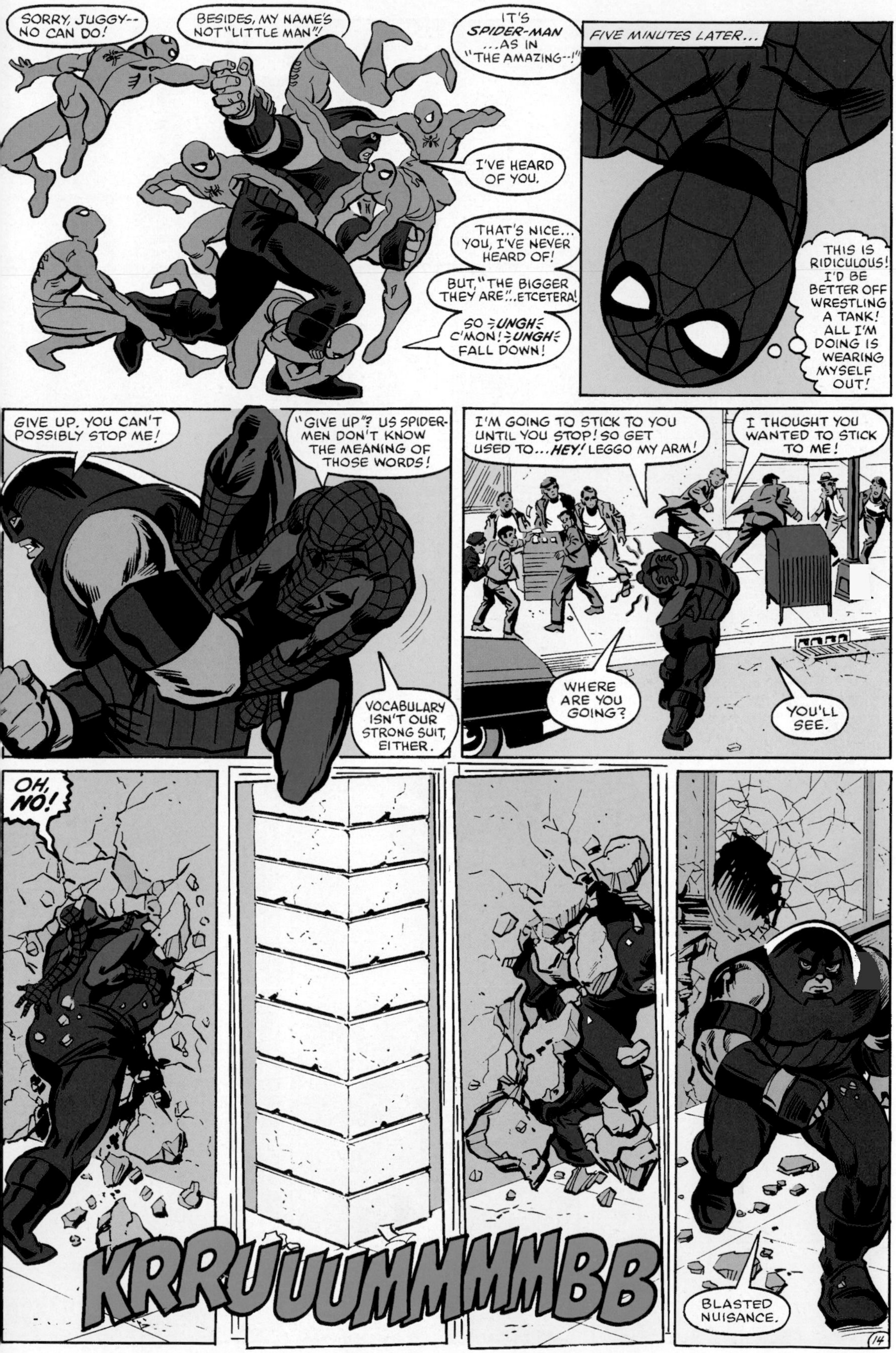
SORRY, JUGGY-- NO CAN DO!
BESIDES, MY NAME'S NOT "LITTLE MAN"!
IT'S SPIDER-MAN ...AS IN "THE AMAZING--!"
I'VE HEARD OF YOU.
THAT'S NICE... YOU, I'VE NEVER HEARD OF!
BUT, "THE BIGGER THEY ARE"..ETCETERA!
SO UNGH C'MON! UNGH FALL DOWN!
FIVE MINUTES LATER...
THIS IS RIDICULOUS! I'D BE BETTER OFF WRESTLING A TANK! ALL I'M DOING IS WEARING MYSELF OUT!
GIVE UP. YOU CAN'T POSSIBLY STOP ME!
"GIVE UP"? US SPIDER-MEN DON'T KNOW THE MEANING OF THOSE WORDS!
VOCABULARY ISN'T OUR STRONG SUIT, EITHER.
I'M GOING TO STICK TO YOU UNTIL YOU STOP! SO GET USED TO... HEY! LEGGO MY ARM!
I THOUGHT YOU WANTED TO STICK TO ME!
WHERE ARE YOU GOING?
YOU'LL SEE.
OH, NO!
KRRUUUMMMMBB
BLASTED NUISANCE.
14

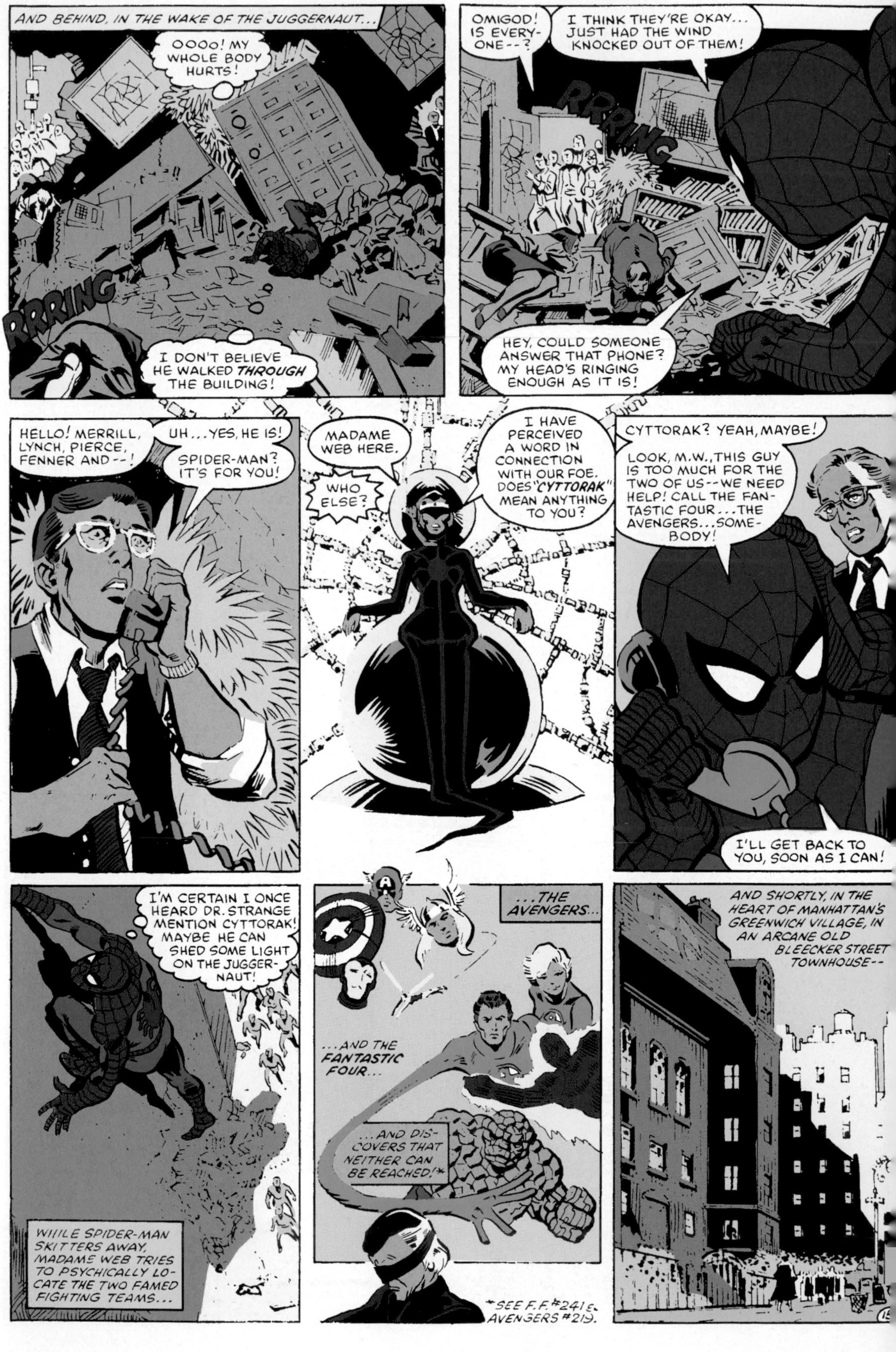

AND BEHIND, IN THE WAKE OF THE JUGGERNAUT...
OOOO! MY WHOLE BODY HURTS!
RRRING
I DON'T BELIEVE HE WALKED THROUGH THE BUILDING!
OMIGOD! IS EVERY-ONE--?
I THINK THEY'RE OKAY... JUST HAD THE WIND KNOCKED OUT OF THEM!
RRRING
HEY, COULD SOMEONE ANSWER THAT PHONE? MY HEAD'S RINGING ENOUGH AS IT IS!
HELLO! MERRILL, LYNCH, PIERCE, FENNER AND--!
UH...YES, HE IS!
SPIDER-MAN? IT'S FOR YOU!
MADAME WEB HERE.
WHO ELSE?
I HAVE PERCEIVED A WORD IN CONNECTION WITH OUR FOE. DOES "CYTTORAK" MEAN ANYTHING TO YOU?
CYTTORAK? YEAH, MAYBE!
LOOK, M.W., THIS GUY IS TOO MUCH FOR THE TWO OF US--WE NEED HELP! CALL THE FANTASTIC FOUR...THE AVENGERS...SOME-BODY!
I'LL GET BACK TO YOU, SOON AS I CAN!
I'M CERTAIN I ONCE HEARD DR. STRANGE MENTION CYTTORAK! MAYBE HE CAN SHED SOME LIGHT ON THE JUGGER-NAUT!
WHILE SPIDER-MAN SKITTERS AWAY, MADAME WEB TRIES TO PSYCHICALLY LO-CATE THE TWO FAMED FIGHTING TEAMS...
...THE AVENGERS...
...AND THE FANTASTIC FOUR...
...AND DIS-COVERS THAT NEITHER CAN BE REACHED!*
*SEE F.F. #241 & AVENGERS #219.
AND SHORTLY, IN THE HEART OF MANHATTAN'S GREENWICH VILLAGE, IN AN ARCANE OLD BLEECKER STREET TOWNHOUSE--

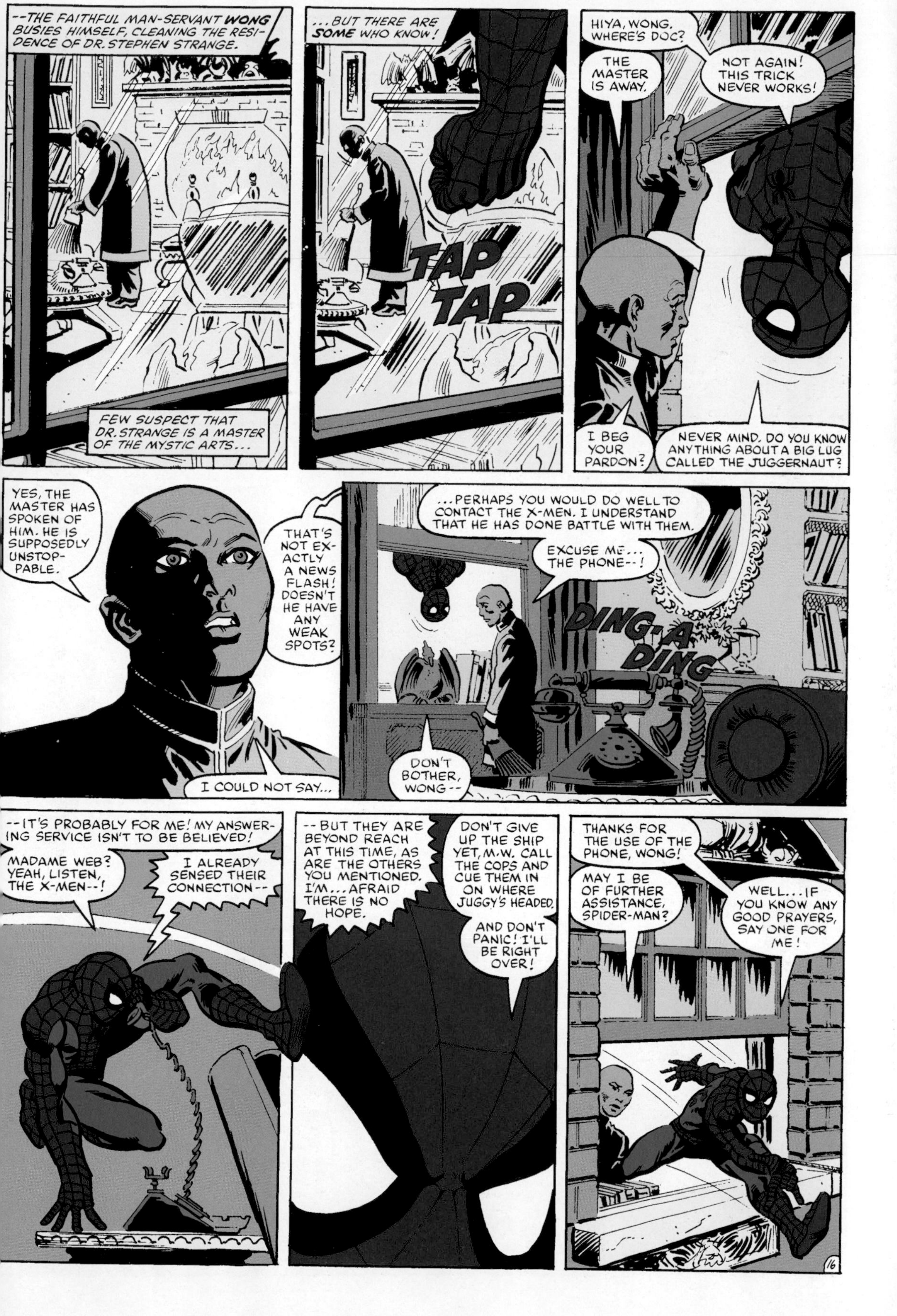
--THE FAITHFUL MAN-SERVANT WONG BUSIES HIMSELF, CLEANING THE RESIDENCE OF DR. STEPHEN STRANGE.
FEW SUSPECT THAT DR. STRANGE IS A MASTER OF THE MYSTIC ARTS...
...BUT THERE ARE SOME WHO KNOW!
TAP TAP
HIYA, WONG. WHERE'S DOC?
THE MASTER IS AWAY.
NOT AGAIN! THIS TRICK NEVER WORKS!
I BEG YOUR PARDON?
NEVER MIND. DO YOU KNOW ANYTHING ABOUT A BIG LUG CALLED THE JUGGERNAUT?
YES, THE MASTER HAS SPOKEN OF HIM. HE IS SUPPOSEDLY UNSTOPPABLE.
THAT'S NOT EXACTLY A NEWS FLASH! DOESN'T HE HAVE ANY WEAK SPOTS?
I COULD NOT SAY...
...PERHAPS YOU WOULD DO WELL TO CONTACT THE X-MEN. I UNDERSTAND THAT HE HAS DONE BATTLE WITH THEM.
EXCUSE ME... THE PHONE--!
DING-A DING
DON'T BOTHER, WONG--
--IT'S PROBABLY FOR ME! MY ANSWERING SERVICE ISN'T TO BE BELIEVED!
MADAME WEB? YEAH, LISTEN, THE X-MEN--!
I ALREADY SENSED THEIR CONNECTION--
--BUT THEY ARE BEYOND REACH AT THIS TIME, AS ARE THE OTHERS YOU MENTIONED. I'M... AFRAID THERE IS NO HOPE.
DON'T GIVE UP THE SHIP YET, M.W. CALL THE COPS AND CUE THEM IN ON WHERE JUGGY'S HEADED.
AND DON'T PANIC! I'LL BE RIGHT OVER!
THANKS FOR THE USE OF THE PHONE, WONG!
MAY I BE OF FURTHER ASSISTANCE, SPIDER-MAN?
WELL... IF YOU KNOW ANY GOOD PRAYERS, SAY ONE FOR ME!
16

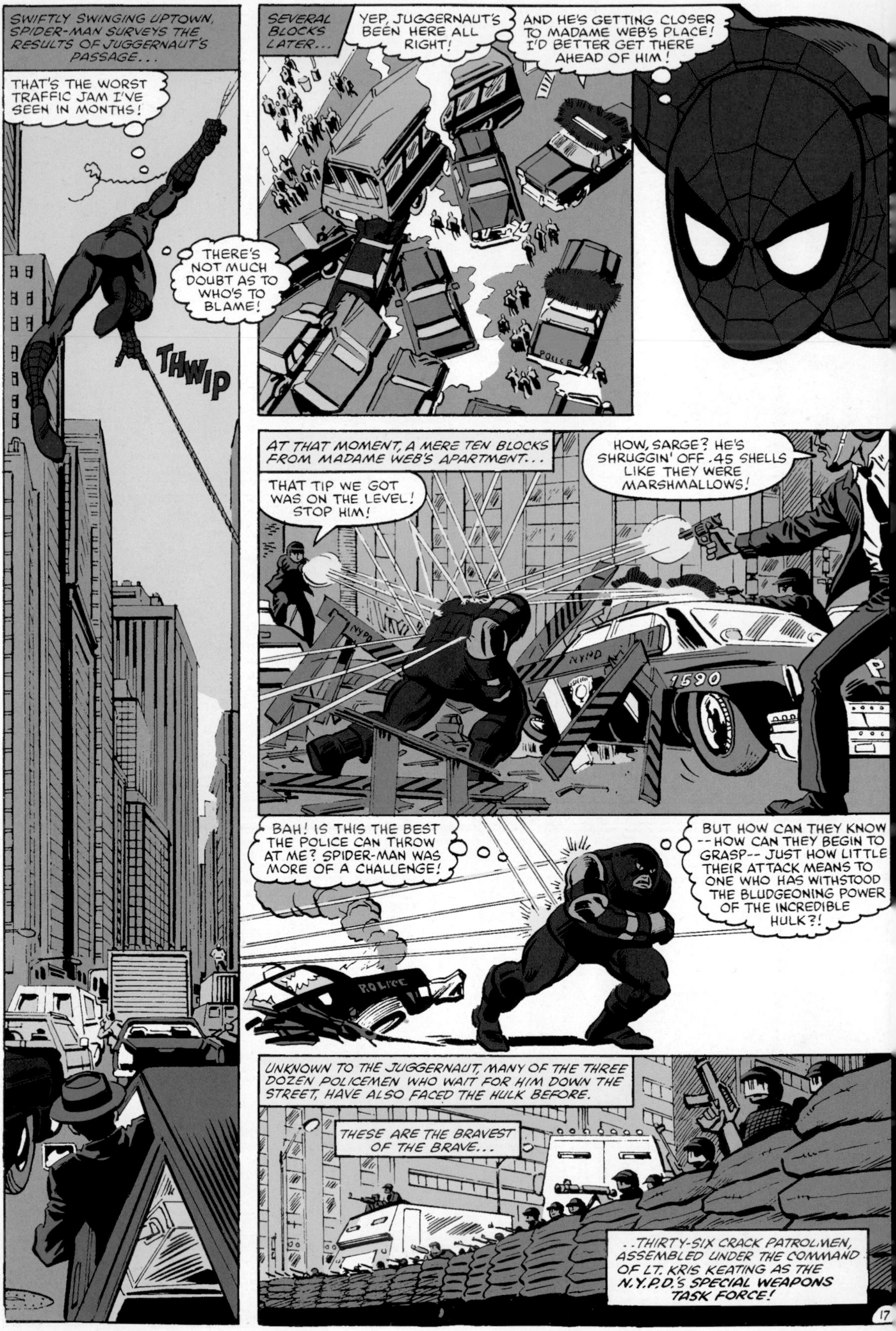
SWIFTLY SWINGING UPTOWN, SPIDER-MAN SURVEYS THE RESULTS OF JUGGERNAUT'S PASSAGE...
THAT'S THE WORST TRAFFIC JAM I'VE SEEN IN MONTHS!
THERE'S NOT MUCH DOUBT AS TO WHO'S TO BLAME!
THWIP
SEVERAL BLOCKS LATER...
YEP, JUGGERNAUT'S BEEN HERE ALL RIGHT!
AND HE'S GETTING CLOSER TO MADAME WEB'S PLACE! I'D BETTER GET THERE AHEAD OF HIM!
AT THAT MOMENT, A MERE TEN BLOCKS FROM MADAME WEB'S APARTMENT...
THAT TIP WE GOT WAS ON THE LEVEL! STOP HIM!
HOW, SARGE? HE'S SHRUGGIN' OFF .45 SHELLS LIKE THEY WERE MARSHMALLOWS!
NYPD
1590
BAH! IS THIS THE BEST THE POLICE CAN THROW AT ME? SPIDER-MAN WAS MORE OF A CHALLENGE!
BUT HOW CAN THEY KNOW -- HOW CAN THEY BEGIN TO GRASP-- JUST HOW LITTLE THEIR ATTACK MEANS TO ONE WHO HAS WITHSTOOD THE BLUDGEONING POWER OF THE INCREDIBLE HULK?!
POLICE
UNKNOWN TO THE JUGGERNAUT, MANY OF THE THREE DOZEN POLICEMEN WHO WAIT FOR HIM DOWN THE STREET, HAVE ALSO FACED THE HULK BEFORE.
THESE ARE THE BRAVEST OF THE BRAVE...
..THIRTY-SIX CRACK PATROLMEN, ASSEMBLED UNDER THE COMMAND OF LT. KRIS KEATING AS THE N.Y.P.D.'s SPECIAL WEAPONS TASK FORCE!

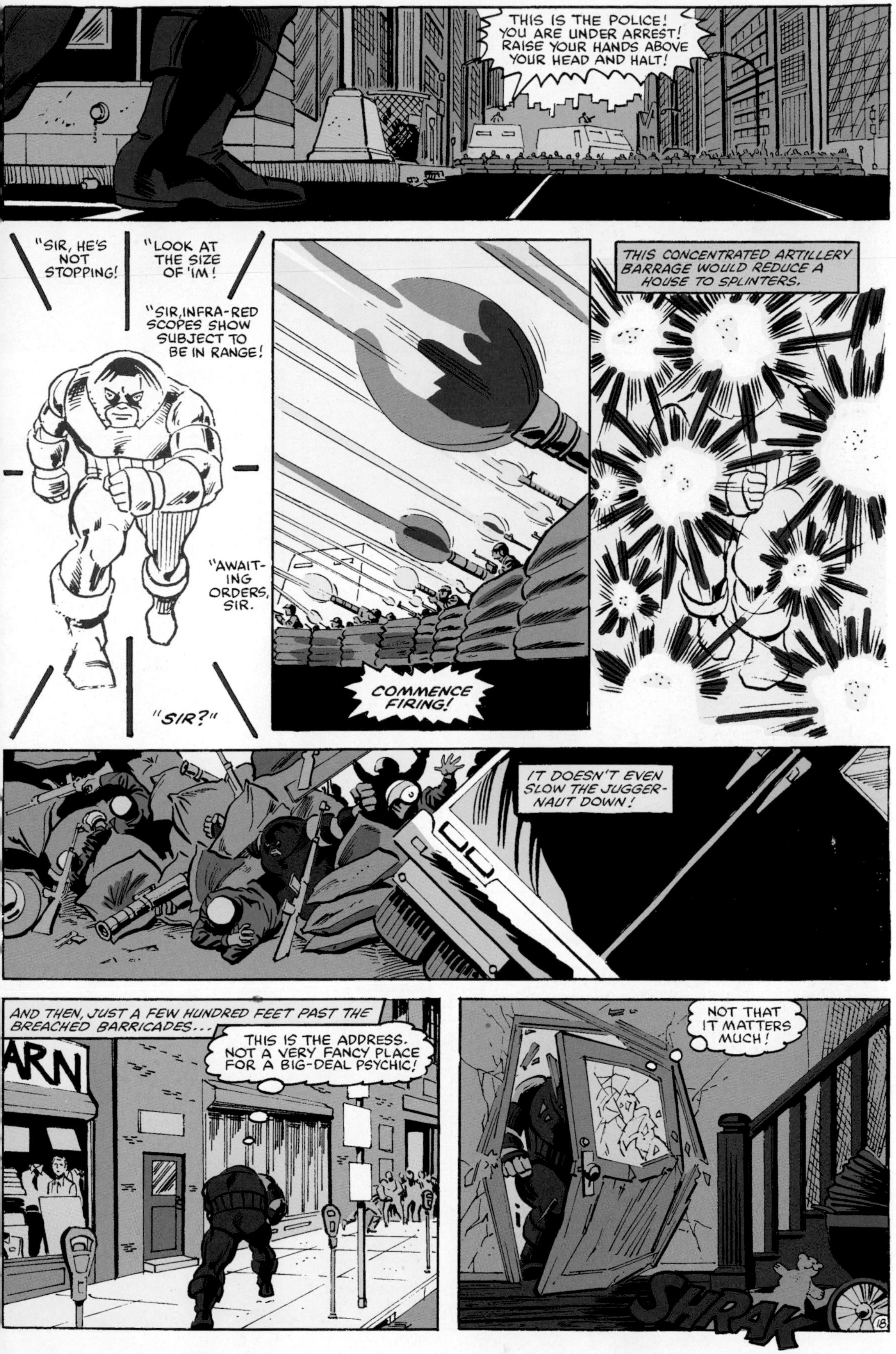
THIS IS THE POLICE! YOU ARE UNDER ARREST! RAISE YOUR HANDS ABOVE YOUR HEAD AND HALT!
"SIR, HE'S NOT STOPPING!
"LOOK AT THE SIZE OF 'IM!
"SIR, INFRA-RED SCOPES SHOW SUBJECT TO BE IN RANGE!
"AWAIT-ING ORDERS, SIR.
"SIR?"
COMMENCE FIRING!
THIS CONCENTRATED ARTILLERY BARRAGE WOULD REDUCE A HOUSE TO SPLINTERS.
IT DOESN'T EVEN SLOW THE JUGGER-NAUT DOWN!
AND THEN, JUST A FEW HUNDRED FEET PAST THE BREACHED BARRICADES...
THIS IS THE ADDRESS. NOT A VERY FANCY PLACE FOR A BIG-DEAL PSYCHIC!
NOT THAT IT MATTERS MUCH!
SHRAK
18

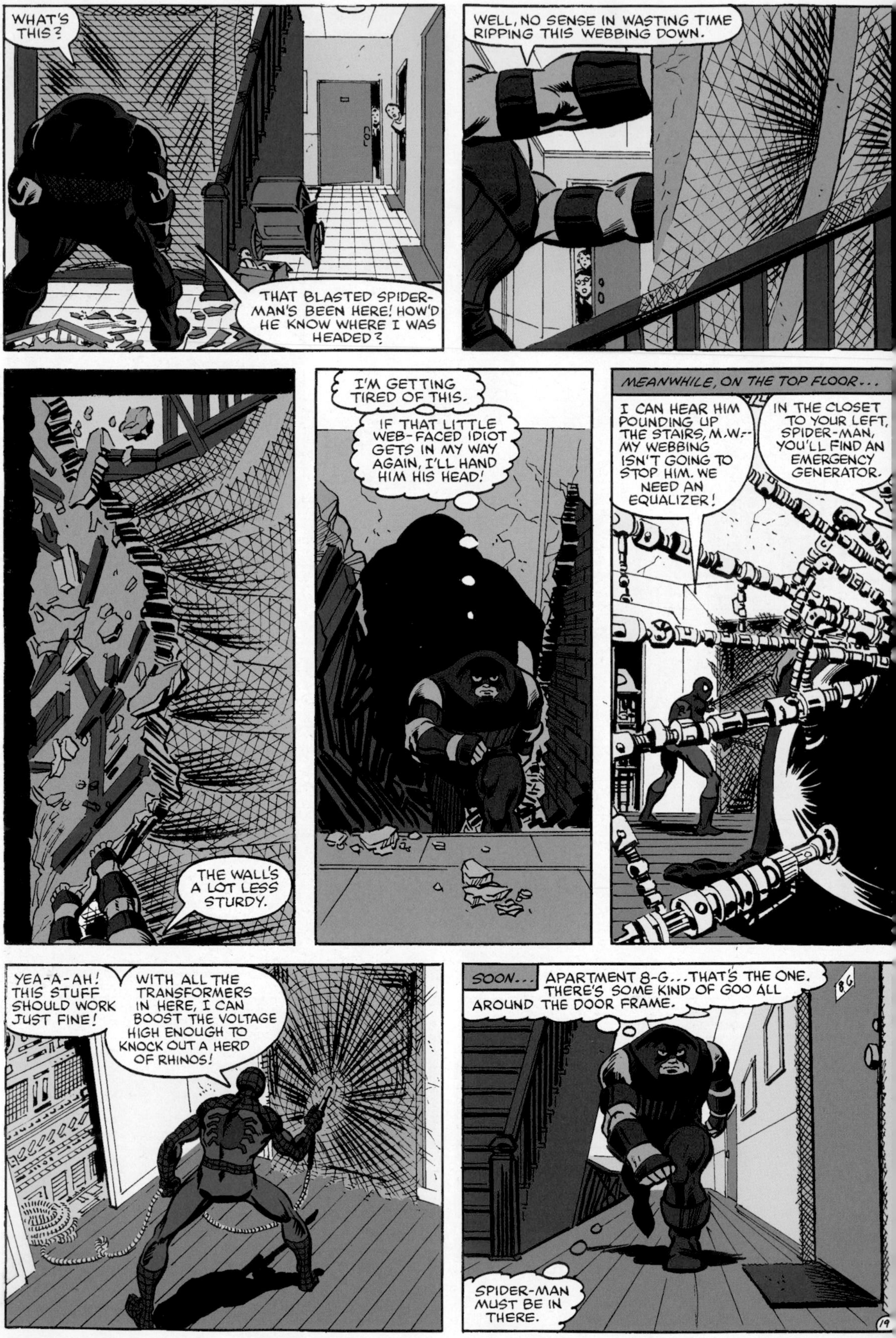

WHAT'S THIS?
THAT BLASTED SPIDER-MAN'S BEEN HERE! HOW'D HE KNOW WHERE I WAS HEADED?
WELL, NO SENSE IN WASTING TIME RIPPING THIS WEBBING DOWN.
THE WALL'S A LOT LESS STURDY.
I'M GETTING TIRED OF THIS.
IF THAT LITTLE WEB-FACED IDIOT GETS IN MY WAY AGAIN, I'LL HAND HIM HIS HEAD!
MEANWHILE, ON THE TOP FLOOR...
I CAN HEAR HIM POUNDING UP THE STAIRS, M.W.-- MY WEBBING ISN'T GOING TO STOP HIM. WE NEED AN EQUALIZER!
IN THE CLOSET TO YOUR LEFT, SPIDER-MAN, YOU'LL FIND AN EMERGENCY GENERATOR.
YEA-A-AH! THIS STUFF SHOULD WORK JUST FINE!
WITH ALL THE TRANSFORMERS IN HERE, I CAN BOOST THE VOLTAGE HIGH ENOUGH TO KNOCK OUT A HERD OF RHINOS!
SOON...
APARTMENT 8-G...THAT'S THE ONE. THERE'S SOME KIND OF GOO ALL AROUND THE DOOR FRAME.
8G
SPIDER-MAN MUST BE IN THERE.

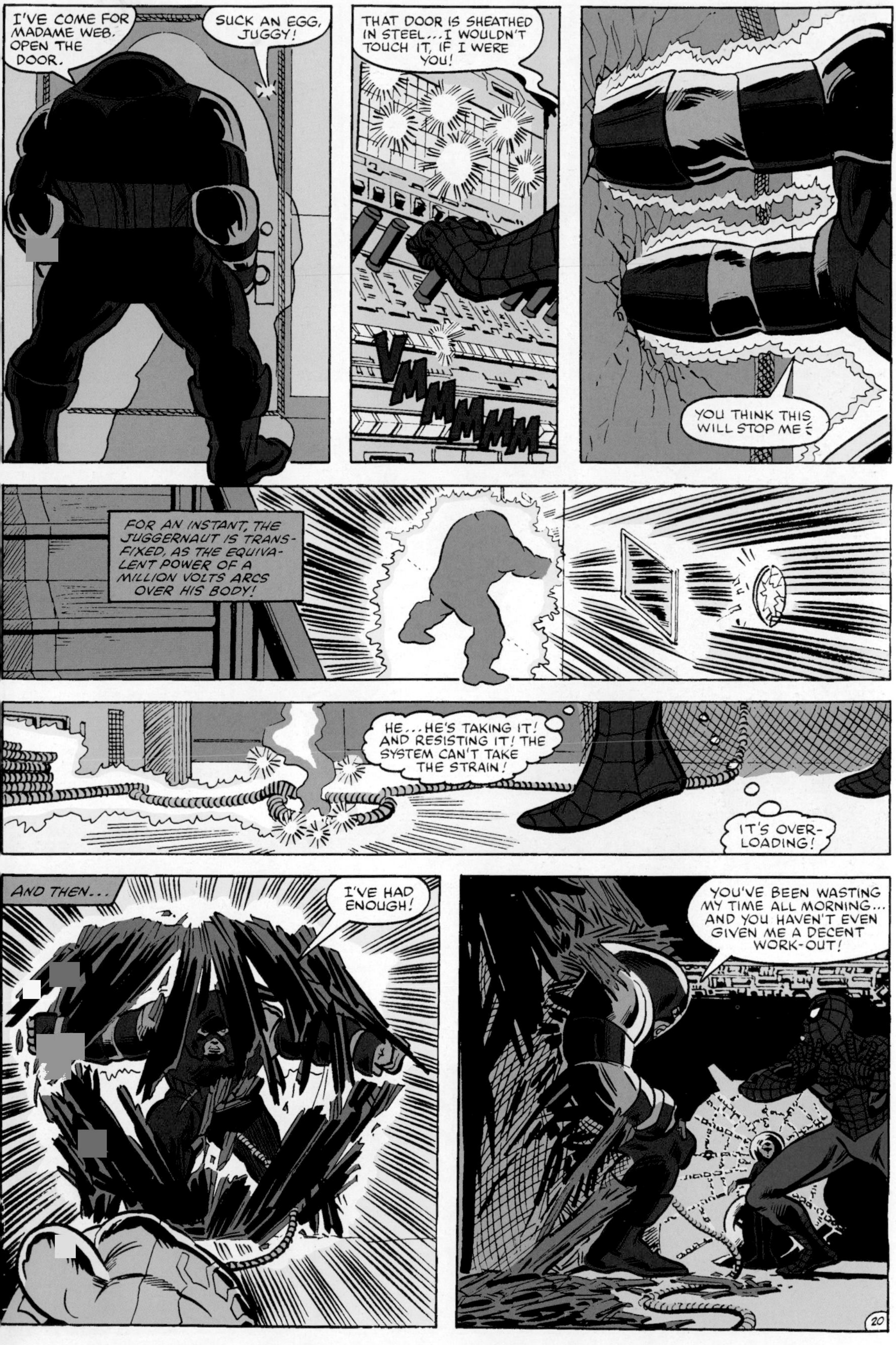
I'VE COME FOR MADAME WEB. OPEN THE DOOR.
SUCK AN EGG, JUGGY!
THAT DOOR IS SHEATHED IN STEEL... I WOULDN'T TOUCH IT, IF I WERE YOU!
VMMMMMM
YOU THINK THIS WILL STOP ME?
FOR AN INSTANT, THE JUGGERNAUT IS TRANSFIXED, AS THE EQUIVALENT POWER OF A MILLION VOLTS ARCS OVER HIS BODY!
HE... HE'S TAKING IT! AND RESISTING IT! THE SYSTEM CAN'T TAKE THE STRAIN!
IT'S OVERLOADING!
AND THEN...
I'VE HAD ENOUGH!
YOU'VE BEEN WASTING MY TIME ALL MORNING... AND YOU HAVEN'T EVEN GIVEN ME A DECENT WORK-OUT!
20

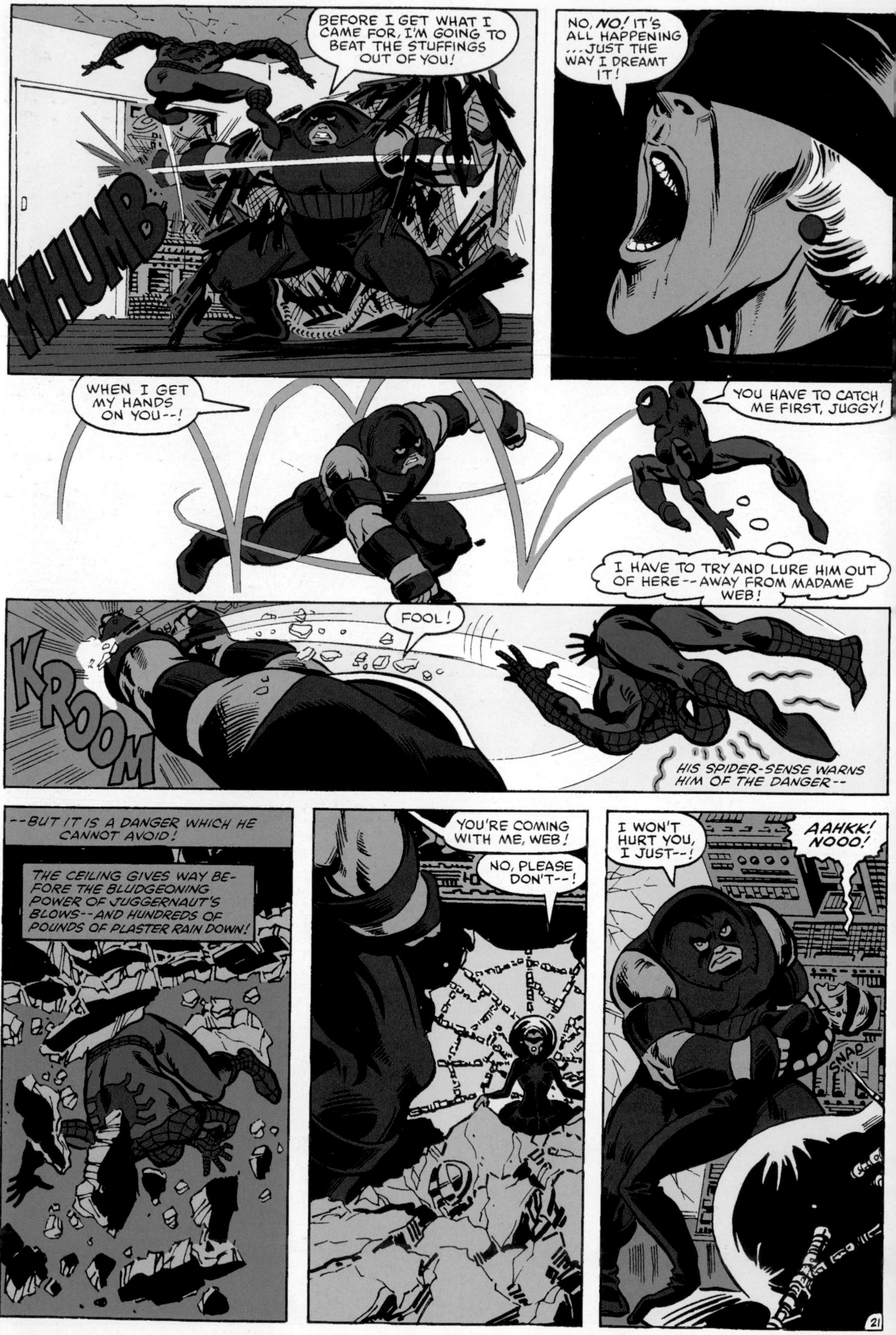
BEFORE I GET WHAT I CAME FOR, I'M GOING TO BEAT THE STUFFINGS OUT OF YOU!
WHUMB
NO, NO! IT'S ALL HAPPENING ...JUST THE WAY I DREAMT IT!
WHEN I GET MY HANDS ON YOU--!
YOU HAVE TO CATCH ME FIRST, JUGGY!
I HAVE TO TRY AND LURE HIM OUT OF HERE--AWAY FROM MADAME WEB!
KROOM
FOOL!
HIS SPIDER-SENSE WARNS HIM OF THE DANGER--
--BUT IT IS A DANGER WHICH HE CANNOT AVOID!
THE CEILING GIVES WAY BEFORE THE BLUDGEONING POWER OF JUGGERNAUT'S BLOWS--AND HUNDREDS OF POUNDS OF PLASTER RAIN DOWN!
YOU'RE COMING WITH ME, WEB!
NO, PLEASE DON'T--!
I WON'T HURT YOU, I JUST--!
AAHKK! NOOO!
SNAP

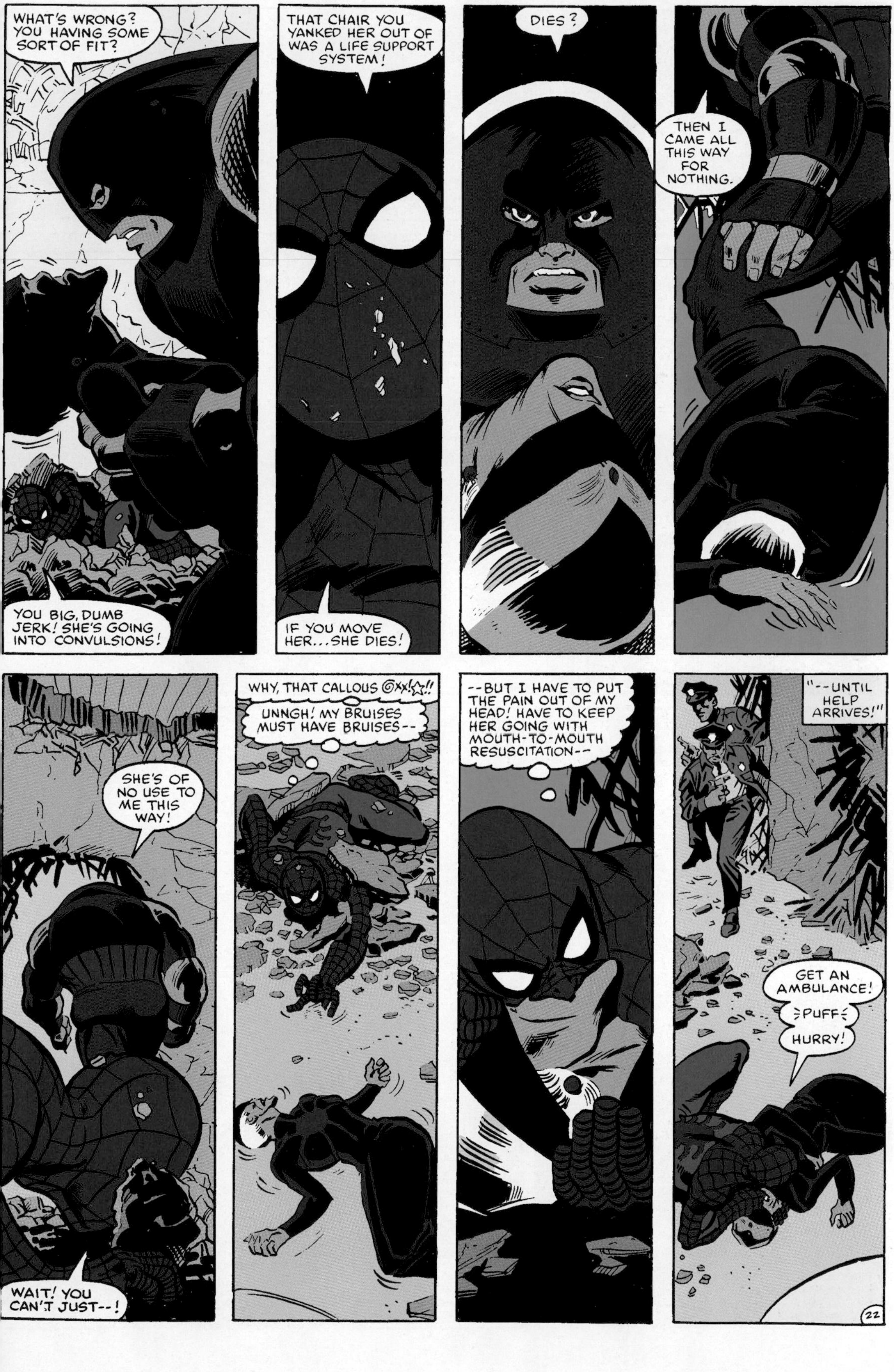
WHAT'S WRONG? YOU HAVING SOME SORT OF FIT?
YOU BIG, DUMB JERK! SHE'S GOING INTO CONVULSIONS!
THAT CHAIR YOU YANKED HER OUT OF WAS A LIFE SUPPORT SYSTEM!
IF YOU MOVE HER... SHE DIES!
DIES?
THEN I CAME ALL THIS WAY FOR NOTHING.
SHE'S OF NO USE TO ME THIS WAY!
WAIT! YOU CAN'T JUST--!
WHY, THAT CALLOUS @XX!☆!!
UNNGH! MY BRUISES MUST HAVE BRUISES--
--BUT I HAVE TO PUT THE PAIN OUT OF MY HEAD! HAVE TO KEEP HER GOING WITH MOUTH-TO-MOUTH RESUSCITATION--
"--UNTIL HELP ARRIVES!"
GET AN AMBULANCE!
PUFF
HURRY!

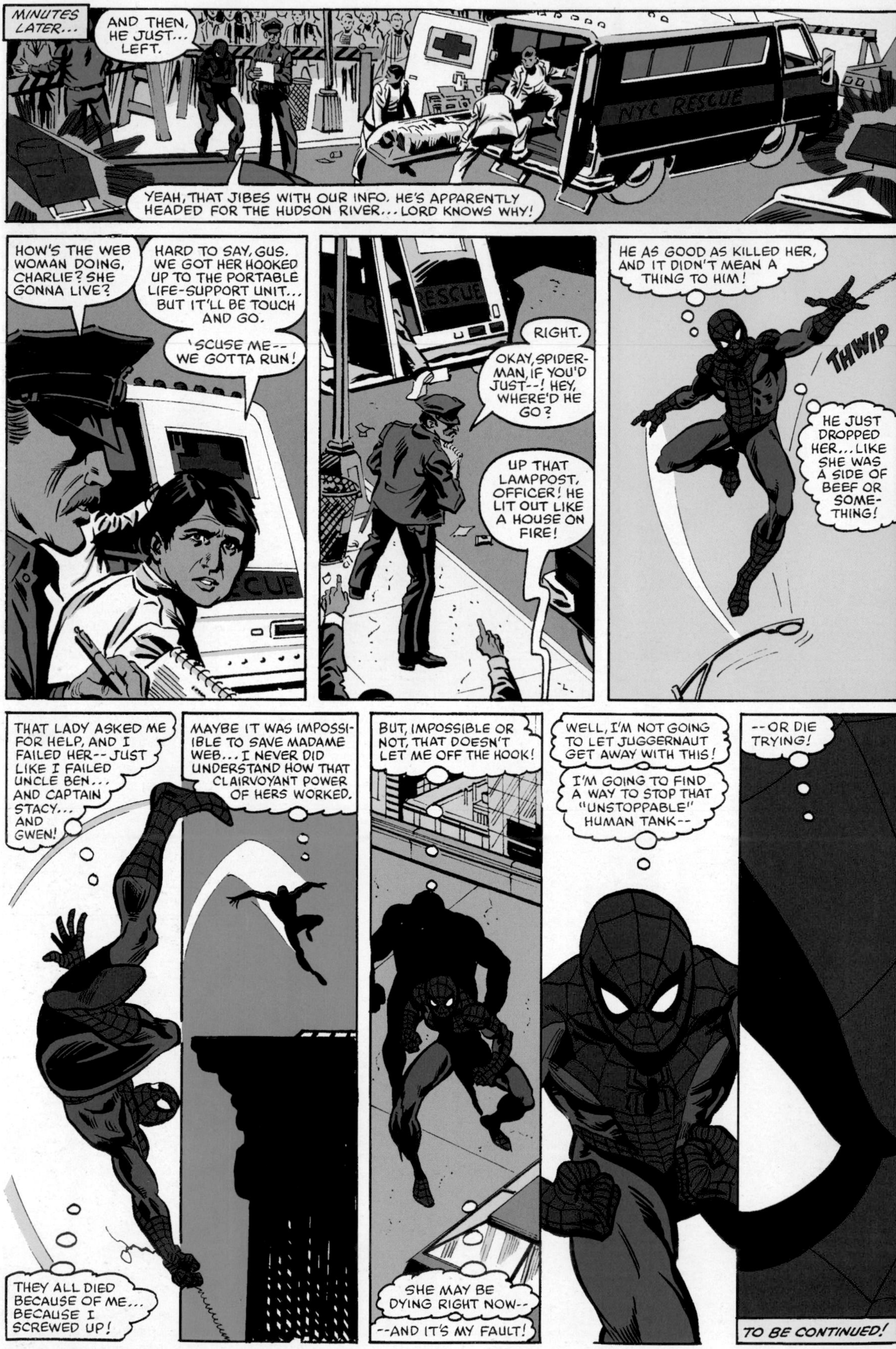
MINUTES LATER...
AND THEN, HE JUST... LEFT.
YEAH, THAT JIBES WITH OUR INFO. HE'S APPARENTLY HEADED FOR THE HUDSON RIVER... LORD KNOWS WHY!
NYC RESCUE
HOW'S THE WEB WOMAN DOING, CHARLIE? SHE GONNA LIVE?
HARD TO SAY, GUS. WE GOT HER HOOKED UP TO THE PORTABLE LIFE-SUPPORT UNIT... BUT IT'LL BE TOUCH AND GO.
'SCUSE ME-- WE GOTTA RUN!
RIGHT.
OKAY, SPIDER-MAN, IF YOU'D JUST--! HEY, WHERE'D HE GO?
UP THAT LAMPPOST, OFFICER! HE LIT OUT LIKE A HOUSE ON FIRE!
HE AS GOOD AS KILLED HER, AND IT DIDN'T MEAN A THING TO HIM!
THWIP
HE JUST DROPPED HER... LIKE SHE WAS A SIDE OF BEEF OR SOME-THING!
THAT LADY ASKED ME FOR HELP, AND I FAILED HER-- JUST LIKE I FAILED UNCLE BEN... AND CAPTAIN STACY... AND GWEN!
THEY ALL DIED BECAUSE OF ME... BECAUSE I SCREWED UP!
MAYBE IT WAS IMPOSSIBLE TO SAVE MADAME WEB... I NEVER DID UNDERSTAND HOW THAT CLAIRVOYANT POWER OF HERS WORKED.
BUT, IMPOSSIBLE OR NOT, THAT DOESN'T LET ME OFF THE HOOK!
SHE MAY BE DYING RIGHT NOW--
--AND IT'S MY FAULT!
WELL, I'M NOT GOING TO LET JUGGERNAUT GET AWAY WITH THIS!
I'M GOING TO FIND A WAY TO STOP THAT "UNSTOPPABLE" HUMAN TANK--
--OR DIE TRYING!
TO BE CONTINUED!

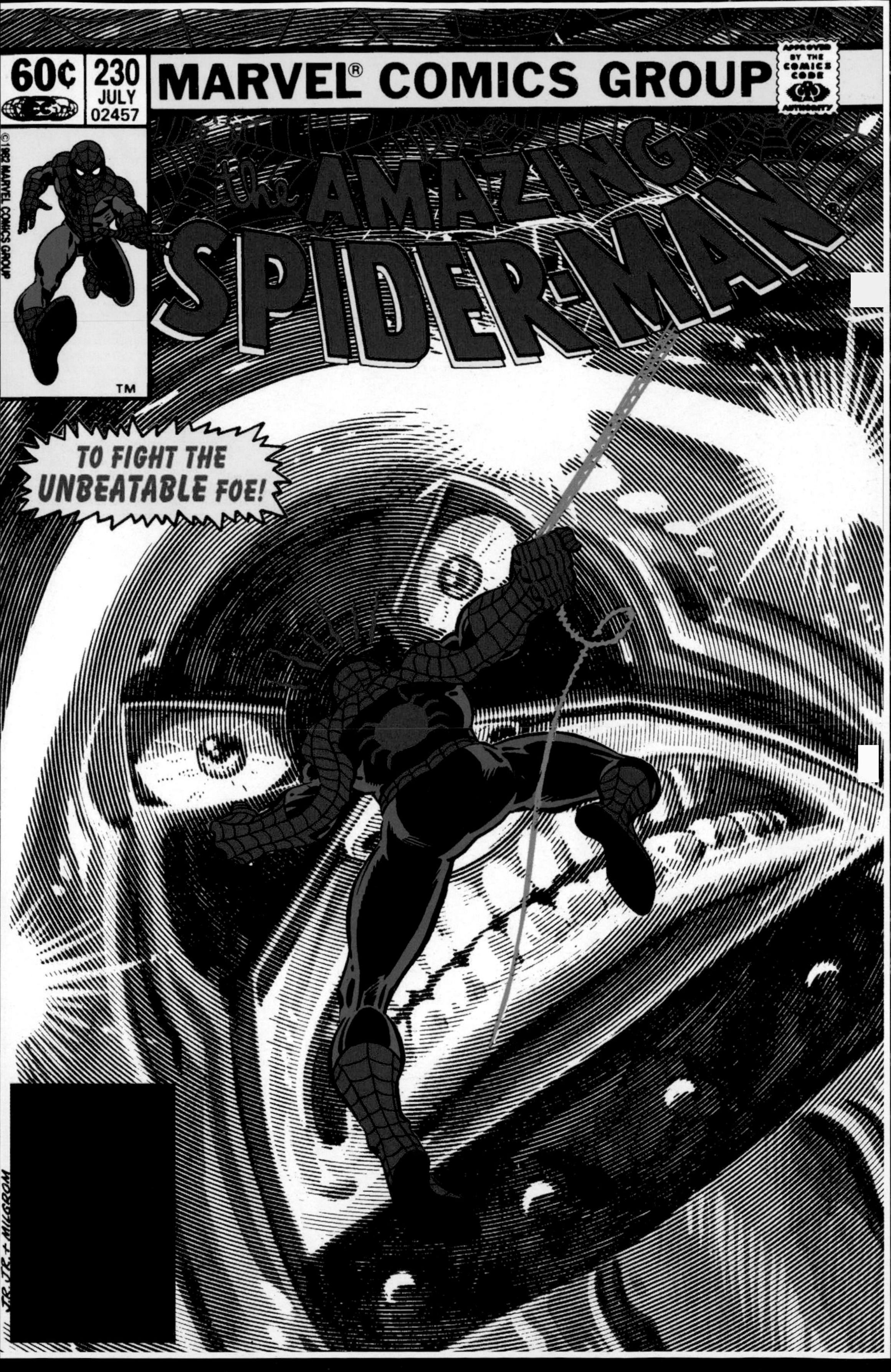
60¢
230
JULY
02457
MARVEL® COMICS GROUP
APPROVED BY THE COMICS CODE AUTHORITY
©1982 MARVEL COMICS GROUP
the AMAZING SPIDER-MAN®
TM
TO FIGHT THE UNBEATABLE FOE!

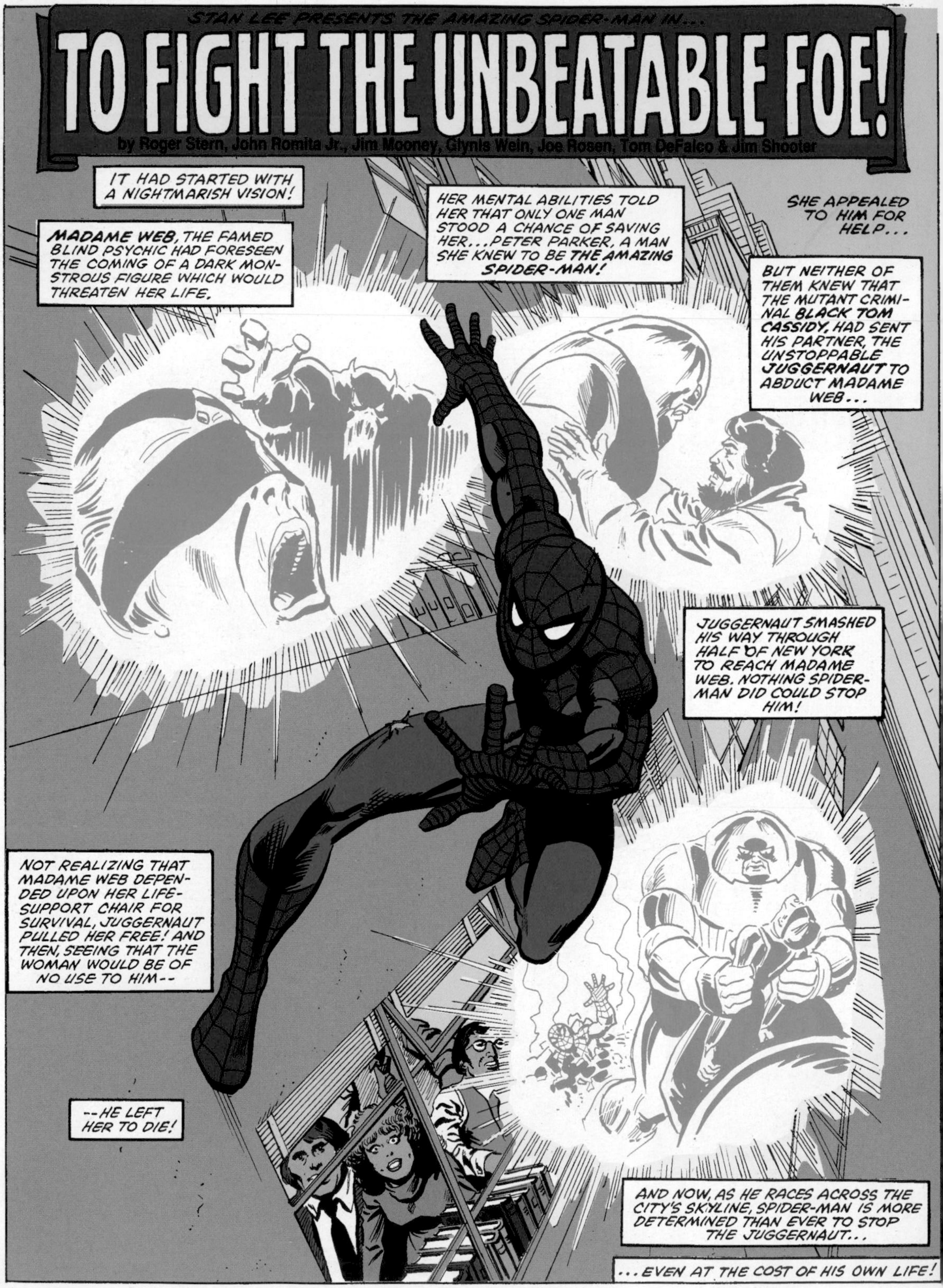
STAN LEE PRESENTS THE AMAZING SPIDER-MAN IN...
TO FIGHT THE UNBEATABLE FOE!
by Roger Stern, John Romita Jr., Jim Mooney, Glynis Wein, Joe Rosen, Tom DeFalco & Jim Shooter
IT HAD STARTED WITH A NIGHTMARISH VISION!
MADAME WEB, THE FAMED BLIND PSYCHIC HAD FORESEEN THE COMING OF A DARK MONSTROUS FIGURE WHICH WOULD THREATEN HER LIFE.
HER MENTAL ABILITIES TOLD HER THAT ONLY ONE MAN STOOD A CHANCE OF SAVING HER...PETER PARKER, A MAN SHE KNEW TO BE THE AMAZING SPIDER-MAN!
SHE APPEALED TO HIM FOR HELP...
BUT NEITHER OF THEM KNEW THAT THE MUTANT CRIMINAL BLACK TOM CASSIDY, HAD SENT HIS PARTNER, THE UNSTOPPABLE JUGGERNAUT TO ABDUCT MADAME WEB...
JUGGERNAUT SMASHED HIS WAY THROUGH HALF OF NEW YORK TO REACH MADAME WEB. NOTHING SPIDER-MAN DID COULD STOP HIM!
NOT REALIZING THAT MADAME WEB DEPENDED UPON HER LIFE-SUPPORT CHAIR FOR SURVIVAL, JUGGERNAUT PULLED HER FREE! AND THEN, SEEING THAT THE WOMAN WOULD BE OF NO USE TO HIM--
--HE LEFT HER TO DIE!
AND NOW, AS HE RACES ACROSS THE CITY'S SKYLINE, SPIDER-MAN IS MORE DETERMINED THAN EVER TO STOP THE JUGGERNAUT...
...EVEN AT THE COST OF HIS OWN LIFE!

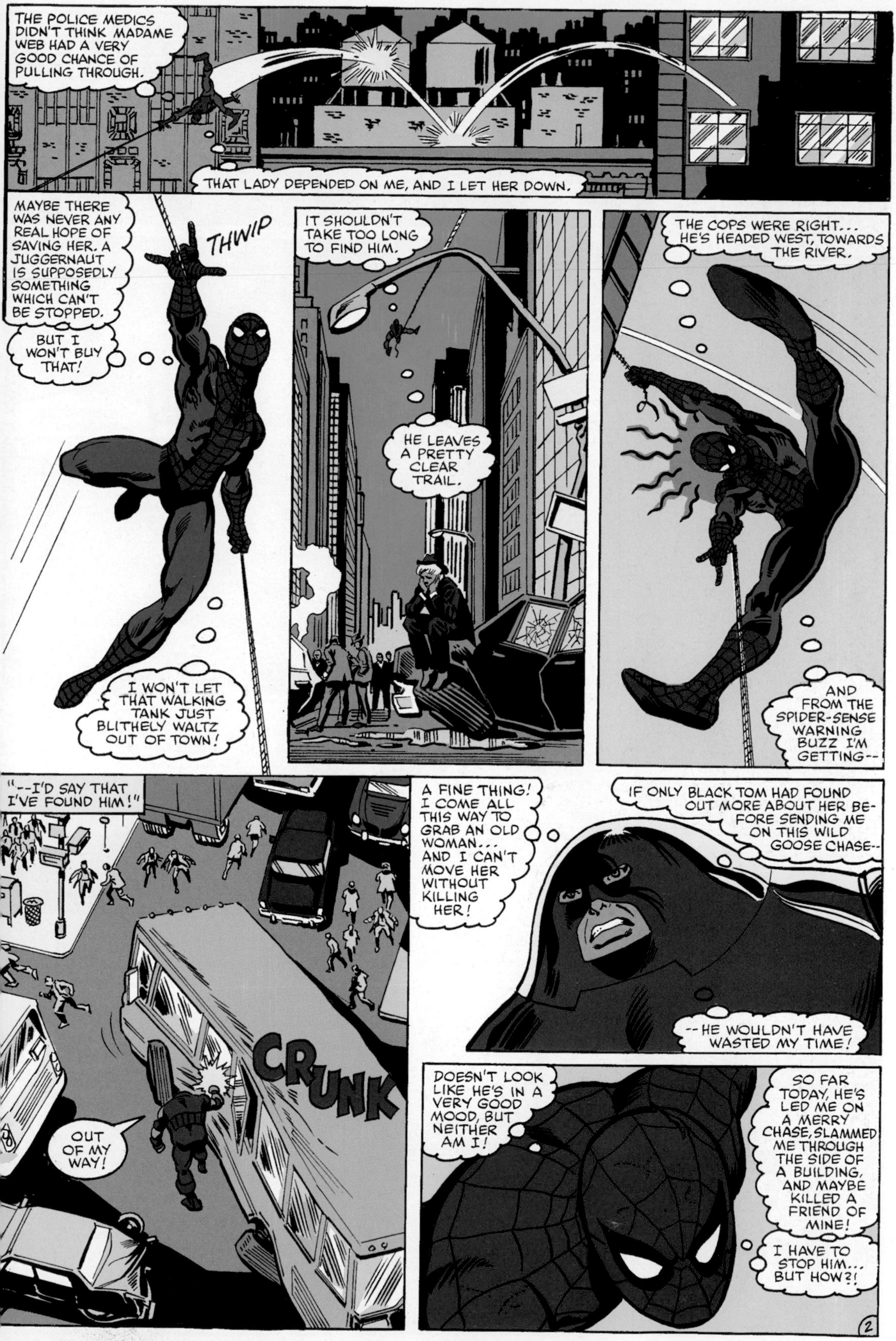
THE POLICE MEDICS DIDN'T THINK MADAME WEB HAD A VERY GOOD CHANCE OF PULLING THROUGH.
THAT LADY DEPENDED ON ME, AND I LET HER DOWN.
MAYBE THERE WAS NEVER ANY REAL HOPE OF SAVING HER. A JUGGERNAUT IS SUPPOSEDLY SOMETHING WHICH CAN'T BE STOPPED.
BUT I WON'T BUY THAT!
THWIP
I WON'T LET THAT WALKING TANK JUST BLITHELY WALTZ OUT OF TOWN!
IT SHOULDN'T TAKE TOO LONG TO FIND HIM.
HE LEAVES A PRETTY CLEAR TRAIL.
THE COPS WERE RIGHT... HE'S HEADED WEST, TOWARDS THE RIVER.
AND FROM THE SPIDER-SENSE WARNING BUZZ I'M GETTING--
"--I'D SAY THAT I'VE FOUND HIM!"
CRUNK
OUT OF MY WAY!
A FINE THING! I COME ALL THIS WAY TO GRAB AN OLD WOMAN... AND I CAN'T MOVE HER WITHOUT KILLING HER!
IF ONLY BLACK TOM HAD FOUND OUT MORE ABOUT HER BEFORE SENDING ME ON THIS WILD GOOSE CHASE--
--HE WOULDN'T HAVE WASTED MY TIME!
DOESN'T LOOK LIKE HE'S IN A VERY GOOD MOOD, BUT NEITHER AM I!
SO FAR TODAY, HE'S LED ME ON A MERRY CHASE, SLAMMED ME THROUGH THE SIDE OF A BUILDING, AND MAYBE KILLED A FRIEND OF MINE!
I HAVE TO STOP HIM... BUT HOW?!
2

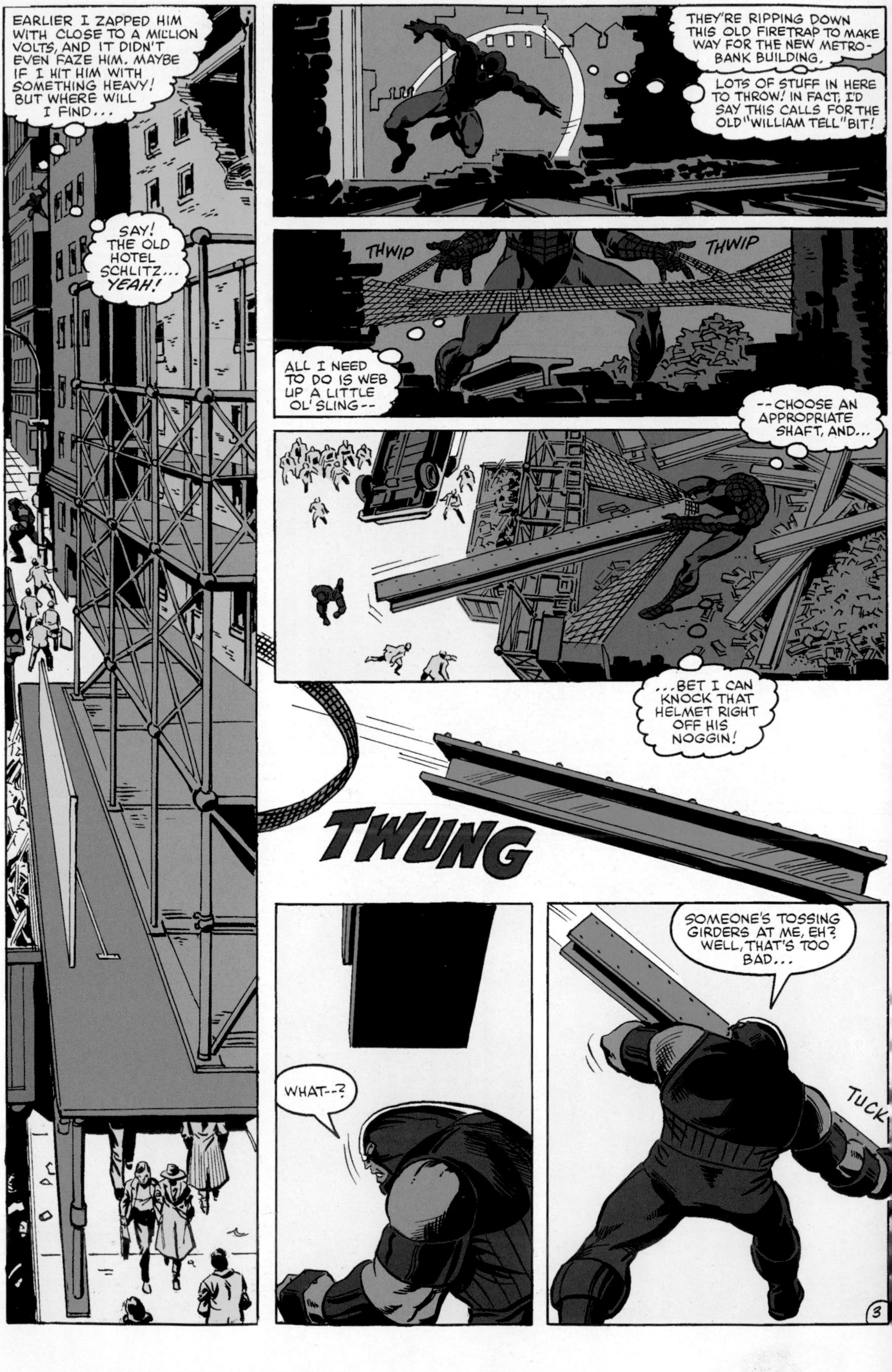
EARLIER I ZAPPED HIM WITH CLOSE TO A MILLION VOLTS, AND IT DIDN'T EVEN FAZE HIM. MAYBE IF I HIT HIM WITH SOMETHING HEAVY! BUT WHERE WILL I FIND...
SAY! THE OLD HOTEL SCHLITZ... YEAH!
THEY'RE RIPPING DOWN THIS OLD FIRETRAP TO MAKE WAY FOR THE NEW METRO-BANK BUILDING.
LOTS OF STUFF IN HERE TO THROW! IN FACT, I'D SAY THIS CALLS FOR THE OLD "WILLIAM TELL" BIT!
THWIP
THWIP
ALL I NEED TO DO IS WEB UP A LITTLE OL' SLING--
--CHOOSE AN APPROPRIATE SHAFT, AND...
...BET I CAN KNOCK THAT HELMET RIGHT OFF HIS NOGGIN!
TWUNG
WHAT--?
SOMEONE'S TOSSING GIRDERS AT ME, EH? WELL, THAT'S TOO BAD...
TUCK
3

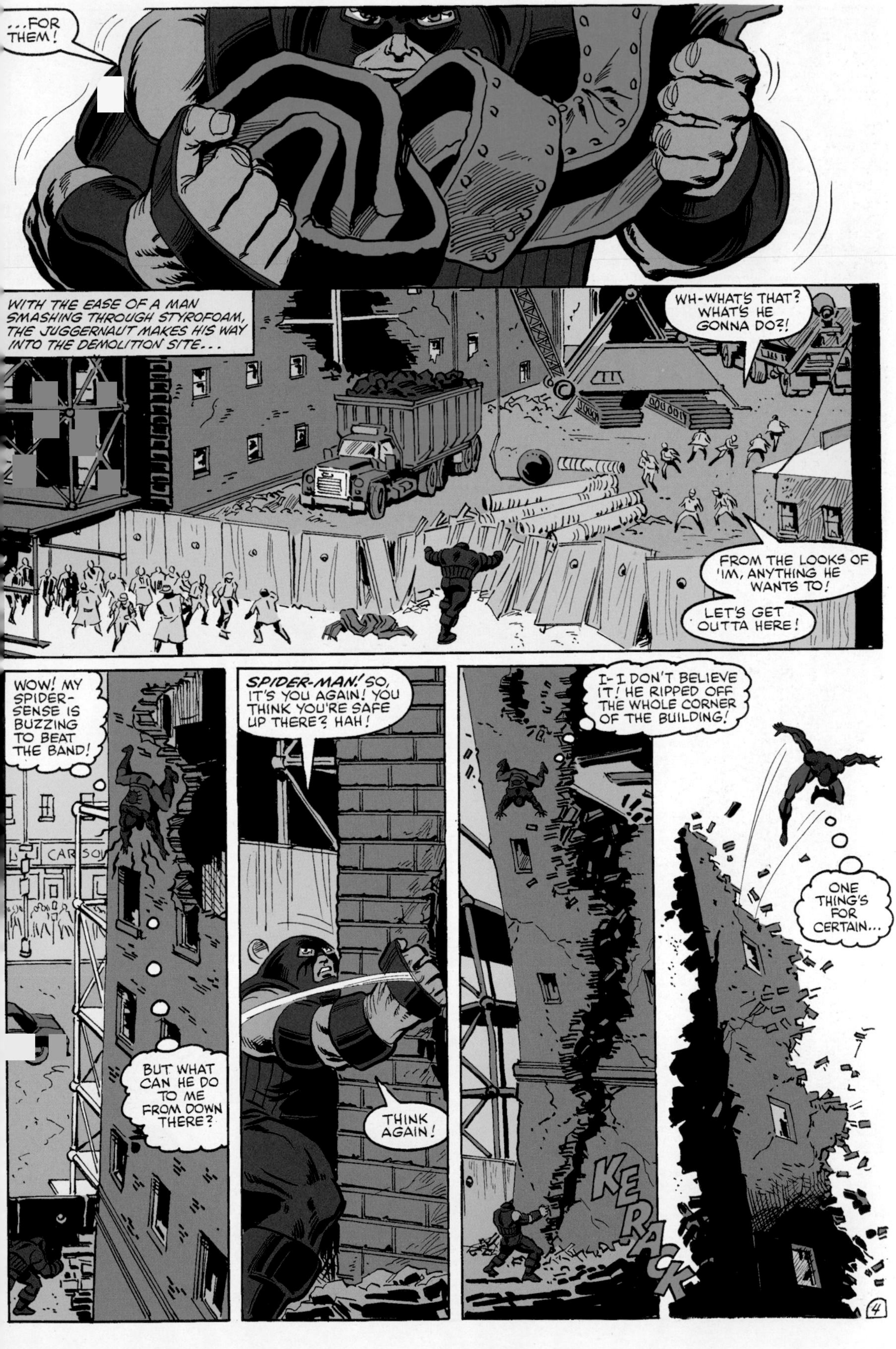
...FOR THEM!
WITH THE EASE OF A MAN SMASHING THROUGH STYROFOAM, THE JUGGERNAUT MAKES HIS WAY INTO THE DEMOLITION SITE...
WH-WHAT'S THAT? WHAT'S HE GONNA DO?!
FROM THE LOOKS OF 'IM, ANYTHING HE WANTS TO!
LET'S GET OUTTA HERE!
WOW! MY SPIDER-SENSE IS BUZZING TO BEAT THE BAND!
BUT WHAT CAN HE DO TO ME FROM DOWN THERE?
SPIDER-MAN! SO, IT'S YOU AGAIN! YOU THINK YOU'RE SAFE UP THERE? HAH!
THINK AGAIN!
I-I DON'T BELIEVE IT! HE RIPPED OFF THE WHOLE CORNER OF THE BUILDING!
KERACK
ONE THING'S FOR CERTAIN...
4

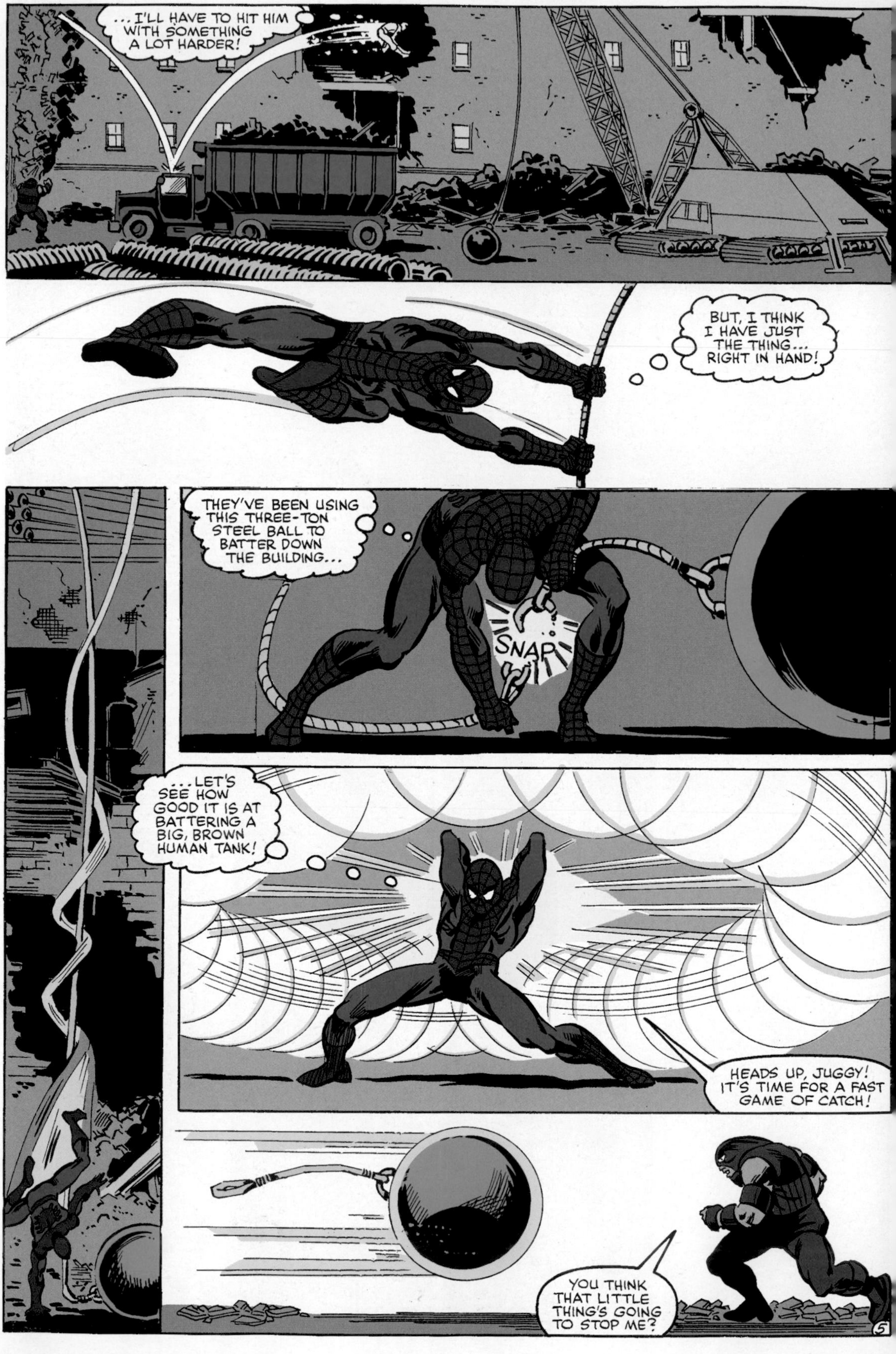
...I'LL HAVE TO HIT HIM WITH SOMETHING A LOT HARDER!
BUT, I THINK I HAVE JUST THE THING... RIGHT IN HAND!
THEY'VE BEEN USING THIS THREE-TON STEEL BALL TO BATTER DOWN THE BUILDING...
SNAP
...LET'S SEE HOW GOOD IT IS AT BATTERING A BIG, BROWN HUMAN TANK!
HEADS UP, JUGGY! IT'S TIME FOR A FAST GAME OF CATCH!
YOU THINK THAT LITTLE THING'S GOING TO STOP ME?
5

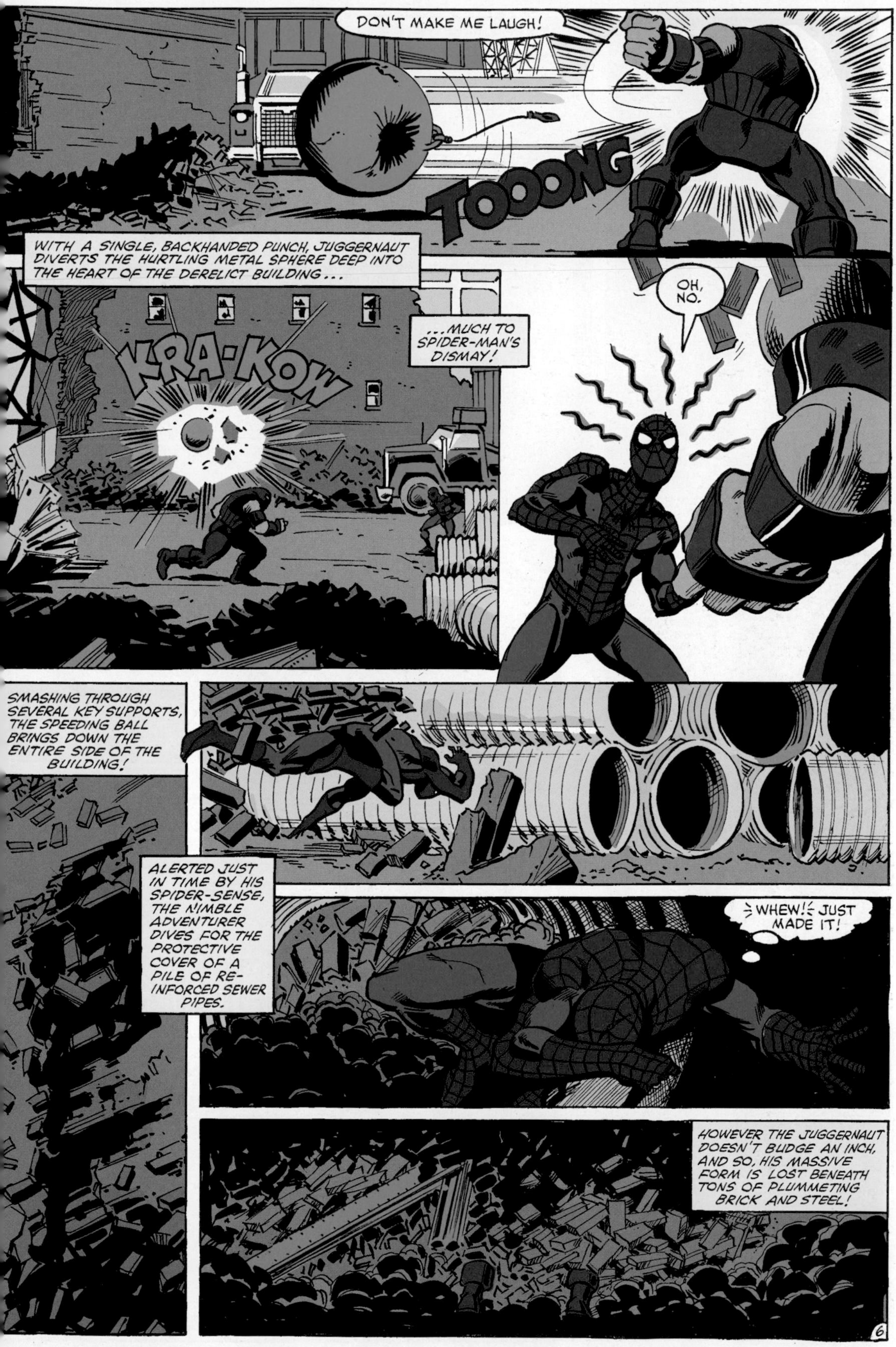
DON'T MAKE ME LAUGH!
TOOONG
WITH A SINGLE, BACKHANDED PUNCH, JUGGERNAUT DIVERTS THE HURTLING METAL SPHERE DEEP INTO THE HEART OF THE DERELICT BUILDING...
KRA-KOW
...MUCH TO SPIDER-MAN'S DISMAY!
OH, NO.
SMASHING THROUGH SEVERAL KEY SUPPORTS, THE SPEEDING BALL BRINGS DOWN THE ENTIRE SIDE OF THE BUILDING!
ALERTED JUST IN TIME BY HIS SPIDER-SENSE, THE NIMBLE ADVENTURER DIVES FOR THE PROTECTIVE COVER OF A PILE OF RE-INFORCED SEWER PIPES.
WHEW! JUST MADE IT!
HOWEVER THE JUGGERNAUT DOESN'T BUDGE AN INCH, AND SO, HIS MASSIVE FORM IS LOST BENEATH TONS OF PLUMMETING BRICK AND STEEL!
6

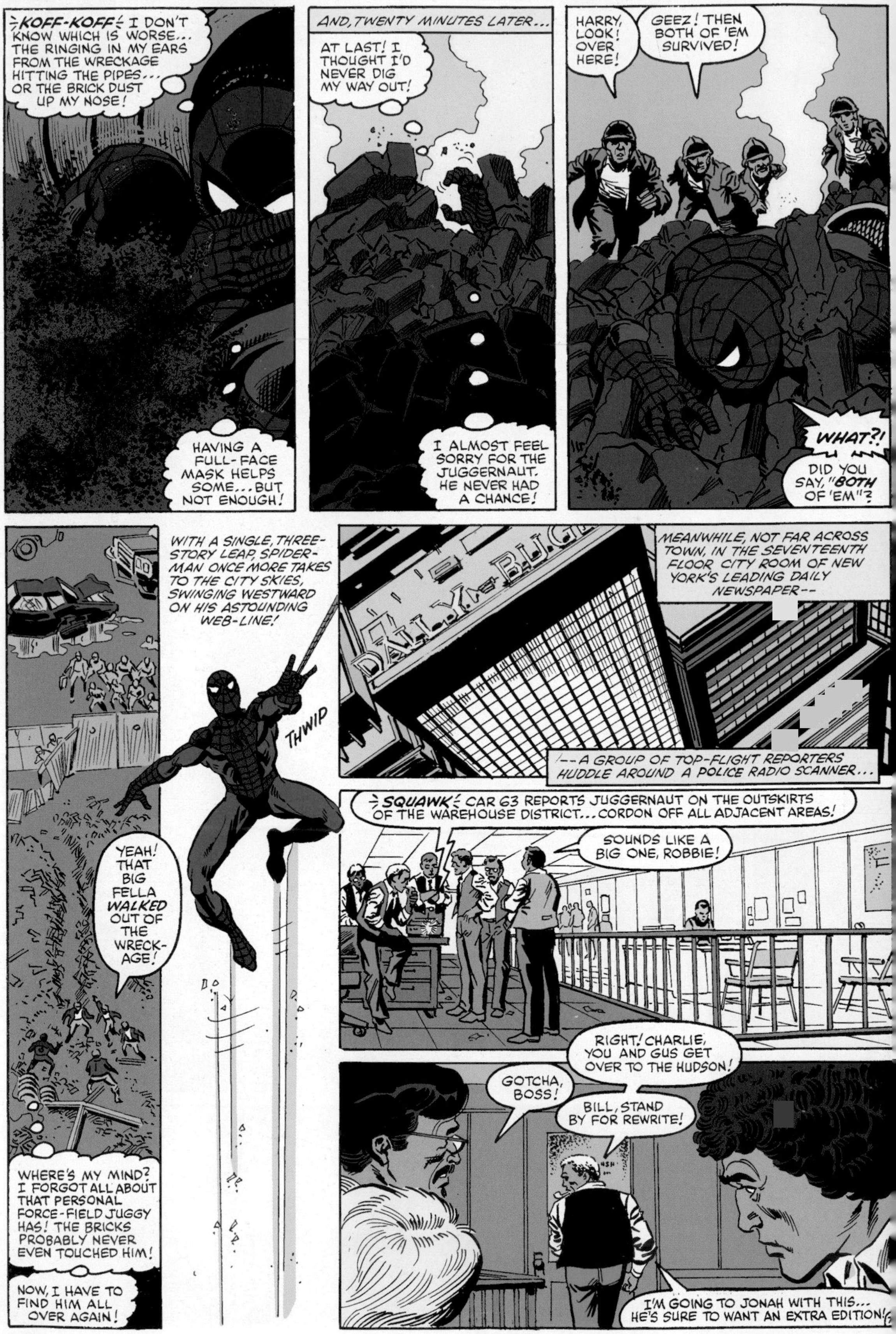

KOFF-KOFF I DON'T KNOW WHICH IS WORSE... THE RINGING IN MY EARS FROM THE WRECKAGE HITTING THE PIPES... OR THE BRICK DUST UP MY NOSE!
HAVING A FULL-FACE MASK HELPS SOME... BUT NOT ENOUGH!
AND, TWENTY MINUTES LATER...
AT LAST! I THOUGHT I'D NEVER DIG MY WAY OUT!
I ALMOST FEEL SORRY FOR THE JUGGERNAUT. HE NEVER HAD A CHANCE!
HARRY, LOOK! OVER HERE!
GEEZ! THEN BOTH OF 'EM SURVIVED!
WHAT?!
DID YOU SAY, "BOTH OF 'EM"?
WITH A SINGLE, THREE-STORY LEAP, SPIDER-MAN ONCE MORE TAKES TO THE CITY SKIES, SWINGING WESTWARD ON HIS ASTOUNDING WEB-LINE!
THWIP
YEAH! THAT BIG FELLA WALKED OUT OF THE WRECK-AGE!
WHERE'S MY MIND? I FORGOT ALL ABOUT THAT PERSONAL FORCE-FIELD JUGGY HAS! THE BRICKS PROBABLY NEVER EVEN TOUCHED HIM!
NOW, I HAVE TO FIND HIM ALL OVER AGAIN!
MEANWHILE, NOT FAR ACROSS TOWN, IN THE SEVENTEENTH FLOOR CITY ROOM OF NEW YORK'S LEADING DAILY NEWSPAPER--
--A GROUP OF TOP-FLIGHT REPORTERS HUDDLE AROUND A POLICE RADIO SCANNER...
SQUAWK CAR 63 REPORTS JUGGERNAUT ON THE OUTSKIRTS OF THE WAREHOUSE DISTRICT... CORDON OFF ALL ADJACENT AREAS!
SOUNDS LIKE A BIG ONE, ROBBIE!
RIGHT! CHARLIE, YOU AND GUS GET OVER TO THE HUDSON!
GOTCHA, BOSS!
BILL, STAND BY FOR REWRITE!
I'M GOING TO JONAH WITH THIS... HE'S SURE TO WANT AN EXTRA EDITION!

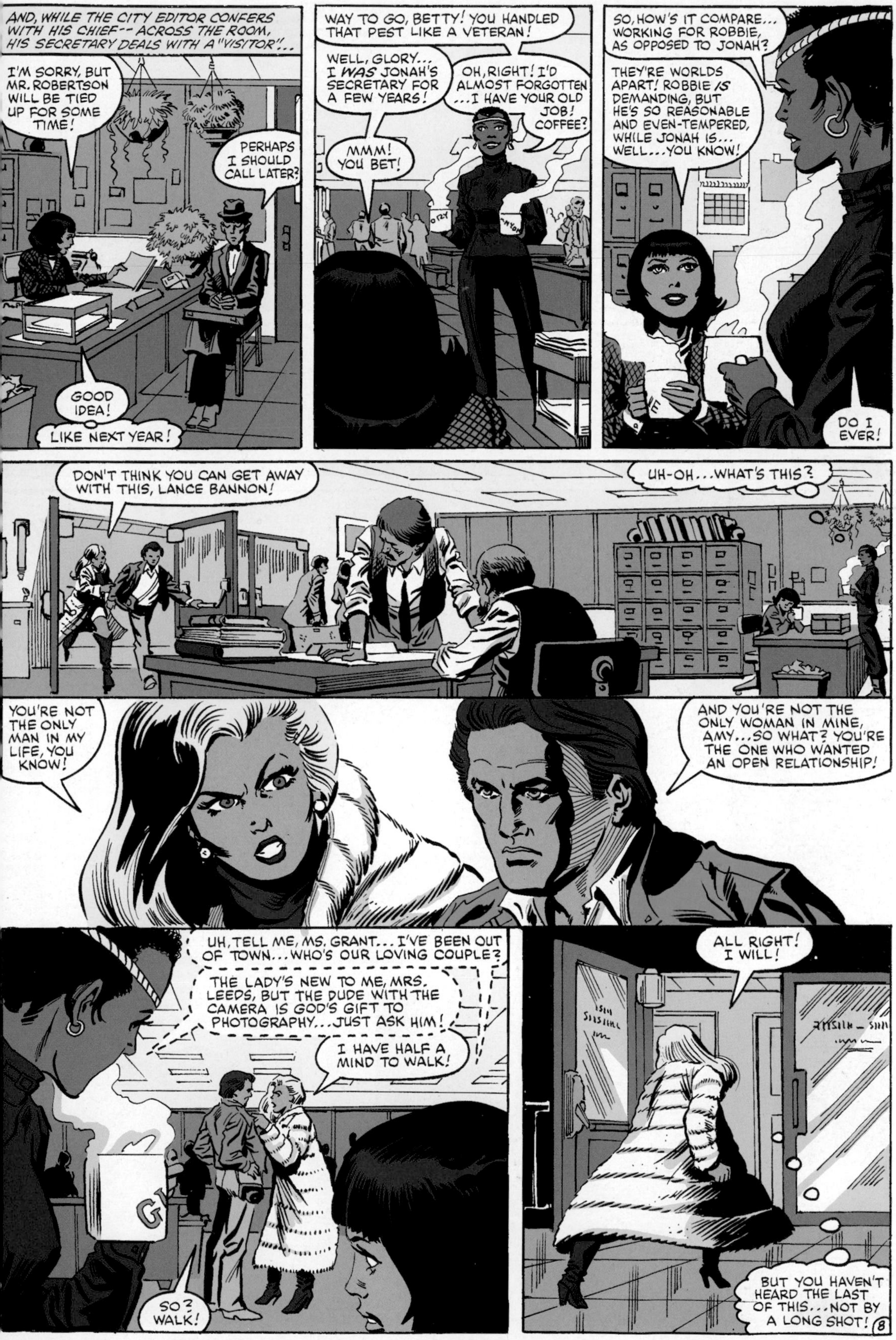
AND, WHILE THE CITY EDITOR CONFERS WITH HIS CHIEF-- ACROSS THE ROOM, HIS SECRETARY DEALS WITH A "VISITOR"...
I'M SORRY, BUT MR. ROBERTSON WILL BE TIED UP FOR SOME TIME!
PERHAPS I SHOULD CALL LATER?
GOOD IDEA!
LIKE NEXT YEAR!
WAY TO GO, BETTY! YOU HANDLED THAT PEST LIKE A VETERAN!
WELL, GLORY... I WAS JONAH'S SECRETARY FOR A FEW YEARS!
OH, RIGHT! I'D ALMOST FORGOTTEN ...I HAVE YOUR OLD JOB! COFFEE?
MMM! YOU BET!
SO, HOW'S IT COMPARE... WORKING FOR ROBBIE, AS OPPOSED TO JONAH?
THEY'RE WORLDS APART! ROBBIE IS DEMANDING, BUT HE'S SO REASONABLE AND EVEN-TEMPERED, WHILE JONAH IS... WELL... YOU KNOW!
DO I EVER!
DON'T THINK YOU CAN GET AWAY WITH THIS, LANCE BANNON!
UH-OH... WHAT'S THIS?
YOU'RE NOT THE ONLY MAN IN MY LIFE, YOU KNOW!
AND YOU'RE NOT THE ONLY WOMAN IN MINE, AMY... SO WHAT? YOU'RE THE ONE WHO WANTED AN OPEN RELATIONSHIP!
UH, TELL ME, MS. GRANT... I'VE BEEN OUT OF TOWN... WHO'S OUR LOVING COUPLE?
THE LADY'S NEW TO ME, MRS. LEEDS, BUT THE DUDE WITH THE CAMERA IS GOD'S GIFT TO PHOTOGRAPHY... JUST ASK HIM!
I HAVE HALF A MIND TO WALK!
SO? WALK!
ALL RIGHT! I WILL!
BUT YOU HAVEN'T HEARD THE LAST OF THIS... NOT BY A LONG SHOT!
8

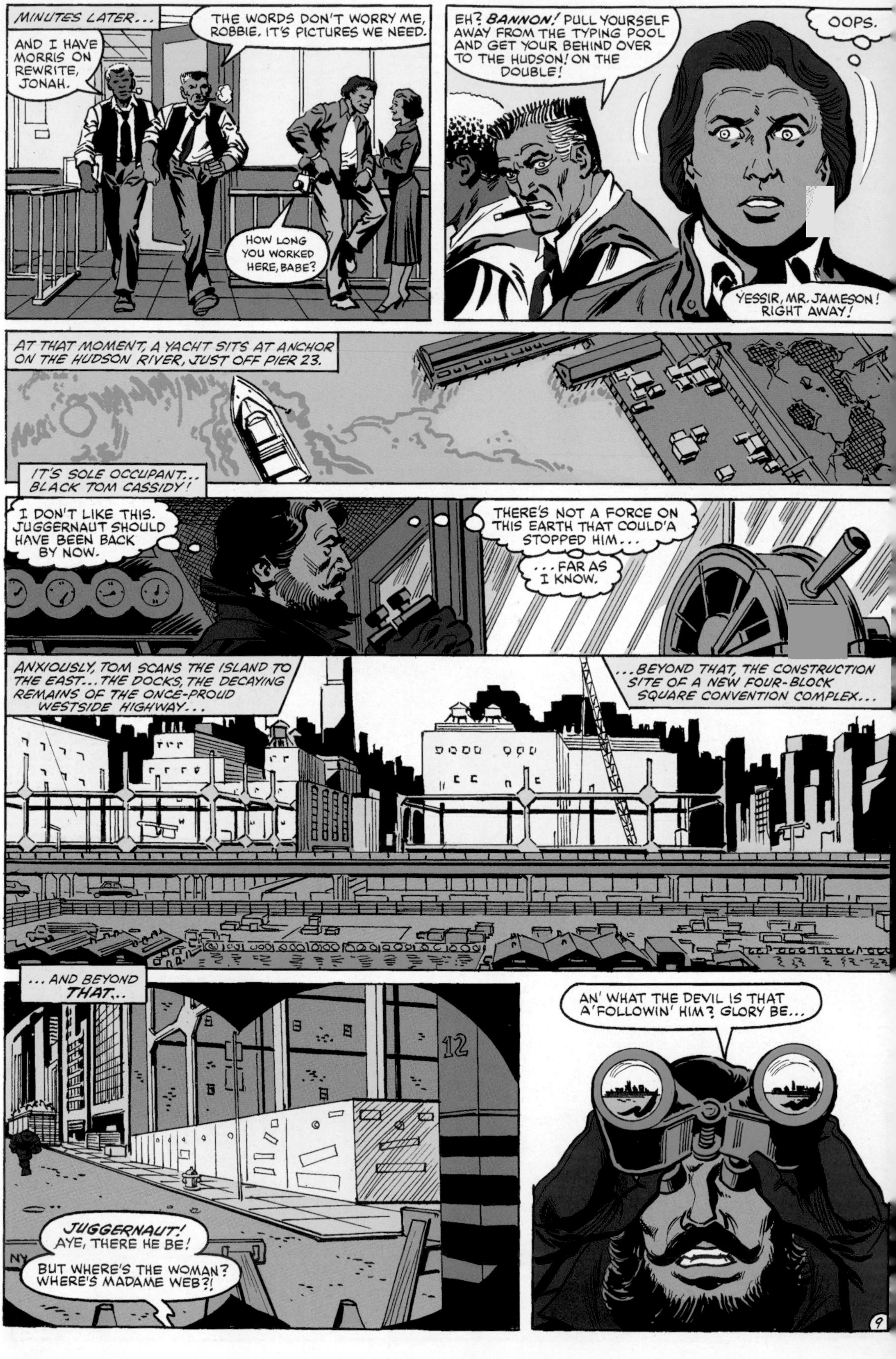
MINUTES LATER...
AND I HAVE MORRIS ON REWRITE, JONAH.
THE WORDS DON'T WORRY ME, ROBBIE. IT'S PICTURES WE NEED.
HOW LONG YOU WORKED HERE, BABE?
EH? BANNON! PULL YOURSELF AWAY FROM THE TYPING POOL AND GET YOUR BEHIND OVER TO THE HUDSON! ON THE DOUBLE!
OOPS.
YESSIR, MR. JAMESON! RIGHT AWAY!
AT THAT MOMENT, A YACHT SITS AT ANCHOR ON THE HUDSON RIVER, JUST OFF PIER 23.
IT'S SOLE OCCUPANT... BLACK TOM CASSIDY!
I DON'T LIKE THIS. JUGGERNAUT SHOULD HAVE BEEN BACK BY NOW.
THERE'S NOT A FORCE ON THIS EARTH THAT COULD'A STOPPED HIM...
...FAR AS I KNOW.
ANXIOUSLY, TOM SCANS THE ISLAND TO THE EAST...THE DOCKS, THE DECAYING REMAINS OF THE ONCE-PROUD WESTSIDE HIGHWAY...
...BEYOND THAT, THE CONSTRUCTION SITE OF A NEW FOUR-BLOCK SQUARE CONVENTION COMPLEX...
...AND BEYOND THAT...
12
JUGGERNAUT! AYE, THERE HE BE!
BUT WHERE'S THE WOMAN? WHERE'S MADAME WEB?!
AN' WHAT THE DEVIL IS THAT A'FOLLOWIN' HIM? GLORY BE...
9

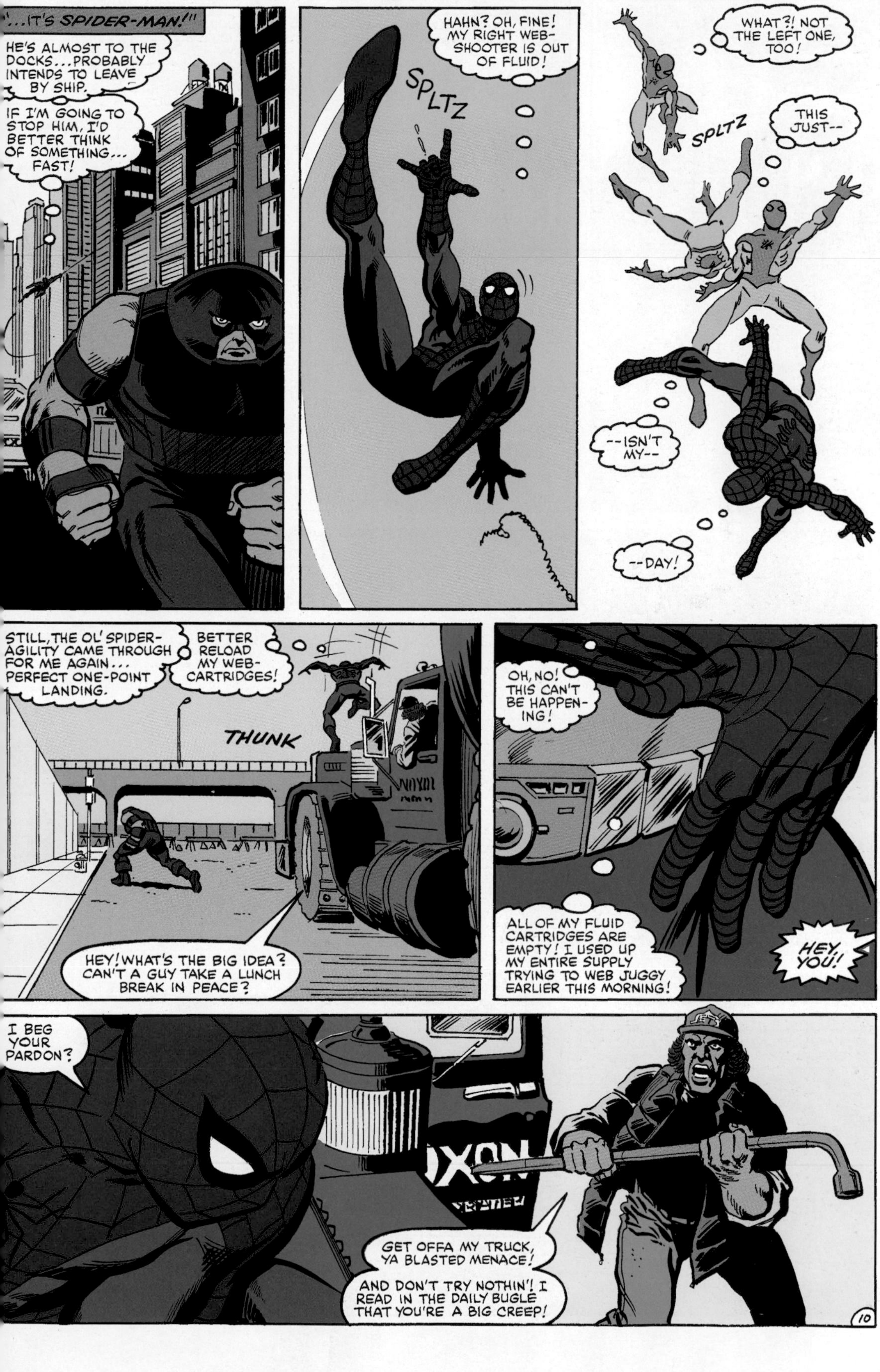
"...IT'S SPIDER-MAN!"
HE'S ALMOST TO THE DOCKS...PROBABLY INTENDS TO LEAVE BY SHIP.
IF I'M GOING TO STOP HIM, I'D BETTER THINK OF SOMETHING... FAST!
HAHN? OH, FINE! MY RIGHT WEB-SHOOTER IS OUT OF FLUID!
SPLTZ
WHAT?! NOT THE LEFT ONE, TOO!
SPLTZ
THIS JUST--
--ISN'T MY--
--DAY!
STILL, THE OL' SPIDER-AGILITY CAME THROUGH FOR ME AGAIN... PERFECT ONE-POINT LANDING.
BETTER RELOAD MY WEB-CARTRIDGES!
THUNK
HEY! WHAT'S THE BIG IDEA? CAN'T A GUY TAKE A LUNCH BREAK IN PEACE?
OH, NO! THIS CAN'T BE HAPPEN-ING!
ALL OF MY FLUID CARTRIDGES ARE EMPTY! I USED UP MY ENTIRE SUPPLY TRYING TO WEB JUGGY EARLIER THIS MORNING!
HEY, YOU!
I BEG YOUR PARDON?
GET OFFA MY TRUCK, YA BLASTED MENACE!
AND DON'T TRY NOTHIN'! I READ IN THE DAILY BUGLE THAT YOU'RE A BIG CREEP!

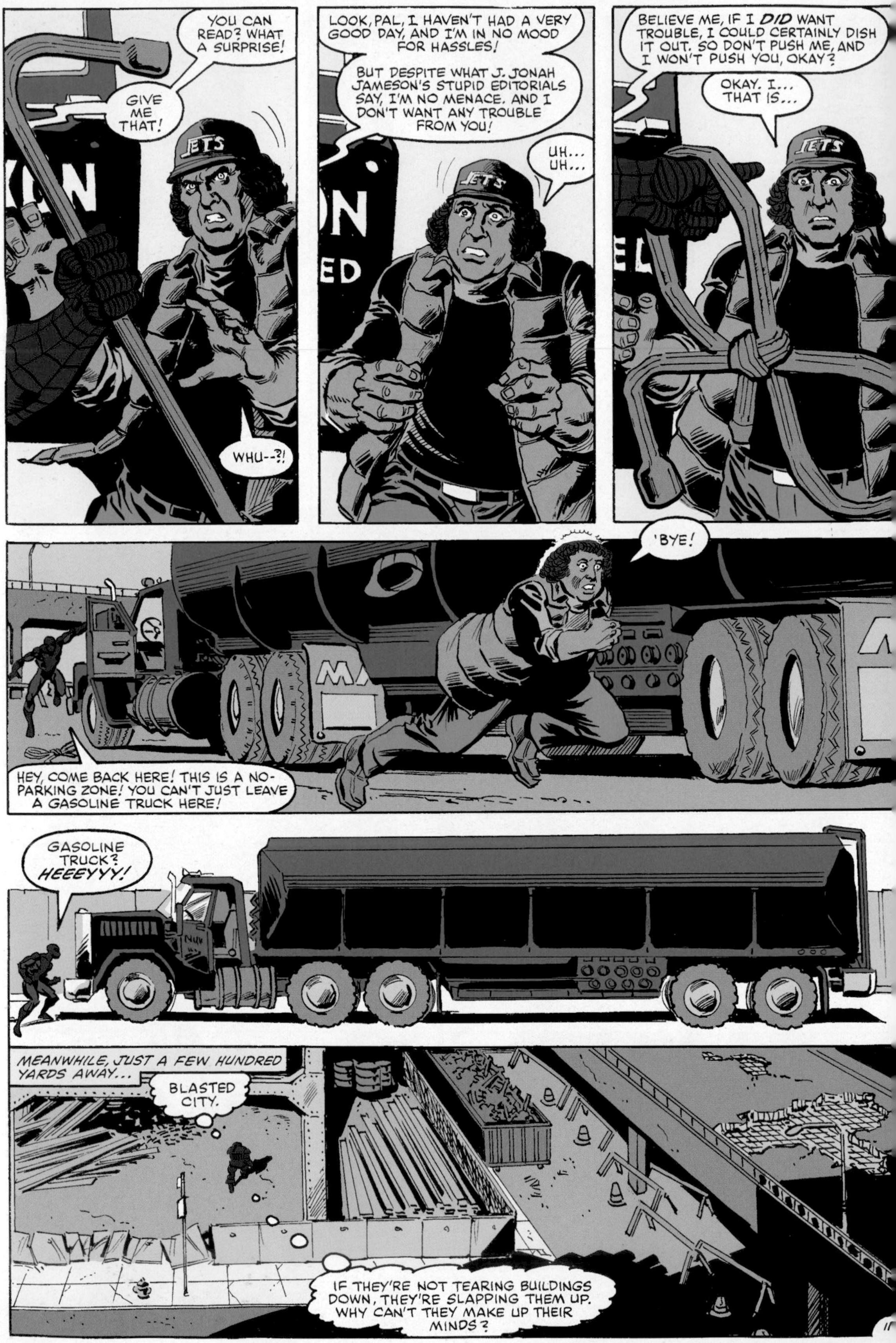
GIVE ME THAT!
YOU CAN READ? WHAT A SURPRISE!
WHU--?!
LOOK, PAL, I HAVEN'T HAD A VERY GOOD DAY, AND I'M IN NO MOOD FOR HASSLES!
BUT DESPITE WHAT J. JONAH JAMESON'S STUPID EDITORIALS SAY, I'M NO MENACE. AND I DON'T WANT ANY TROUBLE FROM YOU!
UH... UH...
BELIEVE ME, IF I *DID* WANT TROUBLE, I COULD CERTAINLY DISH IT OUT. SO DON'T PUSH ME, AND I WON'T PUSH YOU, OKAY?
OKAY. I... THAT IS...
'BYE!
HEY, COME BACK HERE! THIS IS A NO-PARKING ZONE! YOU CAN'T JUST LEAVE A GASOLINE TRUCK HERE!
GASOLINE TRUCK? *HEEEYYY!*
MEANWHILE, JUST A FEW HUNDRED YARDS AWAY...
BLASTED CITY.
IF THEY'RE NOT TEARING BUILDINGS DOWN, THEY'RE SLAPPING THEM UP. WHY CAN'T THEY MAKE UP THEIR MINDS?

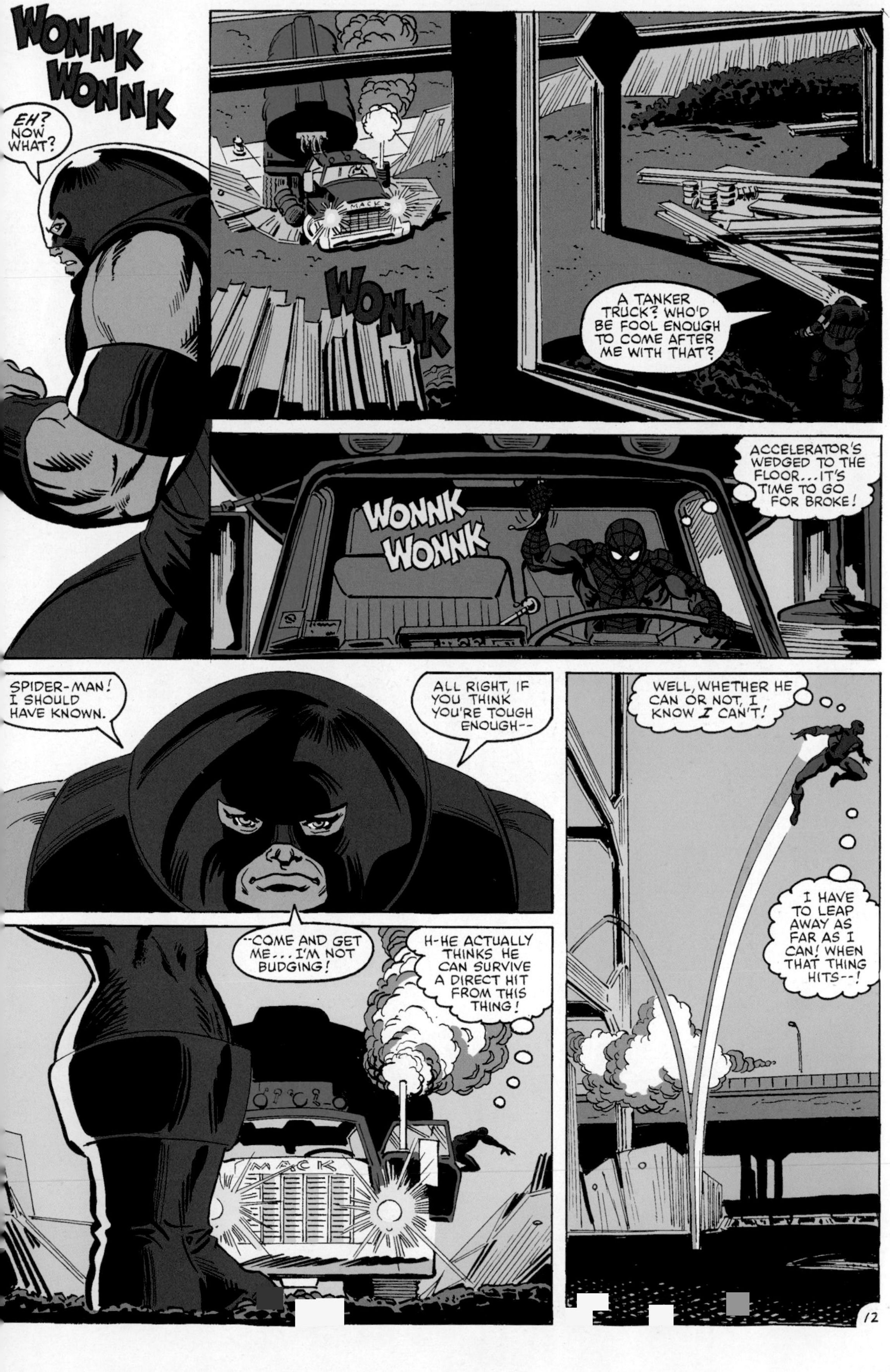
WONNK WONNK
EH? NOW WHAT?
WONNK
A TANKER TRUCK? WHO'D BE FOOL ENOUGH TO COME AFTER ME WITH THAT?
ACCELERATOR'S WEDGED TO THE FLOOR... IT'S TIME TO GO FOR BROKE!
WONNK WONNK
SPIDER-MAN! I SHOULD HAVE KNOWN.
ALL RIGHT, IF YOU THINK YOU'RE TOUGH ENOUGH--
--COME AND GET ME... I'M NOT BUDGING!
H-HE ACTUALLY THINKS HE CAN SURVIVE A DIRECT HIT FROM THIS THING!
WELL, WHETHER HE CAN OR NOT, I KNOW I CAN'T!
I HAVE TO LEAP AWAY AS FAR AS I CAN! WHEN THAT THING HITS--!

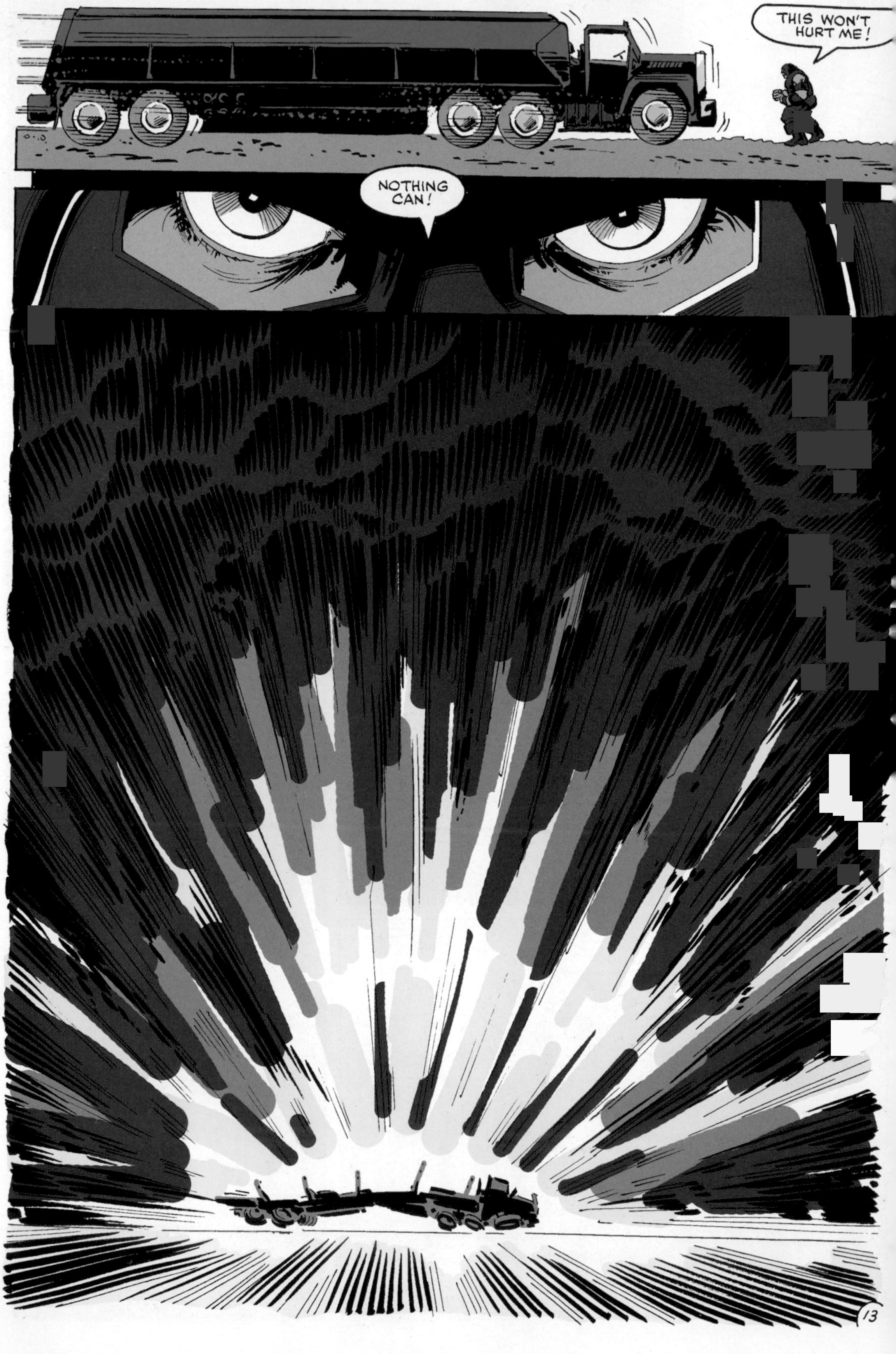
THIS WON'T HURT ME!
NOTHING CAN!

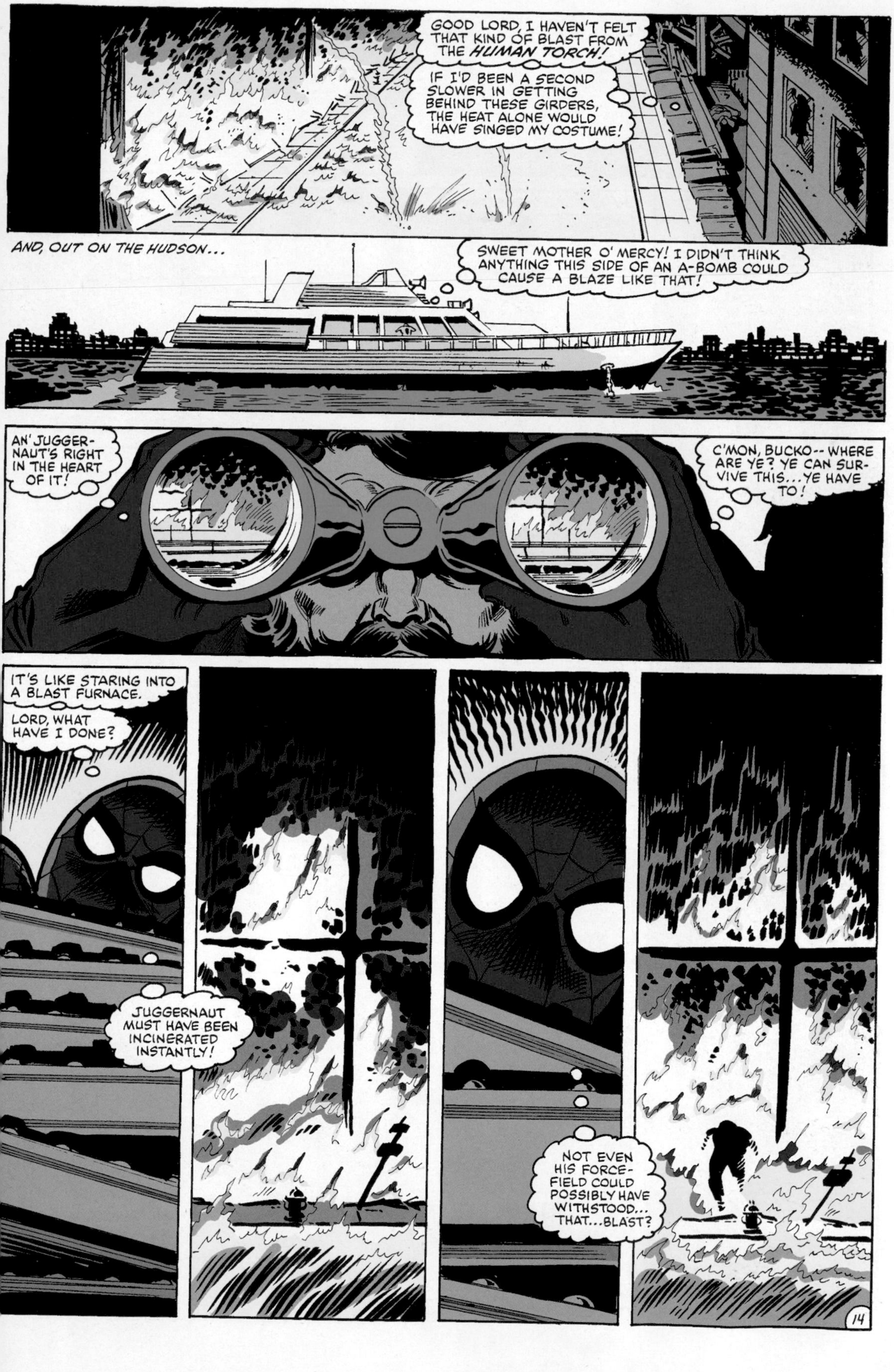
GOOD LORD, I HAVEN'T FELT THAT KIND OF BLAST FROM THE *HUMAN TORCH!*
IF I'D BEEN A SECOND SLOWER IN GETTING BEHIND THESE GIRDERS, THE HEAT ALONE WOULD HAVE SINGED MY COSTUME!
AND, OUT ON THE HUDSON...
SWEET MOTHER O' MERCY! I DIDN'T THINK ANYTHING THIS SIDE OF AN A-BOMB COULD CAUSE A BLAZE LIKE THAT!
AN' JUGGERNAUT'S RIGHT IN THE HEART OF IT!
C'MON, BUCKO-- WHERE ARE YE? YE CAN SURVIVE THIS... YE HAVE TO!
IT'S LIKE STARING INTO A BLAST FURNACE.
LORD, WHAT HAVE I DONE?
JUGGERNAUT MUST HAVE BEEN INCINERATED INSTANTLY!
NOT EVEN HIS FORCE-FIELD COULD POSSIBLY HAVE WITHSTOOD... THAT... BLAST?
14

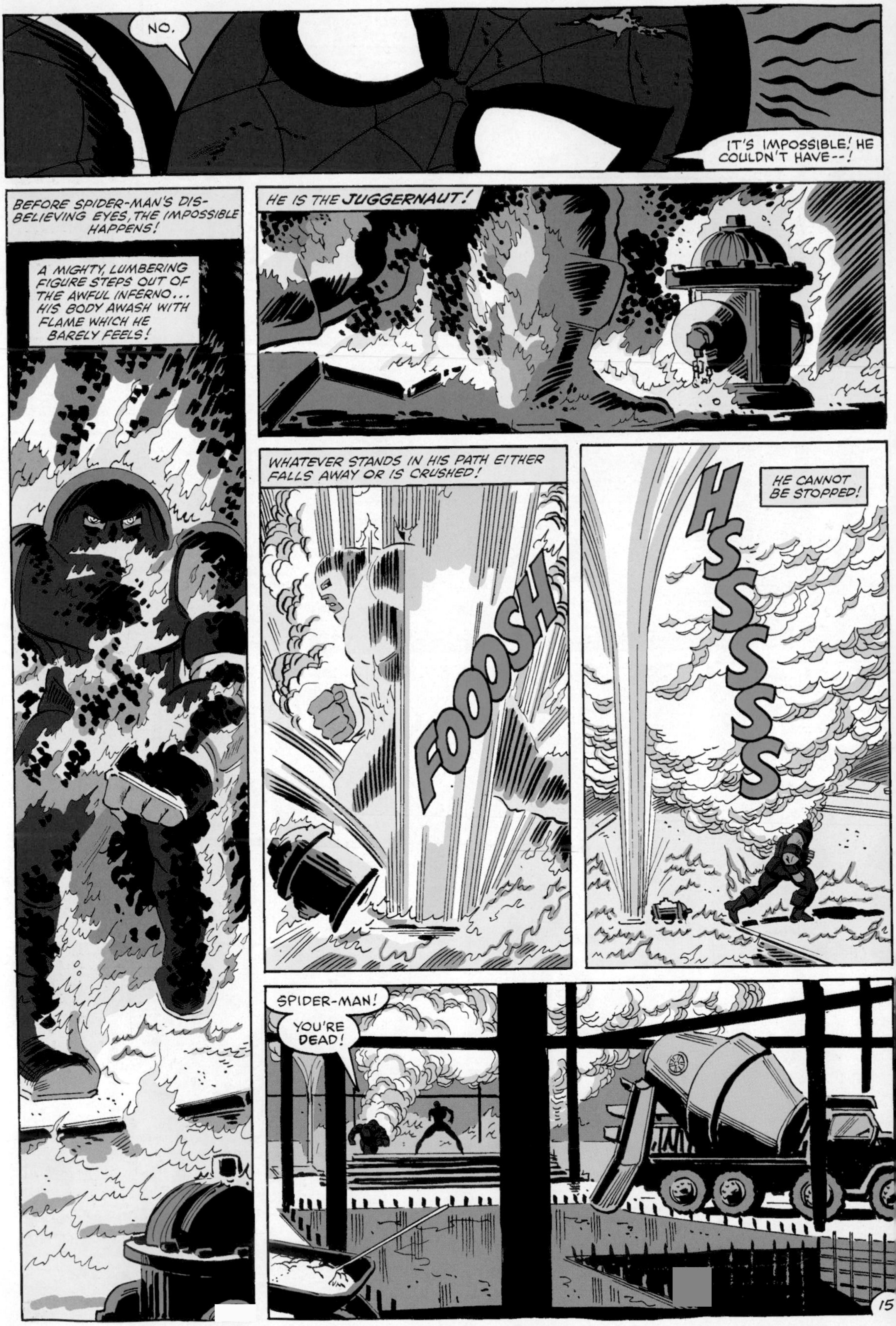
NO.
IT'S IMPOSSIBLE! HE COULDN'T HAVE--!
BEFORE SPIDER-MAN'S DIS-BELIEVING EYES, THE IMPOSSIBLE HAPPENS!
A MIGHTY, LUMBERING FIGURE STEPS OUT OF THE AWFUL INFERNO... HIS BODY AWASH WITH FLAME WHICH HE BARELY FEELS!
HE IS THE JUGGERNAUT!
WHATEVER STANDS IN HIS PATH EITHER FALLS AWAY OR IS CRUSHED!
FOOOSH
HE CANNOT BE STOPPED!
HSSSSS
SPIDER-MAN!
YOU'RE DEAD!

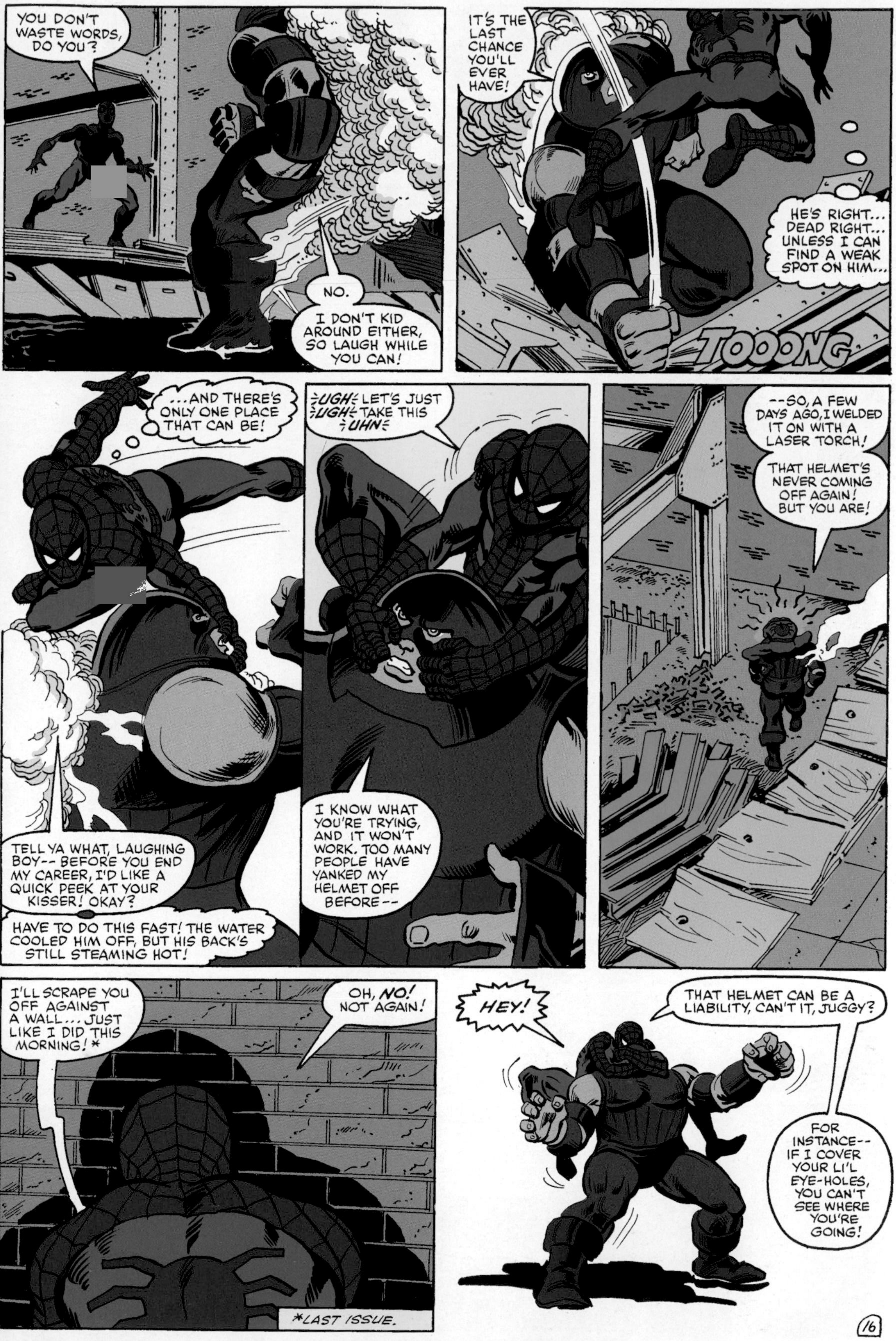

YOU DON'T WASTE WORDS, DO YOU?
NO.
I DON'T KID AROUND EITHER, SO LAUGH WHILE YOU CAN!
IT'S THE LAST CHANCE YOU'LL EVER HAVE!
HE'S RIGHT... DEAD RIGHT... UNLESS I CAN FIND A WEAK SPOT ON HIM...
TOOONG
...AND THERE'S ONLY ONE PLACE THAT CAN BE!
TELL YA WHAT, LAUGHING BOY-- BEFORE YOU END MY CAREER, I'D LIKE A QUICK PEEK AT YOUR KISSER! OKAY?
HAVE TO DO THIS FAST! THE WATER COOLED HIM OFF, BUT HIS BACK'S STILL STEAMING HOT!
UGH LET'S JUST UGH TAKE THIS UHN
I KNOW WHAT YOU'RE TRYING, AND IT WON'T WORK. TOO MANY PEOPLE HAVE YANKED MY HELMET OFF BEFORE--
--SO, A FEW DAYS AGO, I WELDED IT ON WITH A LASER TORCH!
THAT HELMET'S NEVER COMING OFF AGAIN! BUT YOU ARE!
I'LL SCRAPE YOU OFF AGAINST A WALL... JUST LIKE I DID THIS MORNING! *
OH, NO! NOT AGAIN!
*LAST ISSUE.
HEY!
THAT HELMET CAN BE A LIABILITY, CAN'T IT, JUGGY?
FOR INSTANCE-- IF I COVER YOUR LI'L EYE-HOLES, YOU CAN'T SEE WHERE YOU'RE GOING!

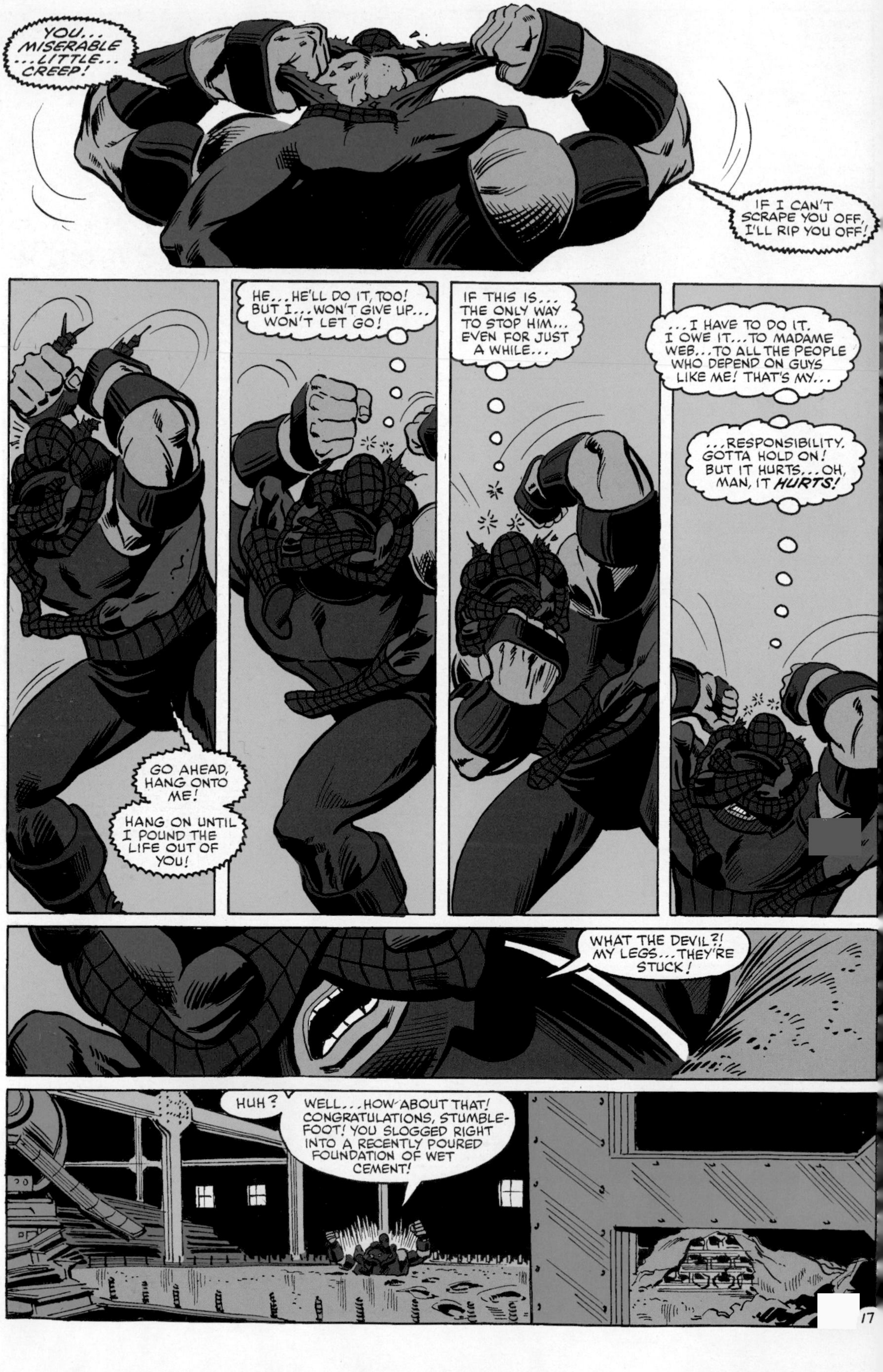
YOU... MISERABLE ...LITTLE... CREEP!
IF I CAN'T SCRAPE YOU OFF, I'LL RIP YOU OFF!
GO AHEAD, HANG ONTO ME!
HANG ON UNTIL I POUND THE LIFE OUT OF YOU!
HE...HE'LL DO IT, TOO! BUT I...WON'T GIVE UP... WON'T LET GO!
IF THIS IS... THE ONLY WAY TO STOP HIM... EVEN FOR JUST A WHILE...
...I HAVE TO DO IT. I OWE IT...TO MADAME WEB...TO ALL THE PEOPLE WHO DEPEND ON GUYS LIKE ME! THAT'S MY...
...RESPONSIBILITY. GOTTA HOLD ON! BUT IT HURTS...OH, MAN, IT HURTS!
WHAT THE DEVIL?! MY LEGS...THEY'RE STUCK!
HUH?
WELL...HOW ABOUT THAT! CONGRATULATIONS, STUMBLE-FOOT! YOU SLOGGED RIGHT INTO A RECENTLY POURED FOUNDATION OF WET CEMENT!

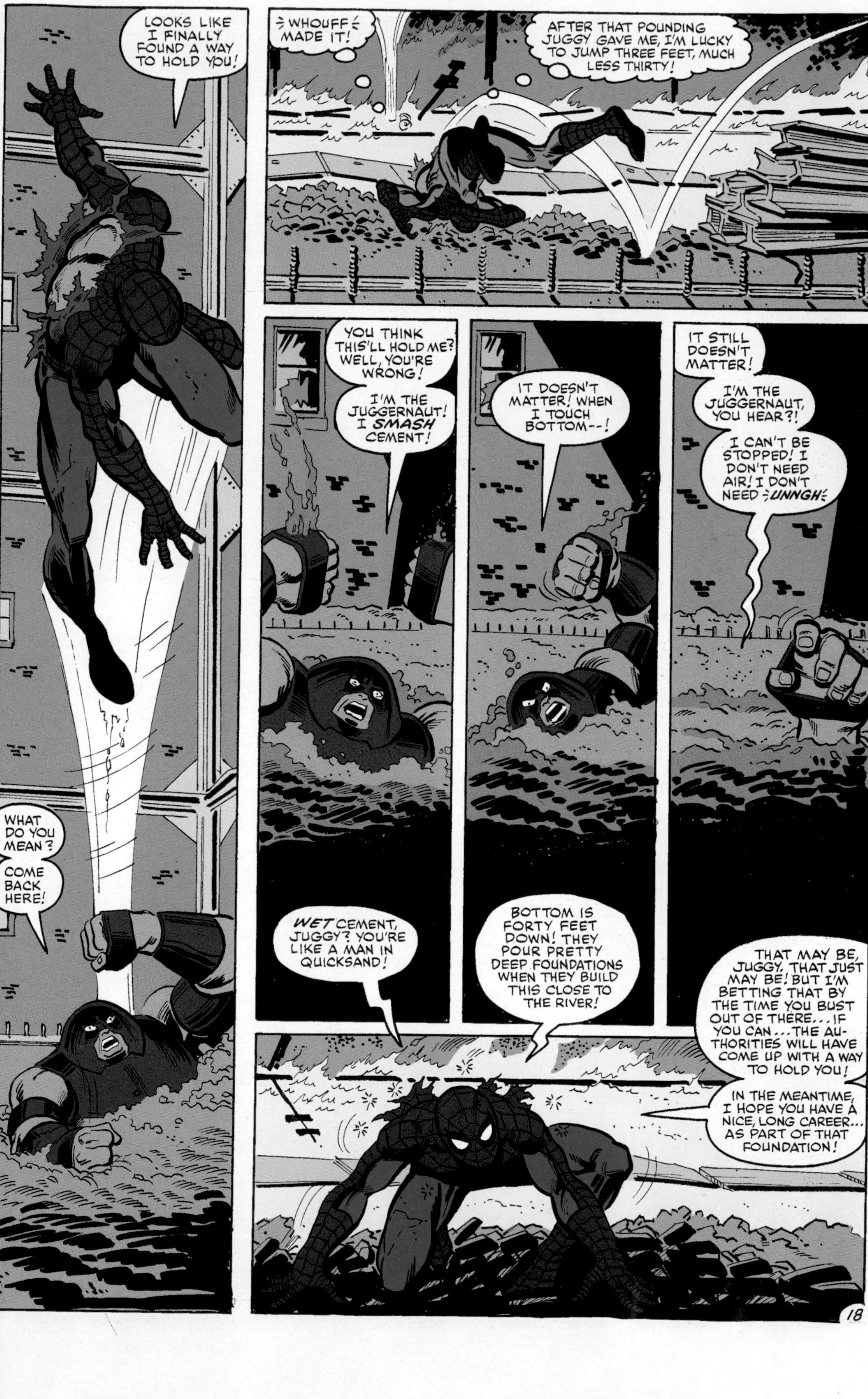
LOOKS LIKE I FINALLY FOUND A WAY TO HOLD YOU!
WHAT DO YOU MEAN?
COME BACK HERE!
WHOUFF MADE IT!
AFTER THAT POUNDING JUGGY GAVE ME, I'M LUCKY TO JUMP THREE FEET, MUCH LESS THIRTY!
YOU THINK THIS'LL HOLD ME? WELL, YOU'RE WRONG!
I'M THE JUGGERNAUT! I SMASH CEMENT!
IT DOESN'T MATTER! WHEN I TOUCH BOTTOM--!
IT STILL DOESN'T MATTER!
I'M THE JUGGERNAUT, YOU HEAR?!
I CAN'T BE STOPPED! I DON'T NEED AIR! I DON'T NEED UNNGH
WET CEMENT, JUGGY? YOU'RE LIKE A MAN IN QUICKSAND!
BOTTOM IS FORTY FEET DOWN! THEY POUR PRETTY DEEP FOUNDATIONS WHEN THEY BUILD THIS CLOSE TO THE RIVER!
THAT MAY BE, JUGGY, THAT JUST MAY BE! BUT I'M BETTING THAT BY THE TIME YOU BUST OUT OF THERE... IF YOU CAN... THE AUTHORITIES WILL HAVE COME UP WITH A WAY TO HOLD YOU!
IN THE MEANTIME, I HOPE YOU HAVE A NICE, LONG CAREER... AS PART OF THAT FOUNDATION!

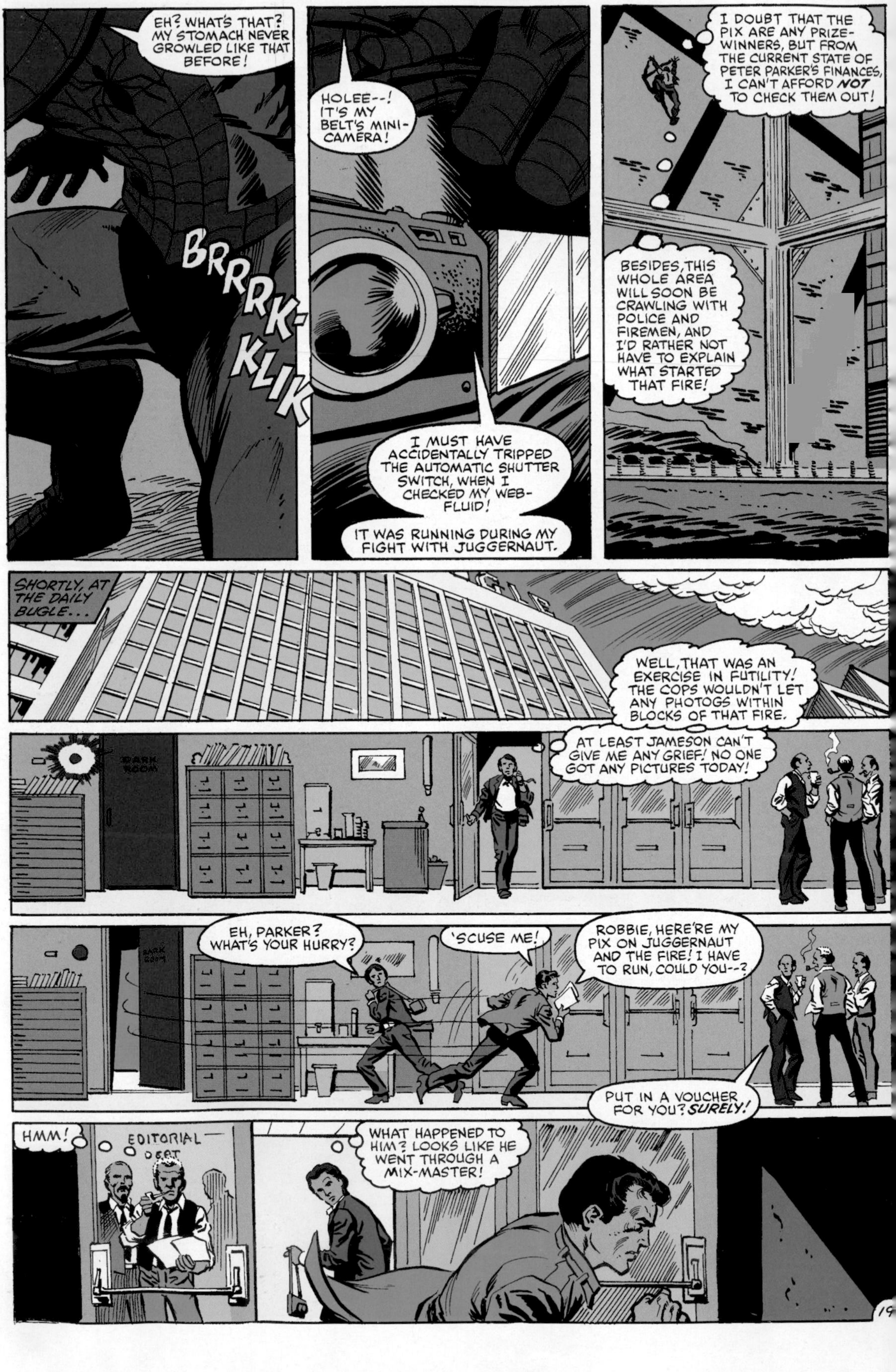
EH? WHAT'S THAT? MY STOMACH NEVER GROWLED LIKE THAT BEFORE!
BRRRK-KLIK
HOLEE--! IT'S MY BELT'S MINI-CAMERA!
I MUST HAVE ACCIDENTALLY TRIPPED THE AUTOMATIC SHUTTER SWITCH, WHEN I CHECKED MY WEB-FLUID!
IT WAS RUNNING DURING MY FIGHT WITH JUGGERNAUT.
I DOUBT THAT THE PIX ARE ANY PRIZE-WINNERS, BUT FROM THE CURRENT STATE OF PETER PARKER'S FINANCES, I CAN'T AFFORD NOT TO CHECK THEM OUT!
BESIDES, THIS WHOLE AREA WILL SOON BE CRAWLING WITH POLICE AND FIREMEN, AND I'D RATHER NOT HAVE TO EXPLAIN WHAT STARTED THAT FIRE!
SHORTLY, AT THE DAILY BUGLE...
WELL, THAT WAS AN EXERCISE IN FUTILITY! THE COPS WOULDN'T LET ANY PHOTOGS WITHIN BLOCKS OF THAT FIRE.
AT LEAST JAMESON CAN'T GIVE ME ANY GRIEF! NO ONE GOT ANY PICTURES TODAY!
DARK ROOM
EH, PARKER? WHAT'S YOUR HURRY?
'SCUSE ME!
ROBBIE, HERE'RE MY PIX ON JUGGERNAUT AND THE FIRE! I HAVE TO RUN, COULD YOU--?
PUT IN A VOUCHER FOR YOU? SURELY!
HMM!
EDITORIAL DEPT
WHAT HAPPENED TO HIM? LOOKS LIKE HE WENT THROUGH A MIX-MASTER!

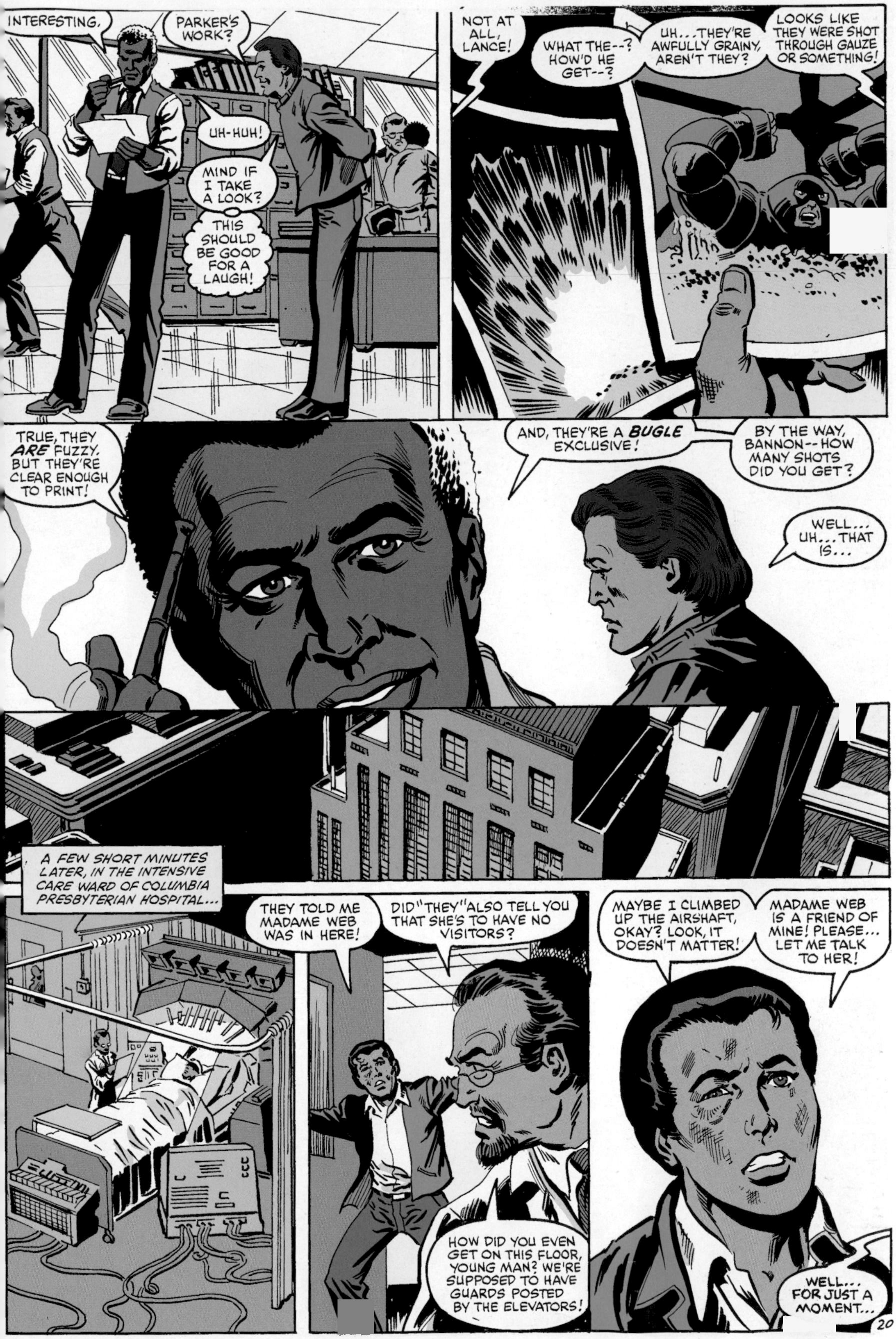
INTERESTING.
PARKER'S WORK?
UH-HUH!
MIND IF I TAKE A LOOK?
THIS SHOULD BE GOOD FOR A LAUGH!
NOT AT ALL, LANCE!
WHAT THE--? HOW'D HE GET--?
UH...THEY'RE AWFULLY GRAINY, AREN'T THEY?
LOOKS LIKE THEY WERE SHOT THROUGH GAUZE OR SOMETHING!
TRUE, THEY ARE FUZZY. BUT THEY'RE CLEAR ENOUGH TO PRINT!
AND, THEY'RE A BUGLE EXCLUSIVE!
BY THE WAY, BANNON--HOW MANY SHOTS DID YOU GET?
WELL... UH...THAT IS...
A FEW SHORT MINUTES LATER, IN THE INTENSIVE CARE WARD OF COLUMBIA PRESBYTERIAN HOSPITAL...
THEY TOLD ME MADAME WEB WAS IN HERE!
DID "THEY" ALSO TELL YOU THAT SHE'S TO HAVE NO VISITORS?
HOW DID YOU EVEN GET ON THIS FLOOR, YOUNG MAN? WE'RE SUPPOSED TO HAVE GUARDS POSTED BY THE ELEVATORS!
MAYBE I CLIMBED UP THE AIRSHAFT, OKAY? LOOK, IT DOESN'T MATTER!
MADAME WEB IS A FRIEND OF MINE! PLEASE... LET ME TALK TO HER!
WELL... FOR JUST A MOMENT...
20

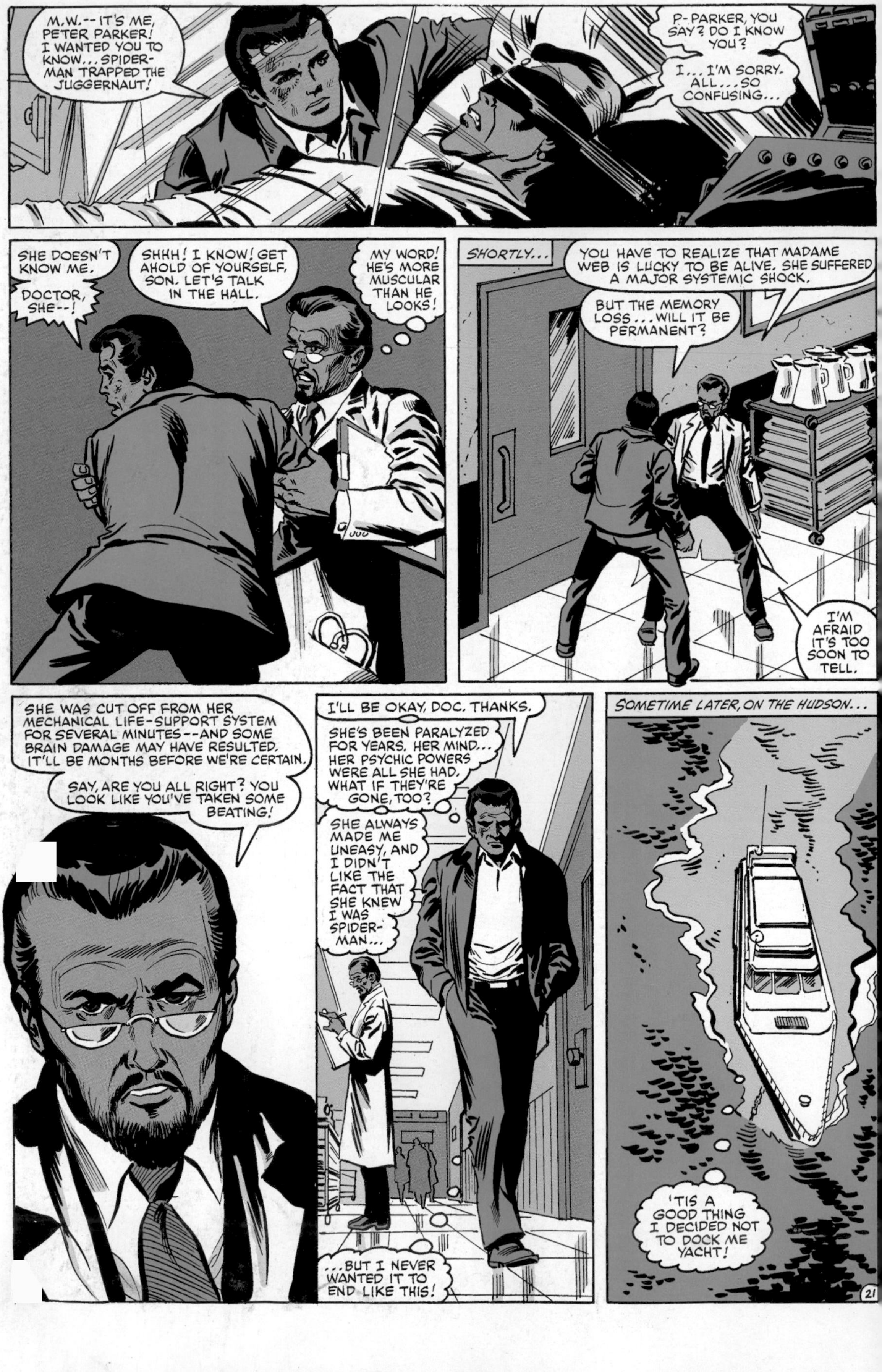
M.W.--IT'S ME, PETER PARKER! I WANTED YOU TO KNOW... SPIDER-MAN TRAPPED THE JUGGERNAUT!
P-PARKER, YOU SAY? DO I KNOW YOU?
I... I'M SORRY. ALL... SO CONFUSING...
SHE DOESN'T KNOW ME.
DOCTOR, SHE--!
SHHH! I KNOW! GET AHOLD OF YOURSELF, SON. LET'S TALK IN THE HALL.
MY WORD! HE'S MORE MUSCULAR THAN HE LOOKS!
SHORTLY...
YOU HAVE TO REALIZE THAT MADAME WEB IS LUCKY TO BE ALIVE. SHE SUFFERED A MAJOR SYSTEMIC SHOCK.
BUT THE MEMORY LOSS... WILL IT BE PERMANENT?
I'M AFRAID IT'S TOO SOON TO TELL.
SHE WAS CUT OFF FROM HER MECHANICAL LIFE-SUPPORT SYSTEM FOR SEVERAL MINUTES--AND SOME BRAIN DAMAGE MAY HAVE RESULTED. IT'LL BE MONTHS BEFORE WE'RE CERTAIN.
SAY, ARE YOU ALL RIGHT? YOU LOOK LIKE YOU'VE TAKEN SOME BEATING!
I'LL BE OKAY, DOC. THANKS.
SHE'S BEEN PARALYZED FOR YEARS. HER MIND... HER PSYCHIC POWERS WERE ALL SHE HAD. WHAT IF THEY'RE GONE, TOO?
SHE ALWAYS MADE ME UNEASY, AND I DIDN'T LIKE THE FACT THAT SHE KNEW I WAS SPIDER-MAN...
...BUT I NEVER WANTED IT TO END LIKE THIS!
SOMETIME LATER, ON THE HUDSON...
'TIS A GOOD THING I DECIDED NOT TO DOCK ME YACHT!

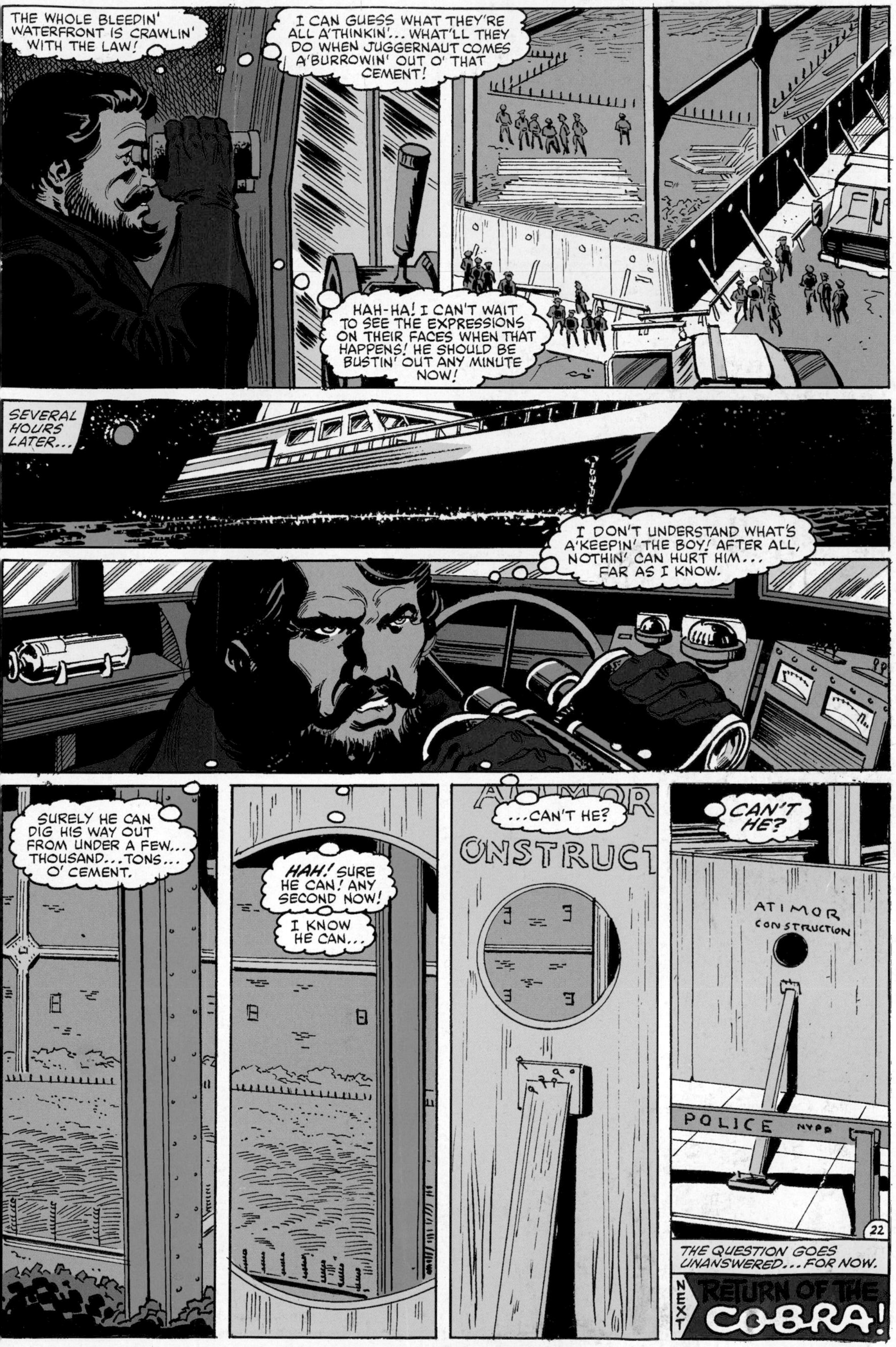
THE WHOLE BLEEDIN' WATERFRONT IS CRAWLIN' WITH THE LAW!
I CAN GUESS WHAT THEY'RE ALL A'THINKIN'... WHAT'LL THEY DO WHEN JUGGERNAUT COMES A'BURROWIN' OUT O' THAT CEMENT!
HAH-HA! I CAN'T WAIT TO SEE THE EXPRESSIONS ON THEIR FACES WHEN THAT HAPPENS! HE SHOULD BE BUSTIN' OUT ANY MINUTE NOW!
SEVERAL HOURS LATER...
I DON'T UNDERSTAND WHAT'S A'KEEPIN' THE BOY! AFTER ALL, NOTHIN' CAN HURT HIM... FAR AS I KNOW.
SURELY HE CAN DIG HIS WAY OUT FROM UNDER A FEW... THOUSAND... TONS... O' CEMENT.
HAH! SURE HE CAN! ANY SECOND NOW!
I KNOW HE CAN...
...CAN'T HE?
ONSTRUCT
CAN'T HE?
ATIMOR CONSTRUCTION
POLICE NYPD
22
THE QUESTION GOES UNANSWERED... FOR NOW.
NEXT RETURN OF THE COBRA!

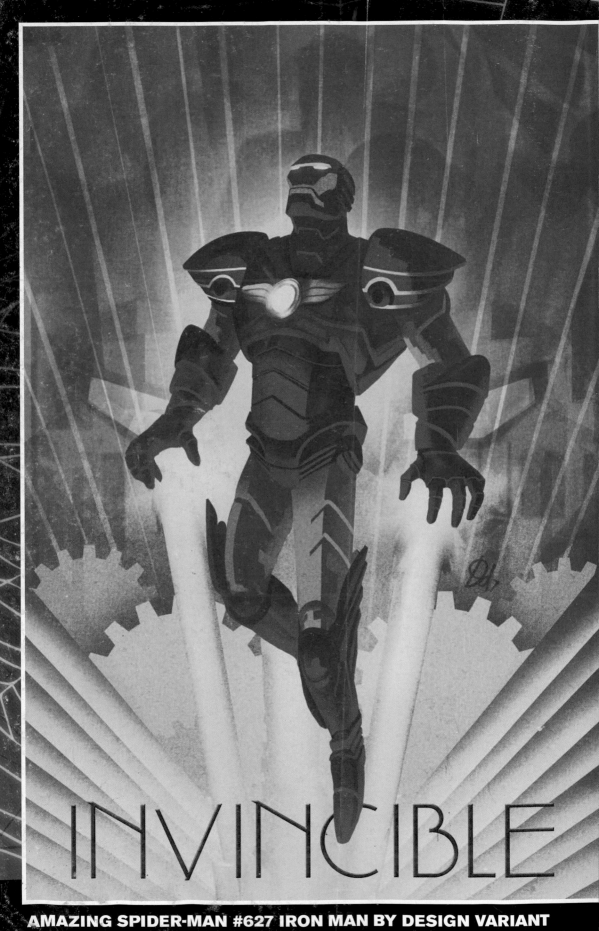

INVINCIBLE

AMAZING SPIDER-MAN #627 IRON MAN BY DESIGN VARIANT
COVER BY MICHAEL DEL MUNDO